S0-AUJ-861

WORKPLACE MOBBING IN ACADEME
REPORTS FROM TWENTY UNIVERSITIES

WORKPLACE MOBBING IN ACADEME
REPORTS FROM TWENTY UNIVERSITIES

Edited by
Kenneth Westhues

The Edwin Mellen Press
Lewiston•Queenston•Lampeter

Library of Congress Cataloging-in-Publication Data

Workplace mobbing in academe : reports from twenty universities /
    edited by Kenneth Westhues.
        p.   cm.
    Includes bibliographical references.
    ISBN 0-7734-6234-1
    1. College teachers--Dismissal of--Canada--Case studies. 2. College teachers--Dismissal
    of--United States--Case studies. I. Westhues, Kenneth.

    LB2335.7.W67 2004
    378.1'2--dc22

                                                        2004059206

A CIP catalog record for this book is available from the British Library.

Cover design photo credit: J. Charles Key
Photo taken on the campus of Carson-Newman College

Copyright   ©   2004   Kenneth Westhues

All rights reserved. For information contact

            The Edwin Mellen Press   The Edwin Mellen Press
                 Box 450   Box 67
            Lewiston, New York   Queenston, Ontario
            USA 14092-0450   CANADA L0S 1L0

                    The Edwin Mellen Press, Ltd.
                      Lampeter, Dyfed, Wales
                    UNITED KINGDOM SA48 7DY

                Printed in the United States of America

Editor's Introduction

On an autumn day in 1991, the eminent mathematician Jack Edmonds, longtime professor at the University of Waterloo, walked across campus to the Department of Sociology. He had been locked out of his office, dropped from the payroll, eliminated from the faculty. Accolades had poured in six years earlier, when he had won the von Neumann Theory Prize, the same laurel worn by John Nash, whose life inspired the film, *A Beautiful Mind*. Now Edmonds's career lay in ruins – not from psychological pathology as in Nash's case, but from some weird organizational pathology. The university itself seemed to have gone mad. For no good reason, it had dumped one of its most beautiful minds. Bewildered and hurt, Edmonds thought sociology might have an explanation of what was going on.

Edmonds did not find me that day but we met soon after. Thus began the most important, challenging and satisfying chapter of my scholarly life, one that continues even now, as I introduce this wonderful, terrifying book. Edmonds got most of his job back in 1993, and returned to his algorithms. I, on the other hand, have worked ever since at identifying and explaining the precise social ill that did him and our university such harm, and that has had still worse effects on other beautiful minds and on other institutions.

Development of this new field of inquiry has been a collaborative effort from the start, initially among professors puzzled and outraged by a series of wrongful dismissals at Waterloo. As the scope of inquiry broadened to include cases elsewhere, the network of researchers of what we came to call *workplace mobbing* enlarged. I did not know initially that anybody earlier had discerned mob behavior in bureaucracies as a distinct focus of study. Learning from my wife Anne Westhues in 1994, that Swedish psychologist Heinz Leymann had not only conceptualized workplace mobbing ten years before I did, but had produced a large body of research on it, counts among the most gratifying moments of my life. Leymann is the giant on whose shoulders I and other researchers of mobbing stand.

Credit for getting the subfield of academic mobbing off the ground goes to another scholarly giant: Herbert Richardson, founder and *lektor* of the Edwin Mellen Press. Richardson read the manuscript of my first book-length report of my research in late summer of 1998. He not only understood what I was saying but thought of ways to help me say it better. This was thanks to his historical and theological perspective on the topic, and to his skill at masterminding. It was also because he had himself been mobbed in the academic workplace, having been ousted from the University of Toronto in 1994, in the most famous dismissal case in Canadian academic history.

Mellen Press published the preliminary report of my research in the fall of 1998: *Eliminating Professors: a Guide to the Dismissal Process.* For the next five years, my research and writing were immeasurably eased by knowing that Mellen was eager to publish a comprehensive report of my work in this area, including a detailed analysis of Richardson's own case. My book was ready for the printer by summer of 2003.

Then, however, instead of releasing the book immediately, Mellen Press embarked on a project for expanding my book's contribution to knowledge beyond my book itself. It published a preliminary edition and invited reactions to it by first-rate scholars in diverse disciplines at universities across North America and beyond. Scores of reactions, long and short, were received. The press accepted 39 essay-length responses for publication. The press's aim, and mine, was fulfilled: to multiply the insights in my book, by letting it serve as a stimulus for other scholars to share related insights of their own.

Nine essays in response, those addressing Richardson's specific case, were published as an appendix to the first Canadian edition of my book, entitled *Administrative Mobbing at the University of Toronto: the Trial, Degradation, and Dismissal of a Professor during the Presidency of J. Robert S. Prichard.* That volume was launched at a reception in Toronto's Sutton Place Hotel on 29 January 2004.

Shortly thereafter, Mellen Press invited me to act as editor of the first separate book of essays in response. We agreed that it should be a stand-alone volume, a sourcebook on academic mobbing that administrators and professors could understand and profit from, with or without a prior reading of my own books. This objective guided our choice of essays for inclusion. The resultant book, the one you hold in your hands, is as good a place to start as any, for understanding the ever-present threat of being mobbed in academe.

The first three of its seven parts describe what mobbing is – the basic, hardest task of this field of inquiry. Participants in this uncustomary social process are ordinarily so caught up in it they fail to see what is going on. They think they are ejecting one rotten apple from the barrel; in fact they are manifesting rot of the barrel itself.

Part One consists of two short pieces of mine that define the concept. The first, an overview of mobbing research in general, is reprinted from *Occupational Health and Safety Canada* 18 (December 2002), pp. 30-36. The second is a checklist of empirical indicators drawn from *Administrative Mobbing...*, pp. 30-35. These two pieces are the jumping-off point, summarizing the line of thought to which the remaining chapters in one way or another respond.

Part Two is composed of three first-person accounts of being mobbed. They are similar in that all three authors are academic stars, ranking easily among the highest-achieving five percent of professors. These authors differ by field (computer science vs. theology vs. surgery) and by the exit door through which each was pushed (disability leave vs. dismissal vs. early retirement). Each account is a variation on basic themes set forth in Part One.

Part Three presents additional variations on the basic themes, but in third-person accounts. The first essay here describes a long series of mobbings at a large university controlled by a major church. The second (reprinted from *New York Academe* 30, Winter 2003) analyzes mobbings at a secular college. The third reviews cases in elementary and secondary schools, adding texture to its analysis by quotations from teachers who were targeted, and including as well an invaluable bibliography of research on workplace mobbing and bullying.

The etiology of a disease is the logical next step after the disease itself is identified. Hence the five essays in Part Four focus on why mobbings happen, though they also describe additional cases. There is first an assertion of general theory by a wise senior scholar, then three essays that explain specific cases in different universities, and finally a young sociologist's grappling with the postmodern context out of which most mobbings today arise.

Part Five concerns techniques. Unlike a workplace geared to routine production of some good or service, a university is a complex maze of overlapping rules, purposes, positions, committees, and codes. The mechanisms by which targets are put down are correspondingly complex. Academic mobbings typically show a lot of ingenuity. The two chapters in this part show even more ingenuity in cutting through subterfuges and exposing the destructive reality.

Part Six is also about techniques, but of a different kind: those by which targets fight back. How does one combat the pathology of workplace mobbing once it has infected the body politic? How is destructiveness overcome? Each chapter in this part offer answers, the first in organizational terms, the second in personal terms.

Part Seven, finally, includes four essays on the difficult problem of how workplace mobbing can be prevented. The first and second essays point to organizational properties of colleges and universities, the third and fourth essays to anti-mobbing laws and policies. A special strength of this concluding part of the book is that the second and fourth chapters take issue with my own views on prevention.

This book belongs to the authors of its constituent essays and to Mellen Press. My editing has been light, and my introductions are brief. I have already had my say in the books to which these essays respond. Here is where other scholars have theirs. I am deeply grateful for their work, glad for their corroboration of some of my contentions, glad also for their disagreement with others. Responses of both kinds are essential for building a body of empirically sound and practical knowledge about a social process that violates truth, hurts people, wastes money, and degrades academic life.

I invite readers, regardless of discipline, to join our effort to understand workplace mobbing in academe: to keep the conversation going by responding to the essays herein, recounting additional cases, and setting forth their own reasoned views. In this way, with luck, we will learn ways to help our institutions serve more effectively their public purposes.

Contents

Part One

The Concept of Workplace Mobbing

Editor's Introduction

Understanding the subject matter of this book requires thinking at a higher level of abstraction than people immersed in conflict at work normally do. Professors are adept at abstract thinking. It is essential to all academic disciplines, from art to zoology. Yet when mired in workplace mobbing, professors have enormous trouble seeing beyond the particular colleague (the jackass, abuser, racist, nutbar, bully, or whatever he or she is called) whom they are trying to eliminate. As in war, hostility for the enemy makes the walls of the mind close in. It becomes hard to see attacks on the target as an instance of a general process. Animosity reduces the ability to think.

First-hand study of many cases has led me to despair of enabling perpetrators to recognize, while a mobbing is underway, the general process they are enacting. "No," they insist, "he deserves whatever he gets. You can ask anybody." Defense mechanisms like demonization of the target, rules of confidentiality, and diffusion of responsibility, prevent mobbers from admitting, often even to themselves, the reality of what they are doing.

Targets recognize the reality more often, but not always. They, too, may be blinded by hate. They may wear the blinkers of revenge. Collective humiliation can leave a target so desolate and alone that he or she cannot imagine that others have undergone a similar ordeal.

Another obstacle to understanding workplace mobbing is its relative rarity. It is not routine. Many academic departments hum along for years, even decades, without a single case, and it is outside the personal experience of many professors.

Mobbing is like a tornado boiling up during stormy, unsettled, inclement times at work. Such times occur in all workplaces, academic ones not least, and everybody knows the signs: disputed decisions, angry words, bruised egos, and tension in the air. Usually such periods of conflict blow over like a summer storm and things settle down again, leaving minor damage to productivity and human relations, damage repaired in subsequent weeks and months.

People who have lived through a tornado, however, know what meteorologists have determined scientifically, that this is not just a "bad storm," but a distinct kind of near-total devastation categorically apart. That is what workplace mobbing is: a destructive social process arising out of unsettled relations at work, similar to the storms of everyday conflict but of such force, fury, terror and ruination as to warrant its own name, separate study, and specific safeguards.

The great benefit of dispassionate, orderly, reasoned study is to help us understand uncommon phenomena that we may never have personally experienced, or that had us so crazed or distraught when we encountered them that we failed to see what was going on. Natural science offers thousands of examples: not just tornadoes but similarly rare plants, animals, diseases, physical and chemical reactions.

Social science serves the same purpose. Most people have never experienced caste relations, blood feuds, wife assault, or child abuse, and many people who experience them deny what is going on. Yet thanks to disciplined empirical research, we have some understanding of these once unnoticed or taken-for-granted aspects of human life.

The two chapters that follow serve this same purpose in the case of workplace mobbing. The first offers a basic conceptualization of the phenomenon and an overview of research on it. The second lists and explains a dozen empirical indicators by which an instance of mobbing can be identified, and distinguished from other kinds of workplace conflict.

Chapter One

At the Mercy of the Mob

Kenneth Westhues

In the early 1980s, a Swedish psychologist named Heinz Leymann identified a grave threat to health and safety in what appear to be the healthiest, safest workplaces in the world. German was Leymann's first language, Swedish his second, but he labeled the distinct menace he had found with an English word: *mobbing.*

Over the next twenty years, news of Leymann's discovery spread across Europe and beyond. Untranslated, the English name he gave it entered the vocabulary of workplace relations throughout Scandinavia and in Germany, Italy, and other countries. All across Europe, not only specialists in occupational health but managers, union leaders, and the public at large came to recognize workplace mobbing as a real, measurable kind of harm, a destroyer of health and life.

Strangely, recognition of Leymann's discovery has been slower in coming to the English-speaking world. *Newsweek* published a popular summary of research on workplace mobbing in 2000, but only in its European edition. In Britain and America, attention has focussed less on mobbing than on the different but related problem of bullying, and, occasionally, on one of its extremely rare possible results: the outbursts of extreme violence, that from time to time make headlines across the country.

Workplace mobbing was almost never discussed in Canada until the coroner's inquest following the murder of four workers at OC Transpo in Ottawa in 1999. In that case, a former employee, Pierre Lebrun, had ended the shooting spree by also taking his own life. It turned out that Lebrun had been ridiculed relentlessly by co-workers for his stutter, and then, after he had slapped one of them in retaliation, been forced to apologize to his tormentors. Had Lebrun been mobbed at work? Was this the phenomenon Leymann had in mind? Media reports and the inquest itself tentatively said it was.

In 2000 and 2001, The *National Post* publicized my research on mobbing in the academic workplace, the process by which even tenured professors are ganged up on, humiliated, and run out of their jobs. While trying to make sense of some bizarre and hugely destructive university conflicts in 1994, I had stumbled upon Leymann's work and found it powerfully illuminating of the data in my files.

In the meanwhile, the concept of workplace mobbing caught the attention of the Ontario Nurses Association, the College Institute Educators Association of British Columbia, and a smattering of other union and management groups, which then sponsored workshops on the topic, much as occurred in Germany a decade earlier.

The Trauma of Being Mobbed

To describe mobbing as possibly the gravest threat most workers face is not to ignore threats posed by slippery floors, dangerous machines, toxic chemicals, and the other material hazards that health and safety committees properly make their top priority.

In practical terms, however, the worst kind of harm most Canadians have to fear at work is the kind that arises from faulty human relations, some kind of glitch in how people treat one another. Montreal researcher Hans Selye won the Nobel Prize for Medicine in 1964, for the best single-word description of today's main workplace ills: stress. This short English word struck a chord in both the scientific community and the public, as mobbing would decades later, and quickly found its way into other languages. By now, research has shown in a thousand ways the stark, even lethal effects of too much of the wrong kind of stress on physical and mental health.

Mobbing can be understood as the stressor to beat all stressors. It is an impassioned, collective campaign by co-workers to exclude, punish, and humiliate a targeted worker. Initiated most often by a person in a position of power or influence, mobbing is a desperate urge to crush and eliminate the target. The urge travels through the workplace like a virus, infecting one person after another. The target comes to be viewed as absolutely abhorrent, with no redeeming qualities, outside the circle of acceptance and respectability, deserving only of contempt. As the campaign proceeds, a steadily larger range of hostile ploys and communications comes to be seen as legitimate.

Mobbing is hardly the only source of debilitating stress at work, and it was not the only one on which Leymann did research. He interviewed bank employees who had undergone the terror of armed robbery, and subway drivers who had watched helplessly as their trains ran over persons who fell or jumped onto the tracks. Leymann documented the depression, absenteeism, sleeplessness, and other symptoms of trauma resulting from such stressful experiences.

Bank robberies and subway suicides were no match, however, for being mobbed by co-workers in the personal devastation that ensued. Not infrequently, mobbing spelled the end of the target's career, marriage, health, and livelihood. From a study of circumstances surrounding suicides in Sweden, Leymann estimated that about twelve percent of people who take their own lives have recently been mobbed at work.

How it Happens

Mobbing is relatively rare, and many workplaces hum along for decades without a single case of it. But by Leymann's and others' estimates, between two and five percent of adults are mobbed sometime during their working lives. The other 95 percent, involved in the process only as observers, bystanders, or perpetrators (though occasionally also as rescuers or guardians of the target), mostly deny, gloss over, and forget the mobbing cases in which they took part. That is one reason it has taken so long for the phenomenon to be identified and researched.

That children and teenagers sometimes join in collectively humiliating one of their number is well known--most people can cite examples from their own school days. The widely publicized deaths of two girls in British Columbia – Reena Virk, beaten and drowned in 1999, and Dawn Marie Wesley, driven to suicide in 2000 – have heightened public awareness of the cruel reality of swarming or collective bullying among both girls and boys.

Leymann's contribution was to document beyond any doubt the same reality among adults, even in the cool, rational, professional, bureaucratic, policy-governed setting of a workplace. The tactics differ. Workplace mobbing is normally carried out politely, without any violence, and with ample written documentation. Yet even without the blood, the bloodlust is essentially the same: contagion and mimicking of unfriendly, hostile acts toward the target; relentless undermining of the target's self-confidence; group solidarity against one whom all agree does not belong; and the euphoria of collective attack.

An Example from a Factory

One of the cases that first opened my eyes to workplace mobbing serves also to illustrate related concepts commonly but mistakenly applied. A former student of mine asked if he and his wife could meet with me. She was being sexually harassed, he said, in the factory where she had worked for most of her adult life.

The label this woman and her husband had placed on her problem fit the facts they presented to me. She was regularly paired for certain tasks with a male co-worker who day after day humiliated her with insults to her work and degrading sexual slurs. Years earlier, when she had threatened to report him to the boss, he had grabbed her arm in a threatening manner.

Yet as this shy, soft-spoken lady shared more facts with me, sexual harassment appeared to be a very partial characterization of her predicament. She had in fact complained to both union and management about the man's offensive behavior, but to no avail. She and her husband were at wit's end. The leader of the union was a paragon of political correctness. A zero-tolerance policy on sexual harassment was posted where all could see. Yet her harasser carried on as before.

Explanation could be found only in the larger dynamics of the work group. This woman ranked at the bottom of the pecking order. She was apart from her workmates in three crucial ways. First, she had a partial disability, the result of an accident at work years before, that under terms of the collective agreement precluded her doing certain jobs. For want of physical dexterity, she was exempt from tasks at which everybody else took a turn. She was also paid at an hourly rate, while most others were on piecework.

Second, though most workers in the group were from immigrant groups, this woman was from a different one than everybody else. Ethnically, she was a minority of one.

Third, while most of her peers sprinkled their speech with obscenities, took crude banter in stride, and seemed to thrive on a relatively coarse workplace culture, this woman did not. She was devoted to her family and her faith.

These and other factors made her an outcast. Her problem was far worse than one man's harassment and bullying. It was the humiliation of daily loathing by her peers. What drove her over the edge were comments from two female co-workers on a hot summer day when job assignments were being rotated. One called out so that all could hear, "I don't want to work with the cripple." Another, distributing sweatbands to combat the heat, passed this worker by saying, "You don't work hard enough to get one."

At that point, this veteran of years of co-workers' hostility began crying then and could not stop. She was taken to the nurse, who sent her home. Her husband took her to the hospital emergency room. She was diagnosed with clinical depression and placed on sick leave. She returned to work months later, was again paired with the man who led the harassment and later suffered a severe heart attack. The formal grievances she had lodged were resolved with her early retirement about ten years after the mobbing began.

The case illustrates the escalation that is essential to workplace mobbing. Each higher level of authority, in both company and union, to which this woman and her husband appealed, was faced with overturning the will of a successively larger group of subordinates. Steadily more and higher-level employees over time voiced the common sentiment: this woman is impossible to work with, she has to go.

Mobbing was exacerbated in this case by its leader's special status in the group. Some female workers found him sexy. He had connections for getting cigarettes and alcohol tax-free, and in this way had forged semi-secret ties with other employees. Acting in the role of chief eliminator, he led the campaign to rob one partially disabled worker of her job, her dignity, and her health. The process took years, but it eventually achieved its aim.

Mobbing versus Other Exits

Why didn't this factory worker quit? In the answer to this question lie clues to why mobbing is more common in some employment situations than others. Mobbing rarely happens to a worker who can easily relocate to a different employer.

Mobbing is also rare in the case of workers on at-will contracts, since they can be summarily fired. A manager faced with ten subordinates who get along and get work done reasonably well, all of whom despise a certain other subordinate and want to be rid of him or her, ordinarily heeds the collective will. If for some reason the manager does not, there is conflict but not mobbing, since opinion about the acceptability of the worker in question is divided.

Further, in situations where a worker can be terminated only for cause, mobbing seldom occurs if legitimate cause exists. On the basis of clear evidence of substandard performance or serious misconduct, workers are routinely terminated – firmly, but often with compassion and regret.

The worker most vulnerable to being mobbed is an average or high achiever who is personally invested in a formally secure job, but who nonetheless somehow threatens or puts to shame co-workers and/or managers. Such a worker provides no legally defensible grounds for termination, yet usually fails to pick up subtle hints and leave voluntarily. An attractive solution, from the majority point of view, is to bring or wear this worker down, one way or another, however long it takes.

As the process drags on, both sides, collective and individual, dig in their heels. It is often as if the targeted worker has grabbed a hot wire and cannot let go, despite the pain and injury it inflicts. The worker's investment of self and sense of having been deeply wronged prevent the one resolution that would satisfy the other side.

Ironically, it is in workplaces where workers' rights are formally protected that the complex and devious incursions on human dignity that constitute mobbing most commonly occur. Union shops are one example, as in the case of the factory worker described above. University faculties are another, on account of the special protections of tenure and academic freedom professors have. It happens in police forces, too, since management rights in this setting are tempered by the oath officers swear to uphold the law. Mobbings appear to be much more frequent in the public service as a whole, as compared to private companies.

Mobbing also appears to be more common in the professional service sector – such as education and health care – where work is complex, goals ambiguous, best practices debatable, and market discipline far away. Scapegoating is an effective if temporary means of achieving group solidarity, when it cannot be achieved in a more constructive way. It is a turning inward, a diversion of energy away from serving nebulous external purposes toward the deliciously clear, specific goal of ruining a disliked co-worker's life.

What to Do about It

As a clinician, Leymann made his priority the healing of post-traumatic stress in those most severely affected by mobbing. With the support of the Swedish health service, he opened a clinic for mobbing victims in 1994, and published detailed research on the first 64 patients treated there. That clinic no longer exists and Leymann himself died in 1999, but 200 patients are currently treated in a similar clinic that opened in Saarbruecken, Germany, this year.

Competent, well-informed treatment of the many mobbing targets who suffer mental breakdown is obviously in order, especially since they have often in the past been misdiagnosed as having paranoid delusions.

Psychiatric injury, however, is but one possible harmful result of being mobbed. Some mobbing targets keep their sanity but succumb to cardiovascular disease – hypertension, heart attack, or stroke. Most suffer loss of income and reputation. Marital breakdown and isolation from friends and family are also common outcomes.

An ounce of prevention is worth a pound of cure, although experts do not agree on the ingredients of the desired ounce. Believers in human perfectibility favor enacting laws and policies that forbid workplace mobbing under pain of punishment. Organizations as diverse as Volkswagen in Germany and the Department of Environmental Quality in the American state of Oregon already have anti-mobbing policies in place. It is too soon to say what effect, if any, such policies will have on the incidence of the phenomenon.

The impulse to gang up, to join with others against what is perceived to be a common threat, lies deep in human nature. It is not easily outlawed. A policy forbidding it may, in practice, become a weapon for convicting some mobbing target of a punishable offense and thereby aiding in his or her humiliation. The evidence is clear by now that policies against sexual harassment have often been used as tools for harassing innocent but disliked workmates. Anti-mobbing policies may turn out to be even more versatile tools for such mischief.

The tiny percentage of mobbing victims – like Pierre Lebrun – who lash back in violent attack would probably have lived out their lives peaceably and productively had they been spared the excruciating pain of relentless humiliation.

All can agree, at least, on the desirability of public awareness of the vital but sad discovery Heinz Leymann made two decades ago, and on the continuing need for careful, critical scholarship that builds on his. The better we understand ourselves, including our darker impulses, the more able we are to keep one another healthy and safe.

Suggested Reading

Two concise summaries of Heinz Leymann's research on workplace mobbing are his articles, "Mobbing and Psychological Terror at Workplaces" (*Violence and Victims* 5, 1990, pp. 119-126), and "The Content and Development of Mobbing at Work" (*European Journal of Work and Organizational Psychology* 5, 1996, pp. 165-184).

For a popularly written application and extension of Leymann's work to the American situation, see Noa Davenport, Ruth Disler Schwartz, and Gail Purcell Elliott, *Mobbing: Emotional Abuse in the American Workplace* (Ames, IA: Civil Society Publishing, 1999).

Chapter Two

A Checklist of Twelve Indicators

Kenneth Westhues

The First, Basic Clue

In lectures on social elimination, I have sometimes said that in every human being are three appetites: for food, for sex, and for humiliating somebody else. The third craving is not ordinarily grouped with the first two. All agree that hunger and sexual desire have a physiological basis, that they drive human behavior in overt and hidden ways, and that they are at times so strong as to preoccupy a person completely, turning him or her into a raging beast, a creature we scarcely recognize as human.

Notwithstanding its less evident basis in biology, the eliminative impulse, the lust to wipe another person out, is categorically similar. It can consume a person to the point of obsession, spread like a virus through a group, and become the driving force behind collective energy. Yet unlike the appetites for food and sex, this one has come to be proscribed in the process of civilization. It is supposed to be held in check by a universal compassion, common allegiance to the "brotherhood of man." The eliminative impulse, when it does seize control of human behavior, is therefore almost always denied, obscured by the pretense of serving some lofty goal. Girard posits a "persecutory unconscious" in those caught up in the snowballing process (2001, p. 126). It is, he says, what Jesus referred to in his prayer on the cross, "Father, forgive them because they don't know what they are doing" (*Luke* 23: 34).

How then can one tell when elimination in its stronger, stricter, narrower sense is underway? Are there identifiable symptoms, empirical indicators that an exclusionary process has escaped the bounds of reason and civilization? Against every professor and teacher a protest has at some time been raised by a student who flunked a test: "You have it in for me." Can the teacher prove otherwise? When an imposter was forced to resign from the faculty of the University of Regina in 2001, after the degrees on her resumé were shown to belong to somebody else, while she herself had no such degrees, her lawyer protested: "It's a real old-boys club around here. She's a foreign-looking person. She has her abrasive side, but she's easy to gang up on" (Perreaux 2001). Was the eliminative impulse, as the lawyer implied, behind the move to get rid of her? If I, like most professors, would defend her ouster, how do I know I am not acting on my own "persecutory unconscious"? Are there reliable signs that elimination in its savage sense is underway?

The first, most basic clue is the eliminators' focus on the targeted person, rather than on the allegedly offensive act. "The guilty person is so much a part of his offense that one is indistinguishable from the other. His offense seems to be a fantastic essence or ontological attribute" (Girard 1986, p. 36). Social order requires pointing out errors, infractions, and offenses, and imposing penalties on their account – including jail, in the case of criminal behavior that threatens public safety. Social order does not require spoiling a person's entire identity, which is what elimination means. An explanation of the need for sanctions that includes personally derisive and humiliating statements about the person on whom the sanctions are to be placed, a statement that break this person's bond with everybody else: this is the basic indication that the eliminative impulse has been unleashed.

Compare two responses parents can make to a child who has just been eliminated from a spelling bee or gymnastics competition. They can say, "This just wasn't your day, we're sorry you won't be going on to the advanced level, better luck next time." Or they can say (what most of us have overhead on some occasion, and winced), "You stupid little shit, what's wrong with you, you've brought shame on your school, get out of my sight." These are radically, categorically different social processes. In the first instance, the child's person is acknowledged and affirmed even in the midst of inadequate performance. In the second instance, a mistake is enlarged to cover and smear the child's whole identity. Only the second instance illustrates the process that is the focus of the present book.

Social elimination reflects what social psychologists call the "fundamental attribution error," the tendency in all of us to overestimate the extent to which behavior reflects underlying personal qualities (dishonesty, for instance, or untrustworthiness) and to underestimate the extent to which it reflects the particular situation or context (see Nisbett and Ross 1991, Gladwell 2000). Some of the most famous experiments in psychology document this tendency. Stanley Milgram, for instance, wondered if some personality defect among Germans was to blame for their acquiescence to and participation in Nazi cruelties. In his research at Yale after the war, he demonstrated that when directed to inflict what they thought were severe, even life-threatening electric shocks on innocent people, the majority of Ivy-League students and ordinary New Englanders did as they were told (1963). The *situation* of being paid to accept direction from a professional psychologist overrode most participants' personal identities, which were presumably as kind and decent as of people in general. It was context rather than character that best explained what people actually did.

The same conclusion is drawn from Philip Zimbardo's study of role-playing in a mock prison he set up at Stanford University (1972). This experiment was done with paid volunteers who had no criminal records and were emotionally stable. Zimbardo assigned these experimental subjects randomly to the contrasting roles of prisoner and guard. He wanted to see how these unaccustomed roles in an unusual setting would affect the behavior of normal young men. The effects were so strong that Zimbardo ended the experiment after just six days. The subjects assigned the role of prison guard had *become* prison guards, taking pleasure in cruelty toward the "prisoners." The latter, for their part, became servile, listless robots; three had to be released in the first few days because of crying, depression, and other symptoms of serious trauma. Even though the participants in the study knew this was just a temporary game, they could not prevent themselves from being held captive by it. What Gladwell calls the "power of context" was so great as to make them act wildly out of character. Zimbardo explained that he called off the project early

> not because of the horror I saw out there in the prison yard,
> but because of the horror of realizing that I could have
> easily traded places with the most brutal guard or become

the weakest prisoner full of hatred at being so powerless
that I could not eat, sleep, or go to the toilet without
permission of the authorities. (1972)

Social eliminations are carried out by people who have fallen deep
into "fundamental attribution error," identifying some alleged offense
so closely with the offender's identity that they cannot see the latter
as a human being like themselves. They have lost sight of the truth
impressed on Zimbardo by his experiment, the same truth Milgram
demonstrated in his research at Yale: that given the right
circumstances, I myself might have done this deed. Oral and written
statements that fail to recognize the essential humanity, the
achievements and virtues, of the one held to be deserving of
exclusion, but that instead characterize the target as personally
abhorrent and despicable, are telltale pointers to eliminative lust.

A Check-list of Ten Specific Clues

Following on the basic clue, here are ten more, none conclusive
but each significant, that an exclusionary process qualifies as
elimination in the strict sense intended here.

A popular, high-achieving target. The person being pursued is
probably average or above by commonly accepted standards of
performance, and respected and popular in at least some circles.
Mediocre performers tend not to arouse the eliminative impulse in
leaders or peers. They do not show others up. If they are let go, it may
be gently, with genuine remorse and out of seeming necessity. When
the person targeted has a record of success, suspicion grows that
something more lies behind the exclusionary move.

Lack of due process. Standard procedures, rules of fairness and
natural justice, and all that the term *due process* includes, hold
eliminative impulses in check and encourage mutual tolerance.
Sophisticated eliminators make a show of being scrupulously fair, but
vigilant outsiders can usually see through it. When evidence suggests
that those leading an exclusionary effort are making up rules as they
go along, or have become a law unto themselves, a process of social
elimination may be underway.

Odd timing. Taking somebody by surprise is a tactic of war, not
respectful co-existence. The timing of actions against a target tells a
lot. Eliminators tend to jump the gun, pounce at an unscheduled,
unannounced, unexpected moment, catching the target off guard and
reducing the odds of successful defense.

Resistance to external review. Reluctant excluders willingly subject ostracizing or penalizing actions to public scrutiny and to possible overturn by higher authority. "Please," they say implicitly, "would somebody show us a way to build this person in, so that we need not throw him out." Impassioned excluders want nothing more than that higher authority and outside agencies stay out of the matter: "We can handle this ourselves."

Secrecy. *Things Which Are Done in Secret* was the title of Marlene Dixon's 1976 book about faculty eliminations at McGill University. Generally, eliminators prefer to keep their proceedings confidential, perhaps cloaking them with privacy or copyright protections under law. Targets may also crave confidentiality, to avoid public shaming. Against these priorities stands Justice Louis Brandeis's dictum that sunlight is the best disinfectant, and Thomas Jefferson's advice to "enlighten the people generally, and tyranny and oppressions of body and mind will vanish like evil spirits at the dawn of day."

Unanimity. The loss of diverse opinion is a compelling indication that eliminative fury has been unleashed. When all decent people agree on the need to put somebody down, when they demand it with one voice in mass meetings, when one by one they put their names to long denunciations, alarm bells should go off. Decency and unanimity seldom coincide. The late French philosopher, Emmanuel Lévinas, liked to quote the talmudic principle, "If everyone is in agreement to condemn someone accused, release him for he must be innocent" (in Girard 2001, p. 118).

Fuzzy charges. In the quintessential elimination case, the charges cited to justify exclusion are vague and numerous. Real or imagined venial sins may be added up to make a mortal sin that allegedly necessitates the target's ouster. Astute outsiders are often struck by this compounding of fuzzy infractions and have trouble pinpointing any actual misdeed requiring punishment. They ask, in effect, "Why, what has he done that is wrong?" The insiders answer in unison, "Can't you see? It's completely obvious."

Prior marginalization. Generally, there is evidence of the target being marginalized, ostracized, and treated with contempt *before* the offenses cited as grounds for formal expulsion and humiliation. In conventional social control, the crime comes first, and only thereafter the apprehension of the criminal. In the elimination process, the devil is identified first; subsequently, the evil deeds he or she has done come to light.

Impassioned rhetoric. The more fervent, excited, and overwrought the language used against the target, the less likely is the basis for exclusion anything but a collective will to destroy. Compelling evidence obviates the need for adjectives like *appalling, preposterous, hideous, repugnant,* and *vicious.* Name-calling, the placing of exclusionary labels on a person, is a common theme, the choice of label depending on the temper of the times. *Heretic* and *witch* were popular several centuries ago, *communist* several decades ago. In recent years, *abuser, bully, nutbar, fraud,* and *difficult person* have served well.

Back-biting. Although the evidence is normally hard to ferret out, malicious gossip and whispering campaigns behind a person's back are common attributes of elimination processes. The usual foundation of formal sanctions is the circulation of rumors and stories that have discredited the target informally, turned him or her into a butt of jokes. "Did you hear what she did last week?"

The Twelfth Clue

If humans were always as physical as Nazi thugs and teenaged ruffians, or as transparent in their scheming as the clique that ousted Gretchen on *Survivor I*, there would be no need for the above list of clues or indicators. The list is tailored to groups and organizations that are generally free of violence and infused with lofty, civilized values, even though still marked by the *Human Stain* (Roth 2000), the impulse to destroy. In settings of the latter kind, universities being a prime example, the list is a reasonably practical guide to deciding whether a given exclusionary process, a given case of somebody losing out, constitutes social elimination.

The list must not be applied mechanically. No checklist or questionnaire could reliably identify which member of a group – which professor on a faculty, for instance – is in process of elimination. Humans weave tangled webs. In a perfect elimination exercise, as in a perfect sting, the target would never even know who pulled it off. Appearances can deceive. One colleague uses overwrought language as a matter of course, but is all talk and would not harm a fly. Another is silent but deadly. A third interprets the slightest criticism as a sign that somebody is out to get him. Only by studying a given pattern of interaction in some detail, taking into account the viewpoints of all participants and the organization's formal goals, can one reasonably assess what is going on and who, if anyone, is out to humiliate whom. Detailed written records permit this in Richardson's case.

One final clue bears mention, because it highlights the complexity of the process. Generally, when a group becomes aroused by the eliminative impulse and puts some individual in the cross hairs, this arouses the same impulse in that individual. The target seeks revenge, lashes back, makes an offensive of his or her own: "Your effort to grind me into the dust entitles me to do the same to you." Social elimination can be like war, a pattern of attack and counterattack, albeit with one side very large and the other very small. The reality in the later stages may be two parties, unevenly matched yet gripped by common passion to destroy. Girard describes this paradox:

> the antagonists resemble one another more and more. They confront one another all the more implacably because their conflict dissolves the real differences that formerly separated them. (2001, p. 12f)

Understanding such a conflict, and all the more resolving it, require studying its origin and tracing its development over time.

Not all targets take the bait. Humans have different amounts of fight in them and different susceptibilities to revenge. Some are so overwhelmed by humiliation that they internalize it and hasten their own disappearance. Some are saints, so full of compassion they scarcely notice their enemies and go like sheep to slaughter. Most targets of elimination efforts sooner or later fight back.

Victor Klemperer, Professor of Romance Languages at the Technical University of Dresden from 1920 to 1935, was such a man. His diaries during and after his elimination from the faculty give insight into the effects of the process on an extraordinarily aware, good-humored, compassionate intellectual. Klemperer was Jewish by birth, vaguely Protestant by choice, a secular thinker, an expert on Voltaire, an opponent of both Nazism and Zionism, a true liberal. He watched helplessly as the number of his students dwindled, as rumors of his department's impending abolition circulated, as colleagues and friends sidled up to the Nazi authorities, and as he himself was targeted for removal. He was 53 years old when the axe fell on April 30, 1935, with the arrival in his mail of an official letter of dismissal.

"At first I felt alternately numb and romantic," he wrote two days later, "now there is only bitterness and wretchedness"(Klemperer 1999, p. 119). The next Saturday he and Mrs. Klemperer hosted a gathering of professors in their home. He was devastated that none of my colleagues bothers about me. ... They took my elimination very lightly. Kühn thought I should complain about the retirement. I was due emeritus status (or "loss of duties," as the new phrase has it). Yesterday I talked to Beste, the dean, about it. He said: impossible to do anything. (pp.121f)

By a year later, August of 1936, isolated now from the university, in straitened financial condition, and with the threat of further antisemitic persecution on the horizon, Klemperer wrote in his diary a sharply more militant sentiment. It was occasioned by reading in the Dresden newspaper a Nazi-friendly article by the aforementioned colleague, history professor Johannes Kühn:

If one day the situation were reversed and the fate of the vanquished lay in my hands, then I would let all the ordinary folk go and even some of the leaders, who might perhaps after all have had honorable intentions and not known what they were doing. But I would have all the intellectuals strung up, and the professors three feet higher than the rest; they would be left hanging from the lampposts for as long as was compatible with hygiene. (p.184)

On account of being married to an Aryan, Klemperer was spared removal to a concentration camp. He survived his elimination from the Dresden faculty and regained a professorship at the University of Halle after the war, holding it until his death in 1960. Dresden awarded him an honorary doctorate in 1952. He continued, without much success, to seek the elimination from universities of professors who had supported the Hitler regime. Kühn, his old nemesis, was appointed to a chair at Heidelberg in 1949. (Chalmers 1999)

Given that so decent and compassionate a target of social elimination as Klemperer showed an inclination to revenge, readers may wonder what lies behind the present book. Its author, as the previous chapter disclosed, was the target of a (blessedly unsuccessful) eliminative campaign at the University of Waterloo. Its main subject, who has cooperated in the research and publication, was the target of a successful campaign at the University of Toronto. Is this book at bottom an instrument of revenge, a way of getting back at the academics who went after its author and the eliminated professors he describes?

From the viewpoint commonly held by mobbers, it cannot help but be. Those who have sought a person's removal from respectable company often interpret anything that person does afterward, even survival, as an attempt at revenge. To those who have tried to silence a person, even friendly words in that person's voice often come across as spite. David Leslie took this viewpoint in a couple of paragraphs of his otherwise cogent review of my earlier book. Westhues, he suggested, "is having his revenge in print" (Leslie 2000, p. 390).

That was not my purpose, nor is it here – not on my behalf, nor Richardson's, nor anybody else's. My purpose has been to rise above the nastier side of life that I and many more have felt at first hand, by subjecting the nastiness to systematic empirical analysis, thereby to enlarge our understanding of elimination as a social process, so that we can collectively learn how to reduce its incidence.

From the average reader's viewpoint, of course, the motives behind this book, whether kind or nefarious, are beside the point. What matters is whether this book delivers valuable knowledge: whether it merits the description a generous reviewer placed on the earlier book, "a remarkably perceptive account of the techniques useful for getting rid of unwelcome academics" (Martin 1999). Substance is what counts: how adequate and powerful is the explanation of events.

Revenge means stooping to the level of good people in their worst moments. In the main, Klemperer did not do that. After the war, he continued his research on language and thought control, and he championed liberal education in the inauspicious setting of communist East Germany. For his part, Richardson has devoted his energies since leaving Toronto to rebuilding and expanding The Edwin Mellen Press, his own instrument for humane learning, which counts among its titles (so I learned long after this chapter's first draft) an annotated edition of one of Klemperer's books. Richardson has established a program at Mellen for publication of studies of administrative injustice. This book and my earlier one (1998) are titles in that program.

One of Richardson's finest moments during the long torment of his ouster was his comment, astonishingly pure of a spirit of revenge, to the reporters who phoned him at home on September 26, 1994, after St. Michael's College had accepted the decision of the Evans tribunal and officially dismissed him. "I'm very sorry not to be able to complete the 33 months remaining to me until my normal retirement," Richardson said. "I'm very grateful to St. Michael's College for having provided me a community to carry on my teaching and my research over 26 years" (van Rijn 1994; see also Wanagas 1994).

References

Chalmers, Martin, 1999. "Preface" to V. Klemperer, *I Will Bear Witness*. New York: Modern Library.

Dixon, Marlene, 1976. *Things Which Are Done in Secret*. Montreal: Black Rose.

Girard, René, 1986. *The Scapegoat*. Baltimore: Johns Hopkins.

Girard, René, 2001. *I See Satan Fall Like Lightning*. Maryknoll: Orbis.

Gladwell, Malcolm, 2000. *The Tipping Point*. Boston: Little, Brown.

Klemperer, Victor, 1999. *I Will Bear Witness, 1933-1941: a Diary of the Nazi Years*. New York: Modern Library.

Leslie, David W., 2000. Review of K. Westhues, *Eliminating Professors*, in *Journal of Higher Education* (May-June): 389-390.

Martin, Brian, 1999. "Want to get rid of an annoying academic?" *Campus Review* 9 (6-12 October): 12

Milgram, Stanley, 1963. "Behavioral Study of Obedience," *Journal of Abnormal and Social Psychology* 67, pp. 371-78.

Nisbett, Richard E., and Lee Ross, 1991. *The Person and the Situation*. Philadelphia: Temple University Press.

Perreaux, Les., 2001. "University eager to hire a minority: Report on Lana Nguyen," *National Post*, May 19.

Roth, Philip, 2000. *The Human Stain*. Boston: Houghton Mifflin.

van Rijn, Nicolaas, 1994. "U of T college fires 'dishonest' prof," *Toronto Star*, September 27.

Wanagas, Don, 1994. "Prof canned, guilty of misconduct," *Toronto Sun*, September 27.

Westhues, Kenneth, 1998. *Eliminating Professors: a Guide to the Dismissal Process*. Lewiston, NY: Robert Kempner Collegium, Edwin Mellen Press.

Zimbardo, Philip E., 1972. "Pathology of Imprisonment," *Society* 9 (No. 6), as reprinted in J. M. Charon, ed., *The Meaning of Sociology* (Upper Saddle River, NJ: Prentice-Hall), pp. 86-88.

Part Two

Narratives

Editor's Introduction

If the chapters in Part One have served their intended purpose, readers now have a conceptual lens through which the similarities among the first-person accounts here in Part Two will come into sharp focus.

At first glance, these three cases of professors leaving their jobs have little in common. A computer scientist at an American university is convicted of crime, imprisoned, and dismissed from his position. A theologian at a Canadian university becomes seriously ill and goes on long-term disability. A surgeon at an Italian university takes early retirement. Different fields, different universities, different countries, different circumstances of departure – connections among these cases seem obscure at best.

Through the lens of workplace mobbing, the key fact in each of these cases becomes startlingly clear: that each professor was ganged up on by colleagues and administrators in his home university, falsely accused of bad behavior, subjected to humiliating rituals, and forced against his will to give up his position. In each instance, the institution was needlessly deprived of a beautiful mind – and in the surgeon's case, of beautiful, healing hands.

Professors are mobbed on any number of irrelevant grounds: wrong skin color, wrong genitals, wrong class, ethnic, or religious background, wrong friendship ties, accent, stutter, tic. Factors like these come into play in all three cases recounted here, but the key factor is even more sinister: that each professor was really good at his job. Pradhan was Texas A&M's highest-paid professor. Meynell was in Calgary's small handful of Fellows of the Royal Society. Cavina, Fellow of the American College of Surgeons and founding president of the European Association on Trauma and Emergency Surgery, worked on the leading edge of laparoscopy and telemedicine.

What gives these accounts their power is that they are written by the ousted professors themselves. Often, in preparing lectures on workplace mobbing, I have racked my brain for ways to convey the terror felt by targets of this process. Sometimes I have quoted a physician who contacted me for advice. He had practiced first in his native country and earned a global reputation for his research. Then his country dissolved into civil war, and he found himself receiving death threats by mail and telephone. He therefore moved his practice and research program to Canada, only to be mobbed in his new home by established colleagues who felt threatened by his intrusion. The nonviolent humiliation in Canada, he told me, was far more debilitating than the threats of mortal violence in his native land.

Sometimes, too, I have recounted the story of a middle-aged nurse who was mobbed in her hospital workplace. Earlier in her life, she had lived for years at death's door on account of a congenital heart defect. She eventually had a successful heart transplant, and she was overjoyed. But that was before her nurse-supervisors ganged up on her and destroyed her life. Her heart troubles were as nothing, she told me, compared to the experience of being mobbed.

Now, thanks to Pradhan, Meynell, and Cavina, I can cite their stories written in their own words. Each of these men knows that his adversaries would dismiss his account as being biased and self-serving, and that he has no defense against such criticism except the honest reporting of evidence. But what a powerful defense that is! Honor to these men for making it. *Honi soit qui mal y pense.*

Readers so trusting of university authority that they cannot take dissenting first-person statements seriously should skip these chapters in Part Two and proceed to the third-person accounts in Part Three.

Pradhan, who by profession writes more code than prose, deserves special praise for hammering out the lines of his essay. So does Cavina, for writing his chapter in what is for him a second language. He and I gratefully acknowledge the help of Toronto journalist Philip Mathias in correcting and smoothing the English sentences.

Chapter Three

A Dream Professorship, Turned Nightmare

Dhiraj K. Pradhan

This is the story of my dismissal from the tenured professorship, an endowed chair, I held at Texas A&M University, in College Station, Texas, from 1992 through 1999. Problems with my appointment began even before I officially took up the position. Multidimensional in nature, these problems included racism and certain elements endemic to the Texas mindset.

Early Years

I begin with information on my background, to give the reader some understanding of my perspective. I moved to the US from India in the late sixties, to pursue higher studies. For me as for many Indian youth, going to the US for education was itself a dream come true. US immigration laws at that time did not encourage settling there permanently. Just to live and attend school there for a brief period was powerfully attractive.

Upon completing degrees at Brown University and the University of Iowa, I was lured by IBM in 1972, with a salary of more than US$18K. This, too, was like living a dream, being hired to a position coveted by many Americans. Granted that industrial positions invariably paid more than academic ones, my starting salary was nonetheless higher than that of my Ph.D. advisor, a tenured professor at Iowa.

On account of antitrust battles suddenly facing IBM, its promise to sponsor me for a permanent US visa was not fulfilled. Newly implemented US labor certification rules, moreover, were sufficiently confusing to preempt efforts to find employment in American academic institutions. Hurriedly, somewhat desperately, I was able to arrange an Assistant Professorship at the University of Regina in Saskatchewan, Canada.

Far from the New York metropolitan area where I had been ensconced with IBM, this small prairie community and its lack of a graduate program hindered my ability to carry out significant research. Shortly after I moved there, on a research visit to Stanford University in California, I met my future wife, a US citizen. It became expedient to move to the US. The Detroit area became our first destination. Having achieved tenure in Canada, I wanted a professional move which would, at least, provide similar job security in the US. With considerable effort, I landed a tenured Associate Professorship at Oakland University on Detroit's northern outskirts.

Oakland had a doctoral program but lacked a strong research environment. With a fairly strong publication record already established, I then sought an academic environment which would facilitate further research. This I found in 1982, in the highly regarded Computer Engineering department of the University of Massachusetts at Amherst. Truly able researchers like Harold Stone and Michael Arbib had helped give the school a name for scholarship. The offer from UMASS included a tenured full professorship – again, like a dream come true. In Amherst, I could interact with people I had greatly admired. UMASS was astute at attracting bright people. An overall environment of open-mindedness enabled me to take on the duties of Coordinator of Computer Engineering, with its professional *carte blanche* to hire talent from industry without regard to cultural background.

The Computer Engineering program grew in status, aided by a forward-looking, progressive administration. I was able, for example, to hire a 25-year veteran of General Electric, of huge respect and stature within the industrial community, as a full professor, despite his not possessing a doctorate.

Chair Offer from Texas A&M University

In the late 80s, one of MIT's associate deans was wooed to Texas A&M University as a dean. Significant monies "oiled" TAMU's desire to create an institution for Texas on a par, say, with Massachusetts Institute of Technology.

With some of those Texas funds, this new dean created several endowed chairs. One in computer science was among the most lucrative. I was wooed for it. Life in Texas seemed far removed from

Amherst's liberal environment. Not surprisingly, I declined TAMU's offer.

The following year, 1990, TAMU asked me to reconsider. This time I allowed the process to go forward, curious about the staggering salary that would come with the chair. Money had become a factor for me, having by then four children to educate.

The then Head of Computer Engineering at TAMU possessed what seemed like a vision for the field, so I made a visit to meet him. He himself had recently moved from the prestigious University of Michigan. TAMU's campus was resplendent with buildings. Its College of Engineering, the largest in America, actually had a separate multi-storied building for each engineering discipline. The furnishings and accoutrements reminded me of an impressive corporate headquarters. Strip malls were connected by highways, and sumptuous homes could be had for about half their cost in the Northeast.

The informal offer, for double my salary at UMASS, was exceedingly attractive. It was, moreover, the highest salary for any TAMU engineering professor, other than the dean. To this foreign-born scholar, it seemed a great honor. In addition, the offer provided that I could make several junior faculty appointments and utilise the chair's generous endowment of nearly $2 million – to say nothing of a significant grant. Still, I had valued Amherst's quality of life, a tough-to-replicate intangible, particularly in TAMU's pointedly conservative milieu.

The formal offer almost scotched the deal. It contained a provision for review of my chair every five years. This review, it seemed, could be used to remove the chair and its accompanying endowment. Finding this condition entirely unacceptable, I declined the offer.

Shortly thereafter, TAMU contacted me with the "surprise" that it was willing to remove the periodic review clause in my case. Such an exception made their offer tantamount to a lifetime appointment. With the university's counter-signature in hand, I plunged ahead. (Only later did I learn – the hard way – that such an appealing deal had been effected without the knowledge or approval of TAMU's Board of Regents.) Four years later, a new dean requested that I "regularise" my chair with the others, by agreeing to review. I did not comply.

I had a sense of foreboding when, relatively soon, the dean who had formerly been at MIT resigned. Also apparent at TAMU from the outset was a palpable sense of resentment toward foreign-born students. This took the form of explicit, pejorative mail (from a supposed colleague), targeting students of Indian origin.

My impulse was to try to assuage venomous feelings, for instance, by circulating memoranda about commitment to improving TAMU's computer science department by drawing on talented students of whatever background – on the model of what had been so successful at UMASS. It was soon obvious that many faculty were not interested in jumping on such a bandwagon. Faculty comments about Third-World students abounded, and strident advocacy that more should be done for Texas-born students.

In retrospect, I recall that during my interview, one department member dared to suggest that I had been fired from another university. Questions followed which were also clearly out of line, concerning my religion and what was perceived as the mixed marriage I had entered into. TAMU's administration, moeover, had held back key information: that a professor had threatened the department that I would be "in harm's way" if I decided to accept the offer, and that the faculty would seek to undermine me in anything I might strive to accomplish professionally.

On the day of my arrival at TAMU in January of 1992, I was nothing short of interrogated by staff in the payroll office regarding my citizenship status. Their attitude of disbelief that I could actually have secured American citizenship a decade earlier smacked of outright racism. Additionally, I encountered innuendo and blatant accusation of nepotism, since a cousin of mine happened also to belong to the department.

There was never any mistaking very marked hostility from various faculty members. That my chair carried with it special privileges, including spending authority on discretionary funds to underwrite activities I undertook to enhance the department and the university, was viewed with unnatural attention. Was this jealousy?

This day-to-day poisoned atmosphere was extremely debilitating. My efforts to gain redress from the administration resulted in empty words. With departmental taunting persisting, I offered what seemed a constructive counter-proposal: that a similar appointment be found for me outside the department. This never materialized.

In sum, from the get-go, I was deliberately made to feel like the outsider. At faculty meetings, colleagues openly questioned the wisdom of hiring foreign-born faculty. Harassment intensified, diverse in form, enabled by covert acceptance of the status quo. Graffiti was pasted on my office door.

To his credit, the department head tried to mitigate the barrage, he, too, being a butt of abuse. He was sensitive, and brought to the situation fair understanding of the abusers' mindsets. The support he consistently offered can best be illustrated by his words on a memo to me in 1995:

> I appreciate the various concerns you have raised. Our environment is indeed much less than many of us would like. It is distressing that some are so opposed to progress. This opposition itself forces and breeds actions that exacerbate the situation; I regret very much the distress that you and others have suffered. I hope that we can work for better situations in the future.

> I want to assure you that you are very highly valued. Your performance was excellent in all major areas of evaluation, research, teaching and external service. You had such a long list of accomplishments that I did not even try to list them all in your evaluation. The brevity of my statements that you were doing excellent was intended to convey the message that the performance was so clearly excellent that it was needless to list everything. Your presence in the Department has made a large difference in our recognition, our ability to attract excellent faculty candidates, and our research contributions. I value your work very highly....

The department contained other elements which I found insupportable, not the least being that certain faculty used their classroom podium as a pulpit to inculcate Christianity in computer science students. My query to the administration about this practice met with the explanation that faculty were essentially free agents. A more vitriolic response greeted my opposition to a major overhaul being proposed, that Electrical Engineering and Computer Science be merged.

Introduction of Post-Tenure Review at A&M

As my working environment degenerated, I contemplated on more than one occasion tendering my resignation. The straw that broke the camel's back was the Post-Tenure Review Policy that the TAMU administration sought to implement. That so sweeping a policy reversal was ushered in *sans* faculty input was bad enough, but to gut the long-established tenure policy, the hallmark of freedom of professional expression, by faculty review every five years, essentially placed seasoned staff on probation (or else forced them to resign). I therefore felt compelled to use my elected position in the Faculty Senate to try to overturn this overreach of micromanagement.

No TAMU administrators supported my dissent. I therefore brought the matter before the faculty, already contravened by retroactive approval of the Post-Tenure Review Policy. No faculty felt they could oppose the policy. Fear of retaliation was too strong. Without other recourse, I sent this memo to the Board of Regents, the university's governing body, on October 14, 1996:

Post-tenure review, as approved by faculty senate, will dangerously dissuade any top scholars from relocating here. This is critical for reputation-building. I must ask that you take heed.

Attracting scholarship is impeded by TAMU's image as micromanaged by outsiders! It is a fact that TAMU has real difficulty luring senior faculty from top universities in many fields, despite million dollar endowed chairs. Tenured professors of true repute from a Stanford, Michigan, Berkeley, or Princeton rarely apply here.

Recent ranking by the National Research Council saw TAMU and the State of Texas fare poorly. Small, new state-supported University of California, San Diego performed much better (than all Texan universities combined!) Such statistics must be taken seriously, as they explain our inability to attract senior faculty. Post-tenure review only raises further roadblocks.

State school systems like the mentioned University of California (UC) excel year after year, their accomplishments proportional to their emphasis on scholarship, as well as aggressively going after scholars from top schools. An attractive early retirement package was recently extended at UC, to usher out those wanting to leave. Similar ideas must be implemented here; our reputation is marginalized with policy that can revoke tenure.

Review of direction/priorities of our own higher education system begins with post-tenure faculty performance discussions; periodic review of research quality by peers may be warranted. Eminent scholars should never feel reluctant to consider TAMU because of this shadow of post-tenure termination. Care and time build reputation, misguided actions dissipate that too easily (see below).

These comments are meant constructively, helpfully; share them as appropriate.

Cc: Faculty Senate

I circulated this memo amongst faculty along with a related article from the *New York Times*. The article delineated how, to counter a similar administrative move at another school, the faculty proposed unionising – which caused their Board of Regents to back down. I hoped to spearhead encouragement, raising consciousness. Full discussion of issues involved in implementing such a policy, I felt, must occur. Dissent by faculty over this policy-implementation had been essentially nil. My own chief consideration was that with such a policy in place, attracting exceptional scholars would be effectively impossible. TAMU's vast potential would, I fervently believed, be reduced to that of the dinosaurs. Consciousness-raising efforts on my part were viewed as "trouble-making," to say the least.

Computer Seized and Documents Removed

While I was out of town in the autumn of 1996, my TAMU secretary was informed that my office was to be visited by a staff member from the System Audit Office, taking "custody" of my desktop computer and confiscating certain documents. She was given express instructions *not* to notify me about this development. The bafflement I expressed on my return was greeted by her reply that my computer had been taken for repair and the missing papers had been "filed." My almost immediate visit to the Head's office let me know that I was in real trouble. He, too, had apparently been left in the dark.

My efforts to explain – by contacting the offices of the dean, the provost and even the university president – got no response, though finally it was confirmed that I was, yes, somehow under investigation. I was then informed that the matter had gone beyond "university business," that the case had been handed to the county District Attorney. Besides failing to get my computer returned, I was further stonewalled as to the nature of the allegations.

Soon, my graduate students were interrogated and told to cease all communication with me. My secretary had been instructed by the university administration to relay every few hours an update of any and all communications with me. Was this spying? All were informed that I was under *criminal* investigation and to cease communication.

The files stored on the computer that was seized have never been returned. Summoning the Open Records Act of the State of Texas yielded only a copy of the letter from the District Attorney to the university, advising against release of my property. Here is a letter I received at the time from the university's director of internal audit:

> Dear Dr. Pradhan,
>
> It has come to our attention that your TAMU Computer Science 489 class was postponed on 11/19/96 due to the purported unavailability of your electronic lecture notes. It was indicated that the notes also maintained on the TAMU Computer Science Department Computer in our possession.
>
> Your past correspondence has made neither mention of specific files nor ownership of the files being requested and therefore, your request could not be processed. In order for us to provide the copies of files maintained on the computer, please refer to the attached memo sent to [the executive engineering dean] on November 12, 1996.
>
> To reiterate, we are willing to expedite your request but the origination of specific files must be firmly established to make certain that they be made available only to the file's originator.

The University somehow obtained copies of my personal bank records, as well as those of my students. It was hoped, I gathered, that material suggesting impropriety like double billing or fraud would be found, but such was not in evidence. Lacking this, the District Attorney could not proceed towards an indictment, which would have given the university "good cause" for dismissal. Instead, TAMU took the rather unconventional step of suspending me from my duties with no hearing. This act earned the university an official complaint from the American Association of University Professors (the letter is reprinted a few paragraphs hence).

The suspension was termed "administrative leave," a euphemism nonexistent in the university's own guidelines. The audit of my professional activities was in fact released to the press before it was released to me. The suspension also caused me to forfeit a much coveted Fulbright Chair in Europe. I was effectively under house arrest.

Here is the confidential memo I directed to the engineering dean on August 25, 1997:

> The administration's response to the audit report is untenable. Your letter states that the auditors never solicited any information from me – either written or verbal –

despite, I remind you, my repeated requests, over the past ten months, to supply such. Steps taken are not only unilateral, but dangerously akin to 'sentencing' prior to trial. (Such action, of course, comes directly on the heels of the Kafka-style indictment proceedings, which have loomed menacingly over my family and me during all of this time). Whatever the content of the allegations, I certainly should have been given opportunity to meet and discuss **prior** to action taken.

Firstly, you demand the postponement of my development leave plan. My leave application, submitted in December of '96, contained a letter from the Fulbright Commission, preferring the Distinguished FLAD chair. Upon the university's acceptance of this leave request, in March of '97, I correspondingly accepted the Fulbright offer. In July of '97, the university approved approximately $8,000 for the university's portion of a portion of my expenses, to be incurred during the period of the development leave. This, of course, was a further confirmation on the part of the university, toward fulfilling the university's commitment and approval.

The Fulbright Commission informs me that it is, indeed, to close to the start-up date to inaugurate, any changes. Postponement would cause very real hardship to the university and students at Aveiro (Portugal). Also, and importantly, this action on the part of the university must adversely impact on future Fulbright awardees to TAMU faculty.

Further, the action on the part of the university to supersede my functions to graduate student advisor at TAMU is already, you should be aware, causing very real concern and disruption among these fine students. It is certainly within their reasonable realm of expectation that a far more responsible handling be invoked, directly affecting, as it does, their very careers and futures.

There is an additional and related issue which, up until this time, I had kept to the background but which now appears to demand bringing forth. You are already aware of racial tensions which have characterised our department's graduate student environment. (Not only overt racial slurs, from fellow white students, but certain staff openly remarking on the sizable number of foreign students within my own group, etc.) It would seem that sponsoring agencies – with whom the university has already –established contractual obligations.

Despite the university's eleven months of investigation, I have been afforded less than one month, in which to furnish comprehensive documentation. The first colleague whom I approached advises me of his instructions **NOT** to communicate with me, must have less to supply a corroborative statement (see attached).

I remind you of my own forthrightness – from the beginning – to clear any and all ambiguities and/or misreading, leading to suspicions of wrongdoing. In keeping with anything resembling good-faith, due-process proceedings, I must insist that no sanctions, as delineated in your letter, be invoked – until ALL facts have **first** been completely and satisfactorily established.

I, of course, appreciate your serious perusal.

I continued to press AAUP for some action as my situation would only make matters worse for all TAMU faculty. In my experience there, the faculty and some administrators lived in fear and suppressed their freedom of expression. Most were afraid to speak up because a tenured position was too precious to risk.

AAUP took action on my request and wrote a letter to the university pointing out flagrant violations of its own rules. With hindsight, I suspect this made TAMU administrators even more determined not to admit any culpability but to prove they were right by bringing criminal charges. They seemed convinced that making an example of me would exonerate them in the eyes of the academic world. Here is the AAUP letter to TAMU's president, Dr. Ray M. Bowen, dated September 18, 1997:

Dr. Dhiraj K. Pradhan, professor in the Department of Computer Science at Texas A&M University, has sought the advice and assistance of the American Assocation of University Professors as a result of the letter, dated August 19, 1997, that he received from Vice Chancellor and Dean of Engineering C. Roland Haden, notifying him that he was being suspended from all academic and other university duties, effective immediately. We understand that the administration's action included postponement of Professor Pradhan's previously approved development leave that was to have begun on September 1, with the result that he is being prevented from taking up a teaching appointment as a Fulbright Chair in Portugal that is to commence at the end of this month. We understand further that the stated basis for this action is a report from the System Director of Internal Audit, alleging financial improprieties on the part of Professor Pradhan.

The interest of the Assocation in the case of Professor Pradhan stems from its longstanding commitment to principles of academic freedom and tenure as set forth in the enclosed joint 1940 <u>Statement of Principles on Academic Freedom Tenure</u>. Derivative procedural standards are found in the joint 1958 <u>Statement on Procedural Standards in Faculty Dismissal Proceedings</u> (also enclosed). We have noted the relevant provisions of the TAMU *Faculty and Staff Handbook*.

Action to separate a faculty member from ongoing academic responsibilities prior to demonstration of stated cause in appropriate proceedings is considered to be a suspension, which is justified, according to the 1958 <u>Statement,</u> "only if immediate harm to the faculty member or others is threatened by continuance." (Similar language may be found in Section VIII. F.4 of the TAMU handbook.) The 1958 <u>Statement</u> and Interpretive Comment Number 9 on the 1940 <u>Statement</u> speak to suspension of a faculty member as a step that may be taken, when justified, pending the outcome of an academic proceeding in which the administration assumes the burden of establishing adequacy of cause before an elected faculty committee. Professor Pradhan, however, appears to have been removed from his academic duties without any statement, let alone demonstration, as to why his continuance might pose a threat of "immediate harm" to himself or others.

With respect to the administration's action in denying Professor Pradhan a development leave and thus the opportunity to take up his Fulbright appointment in Portugal next week, we fail to understand why, if he has no duties or commitments at the university, he should not be free to spend his time where and how he wishes.

The information on the case of Professor Pradhan has come to us exclusively from him, and we realise that you may have additional information that would contribute to our understanding of what has occurred. We shall therefore welcome your comments. If the facts as we have recounted them are essentially accurate, we urge that the administration promptly rescind its suspension of Professor Pradhan and withdraw its objections to his departure for Portugal.

Sincerely,

"Interpretation" of Mentor Graphic's Gift

The University asked that I submit a response to their audit report. Allegations were that I made personal use of university resources, including meeting industry colleagues at a conference to discuss both university business and potential technology transfer of university research. The allegations overlooked that the gift from Mentor Graphics, monies made payable to me, was expressly for technology transfer.

Irony of ironies: I had endorsed the check for this gift *to* the university so as to enhance total department funding. The amount of funds I had allegedly misused was a fraction of the amount *given*, by my endorsement,· to TAMU. Reprinted below is the memo of September 4, 1995, to the Assistant Vice President and Controller from the Head of the Department of Computer Science, on the subject of "Gift from Mentor Graphics":

> Attached is a letter from Mentor Graphics confirming their gift to fund Dr. Dhiraj Pradhan's research. This letter supersedes any other correspondence from the donor relating to this deposit. Also including from Dr. Pradhan's reaffirming that there are no deliverables associated with this gift.
>
> At this time we would like to request that a reverse deposit be made on Interdepartmental transfer #0043819 from account #510902 to account #511423. We would also ask that a budget be set up for these funds in account #511423 for the full amount of $32,000, less than development fee. Through the mix-up in entering this gift, various expenditures have already been made. We would appreciate your expediting this transaction so that travel expenses can be reimbursed.

Invoking a vaguely written law, I was indicted for abuse of official capacity in the spring of 1998. The law's ambiguity invited my appeal to the District Court. By that fall, all charges were dismissed.

Concurrently, I filed a civil suit in federal court against the university. The court in Austin where the lawsuit was filed granted a preliminary hearing in September of 1998. This was one small bright spot in my struggle, since the federal judge reinstated me to my chair, allowing my return to campus duties.

Shortly after that, the unversity made a settlement offer. Not surprisingly, I rejected it as too little too late, and proceeded with the lawsuit asking for damages. The university countered with official notification that my position would be terminated effective July of 1999. The university meanwhile made several motions to dismiss the lawsuit. None was successful.

I was then re-indicted on a single count of abuse of official capacity. Rather than risk the possibility of a lengthy jail term, I accepted a plea bargain that included probation. Interestingly, however, through the discovery process for the civil suit, a copy of the donor's original letter establishing my chair was unearthed. It was incontrovertible proof of the discretionary terms of the monies that came with my chair, and effectively exonerated me of any seeming mismanagement. I promptly filed another appeal to dismiss the criminal charges.

Two months later, however, I was arrested on charges of violation of probation. The charges alleged unauthorized use of university telephone and photocopier. The upshot was my spending thirty days in jail and the end of further monitoring of me by the probation authorities.

Two months after that, my lawsuit against the university went to trial. It lasted a week. From the start, the university made sure the jury was aware of the criminal charges against me. I lost the lawsuit. My recent release from jail made it virtually impossible to convince the jury that my own due process had been violated. We had felt from the start that winning the suit against such a "well-connected" university was a longshot. The financial consequence was hundreds of thousands of dollars in legal bills that had to be paid out of my own pocket, effectively exhausting our life savings. Fighting this costly battle, however, had always been about the critical principles at stake: (a) illegal search and seizure, (b) monitoring of emails and checking accounts of not only me but professional associates all over the country, and (c) suspension and termination of my university position, without a hearing.

The sad truth I reluctantly came to understand is that the words of the US Constitution are only as good as the interpretation of judges, juries, and a local mindset, influenced by geographic location and personal/political association. The saddest truth is that justice, in effect, goes to the highest bidder, that without financial resources to fight in the courts, guilt is essentially a foregone conclusion. All my previous time in the US had fostered belief in the high-mindedness of constitutional rights and their important protective nature.

I have by now become convinced that most of the poor in the US do *not* enjoy such rights. During my own time in the Brazos County Jail, I met poor whites, blacks and Mexicans who were there for a long time because they just could not afford a lawyer more aggressive than the one assigned. One elderly white man had been jailed for ten years for violations of probation for quite a petty crime. A young black man had been incarcerated for months for the negligible amount of marijuana found (or planted) in his home, when it was searched without a warrant. Neither of these fellow inmates, unlike me, had access to attorney representation.

Ironically, the plight of these people made my plight tolerable. It made me dream of establishing a charitable fund to be used to fight for such people. It opened my eyes to how this great nation has more people in its prison system, including those on probation, than the rest of the democratic free world. America's words of freedom ring false when so many of its own citizens are deprived of it. The universally valued American ideal of freedom does not translate into freedom for blacks, minorities, or just plain poor. With crime constantly being hyped and their fears played on, Americans suffer from a frightening desensitization.

For me there was a silver lining: first, getting out of Texas to a position at Oregon State University, then on to a chair at the University of Bristol, from where this account is written.

Chapter Four

Mischief at Muggsville

Hugo A. Meynell

Kenneth Westhues is to be deeply congratulated on the terrifying vision of institutional evil which he has presented to us. Such things are permitted to exist, largely because people cannot believe how bad they are; the great weapon to be used against them is publicity. I myself would find such allegations incredible, but for a case intimately known to myself, some features of which I would like to describe in what follows, with names of persons and places changed.

When Graham Nanton, who had come from an English university in 1981, was elected to the Royal Society of Canada in 1993 – at the time, he was the only member of his faculty to have been so honoured – he might have been forgiven for thinking that he was in reasonably good standing at the University of Muggsville. Nanton was by all accounts quite successful as a teacher, and had the impression that he was generally liked not only by his students, but also by colleagues and staff.

Later in the same year, an endogenous depression which had dogged him since adolescence culminated in an episode so severe that he had briefly to go into hospital, where he was prescribed anti-depressants. He was advised to take some weeks off work, which he declined to do, having always found hard work an antidote to depression (the fall term was about to begin). The psychiatrist who interviewed him wrote a note to his head of department and his dean – this note was not solicited by Nanton himself – asking that he be treated with special consideration due to his depressive illness. What consideration they in fact showed will be the main topic of what follows.

The case seems fairly typical of those Westhues described in *Eliminating Professors* (Mellen, 1998). Most of the "ten specific clues" mentioned in his more recent book characterize this case as well: a "popular, high-achieving target" (at least as compared with the average of his colleagues), absence of due process, odd timing, resistance to external review, and prior marginalization (see *Administrative Mobbing*, Mellen, 2004, pp. 30f). There is no space here for a detailed account of the whole business, so I shall confine my attention to three episodes with their antecedents and fallout: (1) the initial charge of harassment against Nanton in 1994; (2) his temporary ejection from his office and building in 1995; (3) his final expulsion from the university, on the pretext of illness, in 1998.

The Department of Folklore included two female sessional instructors, who were in their thirties. One of them, Susanna Charles, Nanton hardly knew; though on social occasions within the department she gave him a strong impression that she disliked him. Some might have found her attractive; although, so far as Nanton was concerned, her somewhat pre-Raphaelite style of looks was offset by her sulkiness of disposition. The other, Celia Kendal, had been a pupil of Nanton's some years before in a graduate class. She was rather shy in manner, but pleasant-looking. One day in the late 1980s, in the common-room of the department, Nanton had ventured to compliment her on the dress that she was wearing. She took the compliment with evident pleasure, and remarked that her husband always chose her clothes. "Snap!," said Nanton; "my wife always chooses mine." That evening, Nanton told his wife the story; and the latter commented, that it was rather a strange woman whose husband selected her clothes. Nanton said he thought this was rather sexist of her, as she always chose his clothes, and he was very glad that she did so, as her taste was vastly better than his own. Ms. Kendal had shortly afterwards gone to another university to take her Ph. D., for which she had asked for and obtained a reference from Nanton.

It must have been about four years after the incident just mentioned that Nanton took occasion to compliment Dr. Kendal (as she was by now) once again, in the same place and to the same effect. Dr. Kendal just smiled; but later in the week he was summoned to the office of the head of department, Vincent Noseworthy. Dr. Kendal was sitting there, and asked in a constrained voice that Dr. Nanton should not in future make reference to her clothes, as it got her in such a state that she did not know what to put on in the morning. She also asked that Nanton not talk about sex in her presence – which he had no recollection of doing. Nanton was rather disturbed that she had made such an official issue of these matters; why could she not just have let him know her feelings at the time? He reminded her, in an attempt to lighten the atmosphere of the meeting, that he was not Hitler, or even Genghis Khan. Two significant things which he did not know at the time he discovered later. Dr. Kendal's husband had recently left her for another *man*. And he was told years later, by a close female friend and former pupil of his, that while Dr. Kendal was a good teacher, she did seem unduly obsessed with sex.

At all events, Nanton was more distressed by the incident than he should have been, and next day (which was Saturday) walked round to the home of his colleague and staunch friend Herbert Innes, to tell him how upset he was. Innes, and his anthropologist wife, treated Nanton with great kindness, and told him he should not be unduly concerned by the antics of someone whom Innes considered an unduly "uppish" sessional. But Nanton felt more damage control was in order, and rang up another sessional, Dr. Wendy Underwood, with whom he had had many conversations on academic and other subjects. He asked her whether, if she heard unpleasant rumours about him, she would stick up for him, and assure any offended parties that he deeply regretted having annoyed them, however unwittingly. He blurted out, rather to his surprise, that he felt quite suicidal about the matter. He did not mention Dr. Kendal's name, but Dr. Underwood guessed it for herself. She also treated Nanton very kindly, and said she would be glad to discuss the matter at greater length with him as a friend; but she thought he might need professional help. Next he rang up Ms. Charles, who, in spite of her dislike, he thought regarded him with respect, for reasons which would take us too far afield to state. The whole conversation between them could not have taken as much as half a minute. Just as he had done with Dr. Underwood, Nanton asked Ms. Charles whether, if she heard unpleasant rumours at his expense, she would stick up for him. Ms. Charles's reaction was rather disturbing. First she said, in a voice dripping with sarcasm, that it was "not her place" to help Dr. Nanton; and then she shouted, "and don't ring me up at home!" – whereupon she banged down the receiver.

The next Monday morning, to Nanton's amazement, he found that he had been accused, in a letter from Noseworthy to Dean Fetter, of "harassing" Dr. Innes, Dr. Underwood, and Ms. Charles. (Later, Innes and Underwood both denied that they had been harassed by Nanton, the former with indignation; but that made no difference.) This got him what is called a "counselling letter" from the dean, as well as a rather painful interview with him. But the interview ended on a fairly positive note, when Nanton had not only insisted that he had harassed no-one, even on the widest interpretation of that notoriously elastic term, but begged Fetter to consult Innes about what was really going on in the department of Folklore. Fetter assured him that he would do so, as they shook hands. However, when Nanton passed this message on to Innes, the latter, who had a much lower opinion of Fetter than did Nanton at the time, told him that he never would, in spite of his assurances; and Innes turned out to be right.

It was largely Nanton's efforts to get what seemed to him this monstrous and insulting charge of harassment overturned, or at least properly and independently investigated, which led to his expulsion from his department and building a year later, and his ultimate banning from campus. Nanton should, according to a man in the Law Department who later advised him, have officially "grieved" this "counselling letter," as well as another which he received a few months later; but he did not do so, partly because he did not want to annoy Fetter, whom he still regarded as his friend, and acting on misinformation; and partly because he did not realize the degree of danger that he was in. Poor fool, he thought that he was of some value to the university; had not the President thrown a party in honour of himself and a political scientist when they were elected to the Royal Society?

He was forbidden to communicate with either Dr. Kendal or Ms. Charles. He could not, however, always restrain his signs of discomfort in the presence of the latter, though he tried to avoid her as much as possible. On the other hand, he made special efforts to wave an olive branch in her direction by supporting the positions which she took at departmental meetings, a point noted by the ever-observant Innes (who accused Nanton of "sucking up" to her) but overlooked, as it turned out, by the authorities.

For about two years, Nanton had been organizing a conference on the justification of the humanities, where scholars from a wide range of institutions and academic disciplines would discuss this topic, which is surely quite an important one. Early in 1995, his project came to fruition, and the conference seemed a real success; Nanton felt the occasion to be the summit of his career. Fetter and Noseworthy were both invited by him to chair a session, and did so. Soon after the conference, Nanton asked Fetter whether he could have a meeting with Ms. Charles, and Fetter said he would see about it. A week or two later, he told Nanton that he had spoken with Ms. Charles, and that her answer was "interesting." She had told him that while Nanton's behaviour had "improved," he seemed to be deliberately avoiding her in the department, and to show signs of discomfort when they did meet; she found this "demeaning." Fetter's next communication to Nanton was an official "reprimand." Nanton felt desperately hurt by this; though he did not know at the time that it was preliminary to suspension or dismissal. After some hesitation – he still did not want to quarrel with Fetter more than he could help – he rang Teresa Lambton of the Union. Ms. Lambton emphasized what a serious matter a "reprimand" was, and strongly advised him to "grieve" it.

Now we come to Nanton's worst tactical error, which provided Fetter with what Westhues calls the "incident" required for taking Nanton's elimination to the next stage. The letter was handwritten, in considerable agony of mind, between three and four of what was a virtually sleepless night. It was reproachful but affectionate, expressive of the fondness which, in spite of everything, he still felt for his dean. On the advice of the Union, he would "grieve" the "reprimand," grossly unfair as he thought it was; but hoped the dean would not take this personally, since he valued their friendship. In an attempt to lighten the atmosphere, he cited one "William Flake" to the effect that the cut worm forgives the plough. He told Fetter that he was sad that he had not consulted Dr. Innes about the real state of his department, when he had undertaken to do so. But what made the letter a crucial "incident" in this affair, in the sense given by

Westhues, was the end, which had better be quoted in full. "God bless you, Captain Vere. Sincerely, V. Fabrikant (erased but legible) G. Nanton."

The day after next, Nanton was summoned to Fetter's office, where there were seated, along with Fetter himself, Noseworthy (looking distinctly uncomfortable, Nanton thought), and members of the Union. Fetter said that while Nanton's letter on the whole was acceptable, he took strong exception to the end. Then he started shouting at Nanton (colour appeared in his cheeks as he was doing so). "Do you want to kill me? Do you want to kill Dr. Noseworthy? Do you want to kill Ms. Charles?" Nanton said, as calmly as he could, that he wanted to do none of these things, but he admitted that he was desperate. After some half an hour of this kind of thing, Nanton excused himself to go and conduct a class. A young colleague saw him on the way, and said later that he was struck by the intense distress that showed in his face. Nanton hopes that he conducted his class adequately, but has an idea that he did not. These events took place, by the way, on Maundy Thursday, which one might think was rather a bad day for kangaroo courts.

The reader may remember that Billy Budd invokes his beloved Captain Vere in the manner cited by Nanton, when he is just about to be hanged from the yard-arm. The other reference was a deliberate piece of irony; Nanton though that Fetter, as a professor of English, could not fail to recognize it as such. It also might be pointed out that Dr. Fabrikant, at the time of the actions for which he became famous, owned guns, and was proficient in their use. Nanton had not handled firearms of any kind since his military service, which had ended almost forty years before. And as a cousin of his remarked, more justly than charitably, even if he had a gun, he probably would be unable to hit a barn, if you had put him inside and closed the door.

What hurt Nanton most was that he liked Noseworthy, and positively revered Fetter; he was horrified that his foolish joke had been so appallingly misunderstood. After his class, he grasped Noseworthy by the hand. "I'm very fond of you," he said earnestly, "and devoted to Veronica [Noseworthy's wife]; it's hardly likely that I'd put a bullet through your head." He left a note, in the same words, in Noseworthy's pigeon-hole. This was taken as another threat. He left a message on Fetter's home answering-machine, which was to the effect that he was no danger to anyone else's life, and had never been so; not even his own life was in danger from himself at present. That was taken as yet another threat. In the evening, he went to Fetter's office, and waited while Fetter finished work on his computer. He then said, "You make me feel completely worthless." "How can that be?" said Fetter, "Haven't I often commended you for your work?" This was perfectly true.

The following incident appears to be a classic example of the "odd timing" mentioned by Westhues, which seems calculated by administrations to get their victims at an unfair disadvantage.

Shortly after the episode of the letter, Nanton visited Britain for a month during vacation time. (Everything seemed to go well there, and he gave four lectures which appeared to be a success.) When he returned, his daughter had a message from the Union that he would find a request that he should attend a meeting with his dean and head of department. He should on no account attend this meeting, said the Union; if he did, he would almost certainly find himself suspended for six months without pay. They added that the administration was empowered to do this at the drop of a hat, without any inquiry being made. Nanton regarded the warning as paranoid; he "knew" that Noseworthy and Fetter were his personal friends, whose houses he had visited, as they had visited his, on social occasions. He duly found the note, which was friendly in tone, inviting him to attend a meeting to discuss some recent communications which he had had with them. But he took the Union's advice, and attended a meeting which they themselves set up. Fetter, having greeted Nanton very affably outside the door, abruptly changed his tone when they had entered the room and sat down. As the tears streamed down Nanton's cheeks, Fetter said that suspension without pay or dismissal were the only options open for him. The Union begged that, instead of this, Nanton should be barred for six months from his office and building, and promise to undergo intensive psychiatric treatment. Ultimately, though hardly with a good grace, Fetter accepted this proposal.

Nanton was prostrated by what had happened; but his wife Katherine fortunately kept her head. The Union, who had previously advised Nanton not to go to law, suddenly changed their minds, and said that this would be the right thing to do. Katherine had discovered that one of Nanton's colleagues was suing Noseworthy for theft of intellectual property(!); and proposed that she and Nanton should take their case to the same firm of lawyers. The lawyers were extremely sympathetic, and said that they simply could not understand where the university administration were coming from in their treatment of Nanton. However, to quote Hillaire Belloc, "They answered, as they took their fees, 'There is no cure for this disease.'" Nanton had no alternative than to submit to the humiliating conditions which had been imposed upon him. If he defied them, they would have no means of protecting him.

As to going to law against the university, the firm gave its opinion that Nanton did not have the temperament for it. If he did, lawyers for the university would engage in delaying tactics which would halt proceedings for about eighteen months; meanwhile Nanton would be paying legal counsel, presumably without drawing a salary himself. Judging by what Nanton has found out since, eighteen months was a very low estimate. And as Westhues says, unless their victims have very deep pockets indeed, university administrations can always bleed their victims dry if it comes to a legal battle.

Many people, colleagues, students, and ex-students – wrote letters on Nanton's behalf, of course to no effect. One of them especially moved Nanton; it said that he was not only a thoroughly good person, but, in academic terms, perhaps the most valuable member of the faculty. He was, however, rather open in personality and, the writer thought, vulnerable. While he understood that Nanton might make a remark that annoyed someone, he could not believe that he would ever say or do anything that was really insensitive or brutish.

Ed Whiston was a psychiatrist who had been monitoring Nanton's anti-depressive medication sine 1993. He told Nanton that he had been at a meeting with Fetter, on the subject of Nanton, while the latter was in Britain, and had assured Fetter that he was not dangerous, apparently to no avail. (He later told Nanton that he thought he was a remarkably sane person, an opinion Nanton would never have ventured about himself.) For the "intensive psychiatric treatment" insisted on by Fetter, Whiston recommended that he go to Dr. Samuel Huxley, who he said was the most distinguished practitioner in Muggsville. As the University was paying, Whiston remarked, Nanton might profit from the occasion to gain some expert insights into himself. Huxley was going on vacation, but slipped in one session with Nanton before he went; he gave him one more after he returned, after which he submitted his report.

Once in Huxley's office, Nanton very soon realized he was in the presence of a master; he had never felt so thoroughly understood "in the round," and marvelled over and over again at Huxley's insights. Nanton told Huxley, rather ruefully, the story of the erased signature, and said that he must find it rather self-destructive. Huxley raised his eyes to heaven. "Don't give me that psychological jargon," he said, "it was STOOPID" – which Nanton did not venture to deny. The report submitted by Huxley, however, was all that Nanton could have wished. The university, wrote Huxley, had been in danger of losing a distinguished scholar. No doubt Nanton had his eccentricities, but his principal need was not psychiatry but justice. He hoped that Ed Whiston (to whom the report was primarily addressed) would be able to suggest some way in which the authorities who had dealt with Nanton could save face. He himself could hardly envisage Nanton with a gun in his hands; but he thought he might be spurred to truly revolutionary activity if he considered that principles of equity and fair dealing for which he and other academics ought to stand were being violated. The report was evidently not to Fetter's liking; it is a remarkable thing that he said, in Nanton's hearing, "We must find another psychiatrist."

A few weeks after Nanton had moved into his new office, he was walking across campus – he remembers a light drizzle falling at the time – when President Gordon came to meet him, and seized him by the hand. "Are you all right?" cried Gordon. Nanton replied that he had been extremely unhappy, but now was on a reasonably even keel. "Have you gone to law?" asked Gordon. This was irresistible. "Yes. Sir, I have spent nearly $4,000 defending myself against people that I thought were my friends." "I hope you realize it is no doing of mine," said Gordon. A few days later, Nanton came across Gordon in the students' union; the President was wearing a funny hat, presumably for some charitable purpose. There were crowds of students milling about, but Gordon was able to say to Nanton, *sotto voce*, "I'm sure you will be able to find justice without going outside the university." This may, or may not, have had some reference to a statement made by a professor of political science some days earlier, to the effect that Nanton would never find a just solution to his difficulties unless he went outside the institution. Nanton was very grateful for the President's expression of sympathy; but if he really thought that Nanton was being badly treated, why could he not restrain the actions of his subordinates? About a year later, Gordon retired, and almost immediately died of a heart attack; perhaps, if he had been troubled with other cases like Nanton's, the event is hardly surprising.

As to "confidentiality," the authorities clearly wanted, in this case as in most of those discussed by Westhues, to keep their dealings with Nanton as secret as possible. He thought, and thinks still, that this was hardly compatible with good faith on their part. So far as he was concerned, everything about the affair could be be proclaimed from the housetops; if it should turn out that he had really wronged anyone by word or deed, however inadvertently, he wanted to tell them that he was sorry with all his heart.

Immediately after he was expelled from his office and building, he was required to sign an iniquitous "Letter of Understanding" – i.e., gag-order – which stipulated that he tell all inquirers that he was on sick leave. The implication, which was not spelled out, was that he should tell them nothing else. Nanton was compelled to sign this egregious document under the clear threat that, if he did not do so, he would be suspended without pay or dismissed. He interpreted what he had undertaken strictly *au pied de la lettre*; he told inquirers he was on sick leave, and a good deal else, too. He was, of course, duly hauled again before Fetter, and ordered, in stentorian tones, to keep to the spirit rather than the mere letter of the agreement. He has the suspicion that the document contained the loophole that it did due to the fact that the lawyer who composed it knew that, taken in the sense intended by its perpetrators, it was illegal, and in flagrant violation of Nanton's human rights. That forcing him to sign such a document was a morally squalid act should have been, one would have thought, obvious to anyone who had ever learned, or if they had learned had not forgotten, the distinction between good and evil. If the authorities had a clear conscience about the way in which they were treating their victim, they could have had no motive for imposing, with threats, an undertaking of secrecy upon him.

Katherine besought Nanton to do more work at home, since the authorities were so evidently out to "get" him. He passed this opinion on to Fetter, who wrote by way of reply, "I trust you know me and Vincent (Noseworthy) well enough not to put any credence in that view." Still, an article in the *Crier* had quoted "a veteran academic" as saying, "Certainly they are trying to destroy Nanton"; although she or he apparently did not divulge who "they" were.

Once the six months of Nanton's official exile were over, Fetter seemed almost as insistent on getting him back into his former office as he had originally been on ousting him from it. But Nanton was terrified at the prospect of return. By behaving in what seemed to him a perfectly normal and decent manner, he had already reached the end of the university's disciplinary road. Was it not inevitable that, if he spent much time in his department, someone would again take exception to something he had said or done with the best of intentions, and he would be suspended without pay or dismissed? He could come to the department for meetings, and to collect his mail, but he could teach, read and write far more effectively if he remained where he was. He appealed to the Union to this effect, and to Ed Whiston. Whiston told Fetter that, if Nanton returned to his former office, his state of anxiety would make it more or less impossible for him to do any effective work. Fetter countered by demanding that, if Nanton was not to return to his office in the department of Folklore, he should receive a letter from Whiston every three months stating that he was unfit to do so. Whiston replied, rather testily as he told Nanton, that it was very unlikely that the state of things would change significantly for at least a year.

Katherine had never had very good health, and was a borderline diabetic. At about this time, her doctor informed her that she had fully-fledged diabetes, and asked whether she had been going through any stress which might account for this. When she told him how the university administration had been treating her husband, he said that the worsening of her condition was fully accounted for. As Westhues says, university administrators make no scruple to destroy the physical and mental health of their victims.

It is surely rather a remarkable fact that, at this late stage of the game, Nanton still sometimes found himself mediating at meetings between departmental factions, and was once heartily thanked for this by a senior member of the department.

During 1997, Nanton served on a committee which was concerned with the administration of funds provided by a number of churches in Muggsville for a very definite purpose. Noseworthy, supported by Fetter, wanted to use the money in a way which seemed to Herbert Innes a palpable misuse of it, and he was quoted to that effect by the Muggsville *Crier*. But Innes was not on the committee, and he and Katherine both told Nanton that he ought to get involved. Nanton felt wounded and exhausted by his relations with the university administration, and had no wish further to antagonize them. So at first he declined to make a stand; but ultimately was persuaded that he must do so as a matter of conscience. So he roundly told the other members of the committee that what was being proposed amounted to the misappropriation of funds. Representatives of the contributing churches seemed to agree with him; as did a searing comment on Noseworthy's manoeuvre in the monthly *Saskitoba Rambler*. Later, when push had finally come to shove, the administration denied that Nanton's stand with regard to this matter had any relevance to their actions against him; but given his assessment of their overall probity and integrity on other grounds, Nanton has his doubts.

The fall of that year was, as things turned out, the Indian summer of Nanton's teaching. One small class, of about a dozen students, seemed to go especially well. The student reports, which Nanton saw in January, were among the most glowing that he had ever received. He had taken particular trouble over one student, and thought (he now believes wrongly) that he had identified the report which came from her. One day he saw her in the department, and thanked her for her report; she said, "You're welcome."

The student was a mature lady of somewhat porcine appearance (that Nanton did not find her physically attractive seems relevant to what follows), in her late thirties or early forties; we will call her Julia Johnson. Her performance in class and in written assignments was competent, but by no means excellent, and Nanton accordingly gave her marks in the B range. She wanted very much to obtain A's, and asked Nanton to go sentence by sentence through one of her essays, making suggestions about how she could improve her work. Nanton obliged her, though it occurred to him that it would be impossible to pay such attention to more than a very few of one's students. Ms. Johnson used often to come and talk to him privately immediately before and after class, as though there were some special personal relationship between them. Sometimes she would ask his opinion of other members of the class – whether young so-and-so were not very immature, and so on; but Nanton thought it proper not to be drawn in.

One day she came to his office, by appointment; Nanton assumed that the object was further to discuss her work. But no sooner had she sat down, than she started talking about her troubled relations with her husband. Now Nanton did not want to appear in a false light; so he hinted pretty broadly that he himself had not always been as good as he should have been. Thinking that he had made an error of judgment in going so far, he went on to say that her confidences were quite safe with him. She seemed quite unfazed, and continued to talk in her previous vein, while Nanton, who had had a little experience of student counselling in an earlier university setting, listened as well as he could. Later in their conversation, when the matter seemed germane, Nanton said that he considered that too intimate relations between students and faculty were very undesirable; he added that he thought that some university teachers were grievously at fault in the matter. (He had in mind, among others, some members of the faculty of the University of Muggsville, though of course he did not mention this.) Ms. Johnson seemed to need personal encouragement, and to be likeable in character and manner; so Nanton suggested that he should give her lunch, which he did, in a very public area of the university, a week or so later. Their conversation on that occasion, as Nanton remembers it, was pleasant but unremarkable.

Early in February of 1998, Nanton received a note, from the acting dean Flaminia Kuyper, that there had been a student complaint against him. He racked his brains, but could not think what behaviour on his part might have provoked this; Ms. Johnson did not even occur to him in this connection, as relations between them seemed to have been unequivocally cordial. After consultation with the Union, Nanton asked Dr. Kuyper for more details of the complaint, with which she obliged him. The complainant had come to Nanton's office to discuss her work; when she revealed details of her personal life, she immediately regretted having done so. She had found Nanton's own revelations about himself offensive and intrusive. She had felt, however, that she could not decently refuse his invitation to lunch. She mentioned their brief encounter in the department, when Nanton had thanked her for her class evaluation; but claimed that she had been trying to avoid him at the time. Nanton felt surprised that she had not expressed her feelings at their interview in his office, and that she had felt unable to turn down his invitation to lunch; she was, after all, a mature and apparently capable woman, not a nervous and inexperienced eighteen-year-old. But he admitted that he had made a real, if venial, error of judgment, and wanted sincerely to apologise for it to Ms. Johnson. So, once again in consultation with the Union, he asked Dr. Kuyper if he could meet with her, preferably in the presence of a third party who was expert in the unravelling of tangled human relationships. (The university employs such people in its Faculty/Staff Assistance Programme.)

Dr. Kuyper refused his request, in a lengthy note so vitriolic as to be redolent of a severe psychopathological condition on her part; it provoked a kind of temporary emotional breakdown in Nanton. On the morning that he received it, he was supposed to attend a departmental meeting; but when he appeared for it, it was remarked how ill he looked. Before the meeting was called to order, he left, and staggered across campus to the Union. Teresa Lambton calmed him down as well as she could, said "This too shall pass," and recommended that he take stress leave. This Nanton was unwilling to do, partly because, as I have said before, he found work an analgesic; but mainly on the ground that he was due to deliver a paper on the next day in the department, on a topic that he cared deeply about, and on which he wanted to hear the opinions of his colleagues and of students. In fact, he felt at his best in his delivery of the paper, and in the subsequent discussion, where many helpful and instructive points were raised.

That event took place on a Friday in February, 1998. The next Wednesday was Ash Wednesday (how these administrators choose their days!), and Nanton went to Mass before work. In one of the classes that day, which was scheduled for eleven o'clock, Nanton was due to lecture about the thought of St. Anselm. One member of this class had impressed Nanton at once with his philosophical acumen and his religious insight; so Nanton was on his mettle, and at about ten was studying his notes for the forthcoming class. There was a heavy knock on the door; when Nanton opened it, he was confronted by Monty Grossman, the head of campus Security. The latter, as Nanton found then and thereafter, is a thoroughly decent and humane individual; but the first thing that struck him was the troubled look on his face. "I am sorry, Sir," said Mr. Grossman, "but I have to escort you off campus." "This must be terrible for you, Sir," he added after a pause.

Nanton felt that some gallows humour was in order, so he said, "You remind me of the policeman in Gilbert and Sullivan, 'With constabulary duties to be done, to be done, A policeman's lot is not a happy one.'" The troubled face broke into a smile: "I used to be a policeman, Sir." Nanton asked whether he could collect his mail, and write a note on the board apologizing to his class for the fact that he was unable to teach them, as he had been ejected from campus. Mr. Grossman gave his permission, and they walked out together. When they met later, Mr. Grossman was kind enough to tell Nanton that the general opinion around campus seemed to be that he had been treated badly.

A few days after this, Nanton was summoned to appear in a room in a hotel off campus, where he was to meet with Dr. Kuyper and hear the grounds for his expulsion. Dr. Kuyper's diatribe, which was delivered in the presence of Nanton himself, his wife, and representatives of the Union and of the Office of Personnel Management, amounted to a general assassination of his character. No mention was made of any virtue in him, or of any way in which he might be felt to be a credit or asset to the university. Its main burden was that he had made fourteen threats, had broken confidentiality, and had been heard to speak of suicide. A tendency in him to risque conversation was alluded to in passing. Dr. Kuyper's allegations about particular actions of his – like protesting undying love to the secretary of a department and faculty other than his own – were an impressive compound of gross exaggeration and outright fabrication. (The only such secretary that he had been acquainted with at all was in fact one of the signatories to a letter to Fetter complaining of Nanton's treatment when he was first thrown out of his office and building. Nanton had provided her with a sympathetic ear when her husband left her, but he had never proposed, or intended, that they should have sexual relations.) As to "threats," he had certainly said, on one occasion, that he intended to take steps against the university administration for the way in which they had mistreated him, having in mind not acts of physical violence, but appeal to the law or the press. Perhaps enough has been said already about confidentiality in these cases, both in Westhues's books and earlier in the present article. But it seems scarcely kosher to torture one's victims, and then to torture them again for screaming. As to suicide, it is hardly to be wondered at that the ordeal to which Nanton was being subjected, acting in conjunction with a long-established disposition to endogenous depression, would make Nanton feel suicidal. His occasional mention of the fact was based on the hope, admittedly a foolish one, that some evidence of the agony to which they were subjecting him would make the administration treat him with more justice and less cruelty. After all, he had reason to think that he was of some value to the university. But the fact was, as his legal advisor remarked, that his survival was very low on their agenda.

Dr. Kuyper also incidentally accused Nanton of imagining conversations which had never happened – a convenient device, as a sceptical reader might infer, for dismissing out of hand recollections which Nanton might have in support of his own case. She also may have been trying to repress her recollection of a brief encounter which she had had with Nanton some months before. Dr. Kuyper was already Assistant Dean, and Nanton came to meet her when she was walking across campus. A notorious case of bungling by a university administration, where a swimming coach had been sacked for rape, but had overturned the case against him by appeal to hard evidence, was in the news at the time. Nanton suggested to Dr. Kuyper, with some earnestness, that the business seemed to show that the press was sometimes effective in correcting the worst administrative abuses within universities. "Graham," she said in a shocked voice, "if you have anything to say to me, you should make an appointment with me in my office."

By that time, Nanton suspects, Dr. Kuyper's mind had already been poisoned against him, presumably by Fetter, whom she was known to extol to the skies. In one of her letters to the Faculty in her role as Assistant Dean, she had described him as "a Wayne Gretsky among deans." Nanton can hardly blame her much for this, having once, as I have already said, himself had a high regard for that gentleman's character and integrity. According to Westhues, the *coup de grace* in the elimination process is often delegated to a young and ambitious administrator, so that the real eliminators do not have to face the consequences if the process goes awry (*Administrative Mobbing*, p. 198). This formula seems precisely to catch Dr. Kuyper's role in Nanton's degradation and humiliation. Still more than was the case with Nanton's other tormentors, Kuyper's academic achievement was negligible. He had once in good faith, some years before, asked her a question about the evaluation of literature on which he thought she might have something interesting to say; and was taken aback by the vapidity and triviality of her answer. She was said to make elementary mistakes in her teaching of German, which were such that her pupils were easily recognizable as hers by the solecisms that they perpetrated. Of such academic failures are ambitious university administrators made.

The day after Nanton's expulsion, a distinguished German professor came to the university to talk about Nietzsche. Nanton would like to have attended this talk, as he had taught Nietzsche in one of his courses, and had indeed published an article on his thought. When Innes told the visitor what had been done to Nanton, he wrote a letter to the new President Theodore Black, saying that such goings-on were redolent of the Third Reich. President Black may well have taken this as a compliment; Nanton does not have a very exalted view of Black's intellectual attainments, and has never met anyone who did.

Nanton was also directed to go for an interview with the forensic psychiatrist Dr. Quentin Easingwold. Shortly before he went, he spoke with a young lawyer who was a friend of his daughter's; she told him that Easingwold had a very bad reputation in the legal profession. When Nanton telephoned to schedule the interview, Easingwold gave him two options; the required tests and questionnaires could be administered either all at once or at two separate times. Nanton chose the first alternative; in the event. the tests and questionnaires, some of which were administered by another psychologist, lasted from three in the afternoon until ten at night, with a forty-minute interlude while Nanton slipped out to grab some supper. Nanton tried to discount the first impression that Easingwold made on him, which was that of a used-car salesman who was considerably less reputable than the average representative of his profession.

It was in relation to two yes-or-no questions put to him in one of the questionnaires that Nanton smelled a rat. Did he think he was a special person? Nanton's first inclination was to answer "No"; he has always suffered more than most from problems of low self-esteem. But it occurred to him that that very fact would probably be held against him. Then he remembered that he had considerably more publications, over a wider range of subjects, to his credit than the majority of his colleagues; so he answered "Yes." Accordingly, Easingwold wrote in his report that Dr. Nanton considered that he ought always to be treated as a VIP. Nanton is aware of himself as a man of many faults; but he confidently maintains that this one is flagrantly out of character. Another question was whether he believed in telepathy. Nanton thought that it would probably be safer to say no, but was unfortunately overcome by a fit of honesty. He had quite recently been co-editor of a book of essays on the paranormal, one of which he had contributed himself; and was convinced, and remains so, that the occurrence of telepathy is rather strongly attested. So again he answered yes. The report inferred that Dr. Nanton was incurably superstitious. Summing up, Easingwold gave his opinion that Nanton was not fit for any profession whatever.

In the next few weeks, Nanton was astonished and shocked to discover how bad Easingwold's reputation was. The social worker who had been counselling Nanton told him, in confidence, that she had heard that Easingwold's practices were putting him on the windy side of the law, and that the matter would be made public before very long. She expressed considerable outrage that the tests had been carried out all at once over a period of six hours; and did not believe that those university authorities who had chosen Easingwold to deal with Nanton's case were acting in good faith. A friend and former student of Nanton's who had been crippled for some years, as a result of being pinned to a wall by a car, told him how Easingwold had done her out of her disability money. A businessman who had been another pupil of Nanton's reacted with execration to Easingwold's name; and a Catholic professor of management at the university spoke of his steady progression to hell. Some months later, the Muggsville *Crier* carried a long article on how Easingwold made his pile by working for insurance companies, and providing specious reasons why they should not pay out on legitimate claims. In another issue, they described the picketing of his office by patients suffering from fibromyalgia. He himself was not available to answer questions.

There were many more letters written on Nanton's behalf. One of his students, a young man, wrote to the authorities of his dismay in being deprived without warning, in the middle of term, of the best teacher he ever had. The class had been informed that Nanton was sick; but he himself had contacted Dr. Nanton, who claimed and seemed to be perfectly well. What was he to believe? A letter signed by Dr. Kuyper came into Nanton's hands, which was a response to one of the protests which had been written on his behalf. She expressed herself as glad of the concern shown by the writer about Nanton; but when it came to explanation of the administration's action, she or he must understand that the matter was "confidential."

The Press took an interest as they had before, citing several ex-students who attested vigorously to Nanton's decency and integrity so far as they were acquainted with him. Dr. Elizabeth ("Betty") Bettenson, a Vice-President who was employed by the administration for that purpose, assured the *Crier* that the university was not punishing Nanton, and was a "caring" institution. About as caring, one would have thought, as the empire of Chaka the Great, or the kingdom of England during the Wars of the Roses.

Nanton was sixty-two years old at this time. He was officially put on disability leave, and accordingly supported by an insurance company on behalf of the university, until his official retirement over three years later. This seemed to him yet another abuse of funds, as he was perfectly capable of carrying out his university duties, and longed to teach again; but it is always nice to have something to eat.

The Union saw fit to inform Nanton that Fetter was not involved in the final stages of his ordeal – a proposition to which he reacted with some scepticism. Nanton is grateful for some things that the Union did for him, particularly in telling him to "grieve" his "reprimand," and in warning him to avoid going to a meeting where he would have been suspended for six months or more without pay. But in many of his dealings with the Union, he had the feeling that he was a pawn in a game whose rules he failed to understand. He was told by one academic who was working for the Union, that he had probably behaved badly to people, especially female people, in ways that he had forgotten. (Perhaps he was telling him, in a charitable way, that he was lying.) Nanton had heard of cases where professors had acted disgracefully and been defended to the last ditch by the Union. He consistently made it as clear as he knew how that he did not want to be defended on such an assumption; if he had really misbehaved to anything like the extent that seemed to be presumed by his enemies, he would much rather be thrown to the wolves. But he has been sure, from the beginning to the end of this whole affair, that he has not so misbehaved. He insists that he always treated persons on campus, especially women, whether students, staff, or faculty, in a perfectly gentlemanly fashion. That he had ever been guilty of sexual harassment, even in the widest sense of that term, he vehemently denies; and he would like to be confronted with a ghost of evidence that he has ever behaved in such a way.

Basically, his expressions of distress and, occasionally, of anger at the way in which he was being treated, seem to have been interpreted as threats or as signs of mental instability. Apparently some objected to his conversation, which could be risque, though never in the presence of young students; and he was acutely sensitive and responsive to any signs of offence among those with whom he conversed. Furthermore, he can think of a least three academics who were and have remained in good standing with the institution, who took conversational liberties that he found offensive.

Remarks of his that he considers perfectly reasonable, and that he is sure most people would find so, had been reported by Noseworthy, as he found when he consulted his file, as "out of control." A story to rather similar effect was told to Nanton by a former pupil of his. She had heard Dr. Kendal telling Noseworthy how frightened she felt whenever she saw Nanton reaching into his briefcase; and Noseworthy expressed great sympathy for her in this. So is the climate gradually poisoned, in the manner wonderfully described by Westhues, around the victim whom a university administration wishes to eliminate.

Nanton admits that he is, as his sister-in-law once put it, "large and vehement," but he strongly denies that anything he said and did, at any time, could lead a sane and well-disposed person to think that he would ever resort to violence against another. (That his ordeal quite often led to strong suicidal feelings in him has already been admitted.) As a friend and colleague in Classics told Nanton, anyone who was acquainted with him at all knew that he would not hurt a fly.

What were the motives of Nanton's enemies? In the case of Noseworthy, it seems to have been a case of sheer *odium academicum*. Nanton was palpably the better scholar, and he resented it. Shortly after his ejection from his office and building, Nanton looked up three names in the catalogue of the Robarts Library in Toronto, which lists books available throughout the region by author and editor. Nanton's score was 45, Fetter's 2, Noseworthy's 0. Fetter's motivation, to do him justice, was probably a little more complicated. At first he was playing a political game at Nanton's expense, on the basis of the so-called feminist assumption that no man can ever be in the right in a dispute with a woman. Later he feared that he might not be able to bully or threaten Nanton into silence about his disgraceful conduct, and concluded that more draconian measures were in order; it was Nanton's neck or his own.

An academic sympathetic to Nanton suggested that, when Fetter was considering how to deal with his case, a "feminist" was standing at his shoulder, threatening to dish his career if he decided it in Nanton's favour, or even refused to decide it at all due to conflicting evidence. In *Who Stole Feminism?*, Christina Hoff Sommers makes a useful distinction between an "equity feminism" of which she approves, and a "gender feminism" of which she does not. Roughly and summarily, an equity feminist maintains that no woman should in any circumstances be discriminated against on the grounds of her gender; a gender-feminist that when there is any dispute, or conflict of interest or claim, between a man and a woman, one must always decide in favour of the woman, whatever the intrinsic merits of the case. Nanton is no more a gender-feminist than he is any other kind of fascist; but he is an equity-feminist, and proud of it. In fact, a former female student of his, whom he had got to know in the 1980s and has remained a friend right up to the present, remarked, in one of the many letters written to the authorities in support of Nanton after his expulsion from the university, that he had taught her in his classes to be sensitive to gender issues.

One especially sad feature of the whole business was that Nanton used to have a great affection and respect for Fetter, and was sure he would act reasonably and responsibly once he had taken an objective look at the situation. Nanton even used to defend Fetter in the face of those who, as it turned out, had a more accurate assessment of his character and motives. Nanton once met the wife of a former colleague of Fetter's at a social gathering, soon after his troubles had begun. He told her that he feared Fetter might one day undergo a fate like that of Siegfried in Wagner's *Götterdämmerung*; having been elected to the presidency of some women's college on the feminist ticket, he would one day remember his principles, and be stabbed in the back. "Don't worry," she replied; "Fetter has no principles." A little while afterwards she added, "I admit, he does have one value – that is, Fetter." Much later, when Fetter had lied to Nanton and about him; had included a mendacious document about Nanton in his file, and had omitted his rebuttal; had forbidden an independent inquiry into their interactions, and prevailed upon another administrator to sign an official letter to this effect;[1] Nanton was forced, belatedly, to agree with her.

Why was Nanton at first so devoted to Fetter? The reason does Nanton little credit, but seems sufficiently relevant to be mentioned here. Fetter used to flatter Nanton quite fulsomely about his scholarly work. Nanton had not yet read *Without Conscience*, Robert Hare's book about psychopaths, which warns that, if a person is subject to flattery, she is in particular danger from such people.

It is surely a remarkable fact, that Nanton still does not know what Ms. Charles claimed to have against him in the first instance. In discussing the matter with Ronald Slight, an official of the Faculty/Staff Assistance Programme, Nanton suggested that he might remind Ms. Charles of an abusive uncle. Slight looked rather startled, said that this was a shrewd guess of Nanton's, and promptly changed the subject. On another occasion, Slight told Nanton that at his age he should not expect to be treated fairly. One wonders if Jewish people were similarly "counselled" at the time of the Holocaust.

Nanton's case was handled, frankly, with cynical brutality. The administrators concerned seemed to evince total indifference to justice, and to the welfare, or indeed the very survival, of those within their power. There are obvious and urgent questions which arise from the case, in conjunction with those described by Westhues. How can such violations of justice and common humanity be publicly exposed for what they are, and avoided so far as possible in the universities of the future?

---

[1] The sceptical reader will wonder how Nanton came to know this. The answer is, that he did so due to a series of strokes of good luck, which there is no space to go into here. If he has the opportunity to publish a more complete account of his adventures, they will be divulged there. The letter claimed, forsooth, that such an independent inquiry would not be "constructive." As a correspondent of Nanton's, who had some experience of these matters, remarked, this meant that too many administrators would be liable to be embarrassed by it.

Chapter Five

The Mobbing of an Italian Professor

Enrico Cavina

Kenneth Westhues's books show that the mobbing of academics is going on all over the world, causing enormous pain to the victims. A hitherto untold story from Italy demonstrates the wide range of strategies that may be employed by unethical administrators to mob, torment and eliminate their targets. As usual, the actions of the mobbers in this case were sometimes spontaneous and sometimes planned carefully in advance, with the actual mobbing strategy picked carefully out of the many that had been considered. The result was also the same: administrators ganging-up on a professor.

The story I want to tell is based on the deteriorating relationship between the administrators of the Italian Regional and National Health Systems and professors in the faculties of Italian universities. By means of new regulations, the administrators gained powerful influence over the medical schools in particular, and started to eliminate those they viewed as "difficult professors." What the administrators did is a crime against academic freedom, and against individual professors who tried to exercise their professional responsibilities with integrity. I would like to illustrate the broader picture with one story. It concerns the mobbing of Doctor Mal Di Dietro, a professor of surgery who, in order to safeguard his health during a severe mobbing, had to leave the university one year before normal retirement. The mobbers had strictly limited his activities within the university hospital, and had favoured other doctors, either on a political basis, or because they were Freemasons – members of a powerful self-serving secret society. The mobbing of Dr. Mal went on for more than 3 years, often surreptitiously, before the ugly public climax was reached.

This story is fictional, but it captures the spirit of a true mobbing, and incorporates real events from some Italian universities. It begins when my imaginary character, Dr. Mal is driving his car on the way up to his summer retreat in the Valley of Hope, high in the Italian Alps, where he plans to regain his emotional balance after being effectively dismissed from the hospital, a calamity that abruptly changed his lifestyle. Political power in institutions like hospitals is often held by people of mediocre intellect and base ethics, recruited from the bureaucratic apparatus of political parties of every stripe. Dr. Mal's aim on this healing trip is to put his distressing story to paper and use it to encourage other academics to be more aggressive in defending sound institutional values against venal administrators. After arriving at his mountain refuge, Dr. Mal covers his desk with notes, documents, letters, and pages of his diary, and sets out to write the first pages of his book, whose working title is *The Unhappy Experience of a University Professor*. This fictional professor, Dr. Mal ("pain") Di Dietro ("in the back") is the virtual Italian cousin of Dr. Pita (an acronym for "Pain In The Ass.") Dr. Pita is the hero of Westhues's satirical book *Eliminating Professors. A Guide to the Dismissal Process*. Dr. Mal has been in touch with Dr. Pita through Westhues, the book's author, and has also consulted with Brian Martin (an Australian expert on mobbing), who was the first to encourage Dr. Mal to write his story.

After squarely identifying the mobbing phenomenon as an unprincipled "ganging-up" of the mobbers against the victim, Dr. Mal sets out to analyse his starting position from the point of view of the mobbers themselves. He had always been loyal to his duty to encourage talent among the most promising postgraduate students within the team that he headed, but in doing so he had put himself in conflict with the career ambitions of some other students, all of whom, nevertheless, were still indebted to Dr. Mal as their teacher. The notion that Dr. Mal was "against" these resentful students was solely a figment of their imagination. They nonetheless abandoned the high principal of team solidarity under Dr. Mal as the head and "father" of the team and sucked up to the hospital administrators to try to advance their careers. The administrators were eager to believe their stories that Dr. Mal was bossy and overbearing, and they gathered in other "enemies" of Dr. Mal within the university. Together, all these conspirators worked out a strategy to eliminate this "difficult" professor. The tactics they employed are typical of those described in the scientific literature, and pass through the classic pre-mobbing and full mobbing phases.

Dr. Mal was writing his story in the peaceful atmosphere of the Valley of Hope, but after a few days of immersion in such painful memories, he was obliged to take a break to preserve his composure. Only after many encouraging telephone calls from Dr. Pita in Canada did Dr. Mal once again start to enumerate the underlying factors in his own mobbing, one by one. He began reflecting on his own personal success – his development of proficiency in a most difficult discipline, and his introduction of new concepts and techniques in his own hospital and in others. His success led to his being appointed President of the Scientific European Association and at the end of his career, just before his dismissal, as "consultant member" of the Ministry of Health.

To perform this time-consuming international work, Dr. Mal was obliged to delegate many responsibilities to the members of his hospital team, and have faith in their honesty. His team had always been ahead of its academic targets, as set by Dr. Mal. And he had helped many of the students in difficult situations, some of them very personal. Overall, the technical and professional competence of all the team members had grown greatly under his guidance, after many years of surgical experience. In fact, Dr. Mal had created career opportunities for many of the team members from scratch, always in keeping with their individual abilities. But some of the students decided to betray Dr. Mal by putting their futures into the hands of the hospital administrators, along with some academic enemies of Dr. Mal and possibly the Freemasons as well. While all this was going on, an unknowing Dr. Mal continued to encourage talented individuals in the class, and to pioneer new surgical techniques. As Dr. Mal approached retirement age, the ambitions of his despicable antagonists became emboldened, and the pressure for his dismissal became overpowering.

As he relived his troubling experience in his mountain retreat, Dr. Mal suffered symptoms of Post Traumatic Stress Disorder, particularly waking up too early in the morning. During the actual mobbing, he had suffered dangerously high blood pressure, as well as disturbances of the endocrine system, which required surgery one year before his departure from the university. Dr. Mal incorporated these grim medical experiences into his story, because they are typical of the suffering endured by a target during and after a mobbing. Mobbing is a phenomenon utterly without mercy.

The scientific authors, Davenport, Schwartz, and Elliot (*Mobbing. Emotional Abuse in the American Workplace,* Ames, IA, Civil Society, 2000) list the ten elements found in true mobbing, and underline those elements that amount to extreme mobbing or "vulturing."

- A direct assault on the dignity and professional competence of the target.
- Intimidation of the target with hostile and domineering communications.
- Attempts to discredit, confuse, isolate and force the target into submission.
- Driving the target out.
- Representation of the victim's removal from the workplace as the victim's choice.
- Management's refusal to recognise what is really going on.

Many of these factors were experienced by Dr. Mal. The basic strategy of the mobbers was to undermine support for Dr. Mal in every possible way – by reducing his team's resources, by painting a dark future for any doctors and residents who accepted leadership from this "difficult professor," by encouraging Dr. Mal's colleagues to steal his pioneering ideas, and by putting unbearable pressure on any co-workers who remained faithful to him. The administrators also broadcast the slander that Dr. Mal was "always absent," and that he lived in a fantasy world.

One of these supposed fantasies was the introduction of laparoscopy (keyhole surgery) to his university hospital (one of the first in Italy to employ it). Dr. Mal was one of the pioneers in this revolutionary technique, which reduces trauma to the patient, and shortens recovery time. On the basis of Dr. Mal's success, more than 250 surgeons from all over Italy and elsewhere came to Dr. Mal's operating theatre to learn laparoscopy for themselves. The clinical results and the scientific response at both the national and international levels were extremely positive. All this occurred some years before he was stabbed in the back by a cabal of his students. Davenport and her co-authors are right when they say that it's the creative individuals that are most subject to mobbing, because their ideas challenge the mediocre. And so, after a few years, laparoscopy became the key triggering event for the mobbing.

It happened this way. Dr. Mal had just returned from the American College of Surgeons Clinical Congress where he made a presentation on an innovative technique in laparoscopy. The presentation was supported by videotapes of actual surgery. When Dr. Mal returned to Italy he found a nasty surprise lying on the table in his office. While he was in the United States, some of his colleagues had planned a Master-Postgraduate course in laparoscopy, and excluded Dr. Mal from the teaching faculty involved. (Their excuse was that he was always absent.) When Dr. Mal asked his colleagues and the President of the University for a proper explanation, their answers were always evasive, but it became clear that this teaching course had been requested by the Hospital Administrators.

Deeply insulted, Dr. Mal tendered his resignation as Professor of Surgery and as Head of the Department and announced his retirement. From that moment on, Dr. Mal was determined to turn the negative effect of the mobbing into a positive one in order to heal himself, to give support to others, and to defeat the mobbers, who in Dr. Mal's opinion are not worthy to hold positions of authority. When Dr. Mal resigned, Brian Martin emailed him from Australia: "I must congratulate you. You have survived." Yes, Dr. Mal had "survived." But what small comfort!

After receiving a summary of Dr. Mal's story, Kenneth Westhues emailed him from Canada: "The outline you have sent me promises to enrich our understanding of workplace mobbing in many important ways – for instance, the role of Italian party politics and Freemasonry in your particular case, the nature of the triggering incident, your analysis of the phases or stages of the mobbing, the role of the hospital administrators, and so on. What is most important is that the actual facts of these processes in universities – the truth of what really happened – be made public."

Probably the best way to shed light on the mobbing of Dr. Mal Di Dietro (a most "difficult professor") is to present a special chapter of a book-in-progress. *The Unhappy Experience of a University Professor*. This chapter is entitled "Profiles" (of people and events) and is written in the style of a novel. During the evolution of this chapter, an extraordinary meeting of minds occurred and clinched Dr. Mal's determination to submit the story to a publisher. This happy harmony of thoughts occurred some months after Dr. Mal's elimination from the university, when he met with Dr. Pita (his

Canadian "cousin") along with the author of this novel. On the sunny terrace of Dr. Mal's mountain retreat around a big table covered with books, papers, notes, and first drafts of this book-in-progress, the three friends, Dr Mal, Dr. Pita and the author, started reviewing the papers. A fresh breeze blew down the mountains from the sparkling snowfields, which could be seen at the high end of the valley. A high and gloomy forest was cut through by a road that let in the light. A rocky plateau, closer by, lay beside green meadows full of wild flowers and lively streams. The road to the house came up the hill, twisting its way between flowers and bushes, passing a recent landslide full of mud and debris that had settled just behind the village. White clouds against the blue sky were reflected in the surface of a little lake just under Dr. Mal's terrace. It was a wonderful day, full of promise.

The three friends talked cheerfully as if they just woken up from a bad dream, and found that life was happy and full of good things. The lovely valley, the air, the light, the sounds and perfumes of nature all seemed to shout that Dr. Mal and Dr. Pita had overcome adversity. I marvelled at their detachment from past suffering, but I wondered what wounds and scars would remain inside them for ever.

Dr. Mal was the most loquacious: "It seems unbelievable to me that we are all here to talk about this story, and examine all these notes and papers for the details of such depressing events. I am glad we are, of course, but something seems to be missing, and that is the true nature of the deeper human factors at play in mobbing, and why it would happen in an academic setting, which after all, is a place that fosters high intelligence, and learning, and ethics. I, the author, replied that we have indeed spoken about this issue. We had already described the mobbing and sketched in the characters and personalities of the mobbers. " Yes," replied Dr. Mal, "but that's not sufficient if we want this little book to help others to really and truly identify the kinds of people who become the actors and the co-actors in a mobbing drama. We must be more incisive. We must clearly delineate the profile of the stereotypical mobber especially in a university setting."

Dr. Pita interjected: " I have covered this issue in my own book by pointing out that people with brains who are able to control their passions should not be caught up in the kind of 'ethical panic' that characterises mobbing. In other words, intellectual strength should always be able to triumph over the impulse to indulge in immorality. But, of course, this is only an ideal. The urge to mob swamps finer moral instincts and a mobber can indeed be consumed by the fire of uncontrollable passion. Out-of-control mobbing can destroy everything. This is equally true in universities."

"OK, dear friend," Dr. Mal replied, "but every mobbing becomes more destructive when many people co-operate – that's the key to the strength of Freemasonry. The mobbers become intoxicated with their own power and break through all the restraints created by morality and the institution's carefully thought-out regulations. In fact, they turn the truth on its head and say that they are the guardians of ethics. They misuse those very same regulations to pursue their own self-interest, but the real result – as we well know – is only a lawless, immoral ganging-up. I always keep on my table a book by the sociologist Francesco Alberoni entitled *Values* (ed. Rizzoli, 1993) in which he says: 'In the clear light of ethics, evil remains evil, deceit remains deceit, betrayal remains betrayal, cruelty remains cruelty, and goodness remains goodness,' and I have particular faith in this declaration. Evil is the tool of mobbing, and mobbing is the destructive association of wicked people and wicked actions around the fountainhead of power. About eighty years ago, the career of an excellent surgeon was destroyed by the power of Freemasonry. He told his story in a little book entitled *Sunt lacrimae rerum* (Tears are Part of Life). The same kind of tragedy can still occur now at the hands of Freemasonry or other power groups."

At this point, Dr. Mal started to expand on the question of secret societies. "I have always asked myself how there arises in the soul of people of high culture a need to abandon their intellectual freedom to the iron rules of a secret society, where independent opinions are not allowed and the lodge's judgment cannot be appealed. For such people, a sword of Damocles hangs over their professional lives. "Lust for power is the pre-eminent passion," Dr. Pita said. "All these elements appear clearly in your story, Dr. Mal."

"I know. It is true," Dr. Mal replied. "If you remain true to your principles and declare your opposition to Freemasonry as a malevolent factor in society, and if you say these things during a party, or a dinner, or an innocent conversation, there is always someone listening who takes notes and reports your thinking to the lodge. I ask you, how can these people accept absurd ritual liturgies during their meetings? It all seems to me a comedy, though a tragic one. But all this does indeed happen. Sometimes a 'black pope' and his cronies on the board of a lodge have the power to affect your career adversely and decide your future in society. And they probably convince themselves that they are crusaders for justice and a healthy society. This is the same sort of perverse passion that animates many groups of university professors. Did I say 'university?' What kind of 'university' spirit can you attribute to these persons steeped as they are in all their occult powers!"

" Just a moment, my friend," Dr. Pita said, "we must discuss individuals and their stereotypes, not groups."

"Okay, that is true, but this coming together of many different kinds of people around a single goal could be considered the glue that holds together mobbing in the workplace."

"But you, Dr. Mal, how were you able to detect the presence of such people and their networks in your university workplace?

"The local newspapers sometimes published lists of Freemasons, and the persons named issued no denials. And many of these people have more power in their lodge than they ever do in the university. You can find all kinds of people in these membership lists – people who are not very important in society, and others who occupy very important positions in key institutions. It's troubling to think that these people are in decision-making positions and at the same time are subject to the orders of the lodge. You are right, it is not forbidden by law to be a Freemason, but just a few days ago the Supreme Court of Italy ruled that a public administrator – including those in the universities – must declare his involvement in Freemasonry to his employer. Why? Because many people are suspected of being Freemasons but nobody knows for sure. Is their secret connection with Freemasonry a freedom guaranteed by the principles of democracy? I doubt it.

"You meet many of these people every day, and you never know whether your dealings with them are reported to the local lodge for judgment or not. It is very worrying. I have helped many of these people during my academic and professional life, sometimes when they were in great difficulty. And many of them participated in the mobbing process against me." Dr. Pita, who has suffered a mobbing in a different setting in Canada, was interested to know more about what happened in Italy, and he pointed out that some elements of Italian mobbing were the same in North American academic mobbing, and some were not. "Dr. Mal, you say that you helped these people in the past," he said, "and then they acted as mobbers against you; tell me more about them because these are the very people we want to profile."

"We can certainly talk about them and enlarge on their treachery," Dr. Mal replied. "For these people, deceit – which will always be deceit – is fundamental to all their aims. Betrayal – which will always be betrayal – is only perhaps one moment in their life, but it greatly delights them. As for evil and cruelty, these cancers are embedded deep within their souls, and grow more malevolent when their acts of betrayal are effective. All this is neither sophistry nor syllogism. It is a truly malevolent way of life that lies outside the realm of ethics. These people can live moments of kindness, perhaps within their own families, but the virtue of these little acts of goodness is blown away by the wind of their own narcissism. People with such tarnished morals were principals in my mobbing – three or four of them had worked closely with me, and I had diligently built their skills up from nothing as we worked side by side for many years. In some cases, I rescued them from all sorts of personal problems. But then blew that wind of narcissism!

"I have always been loyal to the values of the institution, naïve dreamer that I am, and after the mobbing became stormy and blew itself into my happy little valley, it brought with it piles of mud and rubble, the wastes of the mind and of the body, along with all kinds of lightning and thunderbolts charged with the power of the mobbers' arrogance. But I clung to my credo and my true culture, even though the traitors were snatching away my ideas as vultures would tear a corpse to pieces..."

Dr. Pita interrupted: "I must invite you, Dr. Mal, to return to an objective analyis of the profiles of the mobbers, and put your passion and melodrama aside." Dr. Mal composed himself. "Okay. Let's talk about these "men of power" who use their authority so corruptly, and – perhaps unwittingly – become bad, sometimes wicked themselves. I would like to paraphrase Schopenauer when he said: men of power never understand that the pleasure they take in injustice is nothing to the suffering of the victim."

"Dr. Mal," Dr. Pita replied. "You are talking under the influence of your unhappy experience, but power can be used constructively. Of course, we cannot get into a discussion today of the finer principles of social order, and of the correct government of various institutions, such as urban communities, farms, families, and so on. Let's just say that power is not in itself evil and decision making can be constructive and wholesome, with many benefits for the people."

"I agree," said Dr. Mal. "This is certainly true when administrators are guided by sound ethics and their own inner spirituality and manage power for the benefit of the people, without serving their own personal interest. But in our institutions today, this is rare. Once again, though, we are going too far, becoming too philosophical, if you like. We must return to our actual experiences."

"Dr. Mal, what kinds of administrators have you experienced?"

"Good and bad. Important and insignificant. Friends and enemies. Cain and Abel. But many of them have been slavishly devoted to the principle of "homo hominis lupus" which is to say 'dog eat dog.' For some of them – in my experience – a single bout of 'heavy drinking' of power was enough to satisfy them, for others they drank in power continuously in an effort to become gods or demi-gods over all and everything. These people wake up in the morning and immediately start thinking how much progress they made in their careers by their decision-making the day before, whether by the use of deception or by evil means is not important. Only the result matters to them. They are lost in their egocentricity, always without respect for others, who lie far outside their sphere of self interest. That's the way these people are, nothing more."

"Try to enter more deeply into the souls of these people," Dr. Pita said encouragingly.

"Inside the more important faculties or departments you can often find a "Black Pope" who is usually a professor who does not enjoy great satisfaction in his own discipline and devotes just enough energy to it to hang on to his position, and nothing more. This kind of person really enjoys exercising power and has a great deal of free time to devote to it. His intoxication with dominating other people has many dimensions – secret meetings, pressure on other professors, or the targets themselves, and then perhaps more secret planning, the result of which is presented to the president of the university and the faculty. It's quite usual for him to have his own devoted acolytes within the university. These are sycophants who consider themselves creatures of the Black Pope because they have received past favors, or hope for some kind of advancement. The Black Pope's actions are mostly underground. He hears much and says little, but he can be the supreme architect of the academic destiny of many professors. Often he is a Freemason at the highest level. He doesn't really know what mobbing is, but he is often a mobber par excellence."

The valley and the lake below Dr. Mal's terrace were slowly filling with light from the sun as it crept down the face of the high mountains. The air and light around our friends was most exhilarating, as was their conversation. "I must say that here in Italy,"

Dr. Mal continued, "the men who abuse power are not all that clever or important. Often they are persons who have not accomplished much in their studies and in their professions, but are able to insinuate themselves into political parties where they build their political or administrative careers. And then from that sordid political platform they can grapple with the people that run the institutions, often by making arrogant political decisions. So, from an intellectual point of view, these hangers-on are more little than they are great. They do seem to loom large sometimes, but they soon kowtow to a higher authority when they get a call from party headquarters and then they become obedient, loyal servants of the apparatus and nothing more. This subservience has little to do with intellect or culture."

"But have you found many such people?" Dr. Pita asked. "Oh, yes. I have encountered them in many administrative and academic positions. All of them were persons ready to abandon true principles in favor of other interests, which were often personal. All these people are present in my mobbing story as silent or active accomplices, as actors in the drama directly, as counsellors, as eggers-on, as hangmen, or as gangsters, evildoers, and scoundrels."

"Alright," Dr. Pita said sympathetically, "But let's get to the bottom of this pathological psychology." At this point in the conversation, Dr. Mal started to suffer from labored breathing again, from the stress of his memories, and as a diversion he drew the attention of his friends to a part of the blue sky where a hawk was flying, sometimes hovering, sometimes diving steeply into the green forest. "Look at that hawk. It is not like a vulture, which only looks for creatures in their death agonies. The hawk is fearless and the vulture is as cowardly as many mobbers!"

They drank coffee and then Dr. Mal continued more calmly. "So you would like to know more about the psychology of my mobbers? I am not happy arriving at this point. It is very painful to me. But if everything we say can be recorded and then included in our true-to-life novel, then the actual 'mobbers' might have their consciences pricked, or perhaps start to be afraid that they will be identified and get a demand in law from me to cover my damages. On the other hand, they may stifle their consciences, and perhaps mount a legal action against me for defamation. This could become a tunnel with no light at the end. It is much better to leave them in doubt, asking themselves 'Is it me?' or 'Is it him?' We should only talk about their meanness of spirit without identifying them any further."

Dr. Pita nodded and invited Dr. Mal and the author to join him in reading passages from his book *Eliminating Professors*, specifically the chapters headed: "Techniques of torment" and "Managing moral panic," and "Other outsiders." Then he went on to analyse in depth a chapter from Davenport *et al.*'s book entitled "The psychology and circumstances of the mobbers." It was an illuminating "university lecture" for me.

Now the sunset had arrived, and the colors of nature became softer, the sounds quieter, and the breeze sweeter. From down in the village came the toll of the "Ave Maria" as the church bells called the people of the valley. The three friends ate dinner cheerfully, and went to sleep in the comfortable rooms and warm beds provided within the mountain retreat. Dr. Mal himself fell into a dream. He found himself in a strange theatre and it seemed that he was at the same time the producer, an actor, and a spectator in a stage comedy similar to the one the Italian author Luigi Pirandello called *Six Characters in Search of an Author.*

In his dream, Dr. Mal was covered by a veil of dark semi-transparent voile. He was sitting on a chair looking at the movements – some times jerky, sometimes frozen – of the actors. There were six actors, but sometimes there seemed to be more or less within the dark shadows of this old neglected theatre, with broken wooded floors from which the sounds and voices echoed murkily. Another Dr. Mal was sitting alone on a chair in the deserted stalls, an astonished spectator of this incomprehensible scene. And in the prompter's cabin on stage, yet another Dr. Mal – seemingly the producer – tried to direct the actors, but they were really doing what they liked, out of control. Some actors were huddled together, conspiring, and others were arrogantly waving their canes around in the dusty air screaming: " We will do as we say ! We will never do as he says!"

Dr. Mal observed all this from his observation point. Sometimes he seemed to be weeping, while a beam of light from a skylight in the top of the theatre lit the transparent veil that covered him and made the teardrops on it sparkle. As the dream went on, the scene's atmosphere became oppressive, and Dr. Mal's breathing became labored, as in a Kafkaesque nightmare in which huge faces were in front of him sneering and belching incomprehensible insults. But who were these figures? It seemed to him that they were some administrators, colleagues, and students, the latter dressed for the operating theatre with gowns stained with blood – Dr. Mal's blood. They were shouting: "We love you, shithead, but now you are nothing. Get out! Get out of here for ever! If you don't, we will bury you. Do you understand?" And they were laughing. Dr. Mal, covered by the dark see-through voile, and enveloped in sadness, was imperturbable, with a gaze full of commiseration for them, but he was also weeping tears of ice.

The other Dr. Mal in the prompter's cabin was shouting "Get out, Mal. Get out! Save yourself now, immediately!" And he said to the six actors: "What pathetic figures you are. You little men. You are looking for an author? What author would soil himself with you? Your only author is the devil inside yourselves, a demon dripping with deception and betrayal. Get out yourselves! Get away from here! Sink down into your own evil life. Get out, get out!"

One of the actors walked over hesitantly to Dr. Mal, who said to him "Even you! Here? You ought to be ashamed of yourself. I have helped you many times in your career, and now... this. You are more treacherous than all those others who were ranked against you while I was defending you. And now you are in a gang with them against me. Get away from me! You are dead to me!" The nightmare was becoming more and more oppressive.

The third Dr. Mal, the solitary spectator of the human and professional drama that was unfolding turned toward the first Dr. Mal and looked nervously at the clock as if waiting for the end of the show. Then Dr. Mal the producer waved his hands from out of his little on-stage cabin as if to say "Stop! Stop immediately!" At this moment, a fiery explosion erupted on stage and opened up a deep pit full of excrement and mud and all the actors fell into it. In the corner of the theatre, Dr. Mal took away the dark veil, uncovering a face that showed pain, but also dignity, and he stood up and bowed to the empty stalls. The curtain went down slowly, while thunderous applause came from the theatre, which was now full of Dr. Mal's old friends, his patients and his loyal colleagues, as well as their parents and family members. The black curtain reached the floor and a tragic silence filled the theatre as the lights were switched off.

Dr. Mal's bizarre dream was over. He got up from the bed with a vague sense of having had a bad dream, but nothing more. Opening the window, he enjoyed the sight of the sunrise dissolving away the fogs of night that lay over the valley. He was filled with a great sense of serenity and faith in the future, and out through the window, Dr. Mal shouted to the sky: "Yes, Brian Martin, I survived, and how well I survived!"

Part Three

Case Studies

Editor's Introduction

Most readers will find the first chapter below, about mobbings at Brigham Young University, easier to believe and accept than the three self-reports in Part Two. One reason is that Kendall and Daryl White write as neutral, third-party observers, social scientists analyzing people and events far removed from themselves and their institutions. Adding to their credibility is these brothers' long record of immensely insightful collaborative research on Mormonism.

A further reason the ousters from BYU are more easily recognized as mobbing episodes is that these cases are less threatening to that majority of professors who teach in public or nonsectarian colleges and universities. The BYU cases occurred in a church-controlled institution, and their underlying cause was the targets' insufficient orthodoxy. These cases are similar in this respect to the dismissal of Protestant Herbert Richardson from the Catholic faculty of theology at the University of St. Michael's College in Toronto, the subject of my earlier study. That apologists for a religion, teaching in a corner of academe that is tied to it, sometimes gang up on a colleague too friendly toward science and earthly evidence is not a hard idea for secular academics – that is most of us – to wrap our minds around. It confirms common prejudices about religious institutions.

Appropriately, therefore, the chapter on dismissals at BYU is followed by my essay on the even stranger dismissals at nonsectarian Medaille College in Buffalo, New York. There is no evidence that the perpetrators of injustice and untruth at Medaille acted from religious motives. If anything, the Catholic faith of the one mobbed professor and the Islamic faith of the other contributed to their being mobbed, if only by strengthening their courage to speak out against authoritarian governance – what got them in trouble in the first place.

The objective, to repeat, of these first three parts of the book is to enable readers to abstract from a variety of very different instances of professors being forced out of their jobs, so as to grasp the general concept of workplace mobbing in academe, independent of where, when and how a specific case occurred, and of the particular intrigues, excuses, accusations, and exit door it involved.

The latest news (as of summer 2004) on the mobbings at Medaille College is hopeful. Thanks to the energy and skill of target Therese Warden and other proponents of shared governance among professors in western New York, the American Association of University Professors publicized and condemned the dismissals, and applied intense pressure on the college to rectify them. It appears now that reasonably fair settlements have been reached.

Both the Whites' analysis of the BYU cases, and mine of those at Medaille, document the huge toll mobbings take on the effectiveness of institutions and their ability to adapt to changing times.

The third and longest chapter below, Joseph and Jo Blase's analysis of the mobbing of grade-school and high-school teachers, serves the basic objective of this book in different ways than the first two chapters. First, this one broadens the conception of academic mobbing to include primary and secondary levels of education, where workers have even fewer buffers against persecution and humiliation than do counterparts at the tertiary level.

Second, through dissection of and quotation from interviews with 50 targeted teachers, the Blases provide an amazing albeit horrifying catalog of harassment techniques, a catalog also of their effects.

Third, these authors provide at the start a useful sorting out of the distinct but related terms used in research on mistreatment at work, and they conclude with a comprehensive bibliography. This chapter thus enables readers to situate the study of academic mobbings in the context of research on workplace mobbing in general, and related ills.

Chapter Six

Ecclesiastical Power and the Removal of Professors at Brigham Young University

O. Kendall White, Jr. and Daryl White

Framing the dismissal of theologian Herbert Richardson from St. Michael's College and the University of Toronto in terms of "elimination" and "academic mobbing," Kenneth Westhues (2004) presents a compelling analysis. The concept of elimination, in which someone is singled out, discredited, and finally separated from the organization or community, occurs through "mobbing," where others gradually coalesce, sometimes unwittingly, into clique-like groups that isolate, demean, and ultimately separate the target from others. Entailing similar processes to those involved in the labeling of individuals as deviants, including the retrospective reconstruction of a target's past, mobbing is an especially powerful form of social control. Westhues prefers "mobbing" to "bullying" because the former highlights social processes while the latter emphasizes personality characteristics of the "bully." The distinction is well placed, though the role played by university administrators in the Richardson case underscores the one-sided character of many academic cases. Both bullying and mobbing seem appropriate conceptualizations in many of these cases.

An obvious lesson from Westhues's book is that ritualistic targeting of individuals is not only cruel and potentially devastating, but it also destroys the covenantal social bonds that define community. What it signified in the Richardson case is an institutional transformation from an "academic community," based on mutual respect and the bonds of a covenant, to the university as a corporation with purely contractual relationships. Such transitions are rarely if ever undertaken through democratic processes. New goals, objectives, and criteria are imposed through edict or rituals of humiliation and elimination. Not only do these rituals destroy peoples' lives, but they often generate unanticipated consequences for an institution. The preparation and scheming required to convict and discredit someone through elimination ritual often requires administrators to commit the organization to goals and standards neither they nor others would have selected through a process of rational deliberation.

In the following essay, we describe the use of elimination rituals at Brigham Young University in the context of our research on Mormon intellectuals (see O. White and White 1999). In Thomas F. O'Dea's classic analysis of Mormonism (1957), he argued that in spite of the emphasis on education, Mormonism was not conducive to the development of a vibrant intellectual life because it forced potential intellectuals to become either apologists or apostates. There was no middle ground. We have argued that O'Dea's dichotomy is too simplistic and that a continuum is more useful, ranging from apologists, ardent defenders of the faith, at one end, to apostates, who have rejected Mormonism, at the other. Many intellectuals fall between the extremes. Today's greater intellectual diversity is associated with a growing separation between the LDS church and the Mormon community. If the church and community were coterminous during the nineteenth century, today the community has expanded to include a variety of subgroups asserting claims as legitimate heirs to the tradition. Ranging from fundamentalist polygynist sects and survivalist groups on the right, to liberal intellectuals, feminists, and gay and lesbian Mormons on the left, the number of subgroups claiming the tradition has multiplied with the maturation of Mormonism. While the church is the center of the community, it confronts a chaotic periphery that is becoming more difficult to control. Only by denying legitimacy to its contenders can it reaffirm its claim to be *the* community (see White 1995; D. White and White 1996; O. White and White 1998). Throughout its history, Brigham Young University has been the battleground for reining in the liberal, intellectual propensities of Mormonism. Our continuum identifies the intellectuals who constitute the greatest threat to ecclesiastical control of BYU and explains the use of elimination rituals in the development of hiring and firing practices.

The Continuum

At the extreme end of the continuum, all apologists assert that Mormonism constitutes the fullest embodiment of truth. They "know" that Mormonism is the only true religion. Other religions and sources of knowledge – including science and philosophy – are subordinate to Mormonism. For extreme apologists, Mormonism provides the conceptual framework through which everything is understood. Apostates, by contrast, at the other extreme, reject all things Mormon. In between the two extremes are those who negotiate their identities in terms of internal and external conflicts, placing them on the boundaries of the church and/or community.

Near to apostates are those who may acknowledge a historical and cultural contribution of Mormonism to the formation of their personalities, but who maintain neither a Mormon worldview nor any attachment to the church or community in their everyday lives. For them, Mormonism is understood in terms of some other conceptual framework, typically deriving from historical, philosophical, and/or social scientific perspectives. Mormon truth-claims are denied or not taken seriously. Some may consider themselves "cultural Mormons," but they are not active in the church nor do they believe the theology. These people are unlikely to seek employment or be hired at BYU.

At midpoint, between apologists and apostates, are intellectuals who hold a Mormon worldview while utilizing alternative conceptual frameworks from history, philosophy, science, social science, or literature. Some rigidly compartmentalize their Mormonism and alternative frames of reference while others more or less integrate the two. Rigid compartmentalizers maintain their "naive faith," as some theologians would say, without contamination from their scientific, philosophical, or historical framework. The more or less successful integrators modify either their Mormonism, their alternate conceptual framework, or both. While integrators are closer to apostates, compartmentalizers are nearer to apologists.

Intellectuals who are rigid compartmentalizers cover the spectrum of academic disciplines. Among social scientists who fall into this category are those for whom sociological models are simply useful means of furthering a Mormon agenda and not primarily a way of understanding Mormonism. They may, for instance, use social scientific models of conversion processes to advance proselytizing, but not for understanding Mormonism. The analytical framework is purely utilitarian, adopted if it supports Mormon interests and rejected if it does not.

A number of contemporary Mormon scholars adopt a more integrated yet still compartmentalized use of Mormonism and their alternative perspectives. They apply high professional standards to their study of Mormonism; however, their own beliefs and personal identities lead to religious affirmations that may be incomprehensible to outsiders. These non-rigid compartmentalizers include some of the very best historians, sociologists, anthropologists, textual scholars, and literary critics. They range from those trained in biblical studies who apply textual and contextual analyses to scriptures without allowing this to alter deeply cherished beliefs; to sociologists and anthropologists whose analyses of Mormon belief, ritual, and behavior appear to have little impact on their own religious positions; to the historians who assemble their "facts" to tell stories of Mormon origins and history that are at odds with "official" accounts but who proclaim traditional beliefs in their own religious commitments.

The midpoint of the continuum belongs to those who integrate Mormonism with their conceptual framework by reconceptualizing Mormonism. They retain a Mormon identity, generally participating in the church and community, but "being" Mormon to them differs significantly from what it was in their past or to ordinary Latter-day Saints. Yet Mormonism is not something they are willing to relinquish. For some, this reconstructed Mormonism remains a private choice, but for others the public expression provides the creative force for Mormon cultural development. Included here are important figures in Mormon intellectual history who attempted to reconcile Mormonism with modernity and with challenges posed by religious pluralism. Varying in how they reconceptualized Mormonism – what they would jettison, retain, and rework – they shared a commitment to making Mormonism more socially responsible and intellectually respectable. Had they succeeded, the church would have abandoned its exclusionary racial policy, textual literalism, anti-intellectualism, and authoritarian propensities.

There are contemporary scholars who utilize alternative conceptual frameworks, typically derived from specialized academic disciplines, to redefine Mormonism. Applying their skills in textual analyses, a few scholars trained in biblical studies have concluded that the Book of Mormon is not an ancient document but rather a product of nineteenth-century America. Yet they still claim that it is a sacred text, a scripture, containing divine revelation (Metcalfe 1993). There are theologians whose conceptions of deity, human nature, and salvation approximate classical Christianity and Protestant neo-orthodoxy more than traditional Mormonism, consequently the label of Mormon neo-orthodoxy (White 1987). Others produce a Mormon feminist theology (Toscono and Toscono 1990; Hanks 1992). Even gay and lesbian Latter-day Saints have claimed a niche (D. White and White 1999; O. White and White 2004).

Obviously, compartmentalizers who do not allow other perspectives to affect their beliefs are more likely to be hired and retained at BYU than integrators who create novel versions of Mormon theology. As proverbial wolves in sheep's clothing, integrators may be even more threatening than apostates whose views are easily identifiable. An apparent commitment to the theological tradition hides heretical propensities and may temporarily protect them from harassment and marginalization. However, the moment integrators are identified as departing from the mainstream they engender even greater hostility than acknowledged apostates and are stigmatized as traitors. No longer potentially "discreditable" as deviants from the tradition and community, now they are "discredited" as heretics with a profound character flaw (Goffman 1963). They are the "turncoats" who truly "know better" and, consequently, cannot appeal to naivete or innocence. They come to represent the ultimate threat to the university, church, and community.

Brigham Young University

When Brigham Young purchased the Timpanogos Branch of the University of Deseret in 1875, he sought to mitigate the impact of Protestant influence from public schools that were educating LDS youth. Soon named Brigham Young Academy, the school came under actual church ownership in 1896 (Bergera and Priddis 1985, pp. 2-3). Following a growing emphasis on college-level education in contrast with earlier grades, the academy was renamed Brigham Young University in 1903. With minor variation in the level of tolerance toward unpopular ideas, student diversity, and faculty dissent, the administration has consistently maintained control over what can be taught and whom they regard as appropriate faculty. If a typical mission statement acknowledges the importance of secular education, because the "gospel embraces all truth," it not only subordinates secular education to religious instruction but charges that there should be "advocacy of no principle or standard that is inconsistent with the teachings of the church..." (in Bergera and Priddis 1985, pp. 3-4). Rather typical of religiously affiliated institutions, such mission statements articulate the inherent conflicts generated by constituencies such as ecclesiastical officials, parents, and students who perceive religious indoctrination as the primary goal. Others, including many faculty, parents, students, and outside forces such as accreditation agencies, view these schools as places where the religious tradition is valued and respected, but they believe the religious tradition should actively engage the world – science, philosophy, and perhaps other religious traditions – if students are to enjoy society's imprimatur, a credentialed degree from an accredited institution.

BYU is no exception. The tension between alternate visions pervades its history. From periods of intense sectarianism, when the saints sought to withdraw and separate themselves from the environing society, to periods of conscious assimilation, when they pursued their "quest for respectability" with a vengeance, BYU has vacillated over the ways in which it should insulate, protect, and indoctrinate students. Because of the influence of ecclesiastical officials, the school never has been able to abandon religious indoctrination as a primary objective. The development of secular fields, including the sciences and humanities, has proceeded along the lines of other universities. Church leaders who believed that BYU could become a major university competing with the best secular institutions have never enjoyed the numbers, influence, or vision to move the institution away from its primary goal of religious indoctrination. In fact, there have been a number of occasions when officials debated abandoning BYU because of costs and problems of control (Bergera and Priddis 1985). Not unlike Herbert Richardson at St. Michael's College, in the wake of Catholic retrenchment following the Second Vatican Council, the more cosmopolitan faculty at BYU have experienced comparable problems throughout the school's history and, especially today, following a similar retrenchment within Mormonism (see Mauss 1994). With the excessive ecclesiastical control, church authorities are the principal force in the formal articulation of goals and objectives. Accordingly, every generation of BYU faculty hears some version of Apostle Mark E. Peterson's admonition that "we must seek to convert, never confuse" and "represent only the accepted views and doctrines and practices of the church" (quoted in Bergera and Priddis 1985, p. 4).

So how does an institution like Brigham Young University decide its purpose, determine its goals, and establish the criteria for joining and remaining on the faculty? Obviously, at the point an organization claims to be a college or university, there is some acquiescence to socially defined purposes and objectives; and if legal incorporation is required, then a formal articulation of purpose and goals appears in an organizational charter. Such documents usually identify who may decide matters of hiring and firing, including the criteria for employment. External accreditation agencies have become the major means of enforcing minimal societal standards while internal constituencies – like the board of trustees, administrative bodies, and faculty committees – often reflect more parochial interests as they carry out daily operations. Routinely, a university intent on enforcing orthodoxy, like BYU, may limit speech, restrict assembly, restrain the press, and deny due process for aggrieved faculty and students (Waterman and Kagel 1998).

If criteria have changed for joining and remaining on the faculty at BYU, issues of academic freedom persist. Norms may emerge, change, or become formalized following controversy, through either deliberation or ritual degradation. As the most dramatic means of imposing order on ambiguity or demonstrating the consequence of deviation from extant norms, elimination rituals may reaffirm existing norms or signal the emergence of new ones. However, they do so at real costs to individuals and institutions as they destroy lives, inhibit creativity, and foster self-censorship.

Elimination Rituals and the Articulation of Norms

BYU's first major crisis over academic freedom and the criteria for hiring and retaining faculty occurred in 1911. Joseph Peterson, the school's first Ph.D., was hired in 1905, following his work with the behaviorist John Watson at the University of Chicago. Soon, his brother Henry, who earned a bachelor's degree from Chicago and a master's from Harvard, joined him at BYU along with Ralph Chamberlin, who had been chair of the biology department at the University of Utah. There were now three professors firmly committed to Darwinian evolution and "higher criticism" of the bible. Ralph's brother, William Chamberlin, who had studied philosophy at the University of California and Harvard with Josiah Royce, subsequently joined them. Even the official history of BYU acknowledges their expertise, popularity, and the intellectual excitement they brought to campus (Wilkinson and Skousen 1976, pp. 196-212). However, their progression from "mere exegesis to vigorous advocacy" was more than church authorities could accept (Wilkinson and Skousen 1976:201). Consequently, a committee of church officials summoned the Peterson brothers and Ralph Chamberlin to Salt Lake City on February 11, 1911. Not aware that they were being "singled out" nor cognizant that "the six top dignitaries of the church" were "there to try us," the three were accused of teaching evolution and advocating higher criticism of the bible. They were denied their request for a copy of the charges, and the accused refused to allow either the president or the board of trustees to determine the content of their lectures. Either recant and leave evolution "out of discussion in our church schools" or be fired: this was the ultimatum (Chamberlin 1925; Bergera and Priddis 1985, pp. 134-148).

Ralph Chamberlin informed BYU President Brimhall that for every student allegedly driven from Mormonism by his teaching of evolution, he could produce five who left the church because of the "narrowness" of Brimhall and church authorities. Henry Peterson would later report that were he to be "a good boy" and teach "permitted doctrine only," then he could stay. "Think of it," he wrote, "I was invited to stay as a hypocrite teaching one thing to my students and believing and feeling another" (in Bergera and Priddis, p. 143). Joseph Peterson already had resigned. Though not accused with the others, William Chamberlin found his classes canceled without notification, students sent to the wrong classroom, and some told the class was meeting at a different time. He faced a general climate of intimidation that led to his resignation. After returning to Harvard for study, he taught extension courses for the University of Utah and spent a year at Brigham Young College in Logan, Utah, when he became ill and died in 1921 (Chamberlin 1925).

Embracing conceptual frameworks of evolution and biblical criticism to explain phenomena, including Mormonism, the Peterson's and Chamberlin's are integrators in our continuum. It is their ability to render the tradition meaningful to changing times, both by reinterpreting doctrine in a new context and using the tradition to make sense out of a different world, that makes them integrators who are indispensable to a dynamic community. Integrators keep a tradition relevant. Their creative reworking of the tradition, however, challenges orthodoxy and threatens extant social (power) relations. Since integrators do not reject the tradition, but rather seek accommodation between it and the new cultural environment, they are not easily recognized by "naive" students as "deviant." Their appearance of normality, possibly even embodiment of the best values of the tradition and ability to help others understand a new world, threatens the status quo, tempting the guardians of orthodoxy to label them as deviants and remove them from the community. Ironically, it is in historical moments like these that institutions most need integrative intellectuals, and yet this is when institutions are most threatened by them. The ambiguity and uncertainty accompanying such crises are particularly conducive to the initiation of elimination rituals.

Enthusiastic support for the chastened professors came from the student body and faculty. Over one hundred undergraduates attended a protest meeting "to stand by their teachers," and the *Salt Lake Tribune* reported that four-fifths of the faculty supported the professors. Of the "handful" of faculty and 114 undergraduates enrolled at BYU, over ninety signed a petition backing Ralph Chamberlin and the Peterson's. A few students and faculty declined to return to BYU after the incident. However, the board of trustees approved a new teaching contract requiring loyalty to church authorities as a condition of employment (Bergera and Priddis, p. 147). The limits on academic freedom, at least for those interested in evolution and "higher criticism," were now clear, since neither was to be taught at BYU.

Implications of the elimination of the Peterson's and Chamberlin's would not be lost on others who knew of the degradation and stigmatization that follow from "deviating" from orthodoxy. Reverberations of the "modernism controversy," as the crisis came to be known, were felt a decade later when a new president sought to upgrade the quality of the faculty. He approached Kimball Young to chair the psychology department, but Young, who subsequently became president of the American Sociological Society, declined the offer because of the absence of academic freedom (Wilkinson and Skousen 1976, pp. 242-243). Again in the 1930s, a new president unsuccessfully defended sociologist Lowry Nelson who had questioned the idea of immortality in a private conversation. Nothing had occurred in the classroom, in Nelson's writings, or in his conversations with students. Yet, he too was brought before church officials and informed that a "testimony" of the gospel was a prerequisite to teach at Brigham Young University (Nelson 1985). Nelson left BYU for a distinguished career at the University of Minnesota. It is difficult to imagine that any faculty member familiar with these events would not have felt intimidated if he or she even slightly departed from a perceived orthodoxy. On the other hand, these elimination rituals reinforce a propensity among those who perceive themselves to be orthodox to narrow the boundaries and close the ranks as they ferret out the heretics in their midst.

Given a preoccupation with establishing BYU as a respectable university, which requires compliance with accreditation agencies and the maintenance of faculty whose scholarship is acknowledged by professional peers, the teaching of biological evolution persists as a major concern. The issue emerged again during the 1970s. With frequent tirades by church leaders against evolutionary theory, biologists at BYU became targets of ridicule and derision. Conservative alumni demanded their removal and some religion faculty labeled them heretics. For several years, Apostle Ezra Taft Benson (later church president) publicly derided biology professor Duane Jeffery, without specifically naming him, and a group of zealots launched an aggressive campaign to "rid the church and BYU of all vestiges of Darwinism" (Bergera and Priddis 1985, pp. 165-171). BYU President Dallin Oaks asked the board if they needed to revisit the practice of allowing evolution to be taught as theory but not fact. In a spirited defense of his science faculty, Oaks wrote:

> ...the problem with ignoring this theory is that the theory of evolution currently explains more phenomena that are observed in the physical world than any other theory. Numerous fields of science use the theory and its corollaries, and will continue to do so until a better empirically based theory is propounded. ...If we stopped teaching this theory, within a few years students from BYU would not be admitted to ... graduate schools. At that point we would cease to function as a recognized university and would, in the eyes of the world (especially the world of higher education), be little more than a seminary with added courses in the humanities. I have no doubt whatever that our accreditation as an institution of higher education would be lost. The issue is that loaded. (Quoted in Bergera and Priddis 1985, p. 167).

If this took some immediate pressure off the biologists, the conflict persists. In the meantime, BYU has recognized those sciences employing an evolutionary paradigm as legitimate in its effort to claim the status of "a recognized university."

From the 1920s onward, the criterion of "temple worthiness" – meaning that the individual is certified to enter a Mormon temple based upon interviews with the bishop (pastor) and stake (diocese) president – has been used to control BYU's faculty. Criteria for temple certification include having a "testimony" of the truthfulness of the gospel, compliance with sexual norms and the dietary code, payment of tithing, no affiliation with "apostate" groups, and "sustaining" the authorities of the church. These have generated internal conflict, often because of the ways in which information about compliance was obtained, but they do not pose a problem for accreditation agencies if the criteria appear in writing and are made explicit to professors when they are hired. Private religious institutions may employ denominationally specific criteria for evaluating faculty that would be unacceptable in secular institutions. Such criteria are sometimes manipulated to build the case against a faculty member whom administrators or ecclesiastical officials want removed from the institution.

The decades of the forties, fifties, sixties, and seventies had their conflicts, ranging from disputes over behavioral criteria – including tithing, the dietary code, dress standards, forms of religious participation – and suspect theological and political ideas to the administrative manipulation of students. During the 1960s, the Wilkinson administration recruited students to spy on professors, both during class and in student-faculty consultation, in order to identify those with divergent religious and political ideas. An ultra-conservative Republican, Wilkinson believed that a liberal (Communist) conspiracy was destroying the social fabric of America, and this conspiracy was primarily based in colleges and universities. As he attempted to eliminate political science and history professors whom he perceived as "liberal," he successfully discouraged the hiring of individuals who would qualify as integrationists in our continuum. Due to this atmosphere of intimidation, several professors left BYU for other colleges and universities (Bergera and Priddis 1985; Waterman and Kagel 1998). Nothing is more likely to destroy the covenantal bonds, to which religious institutions typically appeal, more than pitting students against their teachers.

With Wilkinson's resignation and Dallin Oaks' appointment in 1971, the dawning of a new era appeared to be on the horizon. Roughly coterminous with further development of a Mormon intellectual subculture and a movement that came to be known as the "new Mormon history," BYU seemed to be an ideal location to some young professionally trained scholars. However, church officials would not relinquish control. Oaks' vigorous attempt to defend scientists, that we just described, would have less impact when the issue was the study of Mormonism. Here he was guarded. And his successor, Jeffery Holland, who appeared to be more like Oaks than Wilkinson, acquiesced when ecclesiastical officials clamped down on the "professionalization" of history. In 1981, Apostle Boyd Packer condemned the raising of questions and causing doubt among the saints, urging scholars to produce "faithful history" that advances goals of the church and strengthens religious belief. A young historian, D. Michael Quinn, argued that treating church leaders as infallible was akin to "idolatry" and that ignoring the social context giving rise to Mormon experience was professionally irresponsible. *Newsweek* picked up the story in 1982, initiating a conflict that ended with Quinn's excommunication eleven years later (Bergera and Priddis 1985, p. 410, fn. 81).

Quinn is a prolific scholar whose work reflects a willingness not only to examine controversial topics but to do so with professional responsibility, detachment and objectivity. Consequently, his work on Mormon origins portrays a very different Joseph Smith from official accounts and current legends. From Smith's treasure hunting and obsession with magic, to conflicting accounts of his own visions and revelations, to his extensive entanglement with plural wives, some of whom were already married to other Mormon leaders, Quinn (1987, 1994) has documented profound changes in Mormon beliefs and practices. To his credit, he has not hidden what he has found in his decades of research on Mormonism. Nor did he recant, avoid sensitive topics, or censure his work when university administrators threatened his employment and ecclesiastical officials his church membership. Eventually he lost both, resigning from Brigham Young University in 1988, and excommunicated from the church in 1993.

To us, Quinn appears to be closer to the non-rigid compartmentalizers than to the integrators on our continuum because of how he appears to separate his historical materials from truth-claims. He describes himself as both a "New Mormon Historian and an honest apologist for the Mormon faith and experience" (Quinn 1992, p. xiii). In spite of all of the controversy and his accounts of Mormon history, Quinn continually testifies to the truthfulness of the Book of Mormon, the prophetic status of Joseph Smith, the authenticity of the church, and the accuracy of Mormonism's truth-claims. Employing the language and form of typical Mormon testimonies, with a clear understanding of their meaning and ritualistic nature, Quinn (1995) implies that his testimony does not differ from those of other Latter-day Saints on these essentials. If he does mean something different from standard testimonies, what this variation may be remains uncertain from his public pronouncements. Nor is it clear how his own research affects his deeper understanding of Mormonism. At the same time, the price he has paid in loss of job and church membership attests to his commitment to the standard he has set for himself as a professional historian. Even a quite conventional testimony was not sufficient to protect him from academic mobbing.

The same year that Quinn resigned from BYU, David Wright, a professor of Near Eastern studies, was fired for his personal views about the Book of Mormon. While his use of textual and historical analyses of the Old Testament or Hebrew texts potentially could have presented problems, it was what he believed, not what he taught, that led to his dismissal. For he had come to believe, on the basis of his use of historical and textual analyses, that the Book of Mormon was a nineteenth-century product and not an ancient text. On our continuum, Wright is an integrationist. Though he maintains a belief that the Book of Mormon is an inspired sacred text, a scripture containing a divine message, this must be understood in a different context from the official claims of the church. For his elimination at Brigham Young University, the important point is that Wright did not teach the Book of Mormon. These were simply his personal beliefs. Yet they were the basis for his dismissal (see Waterman and Kagel 1998: pp. 177ff.). Though he left the Mormon heartland for a professorship of ancient scripture at Brandeis University, his new local ecclesiastical officials excommunicated him in 1994 (Knowlton 1996: p. 127).

With Rex Lee's appointment as president of BYU in 1989, the administration began wrestling with a formal statement on academic freedom. However, this was in a new context with a burgeoning intellectual subculture. Organized independently from the church, the new Mormon intellectual community was publishing scholarly journals and holding conferences. BYU's 1988 self-study, in preparation for accreditation, questioned the legitimacy of faculty participation in the intellectual community's Sunstone symposia and publication in *Dialogue* and *Sunstone*, independent journals devoted to the scholarly examination of Mormonism (Waterman and Kagel 1998, pp. 179-180). While no official written policy existed, an unwritten practice of proscribing participation was selectively employed to discipline faculty when a convenient pretext was needed. In other instances, participation was ignored. A growing number of BYU professors, which became significant, began participating in the largest of the Sunstone symposia held in Salt Lake City. In response to warnings about listening to "alternate voices" in 1989, and attempts to intimidate participants in 1990, an official declaration warned church members to avoid such symposia in 1991. This brought increased pressure on BYU faculty. Intimidation intensified with the disclosure in 1992 of a special committee keeping dossiers on dissenting intellectuals. Formal disciplinary action against several participants in 1993 included the excommunication of Quinn (see White 1995, D. White and White 1996, and Waterman and Kagel 1998, p. 280). If most BYU faculty were persuaded to avoid Sunstone Symposia, a few continued to participate openly, while others had their names kept off the program or used pseudonyms. Overall, their numbers dropped precipitously as the administration restrained the faculty, and the nascent academic freedom policy made public in 1992 emphasized protection of the institution over the rights of individual professors to pursue their work without undue restraint.

Advocacy of feminist theory and participation in the symposia were pivotal in the two most publicized dismissal cases. Cecilia Farr joined BYU's faculty specifically to teach feminist literary theory in the English Department. However, she was fired during her third-year review. Farr's involvement as co-faculty advisor with the fledgling feminist student group, VOICE, and her pro-choice political views put her in a precarious position. With organized demonstrations, including "take back the night" marches and protest over the handling of a specific rape case, VOICE brought national attention to the campus. Influential alumni and church officials immediately demanded disciplinary action. The situation worsened. At a January 1992 Pro-Choice rally organized to protest Utah's pending abortion legislation, Farr proclaimed her support for the Mormon presidency's opposition to abortion as her personal view while arguing for the right of women to choose. While favoring education, planning, and contraception as preferable measures for dealing with unwanted pregnancy, she refused to impose her personal choice on others. Thus, pro-choice was the appropriate public policy. Church officials and BYU administrators intensified efforts to remove her. Academic Vice

President Stan Albrect read to her a resolution which he claimed had been adopted by the board of trustees that prohibited BYU faculty from publicly advocating a pro-choice position. However, he refused to provide Farr with a copy on the grounds that the board was not ready to release the document (Waterman and Kagel 1998: p. 209).

With her third-year review in 1993, the question of feminism, especially her pro-choice sympathies, led to her elimination. Following publication of her pro-choice speech and an interview in the *Chronicle of Higher Education,* administrators began inserting materials into her departmental review file. Academic Vice President Todd Britsch cited his predecessor's claim of an official policy (still unpublished) prohibiting BYU faculty from advocating a pro-choice position, asserting that she had violated the university's citizenship obligations. He insisted that a copy of the memo be placed in her file. Moreover, she was accused of destroying the faith of students. Since her local bishop reported that he was convinced of her loyalty to the church, even suggesting that her stake (diocese) president shared her personal opposition to abortion while supporting a pro-choice political position, those supporting the removal of Professor Farr did not have the endorsement of local ecclesiastical officials. Provost Bruce Hafen acknowledged his departure from protocol as he inserted letters and materials, highlighting some of her statements, into her departmental review file. Expressing some reservation about interjecting an administrator's views into a "departmental deliberation," he justified his unusual action. "Since we all know that the review process that begins with the department ends with the administration," he wrote, "we can work together better this way than if the reviews at various levels proceed with different information from one another" (quoted in Waterman and Kagel 1998, pp. 211-212). Yet his action, of which he appears cognizant, could compromise the relative autonomy required at different levels in the review process for rational deliberation and just decisions. That this was less of an evaluation process than an elimination ritual, with a forgone conclusion engineered by the administration, is suggested by what President Rex Lee and Provost Hafen told Farr. Implying that they had protected her from church officials, who during the previous year had twice demanded her immediate dismissal, Lee and Hafen had bought her time so she could go through her third-year review under BYU's new academic freedom guidelines (Waterman and Kagel 1998, p. 213). Since the new academic freedom policy actually protects the institution rather than the professorate, the Mormon apostles could be assured that Cecilia Farr would not survive the review.

The pretext for denying renewal of her contract was a charge that her scholarship and teaching did not meet BYU's high standards. However, an Ad Hoc Academic Freedom Committee, established by concerned faculty, including several prominent BYU professors, obtained relevant data to evaluate these claims. Her mean of 6.14 on a 7 point scale for student course evaluations was higher than candidates who were granted continuing status in their third year and those granted tenure in their sixth year. Moreover her scores exceeded both university (5.5) and departmental (5.6) averages. Her three articles in peer reviewed journals with two more submitted clearly exceeded the 1.1 average of successful third year candidates in her department, and numbered beyond the 2.3 average for those receiving tenure. The seventeen papers she had presented at professional conferences were again well beyond the 2.8 average among English candidates approved for continuing status and even the 10.8 for those granted tenure (Waterman and Kagel 1998, pp. 223, 245, fn. 4). These comparisons suggest that BYU administrators were disingenuous in their claims of poor scholarship and teaching when the apparent issues were her feminist perspective, for which she was actually hired, and her political activism. Following a typical pattern of elimination rituals, the administration sought to discredit her. As a colleague in the English Department observed, "it is one thing to find Dr. Farr's activist methods and feminist stances disturbing" but "quite another to try to destroy her reputation..." (quoted in Waterman and Kagel 1998, p. 224). Though she had appealed the decision and was considering litigation, an out-of-court settlement resulted in her resignation and the withdrawal of her appeal. While it prohibited Farr from disclosing conditions of the settlement, the university dropped references to her scholarship and teaching in their news releases. She left BYU as the unanimous choice for a position at the College of St. Catherine in Saint Paul, Minnesota, where she now enjoys tenure.

Though details are somewhat sketchy, there is good reason to suggest that Cecilia Farr would fall closer to Michael Quinn than to David Wright on our continuum. Like Quinn, who maintains a "complex" but apparently quite conventional testimony in which he clearly affirms the fundamental truth-claims of Mormonism, Farr apparently separates her feminist, especially political perspective, from her theological views. Consequently, she is closer to the non-rigid compartmentalizers who value two perspectives, but separate them, than to integrators like Wright whose professional scholarship led to his reinterpretation of the Book of Mormon. Farr once stated that she had never been involved in "*Sunstone, Dialogue,* or in the 'liberal' Mormon tradition." "My Mormonism is fairly separate from what I do as a radical thinker," Farr said, for "I am focused on how to change the world..." (quoted in Waterman and Kagel 1998, p. 209).

Anthropologist David Knowlton's difficulties arose when he presented a paper at the Salt Lake Sunstone Symposium in 1991. Having served an LDS mission in Bolivia, Knowlton was shocked by news that two Mormon missionaries had been murdered in that country. He began research that documented the detonation of sixty-six bombs targeting the LDS church and the assassination of five missionaries in Colombia between 1989 and 1991. Finding a disproportionate incidence for LDS versus other denominations, Knowlton argued that the Mormon identification with America and prevailing beliefs that missionaries were CIA agents were reinforced by the tendency of the church to support established governments, including dictatorships, and national elites. Knowlton hoped his research would help the church address this problem, but church officials greeted his analysis with skepticism and perceived it as a threat to the missionary program. Following the symposium, the Mormon presidency issued its statement, identified above, urging members to avoid symposia that were not sponsored by the church. Knowlton's stake president summoned him for an interview, and media coverage of the incident evoked questions about his status at BYU. As in Farr's case, Knowlton's third-year review occurred in 1993. Following a unanimous recommendation for continued status by the department, the college committee passed him both in teaching and academic citizenship but judged his scholarship to be unsatisfactory. Their vote was split, three recommending "provisional status" and two termination. The grounds: his scholarship was too subjective ("I-centered") and not published in peer reviewed journals. The college dean informed the Faculty Council, the next level of evaluation, that he could not recommend more than provisional status. Voting five to three for termination, the Faculty Council passed the file on to Provost Hafen and President Lee who accepted its judgment. Again the Ad Hoc Faculty Committee on Academic Freedom chastised the council for ignoring peer-reviewed journals outside the United States, his article in *Dialogue* – the source of many "excellent, prize-winning" social science articles on Mormonism, and his chapter in *Contemporary Mormonism,* soon to be published by the

University of Illinois Press (quoted in Waterman and Kagel 1998, pp. 213-222). Following notification of the termination decision, Knowlton began his appeal.

At this point, we became aware of Knowlton's situation and wrote to President Lee. Since the stated problem was scholarship and not his teaching or citizenship, Kendall asked if the administration intended to subject his writing to external review, a common practice of universities. While Lee's reply was evasive, he included with his response the copy of an editorial by Professor Steven Albrecht, a member of the Faculty Council, that was published in the *Salt Lake Tribune* on July 5. Praising the fairness of the process, Albrecht suggested that he personally would have difficulty "accepting a paycheck from the LDS Church and then working to destroy what that church stands for," obviously implying that Knowlton was seeking to destroy the church. Kendall replied (July 23, 1993) suggesting that Albrecht's editorial was an example of the very concern that he had expressed. Did Albrecht "have a set of particular religious beliefs (about which one cannot dissent) that constitute a litmus test for employment at BYU? Are these criteria he invoked while serving on the Faculty Council? Where do they fit among teaching, scholarship, and citizenship?" The letter continued,

> Please forgive me if you have initiated a panel for external peer review. Since your letter gave no indication that you had done so, I (perhaps presumptuously) have contacted three anthropologists and another sociologist (beside myself) to whom I am sending Knowlton's writings. I have requested that they review his work and asked them to send their analyses to you.

While two of the scholars were not from an LDS background, they were highly respected and knowledgeable about Mormonism and the anthropology of religion. Indeed, one was the author of well respected books and articles on Mormonism. The others were established scholars of Mormonism who grew up within the tradition. It is ironic that the principal claim that his work was deficient because of inadequate peer-review could have been easily resolved by sending his writings to external reviewers, which is the responsibility of committees not the candidate. However, BYU chose not to pursue this course. Nor would they consider the external review provided for them by us. There appeared to be less interest in an honest and fair evaluation than in questioning Knowlton's loyalty, impugning his character, and portraying him as a traitor, which is typical of elimination rituals.

In terms of our continuum, Knowlton seems to fit among those integrators who are deeply committed to the Mormon community and church. His own article (1992) on the "native anthropologist as oxymoron," in which he treats his experience as an active Latter-day Saint and a professional anthropologist as a source of tension, illustrates the dilemmas for integrationists on our continuum. While his anthropology marginalizes him among Latter-day Saints, his Mormonism marginalizes him among anthropologists. One foot in each community enables him to see things about both that others often miss. His ongoing efforts to integrate anthropological perspectives with his Mormon tradition will continue to enlighten his scholarship as well as leave him a "marginal man" with cognitive conflict. In the meantime, he is located a few miles from BYU at Utah Valley State University, where some of Brigham Young University's most respected professors relocated as a consequence of the situation described in this essay.

The remainder of the nineties saw an emboldened administration and additional faculty voluntarily leaving BYU. Even greater ecclesiastical control obtained with formalization of a hiring policy in which (1) the board of trustees would be involved in both preliminary and final stages in the hiring of a professor, (2) more attention would be devoted to personal characteristics of "age, marital status, church callings, and bishop's recommendations," and (3) "no factor" would be more important in "assessing the relative strength of competing candidates" than "deep religious faith and loyalty to the church" (quoted in Waterman and Kagel 1998, p. 224). Moreover, in 1996 a church official drawn from the ranks of the hierarchy was appointed president of the university for the first time in BYU's history, and that same year BYU had its first casualty from the "ecclesiastical endorsement" policy that requires formal certification of a faculty member's religious activity by his or her local bishop and stake president. Instead of using poor teaching and inadequate scholarship as pretexts for dismissal, administrators now used BYU's academic freedom policy of prohibiting advocacy of anything believed to undermine church doctrine or policy as stated reasons for removing a professor. The university's response to AAUP investigations and censure has been to forge a closer relationship to national neo-conservative intellectuals who are engaged in broadening the influence of religion in the public square. To preserve its insularity,

BYU ironically appears to be joining forces with conservative Protestant and Catholic intellectuals in their battle with modernity (see especially Waterman and Kagel 1998, pp. 415-453). Fear of secularization unites them.

Conclusion

Today BYU finds itself in the vortex of centrifugal and centripetal forces. Still resisting the secular influences that constituted its very *raison d'etre*, including the early "modernism controversy" over Darwinian evolution and biblical criticism, BYU confronts a new secularism symbolized in postmodernism and feminist and critical perspectives in the social sciences and literary studies. Given the willingness of BYU administrators to forge a coalition with neo-conservative Protestant and Catholic religious leaders, we might infer that secularism is perceived to be a much greater threat than inter-religious challenges. Notwithstanding the retrenchment identified by Armand Mauss (1994), the quest for legitimacy in the eyes of the world remains sufficiently intense to ensure at least minimal compliance with accreditation agencies, professional associations, and the secular environment. On the other hand, the Mormon obsession with peculiarity and exclusivity guarantee that BYU will resist new ideas and perspectives while emphasizing group loyalty.

If BYU originated to protect students from outside secular influences, today it "protects" them from their Mormon professors. The further separation of the church from the community, with the emergence of an independent intellectual subculture, has led ecclesiastical officials to exercise their power to regain control over the Mormon community. Their favored technique is to deny legitimacy to those on the periphery, to narrow the boundaries of acceptable Mormonism. Since the church owns Brigham Young University, it can determine, for the most part, what can be taught and who will teach. It was the growing autonomy of a Mormon intellectual subculture embodied in the creation of scholarly journals, magazines, and symposia that spawned the continuum of intellectuals ranging from apologists to apostates. Using BYU as a battleground, church leaders have narrowed the range of acceptable professors. Obvious apostates, no matter their expertise or personal identification as "cultural Mormons," can neither join nor remain on the faculty, but today the university also excludes those integrators whose creativity keeps a tradition viable in changing times. Even non-rigid compartmentalizers, who insist on rather orthodox testimonies and proclaim their loyalty to the church, have become unacceptable as BYU develops more rigid and narrower criteria for their professorate. The recent formalization of criteria making conditions of employment more explicit to potential faculty members could reduce the use of elimination rituals; however, it may render the occasions when they are employed even more brutal, intensifying the propensity to impugn an individual's character.

Much of the turmoil at BYU is an expression of a broader struggle for control over the Mormon community. Is the church to define the community, or is the community a consensual, covenantal body of participants? Mormon scholar Levi Peterson, advising those marked for disciplinary action (including Quinn), answered this question at the 1993 Sunstone Symposium:

> Finally, if your particular identity and indignation demand a course of action that seems fated to lead to excommunication, well, God bless you and give courage. Even here, I have some advice, which is that excommunication is no reason for withdrawing from Mormonism.
>
> I fancy that if I were excommunicated by a Church court on a weekday, I'd be back sleeping in sacrament meeting on the following Sunday. Presumably I'd be relieved of my duties as home teacher and occasional instructor of the high priest group. Presumably I'd not be called on to pray or preach. But those are petty losses. I'd continue to partake of the sacrament [communion] unless I were expressly forbidden to do so. In that case, I'd attend meetings from time to time in a ward [congregation] where I wasn't known and would partake of the sacrament there....
>
> Though as a corporation the Church may be owned by its legally constituted officers, as a moral community Mormonism is beyond ownership. You and I belong if we choose to belong. I for one choose to belong. I'll not let another human being, however highly placed, drive me from Mormonism (Peterson 1994, p. 39).

References

Bergera, Gary and Ronald Priddis, 1985. *Brigham Young University: A House of Faith*. Salt Lake City, UT: Signature Books.

Chamberlin, Ralph V., 1925. *Life and Philosophy of W. H. Chamberlin*. Salt Lake City, UT: The Deseret News Press.

Goffman, Erving, 1963. *Stigma: Notes on the Management of Spoiled Identity*. Inglewood Cliffs, NJ: Prentice-Hall.

Hanks, Maxine, ed., 1992. *Women and Authority: Re-emerging Mormon Feminism*. Salt Lake City, UT: Signature Books.

Knowlton, David, 1992. "No Man Can Serve Two Masters or the Native Anthropologist as Oxymoron," *International Journal of Moral and Social Studies* 7, 1 (Spring).

Knowlton, David, 1996. "Authority and Authenticity in the Mormon Church" Pp. 113-134 in *Religion and the Social Order* 6, *The Issue of Authenticity in the Study of Religions*, eds. David G. Bromley and Lewis F. Carter. Greenwich, CT: JAI Press.

Mauss, Armand L., 1994. *The Angel and the Beehive: The Mormon Struggle with Assimilation*. Urbana: University of Illinois Press.

Metcalfe, Bruce. L., ed., 1993. *New Approaches to the Book of Mormon: Explorations in Critical Methodology*. Salt Lake City, UT: Signature Books.

Nelson, Lowry, 1985. *In the Direction of His Dreams: Memoirs*. New York: Philosophical Library.

O'Dea, Thomas F., 1957. *The Mormons*. Chicago: University of Chicago Press.

Peterson, Levi, 1994. "The Art of Dissent among the Mormons," *Sunstone* 16, pp. 33-39.

Quinn, D. Michael, 1987. *Early Mormonism and the Magic World View*. Salt Lake City, UT: Signature Books.

Quinn, D. Michael, ed.., 1992. *The New Mormon History: Revisionist Essays on the Past*. Salt Lake City, UT: Signature Books.

Quinn, D. Michael, 1994. *The Mormon Hierarchy: Origins of Power*. Salt Lake City, UT: Signature Books.

Quinn, D. Michael, 1995. "The Rest Is History," *Sunstone* 18, 3, pp. 50-57.

Toscono, Margaret and Paul Toscono, 1990. *Strangers in Paradox: Explorations in Mormon Theology*. Salt Lake City, UT: Signature Books.

Waterman, Bryan and Brian Kagel, 1998. *The Lord's University: Freedom and Authority at BYU*. Salt Lake City, UT: Signature Books.

Westhues, Kenneth, 2004. *Administrative Mobbing at the University of Toronto*. Lewiston, NY: Edwin Mellen Press.

White, Daryl and O. Kendall White, Jr., 1996. "Charisma, Structure, and Contested Authority: The Social Construction of Authenticity in Mormonism," Pp. 93-112 in *Religion and the Social Order* 6, *The Issue of Authenticity in the Study of Religions*, eds. David G. Bromley and Lewis F. Carter. Greenwich, CT: JAI Press.

White, Daryl and O. Kendall White, Jr., 1999. "Mormonism and Homosexuality: A Historical Overview," Pp. 109-120 in *Anticipating the End: The Experiences of the Nineties*; Proceedings of the 1999 Virginia Humanities Conference, ed. Susan Blair Green. Staunton, VA: Mary Baldwin College, 1999.

White, O. Kendall, Jr., 1987. *Mormon Neo-Orthodoxy: A Crisis Theology.* Salt Lake City, UT: Signature Books.

White, O. Kendall, Jr., 1995. "The Church and the Community: Personal Reflections on Mormon Intellectual Life," *Dialogue: A Journal of Mormon Thought* 28, 2 (Summer), pp. 83-91.

White, O. Kendall, Jr. and Daryl White, 1998. "Metaphysics, Epistemology, and the Pursuit of Truth in Traditional Mormon Theology," *Virginia Social Science Journal* 33 (Winter), pp. 1-14.

White, O. Kendall, Jr. and Daryl White, 1999. "A Conceptual Framework for Understanding the Identities of Mormon Intellectuals." Paper presented to the Sociology of Religion Study Group, British Sociological Society, University of Durham, Durham, England, (April 10).

White, O. Kendall Jr. and Daryl White, 2004. "Ecclesiastical Polity and the Challenge of Homosexuality: Two Cases of Divergence within the Mormon Tardition," *Dialogue: a Journal of Mormon Thought* 37, 4 (Winter), forthcoming.

Wilkinson, Ernest L. and W. Cleon Skousen, 1976. *Brigham Young University: A School of Destiny.* Provo, UT: Brigham Young University Press.

Chapter Seven

The Mobbings at Medaille College in 2002

Kenneth Westhues

Since mid-2001, an uncommon but severe organizational pathology has infected Medaille College, an institution serving 2,000 students in Buffalo, New York. Dozens, perhaps hundreds, of individuals at the college have been harmed. Two tenured senior professors, Therese Warden and Uhuru Watson, have all but lost their professional lives.

The harm is needless, serving no purpose but to weaken the college and jeopardize its future. The purpose of this paper is to identify, analyze, and explain, on the basis of publicly available documentation, the precise social ill that has laid the college low. Section 1 summarizes organizational research conducted and disseminated in Europe over the past two decades, but as yet little known in North America. Sections 2-4 apply the research to the Medaille evidence.

The trustees, alumni, administrators, faculty, staff, and students of Medaille are educated men and women with the best interests of the college at heart. Section 5 of this paper invites them all to apply this analysis critically and constructively toward restoring the college to organizational health, lest the lives of two professors be wrongly ruined, and lest a cloud of disgrace hang over the college's future for as long as it may survive. The workplace ill of which Medaille is a textbook case is not beyond remedy. The college may emerge from this episode with renewed vitality, proving true what Nietzsche said, that what doesn't kill you makes you stronger. So favorable an outcome is unlikely without reasoned, well-informed discussion in all of the college's constituencies.

Finally, Section 6 shows the larger significance of Medaille's troubles, by recounting the extraordinary circumstance in which I learned of them and undertook the investigation reported here.

1. Workplace mobbing: the concept

In the early 1980s, the late Swedish psychologist, Heinz Leymann, precisely identified and labeled the distinct workplace ill that occurred at Medaille College in 2001-02. He described it with an English word, *mobbing*, by which he meant "ganging up on someone," "psychic terror,"

> hostile and unethical communication, which is directed in a systematic way by one or a few individuals mainly towards one individual who, due to mobbing, is pushed into a helpless and defenceless position, being held there by means of continuing mobbing activities.... (1996, p. 168; see also 1990)

Leymann took the word *mobbing* from earlier research by ethologist Konrad Lorenz, who had documented "ganging up" among birds. This phenomenon is routine, for instance, in broods of chickens, where a "pecking order" is readily observable. The bird at the bottom commonly dies from the cumulative effect of being shunned, kept from food and water, and physically pecked by the rest.

A similar phenomenon among human adolescents, usually called *swarming* or *collective bullying*, is regularly in the news. Sometimes gradually over many months, sometimes suddenly, teenagers coalesce into a mob that torments, tortures, humiliates, sometimes even murders, one of their number.

Leymann's contribution was to document and study the same phenomenon among adults, even in highly professionalized, rule-bound, ostensibly civilized workplaces. The tactics differ. Workplace mobbing is normally carried out politely and nonviolently. The participants are so convinced of the rightness of their exclusionary campaign that they usually leave ample written records, proudly signing their names to extreme deprecations and defamations, without noticing how thin or nonexistent is the supporting evidence. The object of the process is the same as among chickens or teenagers: crushing the target's identity and eliminating him or her totally from respectable company.

By most researchers' estimates, between two and five percent of adults are mobbed sometime during their working lives. A Swedish study found that about twelve percent of people who commit suicide have recently been mobbed at work (Leymann 1987).

While original in its precision and elaboration, Leymann's discovery echoed time-honored insights into human nature. Asked to comment on the anticommunist witch hunts of the McCarthy era, Harry Truman said:

> You read your history and you'll see that from time to time people in every country have seemed to lose their good sense, got hysterical, and got off the beam. I don't know what gets into people. (in Miller 1973, p. 447)

A century earlier, in *The House of Seven Gables*, Nathaniel Hawthorne drew this lesson from the execution by hanging of a man innocent of crime:

> that the influential classes, and those who take upon themselves to be leaders of the people, are fully liable to all the passionate error that has ever characterized the maddest mob. (1851, ch. 12)

Awareness that fair-minded, reasonable adults sometimes "lose their heads" and wrongly mob a fellow human is older still. René Girard of Stanford University has devoted much of his life to studying the impulse to scapegoat in ancient myths. He calls it the "persecutory unconscious." Girard argues that the Judaeo-Christian myths were unique in calling the urge to scapegoat wrong and in asserting individual dignity in the face of collective persecution, thereby laying the legal and cultural foundation for human rights in Western civilization (see 1986, 2001).

My own research over the past decade (see 1998, 2001; see also Davenport *et al.* 1999, Mathias 2000) has applied Leymann's concept of *workplace mobbing* to academe. I have analyzed by now about a hundred cases in North America, Europe, and Australia, of this hugely destructive snowballing contagion among administrators and professors in colleges and universities. The process runs its course in much the same way as Leymann found in nonacademic settings: first informal ostracization and petty harassment, then some real or imagined incident that is seized upon to justify stigmatization and formal sanctions, leading to termination of the target's academic life, sometimes through formal dismissal (as in the Medaille cases), sometimes through forced retirement, suicide, mental breakdown, or stress-induced cardiovascular disease.

For grasping the mind-boggling character, so bizarre as to be almost comical, of mobbing in the academic workplace, I recommend not only the scholarly literature cited above but also three recent novels. In *The Human Stain* (2000), Philip Roth spins the compelling story of a college ex-dean run out of his job on trumped-up charges of racism. In *Blue Angel* (2000), Francine Prose describes with marvelous humor a spirited campaign to oust an English professor for sexual harassment. In *Never Fade Away* (2002), William Hart recounts how and why an ESL instructor who cared too much for his students gets the boot. Also recommended is *The First Stone* (1997), novelist Helen Garner's nonfiction account of the forced departure of a college master at the University of Melbourne, Australia.

2. Workplace mobbing at Medaille

On February 8, 2002, John Donohue, acting president of Medaille College, formally dismissed from the faculty Therese Warden, professor of human services, on grounds of turpitude, a term whose meaning (to quote my dictionary) is "shameful character; baseness; wickedness."

On April 26, 2002, on almost identical grounds, Donohue dismissed Uhuru Watson, associate professor of social sciences.

From a narrowly legal viewpoint, the key fact in both cases was termination of employment. From the viewpoint of mobbing research, the key fact was not just termination but the stated grounds for it: corrupt personal identity. Warden and Watson were not just dropped from the payroll. They were officially designated as shameful, wicked human beings. Dangerous ones, too, since earlier they had both been suspended with pay and forbidden to come on campus, a penalty allowed by the Medaille College *Faculty Handbook* only if the professor's "continuance directly constitutes an immediate physical or psychological danger...."

A hallmark of workplace mobbing is the personal degradation of the target, the placing upon his or her deepest self the stigma of despicability. This rarely occurs in cases of firing for demonstrated cause. A president has no need to wound personally a professor who has embezzled college funds or failed for weeks to show up for class. The offense is clear. So is the penalty. Invective and disparagement are clues that a clear offense may not be in evidence.

In Warden's and Watson's cases, formal vilification did not stop with Donohue's letters. In the interval between suspension and termination, both professors sought redress in accordance with the *Faculty Handbook*, by appealing to the college's five-member Grievance Committee.

Its decision in Warden's case came on May 21, 2002, three months after she had been dismissed. The committee brushed aside her distress at being accused of turpitude:

> While the committee would like to delve into the definition of turpitude, unfortunately, it is not within the purview of the Grievance Committee since it is limited to matters of procedure by *The Handbook*.

The committee agreed with Warden that she should not have been suspended, and went on to justify the terminal penalty that had replaced the suspension with pay:

> Additionally, the options available to the administration in cases of turpitude are to either ignore the violation or to terminate the faculty member.
>
> *Recommendation*: While we find in favor of Dr. Warden regarding this issue, the fact that the College has dismissed her renders a recommendation moot.

The committee not only dismissed Warden's claim of unprofessional treatment, but rubbed in the stigma already imposed by the acting president:

> As her colleagues, the Grievance Committee is extremely dissatisfied with the behavior of Dr. Therese Warden in regard to the events from which these grievances are derived as well as her actions since the time of her dismissal which we believe have brought discredit to us all.

Finally, after some paragraphs of praise for tenure, shared governance, due process, professionalism, democracy, freedom, the pursuit of truth, and other high ideals, the committee recommended rituals of groveling and humiliation as a possible alternative to dismissal:

> The Acting President can reinstate Dr. Therese Warden, but only upon the mutual agreement of the parties that the following conditions precedent be met:
>
> The parties agree to a written letter of censure by the Grievance Committee to be placed in Dr. Warden's personnel file.
>
> Dr. Warden is prohibited from serving on any confidential committees for five years.

The Promotion and Tenure Committee conduct an annual review for three years of Dr. Warden, which include the area of collegiality especially as it relates to new faculty.

Finally, that Dr. Warden write a letter of apology to the Medaille College community that will be read at a faculty meeting.

More starkly even than Donohue's letters, the Grievance Committee's decision attests the stupendous social force that had been unleashed at Medaille: fanatic resolve to break a professor's professional back, to crush her under collective weight. Coerced public confession has long been outlawed in Western jurisprudence, yet the Committee would coerce from Warden a public apology, a statement of confession plus remorse, if Donohue should deign to receive it.

The Grievance Committee's decision in Warden's case deserves to be read in its entirety. Except for those caught up in Medaille's pathology, readers cannot help but be aghast at the contradiction of which the committee seemed oblivious, between the high ideals espoused and the low conclusions reached.

The same goes for the committee's shorter, three-page report one month earlier, on April 22, 2002, in Watson's case. Watson was at that point only suspended, not yet terminated. The committee judged that suspension was contrary to the *Faculty Handbook*: "The options available to the administration in cases like this are to either ignore the violation or to terminate the faculty member."

In its conclusion, the committee recommended that "the Acting President shall pursue one of the two options described in the Handbook (and as noted above) for cases of this nature," but then immediately contradicted itself by recommending a different alternative to termination: not to ignore the violation but to enforce rituals of humiliation:

Dr. Watson will:

Acknowledge as true, in a manner to be determined in consultation with the Acting President, the facts of the investigation conducted by the Acting Academic Dean;

Authorize the full disclosure of the Grievance Committee's facts and findings regarding the unauthorized distribution of confidential minutes of the Promotion and Tenure Committee at a full faculty meeting.

Apologize in private to the Acting Academic Dean and the Acting President for his conduct during the investigation.

Withdraw any present lawsuits and do not initiate future lawsuits with regard to these matters.

The first of these items, that Watson should be required to "acknowledge as true" ideas with which he obviously disagreed, is especially extreme in a workplace founded upon intellectual freedom. It is an explicit effort at mind control, recalling the voice of tyranny in Orwell's *Nineteen Eighty-Four*:

You are here because you have failed in humility, in self-discipline. You would not make the act of submission which is the price of sanity. You preferred to be a lunatic, a minority of one. Only the disciplined mind can see reality....

(1990, p. 261; first published 1949)

The Grievance Committee's reports in Warden's and Watson's cases highlight a key defining attribute of workplace mobbing, one that distinguishes this pathology from the related and better known pathology of bullying (see Namie & Namie 2000). In the latter, the target is up against a single domineering workmate or manager. In the Medaille cases, although Donohue was the dominant figure, Warden and Watson faced a united front of Donohue and his subordinates: Joseph Savarese, the acting dean who had recommended the dismissals to Donohue in a memorandum of December 10, 2001, the five-member Grievance Committee that joined the eliminative campaign a few months later, plus all those other administrators, professors, trustees, students, and secretaries who gossiped behind the scenes and stood idly by as the campaign progressed. The technical term for the latter is *bystanders*. The peculiarly devastating quality of workplace mobbing consists in the appearance of unanimity, that "everybody who counts knows you are rotten and wants you out of here." As the Grievance Committee declared in the final sentence of its decision on Watson: "These recommendations are offered with the unanimous approval of the Grievance Committee members."

For understanding workplace mobbing, a talmudic principle often quoted by the late French philosopher, Emmanuel Lévinas, is apt: "If everyone is in agreement to condemn someone accused, release him for he must be innocent" (quoted in Girard 2001, p. 118).

3. The course of events

That so many capable scholars could have been caught up in an irrational movement for inflicting permanent harm on two innocent professors is a hard idea to contemplate, so great is our respect for institutions of higher learning as temples of reason and sobriety. Surely Warden and Watson must have done *something* wrong.

In these as in most mobbing cases, elimination was officially rationalized by reference to a critical incident, an alleged instance of grave misconduct ordinarily involving violation of written policies and procedures. To the outside observer of the Medaille conflict, however, the clearest violation was committed not by Warden, Watson, or any other of the punished professors, but earlier, by acting dean Savarese and acting president Donohue.

On June 8, 2001, these two senior administrators convened the college's Promotion and Tenure Committee for the purpose of securing its support for ousting Michael Lillis from his position as chair of business. Savarese presided at the meeting. Attending as a guest, Donohue sought and obtained the committee's support for his determination that Lillis should be replaced.

This meeting violated college procedure and academic custom, since the issue it dealt with was not promotion of anyone to higher rank nor the award of tenure to anyone. Lillis's position as a tenured associate professor was not at issue. The issue was whether he should hold, in addition to his faculty position, the administrative position of department chair. This issue fell outside the committee's mandate. Procedures for appointment of department chairs, as set down in the *Faculty Handbook*, assigned no role whatsoever to the Promotion and Tenure Committee.

As one of the five members of this committee, Uhuru Watson noticed the violation of procedure. He was concerned in particular that Lillis had been the subject of negative comments at the meeting without having opportunity to respond – a standard requirement of the rules of natural justice. In the weeks that followed, Watson registered his concerns with Saverese, other committee members, and the Medaille College Faculty Council.

Thereby Watson acted in a way that is probably the statistically most common root of workplace mobbing: he exposed the wrongness of a decision made by his administrative superiors. He showed them up, implicitly put them to shame (see Wyatt and Hare 1997). They retaliated in kind by shaming Watson, accusing him of having violated the confidentiality of the disputed meeting, and judging this offense to warrant his being humiliated and fired. In colloquial terms, they "went after" him.

In October, 2001, a copy of the minutes of the disputed committee meeting of the previous June 8, appeared in the mailbox of Therese

Warden, co-president of the Medaille chapter of the American Association of University Professors (AAUP), well-known on the campus as a high achiever and nonpartisan advocate of due process. The documentation does not indicate who placed the minutes there. Savarese later claimed it was Watson, and on this basis recommended his dismissal, though Watson did not admit to the charge.

Puzzled by the document and its mysterious arrival in her mailbox, Warden reported the matter to Savarese, who advised her to contact Donohue about it, which she did. She also gave copies of the document to Randy Brown, her co-president of the Medaille AAUP, and to mathematics/science professor Elizabeth Lucyszyn, a member of the Faculty Council. Savarese soon asked all three professors – Warden, Brown, and Lucyszyn – to return their copies of the minutes to him, which they did.

Then, however, Savarese and Donohue "went after" Warden, Brown, and Lucyszyn for the "egregious unethical behavior" of briefly possessing a document that, although not labeled confidential, could be considered so. Savarese recommended, and Donohue concurred, that Warden should be dismissed altogether for passing the document to Brown and Lucyszyn, that Brown (a junior, untenured professor) should be censured and his contract not be renewed, and that Lucyszyn should be censured and removed from her position as chair of the mathematics/science department.

If there were more evidence than that just described of misconduct on the part of Watson, Warden, and the others who were punished, it would be my scholarly duty to report it, but I have found none. The plain fact is that the administrators had no case. In civil proceedings, it could be called a *nonsuit*, or in criminal proceedings, *false arrest*. On the other hand, the evidence seems clear that Savarese and Donohue convened the Promotion and Tenure Committee for a purpose outside its jurisdiction, and that Watson and Warden sought to rectify this policy violation through appropriate channels of college governance. Savarese and Donohue displayed poor administrative skills in convening the Promotion and Tenure Committee meeting of June 8, but nobody involved in the conflict over it committed any grave ethical offense or deserved any kind of punishment.

The conclusion that the two seasoned admnistrators, Savarese and Donohue, in Truman's words, "lost their good sense" on this occasion, is reinforced by a glance at Watson's and Warden's decade-long records of successful work at Medaille. Watson enjoyed such high collegial regard as to have been elected not just to the Promotion and Tenure Committee but to the presidential search committee then underway.

For her part, Warden co-founded the AAUP chapter at Medaille in 1993. As chair of her department since 1995, she had developed successful new certificate programs. On her return from a sabbatical leave during the fall of 2000, Medaille had celebrated her innovative work in community mental health with a lengthy faculty profile and photo in its newspaper, *Horizon* (spring 2001).

4. Origin of the Medaille pathology

Because the documentation reviewed for this analysis begins only in 2001, I lack data on the mobbings' informal stages that probably began years earlier. Watson has spoken publicly of an institutional culture of intimidation. If his and Warden's cases follow the pattern of others in my research, a study of social relations at the college in the 1990s would reveal professional jealousies, factional rivalries, and nefarious coalitions that led to the purge of 2002.

One cardinal fact stands out, however, as weakening the college's immunity to severe pathology: the death in February of 2001, of Kevin Sullivan, Medaille's president for the previous fourteen years, and chair of its board of trustees for seven years before that. In no period of an organization's history is good order more likely to break down than in the interval between sudden loss of a longstanding leader and appointment of a new one. That was precisely the period Medaille found itself in when Watson and Warden were mobbed.

A week after Sullivan's death, Medaille's board appointed Donohue, an accomplished anthropologist then serving as Medaille's vice-president and dean, as acting president, and began a national search for Sullivan's successor. Donohue in turn appointed Savarese, the chair of veterinary technology, as acting dean.

Donohue wanted the Medaille presidency for the longer term. The search committee welcomed his candidacy and included him among the twelve semifinalists selected in December of 2001, then among the three finalists announced in February of 2002.

Donohue must have known his success in the competition depended utterly on his managing the campus well as interim president. He needed to "keep the lid on," keep things under control, not let the college's affairs "go up for grabs" – these being the baseline expectations of any college board.

One can also plausibly assume that when Watson challenged his way of dealing with Lillis's administrative appointment, Donohue felt a greater need than he might otherwise have felt to "come down hard" and "show who is boss." His own vulnerability, one suspects, led to rash, unwarranted incursions on professors' jobs.

Such an explanation of how the college caught the mobbing bug is admittedly speculative, and could only be confirmed by personal interviews with those involved, but such, at least, is the direction in which the documentary evidence points.

On February 19, 2002, as Donohue was preparing for his formal interview for the presidency, a reporter from the *Buffalo News* phoned him for his side of the story of Warden's dismissal, Watson's suspension, and Brown's and Lucyszyn's penalties. Mobbing targets often go public and appeal for outside help; it is their only recourse against the circled wagons of their own institution.

Predictably, Donohue was not pleased. Workplace mobbing is more likely to succeed under cover of secrecy and confidentiality. In a memo to the college community that same day, he said he told the reporter

> the matter in question is an internal personnel issue that is, by nature, confidential. I am not at liberty to discuss it. I noted that Medaille College prides itself on its equitable and appropriate treatment of all its employees.

Donohue wrote in conclusion:

> It's unfortunate that some individuals felt the need to publicize an internal disagreement of this type before letting the processes we have established for review take place. While I am sure that there are people who feel very strongly on either side of the issue, I am equally sure that the procedures and processes in place at the College apply to us all.
>
> Finally, at a time when so many positive things are happening at the College, it's a shame that a few individuals have generated this type of publicity. In their zeal to act, they have hurt us all.

The story in *Buffalo News* appeared on February 20, 2002, and a longer report in *The Chronicle of Higher Education* came out on March 7. Neither article editorialized. Both were factual and clear. Thereby they exposed to the college's two main social environments, its home city and the national academic community, how far out of hand things had gotten in the year since Sullivan's death.

Soon thereafter, the Board of Trustees announced the appointment of Joseph Bascuas, a vice-president of the Argosy Education Group, as Medaille's next president. He took office in July, 2002. Donohue was named vice-president for special programs, but his name no longer appears on the college website.

5. What will happen next

Responding to a series of pleas from Jonathan Knight, Associate Secretary of AAUP, Bascuas said in early August that he was reviewing Warden's and Watson's dismissals. That review is apparently ongoing as of October 2002, since no results have been announced.

According to research on how mobbings in general play out, the statistically most probable action Bascuas will take is none at all. He may remain silent or issue a do-nothing statement about moving ahead and letting bygones be bygones.

Leymann reported "that we have never found a single case where the employer, as the other party, could find himself at fault and give the employee some redress for wrongs suffered" (1990, p. 124). Similarly, John Polya wrote as follows about academic mobbings in Australia:

> One of the most frightening observations in several cases is how new staff and new administrators, not involved in the original witch hunt, join to defend the old errors and injustices. The only explanation for such behavior is that the pressures on certain academics, or perhaps their basic psychodynamics, demand a release of tensions on a convenient scapegoat; it may also be that, by showing a willingness to victimise a scapegoat, they ingratiate themselves with local power elites. (1986, pp. 48f)

When a college or university has officially imprinted on a professor the stigma of turpitude and drummed the person out, it commonly displays extreme reluctance to reverse itself and admit a mistake – even, as Polya pointed out, after leadership has passed to newcomers. It is often as if a new leader contracts on arrival the strain of mobbing virus that has infected the campus, and transmits it further instead of healing it.

Donohue may be gone from the Medaille campus, but those who joined with him in mobbing Warden, Watson, and the others are still there. Subtly or explicitly, most of them can be expected to urge

Bascuas not to "reopen old wounds" but to turn his attention to new projects.

In fact, the wounds are fresh, raw, and festering. If Bascuas digs in his heels behind wrong decisions made before he arrived, he will then have to mount an expensive defense against Warden's and Watson's legal claims. Court proceedings may drag on for five or more years. By American labor law, no court is likely to order Warden's or Watson's reinstatement to the faculty, but an award of financial compensation could put a large dent in the college's resources.

Meanwhile, AAUP is likely to shame the institution, publishing Medaille's name worldwide on the list of colleges and universities under formal censure. Public-affairs journalists may shame the college further with exposés on TV and in the press. Medaille's position as a private college in a harshly competitive institutional environment will probably become more precarious than it is now.

In the meanwhile, the fight to regain their positions and good names will consume the time, energy, money, and possibly the health, of Warden and Watson. They will feel intense stress, not just from bearing institutional stigma but from knowing how much the prospects of getting it legally lifted depend on lawyers' procedural maneuvers and on other vagaries of the justice system. If they win monetary damages in the end, they will not likely see much actual money, on account of their own legal expenses. In any case, as many mobbing targets before them have observed, money cannot compensate for the loss of years of productive life.

In this internecine but statistically probable scenario, nobody wins, no matter what verdict is ultimately handed down or what out-of-court settlement is eventually reached.. All parties, even the lawyers, will in the end feel sick over the waste of resources that could otherwise have gone toward producing knowledge and educating youth – by Warden, Watson, Bascuas, and the college itself.

Even if probable, so destructive a scenario is not inevitable. Several cases reported in my book (1998, pp. 165-170) illustrate the more constructive outcome that may occur also at Medaille, if the leaders of its various constituencies act promptly toward correcting past mistakes and toward making the college whole again.

Neither Leymann nor I have done research on workplace mobbing as a mere academic exercise, but instead with confidence that once managers and workers are informed of it, once we all face up to and understand how wrongly we sometimes behave at work, we thereby become able to prevent and remedy the resultant harm. The present paper provides the information and understanding for the mobbing cases at Medaille College. It can thus be an instrument for restoring the college to health.

What is needed at Medaille now is open, free, blunt, honest, well-informed discussion among all those who care about the school and share an interest in its survival and success: administrators, trustees, faculty, alumni, staff, students, as well as AAUP officials and colleagues in neighboring institutions. Warden and Watson should be invited back on campus to join in the discussion, out of which a solution will emerge that is fair to all sides and serves the college well. The forgiveness, reconciliation, and hope that have been achieved elsewhere are possible at Medaille College, if only people risk exchanging reasoned views.

The initiative should not be left to Bascuas alone. As an administratively skilled outsider, new to the office of president, his role is above all to listen to the varied voices raised, then to draw the discussion to a constructive conclusion. No friend of the college should deprive Bascuas of honest input, lest his presidency be doomed to failure at the start.

The outcome of the mobbings at Medaille will be a test of Bascuas's administrative skills, as it will also be a test of Leymann's and my confidence that an understanding of mobbing enables its prevention and remedy.

6. Origin of this analysis

The outcome will be a test of yet something else: whether the National Association of Scholars (NAS) stands for the classic goals of liberal education or merely for a right-wing agenda just as oppressive as the leftist orthodoxies NAS was founded to oppose. This is the larger significance of the Medaille conflict, as the story of how and why I got involved makes clear.

The analysis set down in this paper began with a question asked by a member of the audience on Friday evening, September 20, 2002, at the opening session of a conference at Medaille College on "Academic Freedom and Intellectual Pluralism: U.S. and Canadian Perspectives." I was in the audience, too. It was my first time on the Medaille campus. I was there to present a paper the next day in memory of Richard Henshel, a sociology professor at the University of Western Ontario who died in 1997.

Henshel had left most of his estate to NAS. I, along with the others to whom Henshel had entrusted execution of his will, had proposed to Stephen Balch, founder and president of NAS, that part of the bequest be spent on an academic conference in Henshel's memory. Balch had graciously agreed, and arranged for the conference to be held at Medaille, where he holds a seat on the Board of Trustees. Now at last, the conference was underway.

The program for the event was remarkable for having brought together the leaders of four major campaigns against political correctness and postmodern fanaticism in higher education. Alan C. Kors, co-author of *The Shadow University* and co-president of the Foundation for Individual Rights in Education (FIRE), had just given the opening address, "The Betrayal of Liberty and Dignity on America's Campuses." Balch had introduced him.

In the audience was Clive Seligman, president of the Society for Academic Freedom and Scholarship (SAFS), the Canadian counterpart to NAS, who would speak the next day on "The Diversity Debate at Canadian Universities." Other prominent opponents of political correctness were also present: conservative philosopher Barry Smith of SUNY Buffalo (the conference organizer), SUNY trustee Candace de Russy, libertarian economist Walter Block of Loyola, New Orleans, and Stanley Rothman of Smith College, chair of NAS's board of advisors.

The most famous of the conference speakers had not yet arrived: neocon provocateur David Horowitz, president of the Center for the Study of Popular Culture (CSPC), who caused a stir in 2001 with paid ads against slavery reparations in the few campus newspapers willing to accept the ads. Horowitz's panel presentation the next day was entitled, "Universities as a Political Base for the Anti-American Left."

It was when the floor was opened for discussion after Kors's talk that John Schedel, a communications professor at Medaille, asked the question to which this paper is in some respects a response. I could tell Schedel was angry but also scared, in the way that one about to ask an embarrassing question often is.

In light of what Kors had just said about liberty and free speech, Schedel asked, what was Kors's opinion about the purge of tenured faculty last spring at this very college? Murmurs of "no" and "be quiet" traveled the assembly as Schedel spoke, but calmly and respectfully, he made his point.

"I don't know about these cases," Kors replied from the podium.

Balch rose quickly to his feet. He said he could not speak officially for the Board of Trustees, but that he knew these cases were not about academic freedom, instead the professors' violation of confidentiality.

Schedel sat down, and discussion turned to generalities.

Weeks earlier, I had seen the article about Medaille in the *Chronicle of Higher Education*: "Actions Against 4 Professors at Medaille College Raise Concern Over Academic Freedom." That was all I knew. Later that balmy night, on the steps of the administration building, Schedel began to fill me in. He described himself as a conservative, a scholar 180 degrees opposite to Warden and Watson on many issues, but nonetheless convinced that they in no way deserved the loss of their jobs and good names.

The more details Schedel gave me, and the more documents I read in subsequent weeks, the more troubled I became about the conference and my part in it. Why was a celebration of academic freedom being held at a college whose administration had just a few months earlier breached academic freedom so flagrantly? Why, when Schedel asked precisely the question that most needed to be asked, did Balch so quickly leap to defend the dismissals? Might the practical effect of our conference be to legitimate the recent mobbings? Might it be an instance of Newspeak, wherein freedom means slavery and ignorance means strength (Orwell 1990, p. 29)?

Two discoveries as I proceeded with research heightened my concerns. One was that ours was actually the second Medaille conference on academic freedom held in 2002. The first one, which I have watched on videotape, was sponsored by the AAUP on February 22. That conference had held the dismissals up to reasoned, critical scrutiny, in light of the standard values of academic and civilized life. Warden and Watson were on hand and allowed to speak. The practical thrust was toward constructive resolution of the conflict. That first conference was originally scheduled to be held in the Alumni Room of the Main Building of Medaille College, but was then apparently forced to move off campus, to nearby Daemen College.

The second worrisome discovery was Balch's column in the *NAS Update* of Winter, 2001-02. It was entitled "Let's Roll" – the famous phrase of the heroic passengers on United Airlines Flight 93 on September 11, 2001, who mobbed terrorist hijackers in a circumstance where mobbing was fully justified. Balch seemed in that column to call for similar aggressive action on American campuses.

"If the intellectual climate of the more politicized domains of scholarship is ever to change," he wrote, "the sorts of people inhabiting them must change as well." Might the Medaille administrators have taken their cue from Balch's rhetoric? Might the panic that followed the September 11 attacks help explain how these administrators mistook two decent professors for wicked, dangerous undesirables who should be sacked?

I have no firm answers to these questions. NAS, FIRE, SAFS, and CSPC have earned my admiration and respect as needed counterweights to the forces of political correctness on American and Canadian campuses. Many if not most of the academic mobbings I have studied in recent years have been rooted in well-intentioned but fanatic and misguided campaigns to purify campuses absolutely of leftist bugbears like sexism, racism, classism, and homophobia.

The Medaille conference, however, left me wondering what the reformist organizations actually stand for. Is it academic freedom or conservative orthodoxy? Is it the curtailment of mobbing or merely a shift from left to right in the direction from which it comes?

Buffalo's magnificent Albright-Knox Art Gallery was the setting for the closing event of our conference on Saturday evening, September 21. After dinner, David Horowitz gave a rousing speech about his battles with the left. I asked him afterwards whether, by his rhetoric and name-calling, he is not as extremist and divisive as the people he opposes. I cited the research Stanley Rothman had presented earlier that day, and Clive Seligman's studies of the social psychology of value-systems, suggesting that humans are not easily divided into polar political opposites, that unless overcome by panic, people's actual behavior tends to be issue- and context-specific.

Horowitz answered politely and thoughtfully. He said my attitude was civilized, but that it was just this attitude that had permitted American campuses to be taken over by the anti-American left.

Horowitz has a point. Yet it is also true that unless his organization (CSPC) and similar ones like NAS, FIRE, and SAFS promote a genuine pluralism in our institutions, reciprocal tolerance of diverse viewpoints and reasoned debate among them, they are as bad as fanatic movements on the left and do not deserve support. What part, if any, the speakers at September's conference at Medaille College play in resolving the college's troubles will be one test, one indication of what the agendas of their respective organizations really are.

Finally, to end on a personal note, this paper springs from my commitment to be true to the late Richard Henshel's will. He would have understood and respected John Schedel's question on the opening night of the Medaille conference. Henshel often asked the same kind of question. Part of what being a professor meant to him was rising in a room full of like-minded people and asking a question that rattled their cage. It was to ensure that academic life continues to have room for such behavior that he left his money to NAS. What lies behind this paper is the sentiment Robert Service wrote in "The Cremation of Sam McGee":

> A pal's last need is a thing to heed
> And I swore that I would not fail.

List of references

Davenport, Noa, *et al., Mobbing: Emotional Abuse in the American Workplace.* Ames, IA: Civil Society Publishing.

Garner, Helen, 1997. *The First Stone.* New York: Free Press.

Girard, René, 1986. *The Scapegoat.* Baltimore: Johns Hopkins University Press.

Girard, René, 2001. *I See Satan Fall Like Lightning.* Maryknoll, NY: Orbis.

Hart, William, *Never Fade Away.* Santa Barbara, CA: Fithian.

Hawthorne, Nathaniel, 1851. *The House of Seven Gables.*

Leymann, Heinz, 1987. "Självmord till följd av förh□llanden i arbetsmiljön," *Arbete, människa, miljö* 3, pp. 155-169 [as summarized in Leymann 1990].

Leymann, Heinz, 1990. "Mobbing and Psychological Terror at Workplaces," *Violence and Victims* 5 (2), pp. 119-126.

Leymann, Heinz, 1996. "The Content and Development of Mobbing at Work," *European Journal of Work and Organizational Psychology* 5 (2), pp. 165-184.

Mathias, Philip, 2000. "Professors Meet Their Waterloo," *National Post,* March 11.

Miller, Merle, 1973. *Plain Speaking: an Oral Biography of Harry S. Truman.* New York: Berkley Medallion.

Namie, Gary, and Ruth Namie, 2000. *The Bully at Work.* Amazon (USA), Chapters (Canada), or by mail from Devon, UK: Roundhouse Publishing.

Orwell, George, 1997. *Nineteen Eighty-Four.* London: Penguin. First published 1949.

Polya, John, 1986. "Commentary" on C. Manwell and C. M. A. Baker, "'Not Merely Malice: the University of Tasmania versus Professor Orr," pp. 48f in B. Martin *et al.,* eds., *Intellectual Suppression.* London: Angus & Robertson.

Prose, Francine, 2000. *Blue Angel*. New York: HarperCollins.

Roth, Philip, 2000. *The Human Stain*. Boston: Houghton Mifflin.

Westhues, Kenneth, 1998. *Eliminating Professors: a Guide to the Dismissal Process*. Lewiston, NY: Edwin Mellen Press.

Westhues, Kenneth, 2001. "'The Difficult Professor,'a Pernicious Concept," with additional commentaries by N. Davenpor, H. Hammerly, H. Klatt, and J. Mueller, CAUT Legal Conference, Ottawa.

Wyatt, Judith, and Chauncey Hare, 1997. *Work Abuse: How to Recognize and Survive It*. Rochester, VT: Schenkman.

Documents related to the Medaille conflict

(Most of these are available online at the New York State AAUP website, www.nysc-aaup.org)

AAUP Chapter at St. Bonaventure University (J. W. Moor, S. Nuttall, J. A. White), 2002. Statement of support for Dr. T.Warden and colleagues at Medaille College, April 16.

AAUP Chapters in Western New York, 2002. Poster announcing symposium, "Crisis! The State of Academic Freedom at Medaille College and in Western New York," to be held at Medaille College, February 22.

AAUP (New York), 2002. Minutes of spring meeting on Long Island, including reports of actions taken toward resolving conflict at Medaille College.

AAUP (New York), 2002. Videotape of symposium on academic freedom held at Daemen College, February 22.

AAUP (Medaille College Chapter), 2002. *The Voice of Academic Freedom Speaking to the Crisis at Medaille College*, "The Facts Regarding the P & T Committee Document," spring.

Auer, Holly, 2002. "Professor Fired after Questioning Panel's Policy," *Buffalo News*, February 20.

Balch, Stephen, 2001-02. "Let's Roll," Column in *NAS Update*, winter.

Brace, Jim, Kim Carr, John Elmore, Robert Johnson, and Ross Runfola (Medaille College Grievance Committee), 2002. Memorandum to Dr. John Donohue stating recommendations on the grievances of Dr. Uhuru Watson, April 22.

Brace, Jim, Kim Carr, John Elmore, Robert Johnson, and Ross Runfola (Medaille College Grievance Committee), 2002. Memoranduum to Dr. John Donohue stating recommendations on the grievances of Dr. Therese Warden, May 21.

Buermann, Barry, and Terry Warden, 1993. Memorandum to Medaille College faculty concerning establishment of AAUP chapter on campus.

Donohue, John, 2002. Letter to Therese Warden suspending her from teaching and forbidding her to come on campus, January 10.

Donohue, John, 2002. Memorandum to Medaille Community about upcoming *Buffalo News* article, February 19.

Drury, Tracey, 2002. "Medaille names John Donohue to acting president," *Buffalo Business First*, February 26.

Drury, Tracey, 2002. "Medaille narrowing search for new president," *Buffalo Business First*, March 7.

Faculty Association of Niagara County Community College, 2002. Resolution supporting AAUP efforts toward "balance of governance" at Medaille College, February 26.

Horizon, 2001. Medaille College newspaper including feature on Dr. Terry Warden and retrospective on the late president Kevin Sullivan, spring.

Horizon, 2002. Medaille College newspaper reporting news since appointment of Joseph Bascuas as president, summer.

Kellogg, Alex P., 2002. "Actions Against 4 Professors at Medaille College Raise Concern Over Academic Freedom," *Chronicle of Higher Education*, March 7.

Knight, Jonathan (associate secretary, national office of AAUP), 2002. Letters to Dr. John Donohue requesting reinstatement of Professors Warden and Watson, February 8, March 7.

Knight, Jonathan (associate secretary, national office of AAUP), 2002. Letter to Dr. Joseph Bascuas requesting reinstatement of Professors Warden and Watson, July 15.

Savarese, Joseph E., 2001. Memorandum to John Donohue recommending dismissals and punishments.

UUP (United University Professors), 2002. Report of delegates' support for Medaille College faculty in struggle for academic freedom, *The Voice*, March.

Warden, Therese, 2002. Memoranda to Dr. John Donohue requesting meetings for informal resolution of conflict, January 2 and 12.

Chapter Eight

Mistreatment of Teachers by School Principals: How Teachers See It

Joseph Blase and Jo Blase

Internationally, systematic research on the problem of workplace abuse, notably nonphysical forms of abuse, has increased significantly during the last two decades in countries such as Sweden, Norway, Germany, Austria, Australia, and Britain. Several of these countries have also enacted legislation against workplace abuse, and private organizations have been created to help victims of abuse (Björkvist, Österman, and Hjelt-Bäck 1994; Davenport, Schwartz, and Elliott 1999; Keashly 1998; Namie and Namie 2000). For most of this same period, organizational scholars in the United States have largely ignored the problem of work abuse, and only in recent years have such scholars begun to address the problem. Indeed, the emerging national literature suggests that workplace abuse may lead to serious deleterious consequences for both employees and organizations (Baron and Neuman 1996; Davenport *et al.* 1999; Hornstein, Michela, Van Eron, Cohen, Heckelman, Sachse-Skidd, and Spenser 1995; Hornstein 1996; Keashly 1998; Keashly, Trott, and MacLean 1994).

This chapter is based on a larger qualitative study of school principals' mistreatment/abuse of teachers and the subsequent destructive effects on them, from the perspectives of teachers themselves. The study is the first empirical study of its kind, and as such, it focuses on types of principal behavior that teachers define as "abusive" or "mistreatment" (teachers in our study used the terms synonymously); that is, it focuses on behaviors teachers experienced as seriously harmful when repeated over the long run. Given space limitations, principal behaviors and the effects such patterns of behavior have on the psychological/emotional and physical wellbeing of teachers are briefly described. For a full description of the behaviors and effects on teachers please refer to *Breaking the Silence: Overcoming the Problem of Principal Mistreatment of Teacher*s (Blase and Blase 2003).

Terms and Constructs

Using a variety of methods, researchers have used a number of terms in the conceptual, theoretical, and empirical literature to describe the workplace mistreatment/abuse phenomenon including *incivility* (Andersson and Pearson 1999), *mobbing* (Davenport *et al.* 1999; Leymann 1990; Westhues 2004), *bullying* (Einarsen and Skogstad 1996; Namie and Namie 2000), *harassment* (Björkvist *et al.* 1994); *petty tyranny* (Ashforth 1994), *abusive disrespect* (Hornstein 1996), *interactional injustice* (Harlos and Pinder, 2000), *emotional abuse* (Keashly 1998), *mistreatment* (Folger 1993; Price Spratlen 1995), *abuse* (Bassman 1992), *aggression* (Neuman and Baron 1998), *deviance* (Robinson and Bennett 1995), and *victimization* (Swedish National Board of Occupational Safety and Health 1993).

In addition, organizational scholars have developed a variety of empirically grounded constructs to define the workplace mistreatment/abuse phenomenon. To illustrate:

- Andersson and Pearson (1999) conceptualize *workplace incivility* as "low-intensity deviant behavior with ambiguous intent to harm the target, in violation of workplace norms for mutual respect. Uncivil behaviors are characteristically rude and discourteous, displaying a lack of regard for others" (p. 457).
- The construct of *mobbing* (or psychical terror), the most common term used in Europe, refers to "hostile and unethical communication that is directed in a systematic way by one or a number of persons toward one individual.... These actions take place often...and over a long period (at least six months) and, because of this

frequency and duration, result in considerable psychic, psychosomatic, and social misery" (Leymann 1990, p. 120). Mobbing consists of humiliating, intimidating, and abusive communication; committed directly or indirectly; to confuse, discredit, intimidate, isolate, and force an individual into submission or out of the workplace (Davenport *et al.* 1999; Westhues 2004).

- Einarsen and Skogstad (1996) define *bullying*, a term commonly used in the United States and Europe, as "...harassment, badgering, niggling, freezing out, offending someone...repeatedly over a period of time, and the person confronted...[has] difficulties defending him/herself. It is not bullying if two parties of approximately equal strength are in conflict or the incident is an isolated event (p. 191)."

- *Work harassment* is defined as "repeated activities, with the aim of bringing mental (but sometimes also physical) pain, and directed toward one or more individuals, who for one reason or another, are not able to defend themselves...." (Björkvist *et al.* 1994, p. 173).

- Ashforth (1994) developed a measure of tyrannical behavior that consists of six dimensions. He defined a *petty tyrant* as "an individual who lords his or her power over others,... acts in an arbitrary and self-aggrandizing manner, belittles subordinates, evidences lack of consideration, forces conflict resolution, discourages initiative, and utilizes noncontingent punishment" (p. 772).

- *Abusive disrespect*, a concept developed by Hornstein *et al.*; (1995), is comprised of eight behavioral dimensions of disrespectful supervisory behavior and specifically refers to "transgressions" by bosses that include deceit (i.e., lying), constraint (i.e., controlling subordinates' actions outside of work), coercion (i.e., threatening excessive or inappropriate harm), selfishness (i.e., blaming and scapegoating subordinates), disregard (i.e., violating standards of politeness and fairness, lack of concern for personal lives of subordinates), inequity (i.e., favoritism), cruelty (i.e., harming subordinates through name calling, personal attacks), and deification (i.e., conduct that communicates a "master-servant" relationship to subordinates).

From comprehensive review of the workplace mistreatment/abuse literature, Keashly (1998) developed a concept of *emotional abuse* that subsumes elements of the constructs defined above. Emotional abuse emphasizes the "hostile verbal and nonverbal behaviors ... directed at gaining compliance from others" (p. 85). Keashly identified emotional abuse with the following: a pattern of abuse (not a single event), behaviors unwanted by the target, behaviors that violate norms of appropriate conduct or an individual's rights, behaviors that are intended to harm the target, behaviors that result in harm to the target, and power differences between the abuser and the target of abuse.

Models

In addition, empirical research has generated a handful of models of mistreatment in the work setting. For example, Baron and Neuman (1996) constructed the three-factor model of *workplace aggression*, which includes expressions of hostility, obstructionism, and overt aggression. Expressions of hostility include verbal and symbolic behaviors such as facial expressions, gestures, and verbal attacks like staring, dirty looks, silent treatment, ridicule, unfair evaluations, and gossip. Obstructionism refers to actions that are often passive-aggressive in nature, such as withholding a resource or behavior. Some examples are not returning phone calls, refusing to provide needed resources or equipment, and failing to warn an individual of imminent danger. Overt aggression, the third factor, refers to threats or acts of physical violence and theft or destruction of an individual's work equipment.

Ryan and Oestreich (1991) produced a model of *abrasive* (i.e., less harmful) *and abusive* (i.e., more harmful) categories of boss behavior, with behaviors (listed from less to more harmful) including silence, glaring eye contact, abruptness, snubbing or ignoring, insults, blaming, discrediting and discounting, controlling others aggressively, making threats about the job, yelling and shouting, making angry outbursts, and threatening physical harm. Ryan and Oestreich contend that any behavior may have greater impact on individuals depending on timing, place of occurrence, and level of repetition.

Finally, a typology of workplace deviance, developed by Robinson and Bennett (1995), indicates that *deviant* workplace behavior varies across two dimensions: minor versus serious and interpersonal versus organizational. Minor forms of deviance were classified into two quadrants including production deviance (e.g., leaving early, taking excessive breaks) and political deviance (e.g., favoritism, gossiping, and blaming subordinates). More serious forms of deviance were classified as property deviance (e.g., sabotaging equipment, lying about hours worked) and personal aggression (e.g., verbal abuse, sexual harassment, stealing from subordinates, and endangering subordinates).

Theoretical Work

Several scholars have specifically developed theories of boss abuse of subordinates. To illustrate, Hornstein *et al.* (1995) constructed a theory of *supervisory disrespect* that draws heavily on symbolic interaction, organizational justice, and the psychological and stress literature. These authors argue that people's feelings of both self-worth and security are affected by how respectfully others treat them; and feelings of self-worth and security, in turn, affect one's mental health and well-being. Hornstein *et al.* (1995) established validity and reliability for the Boss Behavior Questionnaire (BBQ), which uses measurable constructs of respect and disrespect to examine the eight domains of supervisory disrespectful behavior described above.

Ashforth (1994) developed a model of the antecedents and effects of *tyranny* on subordinates. He contends that petty tyranny is an interaction between superordinates' predispositions (i.e., beliefs about organizations, subordinates, and self and preferences for action) and situational facilitators (i.e., institutionalized values and norms, power, and stressors). Ashforth argues that tyrannical management causes low leader endorsement, high frustration, stress, resistance, high helplessness, work alienation, low self-esteem, poor work performance, and low work unit cohesiveness. He emphasized that such effects could trigger a vicious circle that sustains the tyrannical behavior. For instance, the exercise of power may induce a manager to do the following: attribute subordinates' success to him or herself, develop an inflated sense of self-worth, create greater psychological distance from subordinates, and view subordinates as objects of manipulation (Kipnis 1972).

Folger's (1993) work, based on exchange theory and, in particular, referent cognitive theory (RCT), explains how employees come to feel mistreated by management. This theory conceptualizes *employment as both economic and social processes involving the exchange of material things* (e.g., wages for work) as well as the character of "relations" of people (e.g., how management treats employees on interpersonal dimensions, such as politeness and respect). Folger argues that in addition to fair treatment (i.e., in regard to wages and salary) and implementation of policies and procedures (a means obligation), management has a moral obligation to treat employees fairly, with sufficient respect and dignity, and as ends in themselves. During an exchange, respectful conduct by managers reinforces feelings of self-respect, dignity, and worth that are essential to the belief that one has been treated as a person, not a thing; in essence, employees will feel mistreated when they do not receive fair and dignified treatment.

Studies of Workplace Mistreatment/Abuse

Studies of workplace mistreatment have produced a range of nonverbal and verbal/behavioral types of workplace abuse. Nonverbal behaviors include aggressive eye contact and dismissive behavior (e.g., "dirty looks," "the silent treatment," staring, snubbing, and ignoring), as well as physical gestures (e.g., intrusions into physical space, slamming objects, finger pointing, and throwing objects). Examples of verbal behaviors include sexual harassment, yelling and screaming, put-downs, lying, public humiliation, threats of job loss, physical harm, name calling, unfounded criticism of work abilities or personal life, excessive job demands, taking credit for an individual's work accomplishments, blaming, exclusion or isolation, initiating pernicious rumors and gossip, withholding resources, preventing opportunities, favoritism, dismissing an individual's feelings or thoughts, failure to return phone calls, and behavior that implies a master-servant relationship (Björkvist *et al.* 1994; Brodsky 1976; Davenport *et al.*,1999; Einarsen, Hoel, Zapf, and Cooper 2003; Harlos and Pinder 2000; Hoel and Cooper 2000; Hornstein 1996; Keashly *et al.* 1994; Leymann 1990, Lombardo and McCall 1984; Namie and Namie 2000; Namie 2000; Neuman and Baron 1998; Rayner, Hoel, and Cooper 2002; Robinson and Bennett 1995; Ryan and Oestreich 1991; Westhues 2004).

In addition, abuse in the workplace is associated with a host of serious adverse effects on an individual's physical health, psychological/emotional health, work performance, and social relationships. Some *psychological/emotional effects* of abusive workplace behavior are anger, rage, depression, helplessness, powerlessness, distrust and cynicism, self-doubt, guilt, shame, embarrassment, insecurity, poor concentration, disillusionment, lowered self-esteem, revenge, aggressiveness, hypervigilance, panic attacks, and posttraumatic stress disorder (PTSD). *Effects on physical health* include sleep disorders (e.g., insufficient rest or nightmares), headaches, backaches, exhaustion, hyperactivity, weight changes (e.g., significant increases or decreases), irritable bowel syndrome, skin changes, heart arrhythmia, substance abuse (first time use), ulcers, and suicide. Effects of abusive behavior on *work performance* include decreases in job effort, motivation, commitment, and satisfaction and morale as well as increases in absenteeism, turnover, and attrition. Finally, *social effects* identified in the literature include loss of friendships and isolation (Björkvist *et al.* 1994; Brodsky 1976; Davenport *et al.* 1999; Einarsen *et al.* 2003; Harlos and Pinder 2000; Hoel 1997; Hornstein 1996; Keashly *et al.* 1994; Leymann 1990; Lombardo and McCall 1984; Namie and Namie 2000; Namie 2000; Pearson 2000; NNLI 1993; Rayner *et al.* 2002; Ryan and Oestreich 1991; Westhues 2004).

About the Study

What types of principal conduct do teachers define as abusive? What effect does such conduct have on teachers, teaching, and learning? How does a principal's abusive conduct undermine teachers' performance in the classroom and in the school in general? These are among the basic questions we used in our study to examine how teachers experience abusive conduct by school principals.

Over a 1½ year period, we conducted several in-depth interviews with each of 50 teachers who had experienced long-term (6 months to 9 years) mistreatment by their principals. The sample consisted of male (n = 5) and female (n = 45) teachers from rural (n = 14), suburban (n = 25), and urban (n = 11) school locations. Elementary (n = 26), middle/junior high (n = 10), and high school (n = 14) teachers participated. The average age of teachers was 42; the average number of years in teaching was 16. The sample included tenured (n = 44) and nontenured (n = 6), married (n = 34) and single (n = 16) teachers. Degrees earned by these teachers included B.A./B.S. (n = 7), MED./MA (n = 31), Ed.S (n = 11), and Ph.D. (n = 1). The mean number of years working with the abusive principal was 4. Forty-nine teachers resided in the United states and one resided in

Canada. Fifteen of the teachers we studied were with an abusive principal at the time of this study; most others had experienced abuse in recent years. In total, these teachers described 28 male and 22 female abusive principals.

Examination of the personal and official documents submitted to us and reports from those who had worked with and referred us to the veteran teachers we studied suggest that the teachers were highly respected, accomplished, creative, and dedicated individuals. In most cases, they had been consistently and formally recognized by their school and district not simply as effective teachers but also as superior teachers; in many cases, such recognition for their exceptional achievements as public educators extended to state levels.

Symbolic interaction theory was the methodological foundation of our study. This approach focuses on the perceptions and meanings that people construct in their social settings (Blumer 1969; Mead 1934), in other words, "what goes on inside the heads of humans" (Meltzer, Petras, and Reynolds 1975, p. 55). Consistent with research of this nature, no *a priori* definitions of principal abuse were used to control data collection. Such an approach would have limited teachers' freedom to discuss their personal views and experiences of principal mistreatment (Bogdan and Biklen 1982; Glaser 1992, 1998; Strauss and Corbin 1998; Taylor and Bogdan 1998). Our study conformed to guidelines set forth for inductive, grounded-theory research and therefore emphasizes meanings of participants and the generation of descriptive, conceptual, and theoretical results.

All of the findings discussed herein, drawn directly from our data, focus on teachers' perspectives on principal abuse and, in particular, the conduct teachers define as abusive and its adverse effects on their psychological/emotional and physical/physiological wellbeing as well as their performance in the classroom and in the school. The relevant literature is included throughout this chapter in the context of specific findings of our study.

Due to space limitations, we present here a brief summary of categories of abusive conduct and effects for the group of teachers we investigated; individual profiles of principals and teachers are not presented. *Thus, it is important to note that each principal identified by individual teachers engaged in a range of abusive behaviors described in the following pages, and that each teacher, supervised by such a principal, experienced most of the major categories of deleterious effects we describe.* It is also important to reiterate that our study, being exploratory in nature, did not indicate the pervasiveness of the mistreatment problem in the United States.

To investigate the broad question, "How do teachers experience significant long-term abuse by a school principal?" we used a snowball sampling technique to identify teachers who had been victimized by school principals (Bogdan and Biklen 1982; Taylor and Bogdan 1998). Between two and four in-depth structured and semistructured telephone interviews were conducted with each of our research participants. In total, 135 hours of interviews were completed. The personal and official documents we collected were used, in part, to confirm the credibility of teachers' interview data as well as their overall effectiveness as teachers. In addition, we used a variety of techniques to determine the trustworthiness and reliability of teachers' reports. Given the sensitive nature of this study, however, no identifiers (e.g., a teacher's gender, school level, and subject matter specialization) appear alongside verbatim quotes presented throughout this chapter, and pseudonyms are used. (See *Breaking the Silence: Overcoming the Problem of Principal Mistreatment of Teachers* [Blase and Blase 2003] for a full description of our research method and findings.)

Findings: A Model of Principal Mistreatment

From the beginning, he singled me out for criticism. He criticized me publicly and loudly. He criticized my dress as too casual and told me that I couldn't wear Birkenstocks [shoes] because they were gang-related. He would mock me in front of other teachers in his "in" group, with whom he ate lunch. After a fellow teacher and I pointed out a possible solution to a duty problem, he called me into his office and berated me for over an hour on the proper way to show respect to a principal. He called me a troublemaker and told me that I needed to stop changing things and stop being so smart. He ridiculed me in a faculty meeting as someone who was "too smart for your own good." He said that he would never believe a word that I said; he would always take the word of a parent or student against me anytime. (Victimized teacher)

In essence, we have organized the principal behaviors derived from our database according to level of aggression: Level 1 Principal

Mistreatment (indirect, moderately aggressive), Level 2 Principal Mistreatment (direct, escalating aggression), and Level 3 Principal Mistreatment (direct, severely aggressive). Several researchers have conceptualized workplace mistreatment in terms of levels of aggression (e.g., Andersson and Pearson 1999; Einarsen *et al.* 2003; Robinson and Bennett 1995; Ryan and Oestreich 1991), and our model is generally consistent with these conceptualizations of aggression. Ryan and Oestreich (1991), for example, describe behaviors such as silence and glaring eye contact as "abrasive"; shouting, angry outbursts, and physical attacks are considered "abusive" behaviors. Robinson and Bennett (1995) view political deviance, including favoritism and gossip, as "minor," while personal aggression (e.g., verbal abuse and sexual harassment) is seen as a more serious form of deviant behavior. It should be stated that our model does not imply that individual Level 1 principal mistreatment behaviors always resulted in less harm to teachers than Level 2 or Level 3 behaviors; to the contrary, the degree of harm related to any single aggressive behavior varied from one victimized teacher to another, as one would expect. In addition, our study focused on long-term mistreatment (6 months to 9 years); therefore, teachers discussed the "cumulative effects" of a multiplicity of principals' continued, systematic mistreatment/abuse behaviors. Indeed, the importance of a pattern of mistreatment over the long term – with regard to understanding its devastating effects on victims – and in contrast to isolated or occasional incidents, cannot be overstated (Björkvist *et al.* 1994; Davenport *et al.* 1999; Einarsen *et al.* 2003; Einarsen and Skogstad 1996; Keashly 1998; Leymann 1990; Rayner *et al.* 2002).

Level 1 mistreatment, indirect and moderately aggressive, as described by teachers in our study, included nonverbal and verbal principal behaviors. Consistent with the work of others, such behaviors are viewed as subtle and discreet as compared to overt forms of mistreatment (Einarsen 1999; Neuberger 1999; Neuman and Baron 1998). This category of principal behaviors was also considered generally less abusive as compared to Level 2 and Level 3 behaviors, and this finding is consistent with studies conducted with the general population (e.g., Keashly 1998; Neuman and Baron 1998; Ryan and Oestreich 1991). Level 1 behavior was always a part of a more extensive pattern of mistreatment/abuse. At the same time, we found that the frequency of occurrence, timing, amount of negative affect, and the nature of the location in which mistreatment occurred (e.g., public versus private) contributed significantly to the degree of harm teachers incurred from Level 1 behaviors (Keashly *et al.* 1994; Ryan and Oestreich 1991). Level 1 behaviors discussed by teachers were:

- *Discounting teachers' thoughts, needs, and feelings*: Principals ignored and snubbed teachers, exhibited insensitivity to personal matters (e.g., illness, death in the teacher's family), and engaged in stonewalling (e.g., failed to respond to written requests).
- *Nonsupport of teachers*: Abusive principals failed to support teachers in conflicts with students and/or parents. Principals were "shamelessly unfair," failed to investigate problems, blamed teachers for problems, and frequently reprimanded teachers for problems in the presence of students and/or parents.
- *Withholding resources and denying opportunities and credit*: Principals unfairly withheld needed instructional resources, denied teachers opportunities for professional development (e.g., to attend conferences), and took credit for teachers' accomplishments (e.g., grant proposals).
- *Favoritism*: Principals failed to reward targeted teachers; instead, they routinely rewarded "select" faculty and punished and/or neglected other faculty.
- *Unprofessional personal conduct*: Some principals had affairs with other teachers and pursued personal interests during the school day (e.g., working on one's car).

Level 2 principal mistreatment, direct and escalating aggression, included the following behaviors:

- *Spying*: Principals monitored teachers by situating themselves near classroom doorways, listening in on classes via the intercom, and soliciting the services of "favored" teachers and/or parents as informants.
- *Sabotaging*: Principals manipulated other faculty to undermine teacher efforts designed to benefit students or colleagues (e.g., directed other teachers not to help targeted teachers).
- *Stealing*: Principals were accused of stealing teachers' items (e.g., journals, food, equipment).
- *Destroying teachers' instructional aids*: Some principals destroyed instructional aids (e.g., reading lofts) or ordered them removed from classrooms.

- *Making unreasonable demands*: Principals overloaded teachers with extra work responsibilities; in several cases, principals forced teachers to do their (the principals') work.
- *Criticism*: Principals routinely and unfairly criticized teachers both privately and publicly for a wide range of reasons. Criticism was often associated with strong negative affect (e.g., yelling, pounding the desk). Public criticism of teachers occurred in the presence of others at faculty meetings, in the front office areas, in hallways, in classrooms, in the lunchroom, and the school parking lot.

From the foregoing, it is apparent that principals who abused teachers did so in a variety of verbal and nonverbal ways and that such abuse included Level 1 (indirect, moderately aggressive) and Level 2 (direct, escalating aggression) principal mistreatment behaviors. As devastating as these levels of mistreatment were for teachers, principal mistreatment includes even more aggressive and severe forms of abuse: Level 3 principal mistreatment behaviors.

According to our data, victimized teachers believed that most of the principals they described "intended to harm" and even "destroy" them and that many such principals were quite aware of the damage they caused. For instance, most principals failed to investigate issues before "attacking" the teacher. And, when teachers confronted abusive principals about their conduct and its destructive effects on them, such principals typically denied all allegations, blamed the teacher, and engaged in further reprisals against them. Most Level 3 forms of principal mistreatment were strongly associated with various forms of deception; that is, with attempts to mislead victimized teachers as well as others (Bok 1978; Yukl 1994):

- *Lying*: Principals were accused of "blatant lying," that is, repeatedly making statements that conflicted with the teachers' direct experiences. This form of abuse was commonly associated with principals' nonsupport of teachers in conflict with students and/or parents and with unfounded criticism, among other things.
- *Explosive behavior*: During face-to-face interaction with teachers, many principals engaged in loud verbal abuse (e.g., yelling) and negative affect (e.g., pounding fists on a table).
- *Threats*: Principals directly threatened individuals and groups of teachers in attempts to force them to change students' grades, for example; they also threatened teachers

for expressing opinions contrary to the principal's opinions and for confronting a principal for his/her abusive conduct.

- *Unwarranted written reprimands*: Some principals "wrote [teachers] up" for "almost anything," including conduct toward students, a stolen video camera, and going into a storage closet – when there was no wrongdoing by teachers.
- *Unfair evaluations*: In all cases, teachers worked in school districts that required that principals complete "objective" teacher evaluations. According to teachers, abusive principals typically included flagrantly false information on their evaluations. It should be mentioned that, with the exception of beginning teachers, all but one experienced teacher had received superior evaluations from principals before mistreatment began.
- *Mistreating students*: Principals who mistreated students engaged in name-calling, racism, and even physical abuse of students, particularly special education students whom the principals described as "misbehaving."
- *Forcing teachers out of their jobs*: Abusive principals engaged in a variety of unfair actions against teachers such as unilateral reassignments, transfers, and termination.
- *Preventing teachers from leaving*: Some principals obstructed teachers' attempts to leave a school by failing to forward applications (within a district) and writing negative letters of reference.
- *Sexual harassment*: Several female teachers accused their principals of ongoing, long-term sexual harassment. Teachers viewed principals' sexual harassment as obvious assertions of power and control.
- *Racism*: Teachers defined six principals, three Caucasians and three African Americans, as racists.

Thus far, the findings section of this report has described what teachers define as "abusive" principal conduct. In addition, and in contrast to the existing conceptual literature on boss abuse (Robinson and Bennett 1995; Neuman and Baron 1998; Ryan and Oestreich 1991), we have conceptualized abusive conduct as a model composed of three levels of aggression: Level 1 principal mistreatment behaviors (indirect and moderately aggressive), Level 2 principal mistreatment behaviors (direct and escalating aggression), and Level 3 principal mistreatment behaviors (direct and severely aggressive).

The individual behaviors we describe are similar to what others have found in studies of abusive bosses conducted throughout the world (Björkvist *et al.* 1994; Brodsky 1976; Davenport *et al.* 1999; Harlos and Pinder 2000; Hoel and Cooper 2000; Hornstein 1996; Keashly *et al.* 1994; Leymann 1990; Lombardo and McCall 1984; Namie and Namie 2000; Namie 2000; Neuman and Baron 1998; Rayner *et al.* 2002; Robinson and Bennett 1995; Ryan and Oestreich 1991; Westhues 2004).

With respect to our findings, Buss's (1961) model of human aggression is particularly relevant. Buss described three dimensions of aggression: *physical* aggression refers to overt actions against one individual; *verbal* aggression, in contrast, is exhibited through language. *Active* types of aggression involve the performance of a behavior, and *passive* types of aggression refer to withholding some behavior from a target. *Direct* aggression refers to harm aimed directly at the target, whereas *indirect* aggression refers to acts conveyed through another person or by attacking something the target values. Ridiculing an individual during face-to-face interaction illustrates active and direct aggression, and withholding recognition or needed resources are examples of indirect, passive aggression.

As noted, our inductively derived model of principal mistreatment described above consists of three major levels of aggression and a total of 21 categories of abusive behaviors. Level 1 describes low intensity, subtle, and somewhat discreet forms of verbal and non-verbal behavior. According to Buss's (1961) framework, all five categories of Level 1 behavior are passive and indirect, although non-support of teachers contains some active and direct behaviors as well. All Level 2 behaviors are considered active and direct with the exception of sabotaging and destroying teachers' instructional aids, which are active and indirect. Level 3 mistreatment consists of behaviors that are predominately active and direct; only mistreatment of students can be described as active and indirect. *In essence, according to our data, principal mistreatment of teachers is predominately active and direct.* By comparison, Neuman and Baron (1996), who studied the incidence of mistreatment in general – not boss abuse in particular – found that aggression was primarily passive and direct. *The immense power differential (i.e., power distance [Hofstede 1980]) existing between school principals and public school teachers may account, in part, for the greater use of more direct and aggressive forms of mistreatment with teachers.* •

Mobbing

Westhues (2004) has argued that the terms *workplace mobbing* and *workplace bullying* refer to similar organizational phenomena; in many respects they represent the "eliminative process" (p. 44) directed toward targeted individuals. However, *mobbing*, according to Westhues, best describes the "collective expression of the eliminative process" (p. 42); thus, mobbing refers directly to how and under what circumstances administrators and others "gang up" on and harm individuals in formal organizations. Although our study focused on how individual school principals mistreat (i.e., abuse, bully) teachers, there was substantial evidence that such principals frequently influenced others – teachers, parents, students, and administrators – to mob teachers. In this section, we briefly describe how this occurred.

We found that two Level 1 categories of principal mistreatment included evidence of mobbing victimized teachers:

- *Discounting teachers' thoughts, needs, and feelings:* Many of the teachers we interviewed reported that individuals – and sometimes groups – of teachers ostracized them, typically because these teachers feared principal reprisals for association and/or because they were "taking the principal's side" in the ongoing mistreatment ordeal. For example, teachers reported:

  - *I went to my friends, my confidants, and said, "This is miserable, this is terrible." They looked at me as though I had obviously done something wrong and deserved what was happening to me. Their loyalty was to the principal. They were afraid about being mistreated too. They knew to play it safe, and they knew they had better stay away from me.... I feel fearful disclosing things to them anyway.*

  - *I got married that year. Anytime somebody got married or there was a birth of a child, there was some sort of recognition and people would attend the wedding. I had a lot of friends there, but few of them attended my wedding. They were afraid. One of my friends who did attend and stuck with me was treated like crap by the principal. Other teachers just kept their distance. I was the problem child.*

  - *I felt like I was branded. I was even told by two teachers that it would be best if I had my lunch in my classroom. None of the other teachers who were once friendly to me would even turn and look my way or give me a gracious smile or say, "Have a good day," even though I would wave and smile at them in greeting.... They had a baby shower at the school [for another teacher] and everyone got an invitation to the shower except me.*

- *Nonsupport of Teachers*: In addition, we found that abusive principals colluded with parents; they unfairly and routinely blamed teachers for any problem that occurred between them and parents:

  - *I felt like I was not respected by her. She didn't care to listen to what teachers said. If you had a problem with a child and you tried to solve it on your own or with the parent, but the parent got upset and blamed you, not the child, she would take the parent's side against you.*

  - *Parents would show up without an appointment and the principal would call on the intercom and say they are on their way down. I told him repeatedly, in private, that I wanted parents to make an appointment. He would tell me any and every parent complaint that happened that week. I believe hardly any of them ever took place. He said, "I don't want to tell you who it was, you might take it out on the kid." I said, "Give me a break. You call me in here and rake me over the coals, and you aren't going to give me a chance to defend myself or correct the problem?"*

We also found evidence of mobbing that included other faculty, parents, students, and other administrators in Level 2, direct and escalating forms of principal mistreatment:

- *Spying*: Most of the teachers we interviewed indicated that abusive principals solicited the services of favored teachers to "spy" on them:

    The favored group of teachers are wise to the game, cynical, superficial, don't work very hard, report to her on other faculty, and are willing to carry out brutal orders and say hurtful things to people. They are willing to help the principal exercise her authority by extension.

  According to our data, some abusive principals used parents to "spy" on teachers:

It's constant harassment from this man and the parents who are basically snooping for him. He started bringing this woman down to "help" me, supposedly. So, I said, "I do not want any help, there are already 37 people in my half of the trailer." He said she was going to be in there anyway.

- *Sabotaging:* Teachers also disclosed that principals manipulated other faculty to sabotage efforts designed to benefit students or colleagues:

  ▪ *I was asked in a district meeting to give my feedback in reference to developing exploratory classes. Now, if you ask my opinion, you need to be prepared to hear what I'm going to say. I'm not going to kiss up. They asked me and I told them what I thought. The principal didn't like what I said. When I was awarded a grant for a project, she did everything she could to sabotage the project. Word got back to me that the principal said no one was supposed to help me, and she made sure that no one did. In essence, the grant I got was wasted.*

  ▪ *I informally went around to a few people and asked if they would be interested in this project to support teacher development. They were. When she got wind of this, she went around to her inner group and said, "This is a lame brain idea, a very flaky and stupid thing, and anybody who gets involved is a real loser and will be seen as working against the administration."*

  ▪ *He had a group of people who were, in my view, yes people, particularly the coaches. I circulated a letter to all teachers laying out their rights, and that you couldn't be required to serve on committees and so on, and they wrote back across the letter, "Just do it." It's that Nike slogan – don't question, don't argue, don't complain, just charge forward..., we don't need to think or have questions.*

- *Criticism:* In several cases, teachers reported that abusive principals manipulated other faculty to criticize victimized teachers:

  The principal and the pet teacher conspired against the new, young teacher to the point where they got the other teachers to shun her. They had the whole grade level march into this room and sign a form in front of this teacher that said that she lied, and they had never witnessed anything, which was the real lie. The teachers felt terrible that they didn't come forward with the truth, and that they had allowed themselves to be bulldozed by the principal. This new teacher had a nervous breakdown and was hospitalized.

At times, principals were seen as manipulating teachers at faculty meetings in order to "gang up" on mistreated teachers:

I dropped a hint to the school accreditation reviewer that all is not well in Camelot. The next day at a faculty meeting, the principal said that something had occurred that was a cloud on our whole school. She said that the reviewer heard that everything they would see at the school was a sham. She reminded us that if we dared to speak up about anything that was negative about the school, it was grounds for dismissal. The principal said, "How can a Judas betray us like this!" She said she would contact the three teachers on the review committee and get them to tell her who it was. She said that she hoped that the person or persons would be forced to resign. Several teachers were rallying around saying, "Yeah, yeah, let's get them!" Her final words were, "I want all of you to work to find out who this traitor is!" The next day she called an emergency faculty meeting, expecting someone is going to cave in and confess.... At the beginning and at the end of every faculty meeting, she said she did not get mad, she got even. People learned real quick that if you did talk, there were repercussions. I am a single mom and I have got to put my kids through college. I don't want to lose my job. I thought, "That can be the groundwork for her to try and get rid of me."

In other instances, our data point out that abusive principals used what one teacher referred to as "the parent complaint ploy," "to create the impression" that many parents were "upset" with a victimized teacher.

- *She called me into the office and said, "A number of parents have brought to my attention that you were screaming at the children and we can't have that." I couldn't believe that a principal was saying that! She was just lying. I said, "Get those people who told you this, and I want to meet with the superintendent right now!" She said, "I don't quite remember who they are!"*

▪ *He lied. He said five parents had complained about me. The whole thing was made up except for one parent who had actually complained. The principal decided to make this a lot bigger than it was. He said, "You seem a bit defensive about this." He put his elbows on the desk and leaned over and said, "Let me tell you something. If your test scores are not where they should be this year, you will appear before the superintendent." I said, "Fine. I am not afraid to meet with him and tell him what I have done during the year." When I walked out of the office I heard him say to the assistant principal, "Good job," as in "we intimidated her, really scared her."*

Abusive principals also claimed other faculty complained about a mistreated teachers' conduct:

I was called into her office about the fourth or fifth week of the first year. She said another teacher had told her that I had referred to a child as "stupid." Her tone was very harsh. I sat there trembling. (I can feel my insides trembling now.) ... I thought I was going to burst into tears. I said to her as calmly as I could, "I did not say that. I did not do that. I would never do that. That is not a word that I allow the children to use. I certainly would not say that." She would not tell me who had heard this. ... "You are the most negative person on my staff," she said.

In several cases, teachers reported that principals manipulated students to mob them:

▪ *I had put one little girl's head in my hands to get her to look at me. I certainly did not jerk her the way the principal made it sound, like I was a child beater. He called me a liar and said that I was defying him. He got students to testify against me and put a letter of reprimand in my file. He then refused to tell me who testified.*

- *I was unwed and pregnant, and the principal was trying to establish grounds for firing me legally. So, he sent me this letter that had nothing indicating that their reason for termination was because I was pregnant and unwed. It indicated that there was something wrong with my teaching ability. He wanted me to sign it. My students were even being taken out of my classroom, one by one, and encouraged to say that I cursed them, which I didn't. They got a couple of students to say that I cursed all the time and that I used the Lord's name in vain and I used the word that rhymes with duck. I never did. It's not even part of my vocabulary. One time I did tell a child to sit down in his damn seat. One student told them, "I never heard Ms. Atkins curse and I am not going to lie!" Others said the same.*

Teachers accused several principals of soliciting the help of other principals to abuse them:

He's gotten his friends to harass me. He got another principal to write me a letter about my teaching saying, "Let me tell you what you can do to be a better teacher. You are too theoretical, you don't need to apply research in the classroom." I don't even know this woman!

In other cases, abusive principals claimed that other principals found a victimized teacher's professional conduct questionable:

- *My principal had been badmouthing me to other principals. That is why I couldn't get transferred for six years in a row. I tried to transfer out of the building, but I was a prisoner.*

- *The new principal said, "The library was taken away from you for mismanagement!" That was when I broke. I almost got hysterical because I had never been harassed like this before. This guy didn't know me from Adam. I said, "Mr. Prince, I don't know where you are getting your information; the library was neither given to me nor taken away." He also said he talked to my former principal, so I went to him and he said, "That man has never come to me. Does he even know what magic you do in that room?" He [the new principal] was out to get me, and nothing I could do was right. It*

*didn't matter what I said or what I did. He made up
things and acted on his own stories. ... The lies just tore
me apart. I kept thinking, I can't do this. I can't stand in
front of a classroom knowing that my administrator lies
about me. He was getting to me big time. I wouldn't
have gone to attorneys. I would have just totally slipped
into oblivion.*

Finally, we found some evidence of mobbing in Level 3, direct
and severely aggressive abusive behavior:

- *Forcing teachers out of their jobs*: The teachers we studied
  reported that central office administrators frequently played
  a role in mistreating them:

  *I thought, "I had better get out of here and go
  somewhere they would back me." I realized that my
  principal was not going to support me. You get lied to,
  you can't seem to get promoted. But, the fear of this
  woman is so strong in the district. She said that I can't
  get along with people. My friends in high places ran a
  check and found that no one would hire me – they were
  afraid to go against her reference.*

Effects of Principal Mistreatment on Teachers: Brief Description

*I would go home every day and soak in the tub. I probably
soaked my skin off those last four years. At home, I would
lose my temper over nothing. I lost the joy of teaching and I
wasn't enjoying the journey. I didn't sleep. I tossed and
turned in bed. I didn't eat. I was depressed and tried not to
show it at school. That is probably what affected my
marriage. I have been married for 23 years, but for four
years things were very rocky. I don't know if we would have
stayed together if we didn't have a son. I was totally wiped
out every day. My sex life was nil. Other teachers were
depressed, too. If it had not been for having a child and
loving my husband to death, I would have split; I was at
that point. To tell you the honest truth, there was a time I
would go to the grocery store at night and sit in the parking
lot. I remember sitting one time in the parking lot
wondering if I had enough money and could leave and not
come back. It took me a year to recover from the
nervousness after I left that school. (Victimized teacher)*

In addition to teachers' early responses to mistreatment (shock, disorientation, humiliation, self-doubt, and low self-esteem), and beyond collateral damage on teachers' relationships in schools, their classroom work, their participation in decision making, and on their family life (discussed in Blase and Blase 2003), mistreated teachers experienced a range of very severe and often chronic ill effects.

Psychological/emotional effects. Fear is considered a primary human emotion and as such has a "profoundly noxious quality" (Izard and Youngstrom 1996, p. 35); it is essentially an awareness of psychological distress and is considered the most toxic of all human emotions (Tomkins 1962). Our study revealed that intense and chronic fear and anxiety were among teachers' primary long-term responses to principal mistreatment. There were several reasons for this: First, teachers viewed the various forms and patterns of principal mistreatment as extremely threatening and punishing, and they perceived themselves to be particularly vulnerable. Second, teachers tended to internalize their fears and this provoked a chronic state of anxiety, apprehension, obsessional thinking, and hypervigilance regarding the potential of further mistreatment. Third, fear of mistreatment provoked an array of powerful secondary fears, such as fear of losing one's job, losing one's reputation, being ostracized by colleagues, expressing one's opinion, receiving poor evaluations, lack of support from the central office, and failing one's students instructionally and socially. Fourth, fear was experienced as pervasive: It permeated all aspects of a victimized teacher's work life; for many, it also profoundly and adversely affected the quality of their personal and family lives. Said differently, fear dominated teachers' entire "sense of being" for long periods of time ranging from several months to many years. Some terms that teachers used to denote chronic fear and anxiety states were "fear," "scared," "afraid," "dread," and "paranoid."

Also considered a primary human emotion, *anger* is a more or less primitive response to "being either physically or psychologically restrained from doing what one intensely desires to do" (Izard 1977, pp. 329-330). Hence, anger motivates people to prepare their bodies for real or imagined battles and to defend themselves with vigor and strength. Ekman and Friesen (1975) stated that the major provocation to anger is "frustration resulting from interference with [one's] activity or the pursuit of [one's] goals" (p. 78). They noted, "your anger will be more likely and more intense if you believe that the agent of interference acted arbitrarily, unfairly, or spitefully" (p. 78). Indeed, Averill (1982) asserted (as did Aristotle) that anger involves an appraisal that another person has intentionally and unjustifiably wronged one.

All of the teachers we interviewed expressed strong feelings of anger and rage, both explicitly and implicitly. For most teachers, anger was chronic; it was a dominant emotion throughout their mistreatment experiences and, for many, continued long after mistreatment ended. Teachers' anger always included strong feelings of indignation, a form of anger due to the unjust and unfair nature of their victimization by principals. Teachers used many strong words such as "bitter," "hate," "furious," "angry," "enraged," "outraged," "appalled," "disgusted," "despise," "resent," and "hot" to convey the intensity of their anger.

Many teachers admitted that because of their victimization by principals, they harbored feelings of anger towards school administrators in general. Predictably, teachers felt compelled to suppress their anger, given the power differences between themselves and principals, the principals' inclination to use power in abusive ways, and the failure of school district offices, boards of education, and unions to provide help.

A depressive state refers to pervasive, absorbing, and chronic feelings of being out of control. In contrast to anxiety, which is a kind of "mobilization" response to a future threat that may be developing or coming and that, one hopes, can be avoided, depression is a "demobilization" response to a loss, a "static or unlikely-to-vary situation that can no longer (with any hope) be avoided because it has already developed or come to pass" (Riskind 1997, p. 687).

Most of the teachers who participated in our study reported being chronically depressed throughout their mistreatment experience. In describing feelings, teachers used terms such as "depressed," "futile," "helpless," "hopeless," "devastated," "beaten down," "paralyzed," "broken," "worn out," "defeated," "disoriented," "distraught," "trapped," "isolated," "sad," "down," "humiliated," and "despair." Clearly, for most victimized teachers, going to work as well as being at work was a "constant struggle to survive each day." Many teachers' depression was so severe that they sought counseling or psychiatric care for therapy and medication.

In addition, feeling isolated, trapped, and unmotivated was strongly associated with feelings of depression. For example, to avoid further mistreatment, teachers usually withdrew both emotionally and physically (when possible) from social and professional activities (e.g., faculty meetings, committee work, sponsorship of student activities, professional associations). They refused, for example, to volunteer for committee work and sponsorships; when required to attend certain events they did not participate. According to our findings, teachers' protective actions may have inadvertently exacerbated their feelings of isolation and depression. Other factors typically associated with principal mistreatment – showing favoritism, being ostracized by other teachers, and lack of viable opportunities for recourse (e.g., from central office, unions) – also contributed to a targeted teacher's sense of isolation.

Physical/physiological effects. Like psychological/emotional problems, physical and physiological problems were typically chronic; they began with the onset of mistreatment and usually ended when mistreatment terminated. In some cases, problems persisted for several months and even several years later. The seriousness of these problems appears to be related to the longevity of teachers' mistreatment, at least in part. The most frequently identified physical/physiological problems were chronic sleep disorders (e.g., insomnia, nightmares, obsessive thinking), chronic fatigue, stomach aches, nausea, weight gain or loss, neck and back pain, and headaches or migraines. Examples of other severe physical/physiological problems teachers experienced included diarrhea, high blood pressure, blurred vision, nausea or vomiting, respiratory infections, hives, vertigo, heart palpitations, gum disease, auditory impairment, panic attacks, chest pains, and frequent colds and allergies. Our data indicate that in addition to the psychological/emotional problems discussed earlier, individual teachers simultaneously experienced, on average, at least four of the physical/physiological problems previously described throughout their mistreatment experience. Roughly two-thirds of the teachers we studied sought medical treatment for their problems.

In sum, beyond the teachers' responses of shock and disorientation, humiliation, self-doubt, and injured self-esteem, and beyond damage to in-school relationships, classrooms, and impairment of school-wide decision making (Blase and Blase 2003), principals' mistreatment/abuse of teachers resulted in psychological/emotional problems, including severe, chronic fear and anxiety, anger, depression, and a range of physical/physiological effects discussed in the general empirical literature on boss abuse (Björkvist *et al.* 1994; Brodsky 1976; Davenport *et al.* 1999; Einarsen *et al.* 2003; Harlos and Pinder 2000; Hoel 1997; Hornstein 1996; Keashly *et al.* 1994; Leymann 1990; Lombardo and McCall 1984; Namie and Namie 2000; Namie 2000; NNLI 1993; Pearson 2000; Ryan and Oestreich 1991; Rayner *et al.* 2002).

Discussion

Although we used no *a priori* concepts to control data collection (Blumer 1969; Glaser and Strauss 1967; Glaser 1978, 1992, 1998; Taylor and Bogdan 1998), a comparison of our findings with Keashly's (1998) definition of "emotional abuse" – constructed from a comprehensive review of the workplace abuse literature – indicates that teachers' experiences of abuse and, in particular, the conditions under which teachers define a principal's behavior as mistreatment or abusive are consistent with what appears in the extant literature. According to Keashly, individuals will tend to define a superior's behavior as abusive if there is a *pattern* of verbal and nonverbal abuse, behaviors are *unwanted,* behaviors *violate norms for appropriate conduct or an individual's rights,* behaviors are *intended to harm* the target, behaviors *result in harm,* and there are *power differences* between the abuser and the target of abuse.

Several dimensions of Keashly's (1998) definition of workplace abuse (discussed earlier) require discussion in the context of the present study. The statement that abusive conduct constitutes a *pattern* of repeated actions against a targeted individual over the long term (6 months to 9 years in terms of our data base) is critical to understanding the degree of harm teachers incurred as a result of principal mistreatment/abuse. Taken together, such factors produced a set of internal dynamics that had devastating outcomes for teachers. For instance, although we found that one category of principal behaviors (i.e., Level 1) was considered less abusive when compared to other categories (i.e., Levels 2 and 3), and this finding is consistent with the results of other studies (Keashly 1998; Neuman and Baron 1998; Ryan and Oestreich 1991), the individual behaviors contained in Level 1 (e.g., ignoring) cannot be understood in isolation. To begin, less aggressive and less abusive principal behaviors were often accompanied by more aggressive and more abusive behaviors; thus, we found that through simple association, less abusive behaviors could ignite strong emotional responses in teachers. Moreover, a long-term pattern of mistreatment/abuse produced "chronic" emotions in teachers including fear, anger, and depression. Consequently, any abusive behavior by a school principal at any time had the potential to precipitate seriously adverse effects on teachers; strong human emotions such as fear have a particularly long half-life and have the capacity to defy the boundaries of time or place (Harlos and Pinder 2000), and thus have the potential to reinforce preexisting adverse psychological, physical, and behavioral responses in teachers.

Our data also suggest that other factors such as *location* or *timing* account, in part, for the degree of harm teachers experience from principal mistreatment. We found, for example, that a single instance of public ridicule had long-lasting, harmful effects on teachers; such behavior generated additional considerations for teachers including embarrassment, loss of professional reputation, and reactions of others that do not accompany other behaviors such as direct criticism. We also found that timing could be an important factor in understanding the harmful effects of mistreatment. For example, being targeted for repeated classroom observations and evaluations during personal life tragedies (e.g., death, divorce) significantly intensified the degree of harm teachers experienced as a result of such observations and evaluations.

In many respects, public education in the United States has been strongly influenced by the principles of *equity and fairness* (Cusick 1983; Dreeben 1970); indeed, teachers take very seriously *violations of norms of appropriate conduct and human rights,* particularly by school principals (Blase 1988; Lortie 1975). Many researchers have pointed to the significance of fairness to productive school principal-teacher interaction in schools (Blase 1988; Blumberg and Greenfield 1986; Lightfoot 1983). Thus, it was not surprising to discover that teachers victimized by abusive principals primarily experienced "moral outrage" (anger from indignation) in response to the unjust and unfair treatment they received (see Folger 1993); such forms of outrage were reinforced because classroom instruction and students in particular suffered as a result of principals' abusive conduct toward them.

Intentionality with regard to a victim's experience of abuse is considered the weakest aspect of Keashly's (1998) definition of emotional abuse (Hoel *et al.* 1999). However, it should be mentioned that in the context of the present study, teachers' attributions of principals' intent to harm were typically slow to develop; indeed, teachers' responses to being mistreated/abused during the early stages of their experience included disorientation, confusion, self-doubt, and self-blame ("What's wrong with me? Or "What have I done?"), and teachers blamed principals directly and concluded that their actions were intentional only after "repeated attacks" and repeated attempts on their part to address the problem.

The significance of *power differences* between teachers and school principals in accounting for the degree of harm experienced by teachers cannot be overstated. Keashly (1998) points out that administrators in organizations generally have both reward and coercive power; among other things, administrators control performance evaluations, professional development opportunities, and promotions. Indeed, our data demonstrate that abusive principals have access to these as well as other sources of formal and informal power; clearly, the power distance (Hofstede 1980) between principals and teachers is substantial, and this accounts for teachers' vulnerability and inability to reciprocate when mistreated (Keashly and Nowell 2003). The wide range of different abusive behaviors exhibited by principals – both verbal and nonverbal – that emerged from our data, support this conclusion. Even in situations governed by union contracts, teachers reported significant mistreatment/abuse experiences by principals. In fact, we found that teachers rarely complained to district level administrators because they expected to receive "no help" and because they "feared" reprisals. This is consistent with other research that had demonstrated that victims' complaints about abusive bosses typically result in (a) no action (no response) from upper management, (b) efforts to protect abusive bosses, (c) reprisals against victims who complain (Bassman 1992; Davenport *et al.* 1999; Hornstein 1996; Keashly 1998; Keashly *et al.* 1994; Leymann 1990; Martin 1986; Namie 2000; Namie and Namie 2000; Pearson 2000; Rayner 1998). The lack of legal protections for most forms of workplace abuse (with the exception of racial discrimination, sexual harassment, and, in reference to the present data, stealing) may also explain teachers' reluctance to file formal complaints against abusive principals (Yamada 2000).

Further, our findings point out that teachers were often *unable to leave a school* in which they were mistreated/abused, at least not in a timely manner. Several factors of considerable importance frequently result in strong feelings of being "trapped": district policies prohibiting transfers, the high probability of negative letters of reference and blackballing, weak unions, one's need for a job and health insurance, and the chronic effects of long-term abuse itself, i.e., chronic fear, depression, self-doubt, feelings of helplessness, and fatigue – all factors that diminish one's ability for proactive action, particularly in difficult circumstances (Izard and Youngstrom 1996).

With Respect to Gender

In addition to the above discussion vis-à-vis Keashly's (1998) concept of emotional abuse, analysis of our data indicated three *gender* differences related to abusive principals and two gender differences related to victimized teachers; these differences are consistent with those produced by the general research on workplace mistreatment. First, male principals tended to use explosive verbal and nonverbal behaviors (i.e., yelling in public and pounding their fists on tables) more often than female principals (Harlos and Pinder 2000). Second, only male principals were accused of sexual harassment. Third, only male principals were identified with offensive personal conduct (e.g., having affairs).

With respect to the victims of mistreatment, we found that female teachers engaged in severe self-doubt and self-blame during the initial stages of their mistreatment experience; male teachers did so as well but to a much lesser extent. Because experience and positive reinforcement in doing non-routine tasks are related to self-confidence and self-image for women (Dweck, Davidson, Nelson, and Enna 1978), women may be doubly vulnerable to the lack of positive feedback, criticism, and negative feedback from abusive bosses; such mistreatment damages a woman's self-confidence and ability to perform public activities in addition to damaging her in ways directly related to the mistreatment/abuse. Second, no male teacher reported crying during his mistreatment experience, while most female teachers reported crying frequently during their mistreatment experiences; indeed, many of the female teachers wept during the interviews conducted for this study as they discussed the details of their mistreatment experiences.

With Respect to Mobbing

From his research in academe, Westhues (2004) derived 12 indicators of the mobbing phenomenon. Given space considerations, a detailed discussion of such indicators in terms of the present study is not possible. Suffice to say that most of these indicators (e.g., a focus on the targeted person rather than on alleged acts, high achieving targets, lack of due process, odd timing, fuzzy charges, prior marginalization, impassioned rhetoric, and backbiting) were evident in our data as well. However, we found little direct evidence of other indicators, including principals' resistance to external review, secrecy, unanimity to condemn a target, and a target fighting back. We suspect that this may be primarily a function of the research methods employed (i.e., interviews of victimized teacher).

Conclusion

Katzenmeyer and Moller (1996) note that, "Today we face the frustrating task of making massive changes in America's schools while working within an educational system that was never designed for today" (p. 1). In spite of the second wave of school reform efforts in the United States that focused on school effectiveness and recommended a move away from top-down approaches to school improvement (Carnegie Forum 1986; Holmes Group 1986; and National Governors' Association 1986), researchers have found that "variants of structural-functionalism continue to maintain a strong grip on the field of educational administration" (Heck and Hallinger 1999, p. 145) and that school principals tend to resist relinquishing power and persist in authoritarian and control-oriented approaches to leadership (Blase, Blase, Anderson, and Dungan 1995; Drury 1999). Thus, many school principals operate as *managers,* as opposed to school *leaders* (Bennis 1997); they stubbornly maintain this bureaucratic-rational perspective and the status quo, and they effectively block organizational change as well as the on-going growth and development of people and institutions necessary for success (Kouzes and Posner 1987).

In addition, research confirms the critical nature of the principal's role in school effectiveness and improvement (Sheppard 1996; Smith and Andrews 1989); however, principals in general have not broadly realized the recommended development of professional environments for teachers and the decentralization of authority intended to lead to democratic and transformational forms of school leadership that emerged from research published during the1990s (Blase and Blase 1997; Maeroff 1988; Lambert 1998; Schlechty 2001).

The failure of school principals and school restructuring efforts to achieve the promise once held for school effectiveness and improvement is due also to the apparently insurmountable challenges and pressures school principals confront. Their work is characterized by long hours and inadequate compensation (Olson 1999); and they now face an explosion of demands and pressures related to school safety and violence, drugs, diversity, inclusion, site budgeting, aging teaching staffs, and unresponsive bureaucracies (Rusch 1999) as well as new responsibilities linked to school reform including new power arrangements, collaborative planning, evaluation, and accountability (Murphy and Louis 1994a 1994b). School principals are confronted with unique challenges associated with the retention of quality teachers, inadequate facilities and instructional materials, and discouraged, disillusioned faculties (Steinberg 1999). It appears that the press for school reform, combined with such exigencies and challenges, has resulted in dramatic emotional experiences for principals (Ginsberg and Davies 2001); feelings of anxiety, loss of control, disempowerment, insecurity, anger, and frustration are not uncommon (Beatty 2000; Evans 1996). Clearly, it can be argued that conditions have developed that may increase the probability of principal mistreatment of teachers (Hornstein 1996; Yamada 2000).

Difficulties and challenges notwithstanding, the public – and in particular parents, teachers, principals, central office administrators, and school board members – must confront the corrosive problem of principal mistreatment in our schools, a problem that, most assuredly, compounds the manifold difficulties faced by educators and undermines the potential of our youth. Such mistreatment undermines opportunities for principals and teachers to work together collaboratively to reinvent schools. To be sure, collaboration is possible only when school principals build trust – not fear and anger – with and among teachers; trust, in turn, serves as a foundation for open, honest, and reflective professional dialogue; problem solving; innovative initiatives; and, more directly, the development of the school as a powerful community of learners willing to take responsibility for and capable of success (Blase and Blase 2001, 2004). Don Saul, American Association of School Administrators (AASA) Superintendent of the Year 2000, described the link between mistreatment and mistrust:

> Leaders who attempt to work with teachers and principals to promote systemic change within this environment realize district efforts to create a positive atmosphere and common purpose leading to improved student achievement and well-being are hindered by behaviors which create a loss of trust among school professionals. Funding difficulties, curricular narrowing, high stakes testing of debatable utility, special interest advocacy and other factors already conspire to

evoke a feeling of powerlessness and frustration among staff. When these elements are combined with a teacher's perception that "I will probably never truly trust an administrator again," it's hard to imagine how the organizational *gestalt* essential for reform and improvement can be generated and sustained in a district or school. In this vein, the [researchers have] aptly quote[d] Bok, whose statement that "Trust and integrity are precious resources, easily squandered, hard to regain" illustrates what we all know about administrative-staff relations.

For all these reasons, this [study discussed by Blase and Blase] should come with a warning. The challenges implicit in these findings reflect issues affecting the gamut of school performance and the success of related initiatives to guide and improve teaching and learning: abuse and denigration of staff members is seldom dealt with easily or without creative, dedicated effort and courage. The ... findings ... must not be brushed aside as a natural outcome of human interaction in the form of so-called personality conflicts or as grousing from poorly performing staff members. On the contrary, the complexity and depth of change required to assure consistent progress in education demands that the problem of mistreatment of teachers be taken very seriously and that appropriate preventative and corrective action serve as one of the keystones of growth and productivity in district and school cultures. (Blase and Blase 2003, p. ix)

References

Andersson, L.M., and Pearson, C.M., 1999. "Tit for tat? The spiraling effect of incivility in the workforce," *Academy of Mangaement Review*, 24(3), 452-471.

Ashforth, B., 1994. "Petty tyranny in organizations," *Human Relations*, 47(7), 755-778.

Averill, J. R., 1982. *Anger and agression: An essay on emotion*. New York: Springer.

Baron, R. A., and Neuman, J. H., 1996. "Workplace violence and workplace aggression: Evidence on their relative frequency and potential causes," *Aggressive Behavior*, 22, 161-173.

Bassman, E. S., 1992. *Abuse in the workplace: Management remedies and bottom line impact*. New York: Quorum.

Beatty, B. R., 2000. "The emotions of educational leadership: Breaking the silence," *International Journal of Educational Leadership*, 3(4), 331-357.

Beck, L. G., 1994. *Reclaiming educational administration as a caring profession*. New York, NY: Teachers College Press.

Bennis, W., 1997. *Managing people is like herding cats*. Provo, UT: Executive Excellence Publishing.

Bies, R. J., 1987. "The predicament of injustice: The management of social outrage." In L. L. Cummings and Staw, B.M., (Eds.), *Research in organizational behavior*, Vol. 9, pp. 289-320. Greenwich, CT: JAI Press.

Björkvist, K., Österman, K., and Hjelt-Bäck, M., 1994. "Aggression among university employees," *Aggressive Behavior* 20, 173-184.

Blase, J., 1988. "The politics of favoritism: A qualitative analysis of the teacher's perspective," *Educational Administration Quarterly*, 24(2), 152-177.

Blase, J., and Blase, J., 2004. *Handbook of instructional leadership: How really good principals promote teaching and learning* (2nd ed.). Thousand Oaks, CA: Corwin Press.

Blase, J., and Blase, J., 2003. *Breaking the silence: Overcoming the problem of principal mistreatment of teachers*. Thousand Oaks, CA: Corwin Press.

Blase, J., and Blase, J., 2002. "The dark side of leadership: Teacher perspectives of principal mistreatment," *Educational Administration Quarterly*, 38(5), 671-727.

Blase, J., and Blase, J., 2001. *Empowering teachers* (2nd ed.). Thousand Oaks, CA: Corwin Press.

Blase, J., and Blase, J., 1997. *The fire is back! Principals sharing school governance*. Thousand Oaks, CA: Corwin Press.

Blase, J., Blase, J., Anderson, G.L., and Dungan, S., 1995. *Democratic principals in action: Eight pioneers*. Thousand Oaks, CA: Corwin Press.

Blumberg, A., and Greenfield, W., 1986. *The effective principal: Perspectives on school leadership*. Boston: Allyn and Bacon.

Blumer, H., 1969. *Symbolic interactionism: Perspective and method*. Englewood Cliffs, NJ: Prentice Hall.

Bogdan, R. C., and Biklen, S. K., 1982. *Qualitative research for education: An introduction to theory and methods* (2nd ed.). Boston: Allyn and Bacon.

Bok, S., 1978. *Lying: Moral choice in public and private life*. New York: Random House.

Bolman, L., and Deal, T.E., 1995. *Leading with soul: An uncommon journey of spirit*. San Francisco: Jossey-Bass.

Brodsky, C.M., 1976. *The harassed worker*. Lexington, MA: Lexington Books.

Buss, A.H., 1961. *The psychology of aggression*. New York: John Wiley.

Carnegie Forum on Education and the Economy, 1986. *A nation prepared: Teachers for the 21ˢᵗ century.* Washington, D.C.: Carnegie Forum on Education and the Economy.

Charmaz, K., 2000. "Grounded theory: Objectivist and constructivist methods." In N. Denzin and Lincoln, Y., Eds.), *Handbook of qualitative research,* (2nd. ed. pp. 509-535). Thousand Oaks, CA: Sage.

Cropanzano, R., 1993. *Justice in the workplace: Approaching fairness in human resource management.* Hillsdale, NJ: Lawrence Erlbaum.

Cusick, P.A., 1983. *The egalitarian ideal and the American high school: Studies of three schools.* London: Longman.

Davenport, N., Schwartz, R. D., and Elliott, G. P., 1999. *Mobbing: Emotional abuse in the American workplace.* Ames, IA: Civil Society Publishing.

Dreeben, R., 1970. *The nature of teaching: Schools and the work of teachers.* Glenview, IL: Scott, Foresman, and Co.

Dreeben, R., 1968. *On what is learned in school.* Reading, MA: Addison-Wesley.

Drury, D.W., 1999. *Reinventing school-based management: A school board guide to school-based improvement.* Alexandria, VA: National School Boards Association.

Dweck, C., Davidson, W., Nelson, S., and Enna, B., 1978. "Sex differences in learned helplessness: II. The contingencies of evaluative feedback in the classroom and III. An experimental analysis," *Developmental Psychology* 14(3), 268-276.

Einarsen, S., 1999. "The nature and causes of bullying," *International Journal of Manpower* 20, 16-27.

Einarsen, S., Hoel, H., Zapf, D., and Cooper, C., 2003. *Bullying and emotional abuse in the workplace: International perspectives in research and practice.* London: Taylor and Francis.

Einarsen, S., and Skogstad, A., 1996. "Bullying at work: Epidemiological findings in public and private organizations," *European Journal of Work and Organizational Psychology,* 5(2), 185-201.

Ekman, P., and Friesen, W. V., 1975. *Unmasking the face: A guide to recognizing emotions from facial cues.* Englewood Cliffs, NJ: Prentice Hall.

Enomoto, E. K., 1997. "Negotiating the ethics of care and justice," *Educational Administration Quarterly,* 33(3), 351-370.

Evans, R., 1996. *The human side of school change.* San Francisco: Jossey-Bass.

Folger, R., 1993. "Reactions to mistreatment at work." In J. K. Murningham (Ed.), *Social psychology in organizations: Advances in theory and research* (pp. 161-183). Englewood Cliffs, NJ: Prentice Hall.

Fontana, A., and Frey, J.H., 1994. "Interviewing: The art of science." In N. Denzin and Lincoln, Y., Eds.), *Handbook of qualitative research* (pp. 361-376). Thousand Oaks, CA: Sage.

Fontana, A., and Frey, J.H., 2000. "The interview: From structured questions to negotiated text." In N. Denzin and Lincoln, Y., Eds., *Handbook of qualitative research* (2nd ed., pp. 645-672). Thousand Oaks, CA: Sage.

Ginsberg, R., and Davies, T., 2001, April. "The emotional side of leadership." Paper presented at the annual meeting of the American Educational Research Association, Seattle.

Glaser, B. G., 1978. *Theoretical sensitivity: Advances in the methodology of grounded theory*. Mill Valley, CA: Sociology Press.

Glaser, B. G., 1992. *Emergence vs. forcing: Basics of grounded theory*. Mill Valley, CA: Sociology Press.

Glaser, B. G., 1998. *Doing grounded theory: Issues and discussions*. Mill Valley, CA: Sociology Press.

Glaser, B. G., and Strauss, A. L., 1967. *The discovery of grounded theory: Strategies for qualitative research*. Chicago, IL: Aldine.

Glickman, C.D., Gordon, S.P., and Ross-Gordon, J.M., 2001. *Supervision and instructional leadership: A developmental approach*. Needham Heights, MA: Allyn and Bacon.

Harlos, K.P., and Pinder, C.C., 2000. "Emotion and injustice in the workplace." In S. Fineman (Ed.), *Emotion in organizations* (2nd ed., pp. 255-276). Thousand Oaks, CA: Sage.

Heck, R.H., and Hallinger, P., 1999. "Next Generation Methods for the Study of Leadership and School Improvement." In J. Murphy and K.S. Louis (Eds.), *Handbook of research on educational administration* (2nd ed., pp. 141-162). San Francisco: Jossey-Bass.

Hoel, H., 1997. "Bullying at work: A Scandanavian perspective," *Institution of Occupational Safety and Health Journal*, 1: 51-59.

Hoel, H., and Cooper, C., November 2000. *Destructive conflict and bullying at work*. Unpublished report, University of Manchester Institute of Science and Technology, Manchester, UK.

Hoel, H., Rayner, C., and Cooper, C.L., 1999. "Workplace bullying." In C.L. Cooper and I.T. Robertson (Eds.), *International review of Industrial and organizational psychology* (pp. 195-230). Chichester: John Wiley and Sons.

Hofstede, G., 1980. *Culture's consequences: International differences in work-related values*. Newbury Park, CA: Sage.

Holmes Group, 1986. *Tomorrow's teachers: A report of the Holmes Group*. East Lansing, MI: Holmes Group.

Hornstein, H. A., 1996. *Brutal bosses and their prey*. New York: Riverhead Books.

Hornstein, H.A., Michela, J.L., Van Eron, A.M., Cohen, L.W., Heckelman, W.L., Sachse-Skidd, M., and Spencer, J.L., 1995. *Disrespectful supervisory behavior: Effects on some aspects of subordinates' mental health*. Unpublished manuscript, Teachers College, Columbia University.

Izard, C., 1977. *Human emotions*. New York: Plenum.

Izard, C. E., and Youngstrom, E. A., 1996. "The activation and regulation of fear and anxiety." In R. A. Dienstbier and Hope, D. A., Eds.),

Perspectives on anxiety, panic, and fear (pp. 1-59). Lincoln: University of Nebraska Press.

Katz, M.S., Noddings, N., and Strike, K.A., Eds., 1999. *Justice and caring: The search for common ground in education.* New York: Teachers College Press.

Katzenmeyer, M., and Moller, G., 1996. *Awakening the sleeping giant: Leadership development for teachers.* Thousand Oaks, CA: Corwin Press.

Keashly, L., 1998. "Emotional abuse in the workplace: Conceptual and empirical issues," *Journal of Emotional Abuse*, 1(1), 85-117.

Keashly, L., and Nowell, B.L., 2003. "Conflict, conflict reduction, and bullying." In S. Einarsen, D. Zapf, and C. Cooper (Eds.), *Bullying and emotional abuse in the workplace: International perspectives in research and practice* (pp. 339-358). London: Taylor and Francis.

Keashly, L., Trott, V., and MacLean, L. M., 1994. "Abusive behavior in the workplace: A preliminary investigation," *Violence and Victims*, 9(4), 341-357.

Kipnis, D., 1972. "Does power corrupt?" *Journal of Personality and Social Psychology*, 24(1), 33-41.

Kouzes, J.M., and Posner, B.Z., 1987. *The leadership challenge: How to get extraordinary things done in organizations.* San Francisco, Jossey-Bass.

Lambert, L., 1998. *Building leadership capacity in schools.* Alexandria, VA: Association for Supervision and Curriculum Development.

Leymann, H., 1993. *Mobbing* (N. Davenport, Trans.). Hamburg: Rowohlt Taschenbuch Verlag GmbH.

Leymann, H., 1990. "Mobbing and psychological terror at workplaces," *Violence and Victims*, 5(2), 119-126.

Lightfoot, S.L., 1983. *The good high school: Portraits of character and culture.* New York: Basic Books.

Lofland, J., 1971. *Analyzing social settings.* Belmont, CA: Wadsworth.

Lombardo, M. M., and McCall, Jr., M. W., January 1984. "The intolerable boss," *Psychology Today*, 44-48.

Lortie, D., 1975. *Schoolteacher: A sociological study.* Chicago: University of Chicago Press.

Martin, J., 1986. "When expectations and justive do not collide: Blue-collar visions of a just world." In H. W. Bierhoff, K.L. Cohen, and J. Greenburg (Eds.), *Justice in social relations* (pp. 317-335). New York: Plenum.

Maeroff, G.I., 1988. "Blueprint for empowering teachers." *Phi Delta Kappan*, 69(7), 473-477.

Malen, B., and Ogawa, R., 1988. "Professional-patron influence on site-based goverance councils: A confounding case study," *Educational Evaluation and Policy Analysis*, 10(4), 251-270.

Mead, G. H., 1934. *Mind, self, and society.* Chicago: University of Chicago Press.

Meltzer, B. N., Petras, J. W., and Reynolds, L. T., 1975. *Symbolic interactionism: Genesis, varieties and criticism.* London: Routledge and Kegan Paul.

Morse, J. M., 1991. *Qualitative nursing research: A contemporary dialogue.* Newbury Park, CA: Sage.

Murphy, J., and Louis, K. S., 1994a. *Reshaping the principalship: Insights from transformational reform efforts.* Thousand Oaks, CA: Corwin Press.

Murphy, J., and Louis, K.S., 1994b. "Transformational change and the evolving role of the principal: Early empirical evidence." In J. Murphy and L. G. Beck (Eds.), *Reshaping the principalship: Insights from transformational reform efforts* (pp. 20-53). Thousand Oaks, CA: Corwin Press.

Namie, G., 2000. *U.S. hostile workplace survey 2000.* Benicia, CA: Campaign Against Workplace Bullying.

Namie, G., and Namie, R., 2000. *The bully at work: What you can do to stop the hurt and reclaim your dignity on the job.* Naperville, IL: Sourcebooks.

National Governors' Association (Ed.)., 1986. *Time for results.* Washington, D.C. : National Governors' Association.

Neuberger, O., 1999. *Mobbing : Playing bad games in organizations,* 3rd ed. Munich and Mering : Hampp.

Neuman, J.H., and Baron, R.A., 1997. "Aggression in the workplace." In R.A. Giacalone and J. Greenberg (Eds.), *Antisocial behavior in organizations* (pp. 37-67).

Neuman, J. H., and Baron, R. A., 1998. "Workplace violence and workplace aggression: Evidence concerning specific forms, potential causes, and preferred targets." *Journal of Management* 24(3), 391-419.

NNLI (Northwestern National Life Insurance Company), 1993. *Fear and violence in the workplace.* Minneapolis, MN: Author.

Noddings, N., 1992. *The challenge to care in schools: An alternative approach to education.* New York, NY: Teachers College Press.

Olson, L., 1999, March. "Demands for principals growing but candidates aren't applying," *Education Week,* 18(20) 20.

Pearson, C., 2000. *Workplace "incivility" study.* Chapel Hill: University of North Carolina.

Price Spratlen, L., 1995. "Interpersonal conflict which includes mistreatment in a university workplace," *Violence and Victims,* 10(4), 285-297.

Rayner, C., 1998. *Bullying at work.* Stoke-on-Kent, UK: Staffordshire University Business School.

Rayner, C., Hoel, H., and Cooper, C., 2002. *Workplace bullying: What we know, who is to blame, and what can we do?* New York: Taylor and Francis.

Reitzug, U. C., and Cross, B.E., 1994, April. "A multi-site study of site-based management in urban schools." Paper presented at the Annual meeting of the American Educational Research Association, New Orleans, LA.

Riskind, J. H., 1997. "Looming vulnerability to threat: A cognitive paradigm for anxiety," *Behaviour Research and Therapy*, 35(8), 685-702.

Robinson, S. L., and Bennett, R.J., 1995. "A typology of deviant workplace behaviors: A multidimensional scaling study," *Academy of Management Journal*, 38(2), 555-572.

Rusch, E. A., 1999. "The experience of the piñata: Vexing problems." In F. K. Kochan, B. L. Jackson, and D. L. Duke (Eds.), *A thousand voices from the firing line: A study of educational leaders, their jobs, their preparation, and the problems they face* (pp. 29-43), UCEA Monograph Series. Columbia, MO: University Council for Educational Administration.

Ryan, K. D., and Oestreich, D. K., 1991. *Driving fear out of the workplace: How to overcome the invisible barriers to quality, productivity, and innovation*. San Francisco: Jossey-Bass.

Schlechty, P.C., 2001. *Shaking up the schoolhouse*. San Francisco: Jossey-Bass.

Schwandt, T.A., 1994. "Constructivist, interpretivist approaches to human inquiry." In N. Denzin and Y.S. Lincoln (Eds.), *Handbook of qualitative research*, (pp. 118-137. Thousand Oaks, CA: Sage.

Sheppard, B., 1996. "Exploring the transformational nature of instructional leadership," *The Alberta Journal of Educational Research*, 42 (4), 325-344.

Smith, W., and Andrews, R., 1989. *Instructional leadership: How principals make a difference*. Alexandria, VA: Association for Supervision and Curriculum Development.

Steinberg, J., 1999, November 14. "Federal funds for teachers reveal surprising hurdles." *New York Times*, 18.

Strauss, A. L., and Corbin, J., 1998. *Basics of qualitative research: Techniques and procedures for developing grounded theory* (2nd. ed.). Thousand Oaks, CA: Sage.

Swedish National Board of Occupational Safety and Health, 1993. *Statute book*, Ordinance (AFS 1993: 17), Section 1 and 6.

Taylor, S. J., and Bogdan, R., 1998. *Introduction to qualitative research methods: A guidebook and resource* (3rd ed.). New York: Wiley.

Tesch, R., 1988, April. "The contribution of a qualitative method: Phenomenological research." Paper presented at the annual meeting of the American Educational Research Association, New Orleans, LA.

Westhues, K., 2004. *Administrative Mobbing at the University of Toronto*. Lewiston, NY: Mellen Press.

Yamada, D. C., 2000. "The phenomenon of 'workplace bullying' and the need for status-blind hostile work environment protection," *The Georgetown Law Journal*, 88(3), 475-536.

Yukl, G., 1994. *Leadership in organizations*, 3rd ed. Englewood Cliffs, NJ: Prentice Hall.

Part Four

Predisposing Contexts

Editor's Introduction

From the first three parts of this book, readers will have gained a clear, nuanced understanding of what mobbing in the academic workplace is, and of its debilitating effects both on the target, whose life is disrupted at best and lost at worst, and on the institution, whose mission of seeking and sharing truth is undermined.

The stage is now set for five essays that shed light on why mobbing occurs, by identifying conditions and contexts that give rise to it. Most of the five chapters below also recount additional cases, but their thrust is toward answering the crucial question of why.

A kind of explanation skirted by these chapters should be acknowledged in preface: location of the cause in the personal pathology of the mob leader, typically an administrator. Hugo Meynell's chapter in Part One alluded briefly to Robert Hare's book on psychopaths, *Without Conscience* (1993). Hare's viewpoint is not irrelevant. Personal qualities, pathological and otherwise, do matter. The chapters below give priority to what matters more: context, situation, power relations, group and institutional dynamics, and the ideologies prevailing at a given time and place.

First is Melvin Williams's general theory, which is essentially that people seize power and use it to grind others down in order to assuage their own feelings of inferiority, arising in particular out of denial of their animal bodies. Williams places the blame for mobbings more on followers than on leaders. At a time when race and sex pervade campus politics, this African-American anthropologist looks beyond these factors to more basic human propensities.

Yet if enough professors and administrators define race and sex as the real nubs of campus life, these factors have real effects. The next three chapters are all concerned with how race and sex get entangled with pursuit of power, divert attention from educational and scholarly goals, and result in administrative campaigns to punish high achievers and protect lackeys of some favored biological type.

No historian could write a more incisive, gripping account of destructive racial and ethnic politics at Virginia State University these past thirty years than physicist Carey Stronach has done (Chapter 10). One grieves not only for the professors wrongly chased out of VSU, but also for the students wrongly deprived of instruction by them.

Sociologist Martin Loney (Chapter 11), author of *The Pursuit of Division* (McGill-Queen's 1998), shows how obsessions with race and sex have perverted academic purpose at the University of Toronto. His essay is persuasive evidence that religious orthodoxy is not the only kind that leads to wrong decisions and the betrayal of an academic institution's public responsibilities.

In his pungently entitled account of how preoccupation with sexual harassment facilitated disregard of plagiarism (Chapter 12), religious studies professor Irving Hexham exposes a pervasive hypocrisy in colleges and universities, that anti-harassment policies become instruments of harassment by opportunistic administrators.

In the final essay in this part of the book (Chapter 13), sociologist Nathan Young traces much quarreling in today's academic workplace to an extreme postmodernism, an obsession with differentness that makes human connection impossible. Young's balanced, critical appraisal of postmodernism is mature scholarship.

The chapters below do not offer an all-embracing explanation for mobbing in academe. A common direction of their varied searches for explanation is nonetheless discernible: toward the emergence of an administrative caste separate from the professoriate, concerned less with scholarship than management, less with substance than image, less with truth than power, and therefore drawn to bases of decision-making that have little to do with what a university is about.

Chapter Nine

The Power and Powerlessness of Academe: Toward a General Theory of Human Behavior

Melvin D. Williams

The Exercise of Power Is the Only Narcotic for the Temporary Relief of the Inferiority Complex

The Chronicle's Daily Report, 20 June 2003, examined an article in the current issue of *Academic Leadership*. The tongue-in-cheek essay, "How to Demoralize the Faculty: A Six-Step Program That Works," notes that professors are too happy and administrators need to do something about it, says Howard B. Altman, a professor of Modern Languages and Linguistics and a Faculty Development Specialist at the University of Louisville. Altman promises that by following six simple steps, administrators can quickly and effectively lower faculty morale:

1. Close down the lines of communication.
2. Never thank anyone for anything.
3. Always pay outside hires more than their inside colleagues.
4. Stay invisible.
5. Keep the workings of the faculty reward system secret.
6. Change everything frequently.

The plan is "foolproof," Altman says, but he also gives a warning to administrators: "fail to follow these steps assiduously and you, too, can find yourself trying to run a campus burdened by too many contented professors."

I have been in academe most of my adult life and I have written two volumes on the subject – *The Ethnography of an Anthropology Department* and *An Academic Village* (Williams 1993, 2002). Having given considerable thought and analysis to the "prosecution" of professors I have concluded that the central administrative phenomenon involved is power or the fear of its absence (insecurity).

What kind of personalities subjects themselves to years of additional schooling after twelve years of obligatory education? What kind of personalities will endure the torturous years of graduate school? Perhaps, it is those who have severe feelings of inferiority and who are forced to prove to themselves and to others that they are not inferior. How do these kind of people adjust to a little power and authority? Many academics have experienced a youth of relative weakness in athletics and general physical prowess. They have neglected a life of concentrated physical activity for a life of the mind that seemed to be more appropriate to their abilities. Such a youth and subsequent life leaves a gnawing suspicion of impotence and any confrontation physical or political may lead to an imminent threat to one's security. Such a threat often results in administrative overkill as the administrators circle their wagons to protect their fragile authorities and egos and to give a clear signal of their superior power to all who witness their actions.

In addition to the neuroses described above, many administrators have chosen administration to capitalize on their failed scholarly careers. Some mathematicians believe that after age thirty-five their most productive research careers are behind them. Scientists with large research facilities often discover that their most productive grantsmanships are behind them. Teachers discover that they are burned-out in the classroom, have writers block, or no new ideas. Such human resources in academe may have tenure and cannot be retired. They often are accepted into administration. So now you may have insecure administrators who have failed in previous positions.

I do not want to appear overly harsh on academe. Most humans are insecure (Williams 1998). They have animal bodies and spirits that commune with God. They struggle to manage their bodies (e.g., "sex, death, and digestion") or they are victims of "biophobia" all of their lives (Gray 2002, Williams 1996a, 1996b). That struggle keeps them insecure. Such insecurity plagues the human enterprise (e.g., classicism, racism, ethnocentrism, sexism, sectarianism, ageism, nationalism, disableism, and speciesism [CRESSANDS]). Most humans are insecure but for the reasons I have stated academics have even a greater vulnerability.

I have witnessed cruelty in academe that continues to appall me even as I describe it here. A dean at a midwestern university had a friend and running partner in the sociology department. The partner had a wife in the same department that was being reviewed for promotion. The dean wanted to demonstrate his friendship and his power through his support for the wife, as both men were too insecure about their masculinity for such affection and support between them. The dean made every effort to show his support for the promotion of the wife without violating protocol. He was seen eating with her in the sociology building and in other contacts that were clearly designed to send his message to faculty who would vote. But senior faculty in the sociology department were reluctant to be persuaded by the dean and not the dossier. They denied the wife the promotion. The dean took this action as a personal insult, notwithstanding that no one had been told to vote for the wife. He began to pursue all of the vulnerable professors for revenge. They all had tenure so he had to use other approaches. He did. As one example, he had the university foundation cancel a house lease on one of the professors, effective immediately. The professor had one month to move his family and his belongings. He had to move into a hotel and put his belongings in storage until he found other lodging. He had depended on the goodwill of the university and overlooked a clause in his lease that allowed this to occur. The victim never recovered from this violation of academic collegiality. He moved to another university as soon as he had the opportunity.

Another dean at an eastern seaboard university recruited and hired a chair of a department without informing the new chair that he was actively attempting to eliminate the department. In that department he had a tenured associate professor and intimate to whom he had promised the chair and whom he had convinced that the new chair would not endure long. Together they campaigned to make life in the department unbearable for the new chair. The associate professor had been acting chair and he refused to move out of the chair's office. For months the new chair had no office and the dean quietly and calmly assured the new chair that a move was imminent. The department hired a new tenured full professor who secretly was slated to head another department the next year. This full professor and the associate professor organized the departmental faculty to block any efforts of the new chair and each faculty meeting was used to demonstrate that the new chair had no power. The dean was exploiting the faculty to disrupt the department. But the faculty was ignorant of the dean's real objectives. The associate professor continued to believe that all of this disruption would lead to his chairmanship.

A distinguished tenured scientist at a distinguished midwestern university could not tolerate his treatment in his department. The dean placed him in another department. The chairs of both departments were upset that the dean did not allow them to resolve the matter. The new chair and the new faculty began to harass the scientist. His grants and publications suffered. He was punished with the denial of salary increases, graduate students, and laboratory space. They were attempting to force the scientist to resign. The scientist attempted to find another position. He even took a year leave at another university to test the environment. He returned to two student charges of sexual harassment and to faculty refusing to speak when they passed him in the corridors. The chair increased his teaching load. He remained. The chair assigned him a death squad class – a class from which premed students and their parents had driven several professors because the professor purportedly was not adequately preparing the students for medical school. The scientist who was now ailing thought that the department was trying to "kill" him and he feared that they might succeed. He resigned without another position.

At the same university but in another department, three years after a dean hired a new chair the dean retired. The new dean chose to remove the chair from office. The chairperson was understanding and agreed to resign and allow the dean to select her own chair. The dean refused the offer and chose to have an evaluation of the chair as an excuse and alibi to remove the chair. After the evaluation the chair was never informed of the results but he was removed as scheduled. The chair then informed the dean that he had a five-year contract and had to be removed for cause or compensated for the two remaining years. The dean pulled the contract from the files and declared that she had read it and there was no such term. Later the university lawyers corrected the dean. Upset by these events the dean and the assistant provost went after the former chair. After a clandestine search of his office they called the city police and provided them with false information that accused him of a believable felony and had him arrested in the streets as he was walking home. He was thrown to the ground and handcuffed. At the city jail he had his belt and shoestrings taken and was placed in a cell. While in the cell the police captain on duty informed him that it appeared he had been "set up" but that since it was Friday night he could not be arraigned until Monday. He would have to spend the weekend in jail. The case was never prosecuted but the faculty person never recovered from the embarrassment or the evil that lurked at that university. He left for another position.

Staff are not immune to such torturous treatment and I have an example at this same university. This is my whiplash example and the situation requires a staff person who has much longevity on the job. This staff person had been in the department for over twenty-five years. A series of chairpersons had allowed her to manage the records and paperwork of all of the graduate students in the department. She even had a title – the graduate secretary. As a normal human such authority over a number of years encouraged a management style and autonomy that set her apart from the other office staff. Even the chair had little reason to direct her work and some chairs had resented her attitude toward them as not being deferential enough. The other office staff resented her superior attitude. The administration decided that she was too abrasive and too old to continue working but she would not retire. The plan was hatched. During a remodeling for a new rotating chair she was given the largest office in the departmental complex. Her office had the only egress through two different doors and normally would have been the office of the chair. This office assignment surprised most of the office staff and the faculty but it was assumed that the new chair was especially fond of the graduate secretary and that they had been "friends" for many years. The graduate secretary was elated and she decorated her new office with elaborate paintings, pictures, and furniture. After a few months the chair's new administrative associate decided to make the graduate secretary's office a conference room. The chair wore clean white gloves and pretended not to be involved. The office was large and convenient enough. The administrative associate also decided that the department needed a new graduate secretary. The chair opined that he had agreed to allow the administrative associate the authority to run the office and that he could not interfere. The graduate secretary had served the department too long and too well to be dismissed so she was given the position of receptionist. As the receptionist she had no office but sat at a desk near the door that entered into the departmental complex of open space. Ironically, she sat in a position facing the door of her prior office. She was a strong woman but this sudden change devastated her. She kept up her appearance and went about her new job with dignity. She took some of her pictures and put them on the wall above her desk and attempted to make her new job as pleasant as possible under the circumstances. But the administrative associate continued to issue guidelines for her new job. One of the guidelines was that all of her pictures must come down. The receptionist, former graduate secretary, could not endure this continuous "supervision." She took sick leave for stress and fatigue. The administration demanded her medical records and required that their psychiatrist examine her. They were prepared to play the card Professor Westhues calls "mental illness as exit door." I marveled at her ability to withstand the whiplash of her treatment as well as the university's willingness to pursue and punish her.

At an "elite" research university the administration lost its patience with a department that was not "bringing in the grant money" which was deemed appropriate. The department was not ranked near the top nationally and it was not considered to be doing the kind of "cutting edge" research that the top-ranked departments manifested. The department was filled with tenured faculty and the administration saw little hope for change internally. What was there to do? First the administration declared a university-wide budget crisis. The dean of the college that housed the department was ordered to make a sizable cut in his budget. The dean leaked that the department might be affected by the budget crisis. The sophisticated faculty in that department realized that this was a signal that their department would be "axed." They began to look for positions elsewhere. The university had covered itself legally by declaring a financial crisis. However, one faculty member was excluded from the politics and the gossip of a pending elimination of the department. When the call came for a committee to make that decision he was caught by surprise. He was an "outsider" and this was an opportunity to eliminate a tenured full professor that was not doing the "cutting edge" research. By the time the committee had filed its report and the dean had made his decision the entire other tenured faculty had been placed in other departments of the university. The "outsider" had no place to go because of his age and his research record. He was frightened and humiliated. He explained that faculty all over the university began to avoid him and when they could not they had a melancholy look about them. Some of them behaved as if any contact with him might cost them their positions. The faculty member was saved because of the threat of legal action. He was the only member left without a position and this was difficult to explain in a legal action. So, he was placed in another department where his difficulties did not end.

At a small college in the South a tenured professor was being harassed in hopes that he would leave. The president of the college refused to provide the professor an office. The professor filed a grievance. The president responded by designating an outside toilet facility as the professor's office. The toilet was covered with plywood to provide a desk and the professor was told that his grievance had been resolved.

These are brief examples of administrators in academe who torture professors or staff without cause. Of course many of them have been tortured in their own climb to administration and their administrative superiors are torturing many of them. Even without formal actions of dismissal administrators have the capacity to force professors to leave. These are also examples of why it is necessary to examine such human behavior to understand and to explain humans' inhumanity to humans. I attempt this below.

Leadership and Followship

If our "best and brightest" engage in such behavior what can we expect of others? Our heroes and heroines are being exposed daily – Sammy Sosa, Martha Stewart, Catholic priests, presidents, corporate "leaders," and political "leaders." I attempt to explain the behavior in terms of leadership and followship. It does not matter where you find the human behavior – in the academy or in the army it is normal human behavior. Academic administrators perceive themselves as leaders with authority; despite the propaganda that faculty are self-governing. People that "run a campus" are perceived as "leaders" who have power and authority. They pay themselves larger salaries; provide themselves expensive furniture and equipment, and larger offices. They provide themselves large expense accounts, travel first-class, eat at expensive restaurants, and explain to the faculty why all of this is necessary for the survival of the university (Williams 1996c).

Why do faculty tolerate these behaviors of administrators? Many of the faculty have aspirations for administration themselves. They want to safeguard these perks for their own future administrative positions. People in the academy are normal. The administrative perks influence them. Those perks mean that administrators are more valuable than faculty or that faculty are inferior to administrators. Faculty resist such perspectives. Administrators plan and strategize for such resistances. These plans and strategies result in the cruelty that I have described (Epstein 2002).

Administrators work together to control faculty more than faculty do to control administrators. In that collectivity administrators attempt to maintain that power and that fear. Followers often identify with their leaders. The better the leaders look and the more power and influence they possess the more proud are the followers of their leaders and their academy. Administrators exploit such allegiances.

I have observed the same phenomena in churches. Poor members give to their churches and their pastors until it "hurts." Yet they enjoy seeing their churches and their pastors "look rich." They beg in the community and on their jobs to build beautiful churches and to equip them. They do the same to buy their pastors expensive clothes, cars, and houses. They identify with those churches and those pastors notwithstanding their own poverty. The poor members endure many hardships and even abuses from their pastors and the church officers. But year after year they work and support their religious enterprises. Humans are social beings. They thrive in social contexts. They will sacrifice themselves to belong and to participate in "great" social enterprises. Again, academic administrators exploit such allegiances.

Power is a corrosive element in human affairs. Few humans can accrue power without being corrupted. Within universities power is scarce and fleeting. Those who need power are likely to succumb to ruthless measures to get and to keep it. Those who need it are likely to be victims of severe inferiority complexes. The complexes drive them to strive for power all of their lives. They secure enough of it and they are desperately frightened of losing any of it. So in the university where there is little of it even at the pinnacle of university power and there is the constant threat of losing some or all of it, you will find desperate inferiority complexes using extraordinary actions to delude themselves into perceptions of superiority.

The corrective for these abuses are the selections and promotions of people who are secure within themselves. We need people who know themselves and value themselves for who they are and not for what they own and who they control. We must avoid people who are desperate for the accumulation of power. Such people can be terrifyingly brutal for petty administrative gains. They will expend political manipulations and stratagems for the pleasures therein and as ruthless games for petty powers. The driving force of power creates endless cycles of conflict to achieve minor victories. Such people lose any sense of honor, shame, justice, and fairness. They become insensitive to the vulnerability of others as they excommunicate them from their treasured careers, groups, and colleagues. This is a great paradox, to heap great suffering and tragedy upon the intellectual life. But social "superiority" is contextual and very fragile. It requires endless supplies of "inferior" people.

This is not a criticism. I hypothesized that wealth, status, and power are addictive. People must be cured of the addiction. As with most potent drugs the addiction is facile. Humans have been subject to the addiction throughout human history but the addiction has been adaptive. The addiction facilitated bipedalism and human technology. It facilitated the emergence of modern humans in competitive contexts. It enabled the Agricultural, Industrial, and Information Revolutions. Yet the seeds of human destruction were embedded within the same addiction. Our technology now allows the victims of classicism, racism, ethnocentrism, sexism, sectarianism, ageism, nationalism, disableism, and speciesism (CRESSANDS), and yes, even administrative mobbing, to retaliate with weapons of mass destruction. Soon an individual will be able to carry an atomic device in a briefcase. The global and transnational exploitation of people in the second and third world for the wealth and power of a few in the first world threatens our cradle and our tomb. Terrorism is another form of global racism and transnational CRESSANDS. This addiction of wealth, status, and power must be treated if we humans are to survive. Prime Minister Tony Blair, in his address to both houses of Congress (July 17, 2003) concedes, "Our ultimate weapon [against terrorism] is not our guns but our beliefs."

I offer my resolution of the problem. The addiction is fostered by the human attempt to escape his/her own biological trappings – sex, death, and digestion. Women have been treated as inferiors for three million years because they process more water than men (Williams 1998a). Let me offer a graphic vignette. An old "ugly" man goes to his faculty office every day to discover that his colleagues and associates treat him as an inferior. In words and body language they communicate that he is too old, too behind in research, teaching, and writing to be among them. They also remind him that his Ph.D. university, his social class, his ethnic group, his residential neighborhood, his taste in music, art, and "culture" are all "inferior" (Epstein 2002). The old man continues to work. But each evening when he returns home to shower, brush his teeth, and prepare for bed he is vividly reminded that he has an animal body. He has odors emanating from under his arms and between his legs, from the products that come from his rectum and his urethra, from his mouth and his feet, from the products from his ears and his nose, and from the perspiration in his head and all over his body. His society insists that all of these odors are undesirable (Gray 2002, Miller 1997). The old man is a strong human being and he can handle his job or his body. But to deal with both of them every day and refuse to succumb to pathological feelings of inferiority taxes his mind, spirit, and body.

Religions of the world have enabled many to rise above their biological trappings. Yet most people in the world have not been converted. They must demonstrate their superiority to all the other animals by wealth, status, and power. In this process the zeal of these demonstrations expand to include all of the "inferior" people as well. Administrative mobbing is just another form of creating "inferior" people by trial, degradation, and dismissal.

Humans must be reared and socialized to accept themselves, to believe in themselves, and to support themselves and others. No human is inferior. Some of us are blessed and others have misfortunes. But death comes equally to all of us and when it comes it makes all of us equal. Many will be harried, hungry, sick, lonely, and bored in a lifetime, but none of us are inferior to others. The Earth is our home, our nest. We must care for it and our fellow humans or they will be the basis for our extinction. In the Ecological Revolution AmeriCorp and the Peace Corps will no longer be small American programs but the basis for all human societies. We must work and wait.

Meanwhile, academic mobbing and scapegoating will continue. Academic administrators maintain bureaucracies. Bureaucracies attempt to create, manipulate, and control power. There is relatively very little power in academia. Thus we must expect petty and insecure academic administrators to mob and to scapegoat until we attract secure and better socialized people into those positions.

Leadership and Followship: The Search for Fundamentals in Human Behavior

My research career has been a series of exposures to church leadership and followship in Pittsburgh, Pennsylvania, and Lafayette, Indiana, as well as academic leadership and followship at Pennsylvania, Indiana, Maryland, and Michigan. But as most ethnography my work has been designed to understand the larger picture of general human conduct. It has taken me a long time to get where I wanted to go. I may not be there yet. Such efforts seem always preliminary and merely await the next set of circumstances to disprove them.

The psychologist Alfred Adler (1918, 1927, 1964) told us we all feel inferior and carry with us a lifetime inferiority complex that dominates our behaviors. Perhaps we see similar proclivities among other mammals and primates in their territoriality, food chain hierarchies, sexual competition, and dominance behavior. Many humans spend their lives attempting to prove to themselves and to others that they are not inferior. Regardless of the evidence they fail to believe for long. The drives for status, prestige, wealth, power, fame, recognition, money, property, material possessions, titles, symbols of superiority, and for success in sex, games, and careers fill our daily lives. If we are to understand ourselves we must continue to examine these behavioral dynamics. Like incest and homosexuality, the inferiority complex is disconcerting even in scholarship.

I approach the inferiority complex by way of the ethnographic record. I analyze the leadership and the followship of the pimp, the politician, the academic, and the preacher. One must understand the images created and the spectacle needed for leadership and followship. One must examine the nature of status, and the godfather, the academic-scholar star, the "key" administrator, the dictator, the star entertainer, and the sycophants that court such status.

A General Theory of Human Behavior: Institutional Inferiority

As with the physical sciences, the ultimate goals of the social sciences are to arrive at general theories that explain most behavior in the universe (Wilson 1998, 2000). The social sciences have railed against a theory of human behavior because of the "complexity" of such behavior. Much of that excuse is a result of being human and the denial of animalism. It is somewhat of a status phenomenon. Anthropologists once described their subjects as "primitives." When that was deemed to be pejorative they used the term "simple societies." The complexity of an "upper" animal is such that you cannot understand its behavior within a simple theory. That is a social science bias and a human myth. It is a comprehensible bias and myth (Becker 1968, 1973; Miller 1997).

Humans are animals whose self-consciousness appears to find such existence repugnant. Most human behavior seems designed to deny its animal origin and substance. This is an epigenetic rule (Wilson 1998, 2000). Most human actions can be explained with such a perspective. So I am working to find human behaviors that cannot be understood from an animal denial basis. Such work meets tremendous resistance. Scholarship has vested interests. Scholarship has power enclaves. Any new ideas can threaten. I have already stated the problem of the bias and the myth. Most humans believe myth. A general theory of human behavior would undermine further those myths as the theory of evolution has already commenced to do. Many of those myths allow power and privilege to be distributed arbitrarily (e.g., classicism, racism, ethnocentrism, sexism, sectarianism, ageism, nationalism, disableism, and speciesism [CRESSANDS], which are disguised as mere classifications). Finally, I am a Black American who is arbitrarily defined as inferior and who could not possibly work on a general theory of human behavior that could be worth the consideration of the white scholarly establishment. My work is difficult to teach, publish, distribute, and critique. That is the essence of scholarship and mine is ignored. Perhaps it is better ignored than bitterly denounced.

Most social animals appear to be instinctively followers. They test one another to determine dominance of the leader (e.g., queen), which is determined at birth, and then they follow.

Self-conscious humans with animal bodies are surrounded by social institutions that declare these humans inferior. It requires great wealth, power, and privilege to disguise their animal bodies. Few humans have such wealth, power, and privilege. Those that have it are reluctant to spread it because their own is relative to those who do not. So if one can successfully identify with someone who has the resources to be "superior" one can escape one's animal "inferiority" by following. Children are socialized to be followers in the family and the schools. If they are fortunate they will attend colleges and postgraduate universities where insecure faculty will demand that they follow.

Most humans are poor and victims of CRESSANDS. Such people do not possess the self-confidence to lead. If they do, it is often in violent and anti-social behavior that is severely punishable by the "real leaders." Poverty and CRESSANDS are the basis of institutional inferiority. They keep most humans "inferior." The best they can expect from life is to have a capable "leader."

Most humans are followers. We will never have the wealth, power, and privilege to lead. We will always have our animal bodies, which we do not have the resources to disguise. We see ourselves as the animals we are. We are socialized into humility. But in the Ecological Revolution humans will learn to admire and respect their bodies. They will know that all of the "leaders" of the world have the same kind of bodies as they do. They will know that death comes equally to all of us and when it comes it leaves all of us equal; that all of our "leaders" have feces in their underwear and began life's journey in the vagina of a woman (sex, death, and digestion). They will ignore the rich clothes, cars, boats, houses, degrees, and privileges that attempt to disguise the bodies of the rich, powerful, and privileged. They will look to good character, community commitment, and wisdom as the values of the global village and as qualities of good leadership for good followship.

Recently the University of Michigan International Institute held a symposium titled, "For a University of the World: Academic Symposium of University of Michigan Presidential Inauguration," March 27, 2003. In that symposium the faculty continued to give lip service to globalization, diversity, otherness, a diverse humanity, a university engaged in the world, and two-way visions. Faculties are fascinated with words that pretend to be their ideas, values, and goals. Often such words are merely to manipulate, articulate, and create intellectual boundaries for themselves with concomitant modes of securing identities within the "intellectual" world. They are mere reflections of the insecurity rather than the signs of a quest for discovery and innovation (Shweder 2003). It is this very insecurity that must be conquered if we are to connect the global poor with the rich and treat the instability, scarcity, deprivation, disease, and hunger that left untreated will result in the terrorism that will render our species extinct.

I have attempted to examine leadership and followship in order to explain my general theory of human behavior. That theory has a real global reach. It is globalization of anthropology (macroanthropology). It attempts to explain the human search for meaning and security that is the foundation of human behavior. Scholarship, too, must recognize its prejudiced lenses and look back through the windows of others. Anthropology must cease to fetishize otherness and begin to recognize their different windows of vision. And looking back through their windows, see a general theory of human behavior that our social science projections on the world have prevented (Wilson

1998, 2000). Such a theory will teach us that human insecurity must be treated with global access to credit, high quality health care, and free education. This is access without ownership for the poor. It is fair chances not favors. Anthropology specifically and the social sciences generally must begin to think out of their boxes. We must build confidence (not insecurity) among the non-privileged in order that they can use their own lenses to help themselves and even help the privileged to insure continued human survival.

Scholars as other humans often see the forest and ignore the trees, as well as vice versa. The University of Michigan business school professor, Coimbatore K. Prahalad proclaimed commercial enterprises from his native India that operated from personal computers inside of one-room shacks of the poor. He praised their delivery system that rivaled United Parcel Service. He railed about the ten-dollar cataract operations in south India that had greater quality surgery than similar operations in the United States. He cited the oppressed women of the developing countries that spearhead development there. He gave the examples of the peasants in the countryside using color-coded cards to identify diseases and the United States Defense Department copying the technique to identify smallpox on the battlefield. University of Michigan President Mary Sue Coleman responded about the women of Bangladesh who have succeeded in birth control and commercial enterprises.

Everyone agreed that this was global knowledge that came from the bottom of the pyramid and served the privileged top. Yet how many were aware of the fifteen years that a Black scholar in their own midst had attempted to proclaim his general theory of human behavior without notice or much assistance? This is a problem of race. Race was created by, for, and of racism. As whites discovered the globe they created inferior categories of humans – others: Black, Brown, Red, and Yellow – to dominate and to exploit. They used guns and other technology of violence, biological warfare and deception to take the land, the natural resources and the people (slaves). They created race, one of the greatest stories ever told, in order to conceptualize the inferiority of other populations. Over fifty years ago (1942) Ashley Montagu wrote that race was *Man's Most Dangerous Myth*. He was persecuted the remainder of his life by scholars and intellectuals. Now whites dominate the earth and even the universe. Such behavior may soon provide the extinction of our species (Soulé and Lease 1995).

Sex creates life; death holds its meaning; and digestion its measure. If humans can conquer their aversions and fears of sex, death, and digestion they can extend their time on the planet. Sex, death, and digestion are to macroanthropology as time, space, and motion were to physics.

Fear and aversion (biophobia) have resulted in humans attempting to be superior to themselves, which is an impossible task and results in the inferiority complex and CRESSANDS. Marilyn Monroe said it best. She said I go to bed as Marilyn Monroe and I wake as Norma Jean who has to go eliminate. She is explaining that in the morning when she awakens, the makeup, perfume, lotion, hair style, and designer clothes are gone. The fermentation in the mouth and other digestive organs creates bad breath and other gases. As Marilyn she was superior to herself (Norma Jean) but in the morning she returns to herself.

Humans have attempted many devices to institutionalize their superiority to themselves. None of these devices conquer their biophobia. So why do we expect money, status, and power to succeed? It is never how much you possess but how much more that others have. These are the problems of macroanthropology. There must be a concerted effort to socialize ourselves to accept ourselves.

Sex, death, and digestion are the signal markers of human behavior. The horny, the harried, and the hungry seek salvation in dissipation, eternal life, and gluttony and yet remain sick, frightened, lonely, jaded, and bored. Humans reach for that addictive drug of status and power to assuage the human predicament. Dominance, territoriality, sex, and food competition find their way into human affairs (Heimberg, *et al.*, 1995, Williams 1998) – MacArthur, the Roosevelts, Stalin, Hitler, Saddam Hussein, the Bushes, etc. – have won their places in history by ruthless animal behavior that determined their "leadership" and their followship. My colleague calls them sociopaths but millions of people have lived and died because of their influences. Their sociopathology appears to be their willingness to succumb to their animal proclivities rather than to the virtues taught by their societies. I suspect that such vulnerability to those proclivities is hard-wired so I do not render criticism but a plea for understanding the problem (Soulé and Lease 1995).

Finally, let me assert that all of the social problems that I have discussed above are connected by the human insecurity that human societies have not been able to resolve in intelligent ways. So the disparate dilemmas that I have discussed are vitally related to feeling of inferiority that drives humans to "supremacy narratives and performances" (Williams 1997). If we are to confront one of these dilemmas, "administrative mobbing in the academe," we must confront all of them. That is my message. That is my mission.

References

Adler, Alfred, 1918. *The Theory and Practice of Individual Psychology.* New York: Harcourt Brace.

_____, 1927. *Understanding Human Nature.* New York: Greenberg.

_____, 1964. *Social Interest: A Challenge to Mankind.* New York: Capricorn Books.

Becker, Ernest, 1968. *The Structure of Evil: An Essay on the Unification of the Science of Man.* New York: George Braxiller.

_____, 1973. "The Denial of Death." New York: The Free Press.

Blair, Tony, 2003. *Congressional Record.* 108th Cong., 1st sess. H7060.

Epstein, Joseph, 2002. *Snobbery: The American Version.* New York: Houghton Mifflin.

Gray, John, 2002. *Straw Dogs: Thoughts on Humans and other Animals.* London: Granta Books.

Hall, Stephen S, 2003. "Merchants of Immortality: Chasing the Dream of Human Life Extension." New York: Houghton-Mifflin.

Heimberg, Richard G., Michael R. Liebowitz, Debra A. Hope, Franklin R. Schneier, eds., 1995. *Social Phobia: Diagnosis, Assessment, and Treatment.* New York: Guilford.

Miller, William Ian, 1997. *The Anatomy of Disgust.* Cambridge: Harvard University Press.

Montagu, Ashley, 1942. *Man's Most Dangerous Myth: The Fallacy of Race.* New York: Columbia University Press.

Shweder, Richard A, 2003. *Why Do Men Barbecue? Recipes for Cultural Psychology.* Cambridge: Harvard University Press.

Soulé, Michael E., Gary Lease, eds., 1995. *Reinventing Nature? Responses to Postmodern Deconstruction.* Washington, D.C.: Island Press.

Williams, Melvin D, 1993. *An Academic Village: The Ethnography of an Anthropology Department 1959-1979.* Ann Arbor: San Serif.

_____, 1996a. "Biophobia and the Human Body: Another Approach in Medical Anthropology." *Journal of Social and Evolutionary Systems* 19(1):55-80.

_____, 1996b. "Biophobia, Social Boundaries, and Racism." *Journal of Social and Evolutionary Systems* 19(2):171-86.

_____, 1996c. "Supremacy Narratives and Performances." *Journal of Social and Evolutionary Systems* 19(4): 313-19.

_____, 1998a. "Water, Power and Human Nature: In Search of Humans Evolving." *Journal of Social and Evolutionary Systems* 21(1):7-18.

_____, 1998b. *Race for Theory and the Biophobia Hypothesis: Humanics, Humanimals and Macroanthropology.* Westport, CT: Praeger.

_____, 2002. *The Ethnography of an Anthropology Department (1959-1979): An Academic Village.* Lewiston: The Edwin Mellen Press.

Wilson, E. O, 1998. *Consilience: The Unity of Knowledge.* New York: Alfred A. Knopf.

_____, 2000. How to Unify Knowledge. Keynote Address at the New York Academy of Science Conference on "The Unity of Knowledge: The Convergence of Natural and Human Science," 23 June.

Chapter Ten

The Campus CEO, State Politics, and the Mobbing of Exceptionally Competent Professors

Carey E. Stronach

The Way of the Transgressor

"I was never in the Vlasov Army. I was never in anyone's army." This was not the pleading of a Ukrainian peasant before a Soviet tribunal in 1945, who may have joined the losing side of World War II. This statement was made by Dr. Filimon D. Kowtoniuk, a tenured associate professor of foreign languages at Virginia State University, speaking out against false rumors of his alleged pro-Nazi activities, in 1970. Dr. Kowtoniuk, as one might guess, had been proscribed for elimination by the inner circle of VSU administrators and senior faculty.

Dr. Kowtoniuk, a Ukrainian immigrant to the USA, thought that he had finally found his calling, and a secure niche in American society, when the chair of the foreign language department of historically-black Virginia State College (now University) invited him to teach German and Russian at VSC, first on a part-time basis in 1961, then full time in 1965. Little did he know that his appointment generated deep resentment among two elements on the campus, some old-guard black faculty who wanted VSC to remain all black, and some young left-wing faculty who disagreed with Kowtoniuk on the war in Vietnam and a variety of domestic political issues.

This resentment boiled over in 1970. Dr. Kowtoniuk held the not-surprising new immigrant's belief in America as the land of freedom and opportunity. He not only let it be known that he was of the Republican persuasion, he organized a chapter of the Young Republicans, a first for VSC. It is not too surprising that the faculty adviser of the VSC Young Democrats, Calvin Miller (an associate of then State Senator L. Douglas Wilder), became Kowtoniuk's most vociferous enemy. In addition, Kowtoniuk had the misfortune to become director of a small grant that was to provide summer employment to some (supposedly) needy students. Kowtoniuk saw to it that those summer jobs went to truly needy students who showed academic promise. Later he learned that he had been expected to give the jobs to children of VSC administrators and senior faculty.

So what happened to Kowtoniuk? The VSC administration accused him of forging his Ph.D. degree (from the Free Ukrainian University, then located in Munich) and summarily dismissed him. But Kowtoniuk's insistent demands for an investigation caught the ear of a *New York Times* reporter. The *Times* had its correspondent in Munich visit the Free Ukrainian University, who found Kowtoniuk's degree to be fully valid. Kowtoniuk went to court and the judge ordered him reinstated. But the VSC administration didn't stop there. When Kowtoniuk went to meet his classes the following week he found another faculty member (an Instructor without a terminal degree) teaching his classes. An argument ensued in front of the students. So the VSC administration fired him again, charging him with unprofessional conduct. He went back to court, but he could not readily shake the accusation of unprofessional conduct, although it was obvious to all unbiased observers that he was set up.

Kowtoniuk ran out of money, and was unable to obtain adequate legal counsel. The VSC administration had the full weight of the Virginia Attorney General's office behind it, and Kowtoniuk was forced, for lack of resources, to abandon his case. (The Attorney General at that time, Andrew P. Miller, had been elected with strong support from the black community. Much later, Kowtoniuk had his revenge on Miller.) So in 1971, at age 48, Kowtoniuk's academic career was over. He did obtain a part-time position at the Roanoke Bible College, and led some tourist groups to the Soviet Union. But he was a broken man, had several heart attacks in the 1980s, and died in a nursing home on Medicaid at age 68 in 1992.

Kowtoniuk did obtain some Schadenfreude at the expense of Andrew P. Miller in 1978. Miller was the Democratic Party nominee for the United States Senate from Virginia. The Republican Party nominee was John W. Warner. The contest was very close and the GOP was concerned that, because of Warner's marriage to the four-time divorcee Elizabeth Taylor, the rural conservative Christian community would not support him. Kowtoniuk saved the day; his Christian fundamentalist friends saturated the rural churches with leaflets pointing out that Andrew Miller had supported black militants and anti-war radicals in their vendetta against this law-abiding Christian conservative professor. Warner won by 4000 votes out of over two million cast.

In addition, the conservative syndicated columnist Russell Kirk wrote a column about the persecution of Dr. Kowtoniuk, "The Way of the Transgressor," that appeared in dozens of newspapers around the country in 1970. A play, *Magnolia Aftershock*, by "Elliot Lake," is based loosely on the Kowtoniuk case.

Slowly Going to Hell in a Handcart

So here we have seen a case of mobbing and elimination of a professor at VSU in 1970-71, when this observer was a young assistant professor (starting in 1965). It occurred under the presidency of Wendell P. Russell (1970-74). Russell was succeeded by Thomas Law (1976-82), Wilbert Greenfield (1983-87), and Wesley McClure (1988-92). During this period there was no major case of mobbing of a faculty member (apart from the firing of several agricultural research faculty from the university farm in 1984), even though these were years of turmoil. But the turmoil was between the faculty and the administration, and the relative solidarity of the faculty against administrative incursions damped out intra-faculty controversies that might have led to an elimination campaign.

In 1992, then Governor of Virginia L. Douglas Wilder manipulated the ouster of Wesley McClure, a relatively apolitical mathematician with Republican leanings. He subsequently manipulated the appointment of Eddie N. Moore, Jr., his appointee as State Treasurer, to the presidency of VSU. If the Kowtoniuk case can be viewed as an analogy to the Spanish Civil War, World War II was about to begin on the VSU campus.

During the two decades from about 1968 to 1988, Virginia State University was an institution adrift, on a meandering downhill slide. Prior to 1968, VSC had been the one and only state-supported institution open to blacks. Its fortunes had fluctuated during the nearly nine decades since its founding as Virginia Normal and Collegiate Institute in 1882. After the failure of the populist rebellion (in prim and proper Virginia, the "Readjuster" movement), an era of strict segregation and white supremacy began, and in 1902, the institution lost its college program and was renamed the Virginia Normal and Industrial Institute. During the 1920s the college program was gradually reinstated and the name was changed to Virginia State College for Negroes. In 1946, it became simply Virginia State College, and a branch was established in Norfolk. Anyone who wants a complete account should refer to *Loyal Sons and Daughters*, by Edgar A. Toppin.

But after the passage of the major civil rights legislation in 1964 and 1965, the mission of VSC became less clear, as the best and brightest African-American youth were not only admitted, but provided handsome scholarships to the University of Virginia, Virginia Tech, William and Mary, and the other predominantly white public colleges and universities in the state. The Norfolk branch was separated from VSC and became Norfolk State College. Suddenly Virginia State had competition, tough competition, for its top prospective students.

In the late 1960s, some of the truly excellent faculty and administrators wanted VSC to strike out and become a high-quality integrated college. This hope was shattered by three external factors: (1) the expansion of upper-level and graduate programs at Richmond Professional Institute, which became the Academic Campus of Virginia Commonwealth University; (2) the establishment of John Tyler Community College near VSC, which drew many potential white students seeking an inexpensive education; and (3) the announced expansion of neighboring Richard Bland College (a branch of William and Mary) from two-year to four-year degree-granting status. The last of these was thwarted by a protracted law suit that was eventually settled by the United States Supreme Court.

As a backdrop to the Kowtoniuk case, in 1969 the State Council of Higher Education in Virginia directed that the VSC School of

Agriculture be transferred to Virginia Tech. The VSC student body, with the help of some faculty, protested the move and the upshot was that the state legislature rescinded the transfer and VSC President James F. Tucker (known as "Tom Tucker" to the students) resigned. The successful law suit against the expansion of Richard Bland College was a product of this movement also, with considerable assistance from the NAACP Legal Defense Fund.

The Thermidor of the VSC revolt came in 1970, with the appointment by the VSC Board of Visitors of Dr. Wendell P. Russell as successor to Tucker. Russell took a strong black-separatist stand, which alienated him from much of the faculty and eventually led to his resignation in 1974 (probably the direct consequence of fiscal irregularities discovered by state auditors). But the Russell administration did set the path of VSC for the next fifteen years. That is, instead of taking an innovative path, *any* innovative path, VSC delved deeper and deeper into a diminishing pool of prospective black students, letting the best go elsewhere without doing much to combat this brain drain, lowering admissions standards to maintain enrollment numbers, and increasingly recruiting from inner-city high schools in the Northeast.

The administrations of Thomas Law (1976-82) and Wilbert Greenfield (1983-87) were dominated by a slow downhill slide and many turf fights between administrators and faculty. These years were largely forgettable at VSU, although there was a change to the current name, Virginia State University, in 1979, and there was a mass firing of agricultural research faculty in 1984-85. A novel technique was used to eliminate Dr. Mohamed Latheef, whose name correctly implies his Muslim faith. He was reassigned from botanical research to the swine laboratory. He refused to accept this on religious grounds, and was consequently fired.

Prague Spring

VSU had its "Prague Spring" from 1988 to 1992, with the arrival of Greenfield's successor, Dr. Wesley McClure, who came to VSU from Southern University in Louisiana, where one of his greatest achievements had been to fight the state all the way to the U.S. Supreme Court over racial discrimination and the state's dual system of higher education. During the McClure years an honors program was established, and scholarly activity and research were emphasized. McClure brought with him a number of new people from Southern University, including Fathy Saleh, whose task was to develop an environmental science program and a multi-institutional consortium called WREMCON (short for Water Resources and Environmental Management Consortium), which would have consisted of 22 of the nation's leading historically black and minority institutions. Saleh, a native of Egypt and naturalized U.S. citizen, holds a Ph.D. in environmental engineering from Iowa State University. Saleh's enthusiasm and forthright manner quickly made him a lightning rod for all the resentments of the old-guard African-American faculty, who saw themselves being left behind in the dust of the fast-moving McClure administration.

No Good Deed Goes Unpunished

One cannot understand the events that followed at VSU without understanding the role of L. Douglas Wilder, who was elected Governor of Virginia in November 1989, the first African-American governor elected in any state in American history. A naive observer might expect that VSU would have entered a golden age during the four years of the Wilder administration. Then again, a naive observer would not know that Wilder flunked out of VSU in the early 1950s. Instead of a golden age, VSU entered a period of stagnation, infighting, and rock-bottom morale.

Wilder was a Democrat whose slash-and-burn take-no-prisoners cronyism politics rivaled that of Northern city bosses such as Richard Daley of Chicago and Frank ("I am the law in Jersey City") Hague. McClure was a relatively apolitical academic with Republican leanings, who had the audacity to stay out of the gubernatorial election without supporting Wilder (or his Republican opponent). Jean Cobbs did not support Wilder either, but we will discuss her troubles later.

Because terms on the VSU Board of Visitors are staggered, it took Wilder until 1992 to appoint a majority in opposition to McClure. While stacking the Board against McClure, Wilder at the same time persuaded him that Wilder's state treasurer, Eddie N. Moore, Jr., as a leading black government official, should receive an honorary doctorate from VSU. This enabled Moore to appropriate the title "Dr." Thus the ground was prepared for a coup. The state comptroller, Walter Kucharski, a close associate of Moore, told the

McClure administration that the VSU financial system should be converted from a semi-manual operation to a fully automated computer-based system. VSU was given three years to complete this task. But after only one year the comptroller's office sent a tiger team to VSU and ordered that the new system be turned on. Of course, this was impossible. The tiger team left, claiming that the system was in disarray and dysfunctional. This provided the excuse to fire McClure, and to justify bringing in a replacement with accounting experience.

Wilder obtained his Board of Visitors majority in July 1992, and McClure was fired the next month amid accusations of fiscal mismanagement and of generally being a bad person. So here we see the mobbing of a politically incorrect university president by state government officials. It may be noted that McClure had no difficulty finding another presidency, that of Lane College in Jackson, Tennessee, where he remains as of 2004.

A search was begun for a new president. There were 126 applicants, 125 of whom held an earned doctorate. The one who did not was chosen: Eddie N. Moore, Jr., Wilder's state treasurer. Moore had never held an academic position. Serving as the comptroller of William and Mary for two years was his closest approximation.

The selection of Moore was turbulent and full of high drama. There were numerous student demonstrations on behalf of other candidates. The process was capped by Doug Wilder landing on the campus quadrangle at VSU aboard the state helicopter. He marched into a meeting of the Board of Visitors. Board members not in support of Moore were forced to resign. They are appointed for fixed terms, so Wilder did not have the legal authority to do this, but he did it anyway. Moore was appointed president, effective June 1, 1993. This date is considered by some campus observers as the VSU equivalent of January 30, 1933.

A Line is Drawn in the Sand

Moore, who prefers to be called "The CEO" rather than his official title of "President," put his team together rather quickly. Dr. Martha E. Dawson, a retired provost from Hampton University and a graduate of VSU (class of 1943) was named Provost and Vice President for Academic Affairs. Dawson, who had considerable experience as an educator and administrator, was basically capable, but her advanced age and lack of experience outside the HBCU realm, led her to limit appointments to African Americans and to follow outdated educational concepts, which discouraged innovation and research. The most damaging aspect of her tenure as provost was her reliance on very militant African-American female faculty for advice.

Moore made several other questionable appointments. An agricultural extension agent who is a member of Moore's social fraternity was leapfrogged into the newly-created position of Dean of Agriculture, Science & Technology. Several of Wilder's political appointees were brought on board as administrators, as Wilder's administration was coming to an end.

Thus, as the 1993-94 academic year began, the political chess board at VSU came into focus with Moore, his ne'er-do-well administrators, Democratic party hacks, and the militant African-American faculty on one side. Facing them were the active research faculty, members of the National Association of Scholars, the handful of openly Republican faculty and staff, and those who had crossed Wilder in the past. It soon became clear that Moore meant business. A decade-long night of the long knives had descended upon VSU.

Among the first to go in the ensuing reign of administrative mobbing were untenured staff. The long-time VSU purchasing agent, Thomas W. Darby (who was Chairman of the Republican Black Caucus of Virginia at the time), and his wife Eileen, a secretary at VSU, who had both received outstanding performance evaluations for many years, were simultaneously given unsatisfactory ratings and fired. The Darbys went to court and obtained an order overturning their dismissals. They retired shortly thereafter, and the new (Republican) Governor, George Allen, appointed Tom Darby to the VSU Board of Visitors. Another conservative black Republican and former policeman, Bernard L. Jones, was fired from his position in the accounting office.

During this period a number of eminent faculty, both black and white, saw the writing on the wall, quietly packed their bags and left. For example, the Chairman of Governor Allen's Minority Task Force, Dr. Charles Whyte, had the *Center for Minority Business Development*, which he had founded, taken away from him. In addition, two newly-awarded projects to Whyte's center from the *Agency for International Development* (USAID), were rejected by the Moore administration. Whyte took a position with the USAID. A white economics professor, Dr. David McLean, (operating under the radar screen) received approval to take a one-year sabbatical at Johns Hopkins University, but when he received an even better sabbatical offer from MIT, was told he couldn't change his sabbatical institution. He went to MIT and never returned to VSU. Thus various techniques of harassment were used to inch out the targeted faculty and staff.

Apart from killing WREMCON and Charles Whyte's *Center*, the Moore administration apparently tried to kill off every scholarly initiative, venture, intellectual effort, or major funding opportunity that was, or appeared to be, associated with faculty and administrators considered to have been part of the "McClure team." These included a potential multi-million dollar computer science and software development contract with the BDM Corporation, a similar project with the Computer Sciences Corporation, and others from a number of federal agencies, including NASA. The reason given by CPA Eddie Moore for rejecting these projects? That VSU did not have the fiscal management capability to handle these projects.

But the really bitter fights were those involving foreign-born faculty and Jean Cobbs. An accusation had been made by a militant psychology professor, Florence S. Farley, that *our* students can't understand the accents and customs of foreign-born faculty; that African-American students should be taught by African-American faculty. Farley is also reputed to have said in a faculty meeting that we really didn't need to teach skills to our students – they would get jobs through affirmative action – we only needed to teach them about racism.

Bad things started happening to Nigerian-born accounting professor Emmanuel Amobi (an outspoken Republican with ties to Oliver North), to Pakistani-born biology professor Shaukat M. Siddiqi (another Republican), to Indian-born microbiology professor Janeshwar Upadhyay, to Nigerian-born chemistry professor Godwin Mbagwu, and to Egyptian-born engineering professor Fathy M. Saleh (yet another Republican). This observer puts Upadhyay in another category. In my opinion Upadhyay (once pictured on the front page of *The Times-Dispatch* as the most notorious slumlord in Richmond) should have been dismissed years before Moore arrived.

Amobi, Siddiqi, and Upadhyay filed law suits and, after much foot-dragging by the state, received substantial out-of-court settlements. Amobi and Upadhyay left VSU, the former going to

(Jerry Falwell's) Liberty University, the latter to tend to his real-estate interests.

The VSU administration refused to budge on the Saleh and Mbagwu cases, and they went to trial in Federal District Court, Eastern District of Virginia, Judge Robert Payne presiding, in the spring of 1999. The VSU administration was initially quite confident because they had the full support of the attorney general's office. This had been used to wear down other VSU faculty litigants, such as Filimon Kowtoniuk. But Saleh had connections: Mays and Valentine LLP, the second-largest law firm in Virginia (later merged with Troutman Sanders LLP of Atlanta). His high-profile team of lead attorneys Jim Crockett, Sam Brock, and Tony Troy (a former Virginia Attorney General), with their considerable resources, uncovered massive quantities of damning evidence. For example, Florence Farley was asked in a deposition if she had tried to have Saleh's tenure revoked. She replied that she hardly knew who Saleh was, and that she had not done anything of the kind. Saleh's legal team proceeded to subpoena audio tapes of a Faculty Council meeting in which Farley had issued forth with a lengthy diatribe against Saleh and vowed to take away his tenure.

Godwin Mbagwu's case was joined with Saleh's for economy of the court (and lawyers). His case was not as bitterly fought as was Saleh's, and it centered on a bad evaluation of his performance that was based not on his knowledge of chemistry nor the quality of his course material, but on his accent. It was brought out that Farley had made public references to "African trash." This displayed the cultural gulf between the African-American faculty (Jean Cobbs was a glaring exception), who generally favored affirmative action, welfare rights and reparations for slavery, and the immigrant African faculty, who were generally entrepreneurial and favorable to free-market economics.

In May 1999, the jury found in favor of Saleh and Mbagwu, and awarded them a total of $350K in compensatory and punitive damages. The judge, Robert Payne, later awarded the lawyers for Saleh and Mbagwu approximately $1.3M in legal fees. Eddie Moore's lawyers appealed the verdict and the $1.65M awards. The appeal process took nearly a year, but in May 2000 the Fourth Circuit Court of Appeals unanimously upheld the verdict and awards. With interest added since the initial verdict (plus additional legal fees), the net judgment came to slightly more than $2.0M. What followed was an amazing episode that demonstrates the evolving absurdities in racial politics in Virginia.

When a state official loses a civil suit that relates to his/her official duties, the state usually pays the compensatory damages, but the official has to pay any punitive damages out of his/her own pocket. In this case, however, then Virginia governor Jim Gilmore paid the entire judgment out of state funds while declaring the entire judgment to be compensatory. Therefore Eddie Moore and his co-defendants (former Provost Martha Dawson, Dean Lorenza Lyons, then Chemistry Department Chair Thomas Epps, and then Faculty Council Chair Florence Farley), having cost the Commonwealth of Virginia the $2M owed Saleh, Mbagwu and their lawyers, plus well over $1M in their own legal expenses, came out of these proceedings without paying one penny from their own pockets. The VSU Board of Visitors gave Moore a substantial raise and a new five-year contract (extended six more years in 2003). Bradley Cavedo, Moore's losing lawyer, was given a judgeship.

After this suit, the VSU administration made peace with Godwin Mbagwu and promoted him to the newly-formed position of Associate Dean for Research. This position may turn out to be a setup for failure, however, because the rotten treatment accorded researchers during the first seven years of the Moore administration had resulted in the resignations of a number of research-oriented faculty, while others had decided they would stick to the classroom.

The Iranian Connection

Eddie Moore is, if nothing else, a clever politician. After having had his knuckles rapped for having discriminated against foreign-born faculty, it seems as if he said to himself, "Alright, if they want foreigners, I'll give them foreigners up to their ears." Moore then developed a relationship with one ethnic group that had lain low during the Saleh-Mbagwu crisis, the Iranian faculty. In particular, more and more authority was handed to a hitherto obscure mathematics professor, Mohamed H. Moadab. Moadab had some knowledge of computers and this led to his appointment first as Director of the Academy for Faculty Development, and then Dean of Engineering, Science & Technology. His close associate, Ali A. Ansari, was appointed Chair of the Engineering & Technology Department.

The rise of Hadi Moadab is one of the most peculiar events to occur during the Moore administration. During the fall semester of 2000, Moadab's wife had an altercation with one of the administrators of the VSU computer center, where she worked. It is important to note that the computer center was operated by a private corporation under contract to VSU. It was alleged that the fight she had with her supervisor was over her provision of financial records to her husband, Hadi Moadab. After this fight occurred, Hadi Moadab told a number of faculty, this observer included, that he had enough evidence to send Moore and Ed Mazur (the financial VP) to jail for five years. At least one professor claims that Moadab showed him documents that suggested embezzlement and kickbacks. Another senior professor claims to have heard, while waiting in the ante-room of Moore's office, a discussion in the president's office, presumably between Moore and Mazur, about how much evidence Moadab might actually have.

Moadab was told by a senior faculty member that if he had evidence of the commission of a felony, he was required by law to provide that information to law-enforcement officials. Failure to do so is an offense called *misprison of felony*. Within a few days, however, there was a meeting of Moadab with Moore and (presumably) Mazur, and all of Moadab's complaints stopped. Shortly thereafter, Moadab was named Interim Dean of the School of Engineering, Science and Technology, and his wife was given a job in the VSU personnel office. (It is against state law for a private contractor doing business with the state to go onto the state payroll for at least a year after the completion of the contract work.) The supervisor with whom she had the altercation left the VSU campus.

In 2001 and 2002, following the appointments of Moadab to the deanship and of Ansari to the department chairmanship, there was a substantial influx of Iranian faculty into the ES&T School and, especially, into the Engineering and Technology faculty. Now there were more Iranian ES&T faculty than either African or European Americans. And round two of the Saleh case began.

Saleh Redux

In the spring semester of the 2000-01 academic year, the E&T department chair (Ansari) gave unsatisfactory ratings to two faculty, Saleh and Dr. Raymond Kliewer (the only licensed Professional

Engineer in the department). This led to the placement of Saleh in post-tenure review and the termination of (untenured) Kliewer's appointment effective May 2002. The administration then attempted to place Saleh in the School of Agriculture. At this point Saleh's lawyers returned to federal court and accused the administration of contempt of the previous order from Judge Payne in May 1999, which enjoined the administration from further maltreatment of Saleh and Mbagwu, in addition to ordering payment of compensatory and punitive damages. At this point, during the summer of 2002, the administrators promised the judge that they would cease harassing Saleh, but continued to do so anyway, and that they would take a number of actions to provide relief for Saleh. The latter included a stipulation that a panel of three full professors (Carey Stronach of Physics, Shaukat Siddiqi of Life Sciences and Ben Nwoke of Industrial Arts Education) re-evaluate Saleh's performance for 2000-01 (Ansari had rated him Unsatisfactory). This stipulation was set in place in October 2002, but the VSU administration did not convene the panel. Therefore, in May 2003, his lawyers asked Judge Payne that criminal contempt of court charges be brought against Moore, then-Provost Earl Yarbrough, and Moadab. But before bringing the Saleh case up to its present status, we must look at one of the most bizarre events seen anywhere in academe.

Anonymous letters, many of the most scurrilous type, have a long and dishonorable history at VSU, but they provide glimpses of what is really happening on the campus, where information and speech are tightly controlled. A *samizdat* collection of them would give a view of VSU that is perhaps more perceptive than this article. But the one that surfaced on July 31, 2002, really took the cake. A letter apparently written and signed by Provost Earl Yarbrough and addressed to Dean Mohamed Moadab appeared in the mail received by Judge Robert Payne. It read as follows:

MEMORANDUM
TO: Dr. Mohamed H. Moadab
FROM: Earl G. Yarbrough, Sr., Provost/
                 Vice President for Academic Affairs
DATE: November 12, 2001
SUBJECT: Meeting with Dr. Saleh
The President wants us to meet with Dr. Saleh as he requested but we must keep the pressure on. He does not want us to back down. Also, Dr. Saleh's evaluation must not show

improvement next year either. Since Dr. Saleh claims that you and I are out to get him, shifting him to Dr. Young (an impartial chairperson) would take care of his concern. I can get her to follow through with what you started. When we meet with Dr. Saleh, we must get him to agree to the move.

EGYSr:adj

This memorandum gave VSU more publicity than if the football team had won the conference championship, but not the type the institution would like to have. The memo was printed verbatim in *The* (Richmond) *Times-Dispatch* and *The* (Petersburg) *Progress-Index*. It was shown on the local TV news. And it prompted a witch hunt of major proportions on campus. The administration declared it to be a hoax, and was determined to pin it on one or more of its faculty adversaries. In a pretentious investigation a large number of computers were confiscated in hopes of finding the tell-tale file. The computers in the offices of the officers of the erstwhile VSU Faculty Council (which Moore convinced the Board of Visitors to abolish in August 2001), the officers of the VSU AAUP chapter, and all campus members of the Virginia Association of Scholars, among others, were confiscated. This observer (CES) had the computer in his office forcibly taken from him by the campus police. Judge Payne was very angry about this memo being mailed to him anonymously and requested that the United States Attorney investigate. The U.S. Attorney is doing so, with the assistance of the U.S. Postal Inspector. As of this writing, no charges have been filed. However, Earl Yarbrough resigned as Provost in November 2002, effective June 30, 2003, obviously under pressure, and took a demeaning job teaching shop in the industrial arts education area at VSU. He was succeeded by Dr. Eric Thomas. The secretary who allegedly typed the memo, Angela Johnson, has refused to speak with Saleh's lawyer and has been given a new job in the president's office with much higher pay.

In late summer of 2003, Dr. Saleh's lawyers completed negotiations with lawyers from the state attorney general's office to work out a settlement of his case. Although the details are confidential, it is clear that Saleh was given a sabbatical at full salary for the 2003-04 academic year, promoted to the rank of Full Professor, and given a generous financial settlement plus payment of all his legal fees. He had the choice of returning to VSU with a nine-month salary of approximately $85,000 or resigning and taking a one-time payment of approximately $250,000. Thus Eddie Moore escaped by the skin of his teeth having to face Judge Payne on charges of (possibly criminal) contempt and a possible jail sentence.

Collateral Damage

Raymond Kliewer thought that teaching mechanical engineering technology at Virginia State University would be the capstone of his professional career. Instead, it turned out to be its tombstone. After a distinguished career in metallurgy, with over 25 years of experience with Brown & Root (now part of the Halliburton Corporation) and Inland Steel, Dr. Kliewer took early retirement from Inland in 1999 at age 57 and accepted an assistant professorship in the VSU engineering technology department. He worked hard, became popular with students, and was the only licensed Professional Engineer in the department (this was important for accreditation). But he made one mistake. He developed a cordial friendship with the occupant of the adjacent office, Fathy Saleh, and they frequently went to lunch together. When the department chair, Ali Ansari, began attacking Saleh in departmental meetings, Kliewer supported Saleh. Consequently, Ansari gave Kliewer an Unsatisfactory rating for the 2000-01 academic year. Officially, this was based solely on the fact that one dilatory student assigned to Kliewer had not completed his senior project. He was informed by the Provost (Yarbrough) in December 2001 that his appointment would not be renewed after his then current contract expired in May 2002. Kliewer filed an appeal, which was blocked by Yarbrough and Moore. This action led in large measure to the resignation of Dr. Christopher Barat (see below).

As previously mentioned, the second Saleh suit resulted in an order that a special panel of senior tenured full professors (Ben Nwoke, Shaukat Siddiqi, and Carey Stronach) review the evaluation of Saleh for the 2000-01 academic year. Although the VSU administration ignored the order for eight months, the panel was assembled in June 2003, after Saleh's lawyers filed criminal contempt-of-court charges against Moore, Yarbrough and Moadab. The panel completed its deliberations in early August. It decided to extend the evaluation to all faculty in that department, so that a comparative study could be done. The results were that the three faculty whom Ansari had rated Outstanding were found to be Satisfactory, and Saleh and Kliewer, both rated Unsatisfactory by Ansari, each received two ratings of Outstanding and one of

Noteworthy from the special panel. Armed with this report, Kliewer has renewed his efforts to attain reinstatement but, as one would expect, he has been stonewalled. Another law suit appears to be on the way.

Kliewer and Saleh were removed from the Engineering Technology department during the year prior to the preparation of a re-accreditation application submitted to the Accreditation Board for Engineering and Technology (ABET) in July 2002. Even though they were no longer in the department (Saleh was reinstated by Judge Payne in September 2003), their cv's were included in the application as if they were still active members of the departmental faculty. Why? The chair and the dean apparently realized that the department didn't meet minimal accreditation standards without Saleh and Kliewer. They had to have a licensed Professional Engineer, a distinction only Kliewer held; and Kliewer was a certified accreditation reviewer for ABET as well. On the strength of the Saleh and Kliewer vitas, re-accreditation was obtained. Might a whistle-blower be needed here?

One more unfortunate byproduct of this internecine campus warfare was the resignation of Dr. Christopher Barat, Associate Professor of Mathematics. Dr. Barat had assumed the leadership of the new faculty organization that had replaced the Faculty Council. This organization was appointed by President Moore, and was not elected by the faculty. But Dr. Barat secured from Moore a commitment to permit this organization to operate freely without interference from the administration. However, shortly after it was formed, Fathy Saleh, Raymond Kliewer and Jean Cobbs filed grievances with this organization and requested that it function as the Faculty Affairs Committee of the old Faculty Council would have done. Barat tried to follow the handbook and provide due process to the three pariahs, but the administration would not cooperate. Moore ordered that the grievance process be aborted in all three cases. Therefore the dismissal of Kliewer stood, Saleh's "Unsatisfactory" rating at the hands of Ansari and Moadab stood (and the administration continued to ignore the stipulations of the federal district court), and Jean Cobbs' most recent "Unsatisfactory" rating at the hands of sociology department chair Mokerrom Hossain and Dean of Liberal Arts and Education Leon Bey (a physical education instructor and Nation of Islam member) stood.

This was the last straw for Chris Barat, a Phi Beta Kappa graduate of Brown University and one of the finest scholars to serve on the VSU faculty in recent memory. He found another position at Villa Julie College, near Baltimore, and left VSU in May 2003. His letter of resignation listed seventeen particulars, including the failure of the administration to consider the grievances filed by Fathy Saleh, Raymond Kliewer and Jean Cobbs. True to form, a number of poison-pen e-mail letters were sent from VSU to the Villa Julie administration slandering Dr. Barat. He did some investigating and found that these e-mails originated from the office of a high-ranking VSU administrator.

Another change brought about by the Moore-Yarbrough-Moadab administrative troika was the retirement of Dr. Florence Farley. During the 2001-02 academic year she was relieved of her position as Chair of the VSU Psychology Department. Faced with a new, white, department chair, she retired in May 2003, but also filed a law suit against the VSU administration. Her attorney was disbarred shortly thereafter.

To be fair, it should be noted that Dr. Moadab has put considerable effort into improving the physical facilities for the School of Engineering, Science and Technology. The computing facilities have, in particular, been upgraded, and he did use some end-of-the-year funds to provide additional computing capabilities for the Center for Interactive Micromagnetics, a physics research laboratory sponsored by the Air Force Office of Scientific Research.

In 2002, the *Richmond Times-Dispatch* published a study of state institutions of higher education based on analyses done by the State Council of Higher Education for Virginia (SCHEV). It listed the percentages of state funds that the schools used for educational activities, as opposed to administrative overhead. VSU wound up in the cellar, with only 48 percent of its income used for instruction. Most institutions scored in the sixties and seventies. The study was a source of deep embarrassment, but the administration made no public response, acting as though the study had not taken place.

An American Dreyfus Affair?

As bad as has been the harassment of Dr. Saleh and some others mentioned here, it is eclipsed by the heart-rending persecution of Dr. Jean R. Cobbs, an African-American professor of sociology and social work at VSU. This observer wrote an essay about her case, *The Strange Case of Professor Cobbs - An American Dreyfus Affair?* in 1998. The document appeared on the FIRE web site at the time, from which the following (updated) description of her torment draws heavily.

Dr. Cobbs is one of the most eminent scholars on the VSU campus. A faculty member since 1971, a program director for 24 years, and department chair for 12 years, she earned her baccalaureate degree from Elizabeth City State University (NC), her master's degree from Virginia Commonwealth University, and her doctorate from the College of William and Mary.

Cobbs, after joining the VSU faculty in 1971, advanced through the ranks to tenured full professor. She founded the Social Work Program at VSU, got it accredited by the Council on Social Work Education, and kept it accredited throughout the 24 years she directed the program. She also founded the VSU chapter of the Alpha Delta Mu social-work honor society, which flourished under her advisement. And she was successful in soliciting grants for her department.

But Dr. Cobbs is a bit different from many VSU faculty, not to mention most in the sociology and social work disciplines. That is, she is a Republican and an objective scholar who takes a dim view of the political correctness scourge, and of those who use the classroom to indoctrinate students into radical (Marxist/black separatist) politics. For this she should be applauded, but instead, it has been the undoing of her career at VSU.

Dr. Cobbs received very high performance ratings from 1971 to 1993. The militant/Marxist/separatist element of the faculty of the social sciences disliked her, but with fair-minded deans, provosts and presidents, they were unable to retaliate against her effectively.

Enter Mr. Eddie N. Moore, Jr., who was appointed president of VSU in 1993 by the same Board of Visitors that had previously fired Dr. Wesley C. McClure, president of VSU from 1988 to 1992, a relatively apolitical mathematician with Republican leanings.

Mr. Moore has no earned doctorate, and had no experience in academia (which quickly became obvious). He is a CPA who had been state treasurer under Wilder, and is so proud of his combined SAT score of 920 that he put it on his automobile license tags. (What is truly sad is that Moore's 920 was the highest combined SAT score of any graduating African-American senior in the Philadelphia school system that year.)

Although the details are murky, it has become apparent that some sort of deal was cut between Mr. Moore and the militant/Marxist/separatist element of the faculty. The evidence is circumstantial but extensive. As mentioned earlier in this article, almost immediately upon Mr. Moore's arrival, foreign-born faculty, conservative and Republican faculty and staff, and faculty who were heavily engaged in research began to have difficulties with the VSU administration. Those harassments and employment terminations have already been discussed. As reprehensible as all these actions are, they pale before the treatment accorded Dr. Cobbs. A full narrative would fill a short book, but the main points are as follows:

- In 1994, when Dr. Cobbs was working on the re-accreditation study for the Social Work program, the provost (Martha Dawson) ordered the secretaries who would normally type the study, not to provide typing support to Dr. Cobbs. Cobbs wound up paying a typist out of her own pocket. When she sent the typed report to the printers for duplication, the University administration canceled the purchase order. Also, the VSU administration refused to pay Dr. Cobbs overtime for her work on the self-study report.

- In the summer of 1994, Dr. Cobbs was forced out of the sociology department chairmanship and was hit with a 25% reduction in salary.

- In November 1995, one month after riding on the Republican float in the VSU homecoming parade (the only African-American to do so), Dr. Cobbs was fired from the position of director of the social work program.

- Beginning in 1994, Dr. Cobbs began receiving "Unsatisfactory" performance ratings (as opposed to the "Outstanding" ratings she had received previously). She was placed in post-tenure review, under which she could have been dismissed. However, the post-tenure review committee ruled unanimously in her favor, but the VSU administration never acknowledged that finding.

- In April 1996, Dr. Cobbs (a tenured full professor) was given a terminal contract by the VSU administration. A close friend in the community, (ironically, the president of the local chapter of the Sons of Confederate Veterans), who knows former Governor (now Senator) George Allen well, contacted then Governor Allen and, working through the Attorney General's office, forced the VSU administration to replace the terminal contract with one respecting her tenured status.

- In a secret meeting held without Dr. Cobbs' knowledge, the VSU administration banned the Alpha Delta Mu social-work honor society from the campus. (Dr. Cobbs founded and served as faculty adviser to this chapter.) No reason has ever been given for this action.

- On March 2, 1997, one of the militant separatist faculty members (a large man almost twice Dr. Cobbs' size) physically assaulted her in the campus dining hall. No disciplinary action has ever been taken against her assailant.

- Dr. Cobbs has systematically been denied fair cost-of-living raises since 1994. In 1998 she received zero salary increase. In the other years since 1994 she has received a 1.2% increase or less. The university averages were about 5% for each year.

- Dr. Cobbs has been called "crazy" and "a traitor to her race" by militant faculty, and has been told to "watch your politics" by the chair of another department a few days after she attended a reception for Oliver North.

- Many acts of petty harassment have been committed against Dr. Cobbs. Her department chair refused to provide her with a computer (from grant money brought to VSU by Dr. Cobbs; computers were provided to every other faculty member in the department except Dr. Cobbs), then even refused to provide a new ribbon for the printer on her old computer, has given her the worst teaching schedule in the department (in the least desirable classrooms on campus), refused to order desk copies of textbooks for her classes, and refused to process routine travel requests for Dr. Cobbs.

- Under the new chair and social work director, the social work program lost the accreditation that Dr. Cobbs originally obtained and kept for 24 years. No action has been taken against these persons for loss of the accreditation. The VSU administration subsequently eliminated the social-work major.

- The University Office of Business and Finance has failed to reimburse her $500 for a course her daughter signed up for but dropped less than an hour later after her daughter's faculty adviser (from Old Dominion Univ.) advised her that it was not the proper course to take.

What has Dr. Cobbs done to deserve all this? First, she is a conservative Republican who has been active in the Republican party. She put Republican signs in her front yard. She refused to donate $1,000 to L. Douglas Wilder's campaign, as she was asked to do by a left-wing colleague. When department chair, she turned down an extremely militant social work faculty member for tenure, based upon unsatisfactory work performance and a failure to complete the doctorate within an expected time frame. And when serving as chair of the search committee for a new provost in 1992, she voted against another extremely militant faculty member who had applied. In this latter case the applicant confronted Dr. Cobbs and called her a "nigger."

An American Dreyfus affair? Indeed, it is fair to posit that the VSU militants and cowardly administrators would ship Dr. Cobbs to Devil's Island if it were in their power to do so.

Because of the unique nature of her case and the fact that she didn't actually lose her job, Dr. Cobbs had a difficult time in court. She was offered a settlement that would have required her resignation from VSU, which she rejected. But petty harassment and a stubborn refusal by the administration to increase her salary (she is now by far the lowest-paid full professor on the campus, with 32 years of seniority) have continued.

Perhaps the most sickening episode in the persecution of Dr. Cobbs is currently underway. Her husband Alfred was diagnosed with stomach cancer in the summer of 2003. His health failed rapidly. Dr. Cobbs took considerable leave time, without pay, to care for him. He died in January, 2004. The chair of the sociology & social work department, Dr. Mokerrom Hossain, gave Dr. Cobbs an "unsatisfactory" rating for the year, referring to her frequent absences from class. She was then informed that she was being placed in "post-tenure review," that unless she submitted a research plan satisfactory to Dr. Hossain and the dean, she would not receive a contract for the 2004-05 academic year. She submitted a plan, under protest, on April 30, 2004, but it was rejected. She then received a registered letter informing her that unless she submits a "satisfactory" plan by July 15, 2004, she will be dismissed from the faculty. She requested a meeting with the department chair, dean, and provost, to discuss why her previous plan was rejected, but has received no response as of this writing (June 13, 2004). She has filed a complaint with the EEOC and a lawsuit in federal court.

The Hinge of Fate

Several other African-American female faculty, including Florence Farley herself, filed suit against the Moore administration during the 2002-03 academic year, claiming gender and in some cases age discrimination (they had applied for administration positions that were given instead to African-American males with lesser credentials). As noted above, Farley subsequently retired in May, 2003. An inquiry under the Virginia freedom-of-information act revealed that as of August, 2003, there were seventeen law suits filed against Eddie Moore and the VSU administration.

During the summer of 2003, the Dean of the School of Business, Dr. Sadie Gregory, was pressured to resign for undisclosed reasons. The unofficial rumor coming from administration sources was that it had to do with the failure of the business school to attain accreditation. Other sources have suggested that it was because Dr. Gregory refused to recommend President Moore for a tenured professorship (which he may need if the results of one or another of these suits force him to resign the presidency). She was replaced by Dr. David Bejou, an Iranian who has served as assistant to the provost for several years. There has been a rising tide of complaint that the School of Business is being taken over by Nigerians, and that the School of Engineering, Science and Technology is being taken over by Iranians. Gregory has recently been appointed Provost of Coppin State University in Baltimore. Under Bejou there has been a concerted attack on the Nigerian faculty, some of whom were placed in post-tenure review and fired.

Dr. Ali Ansari, associate professor of engineering technology and an Iranian, was given an award as "Outstanding Faculty" at the opening convocation in September 2003. This award was a puzzle to most faculty, because the only activity of note in which he had been engaged was the war against Fathy Saleh and Raymond Kliewer. More recently, he was appointed Dean of Graduate Studies, even though he has never served on the graduate faculty nor advised a thesis student – his discipline does not offer graduate degrees at VSU. His replacement as department chair, a Dr. Rashidi, is also an Iranian. With the appointments of Ansari and Bejou in addition to Dr. M. Hadi Moadab as Dean of Engineering, Science & Technology, three of the five deans at VSU are Shiite Muslim Iranians.

One Iranian employee has recently fared less well. Dr. Djavad Djavadi, a native of Iran and a British citizen, worked as a media expert in the VSU audio-visual center. His visa and work permit came up for renewal in the spring semester of 2004. He filled out the appropriate forms, then submitted them to the VSU personnel office for that office to complete and send to the INS. It failed to do so – something Djavadi discovered too late. Following his attendance at a workshop in El Paso, Texas, he went to the airport to board his return flight. INS officers were checking the papers of the passengers. His were found to be expired. Because his name is vaguely similar to that of a known terrorist, he was placed in detention. When the VSU administration learned of this, it neither supported this ten-year employee nor reprimanded the personnel office for its cavalier and sloppy treatment of his document. Instead, it fired Djavadi. As of this writing, he is unemployed and fighting a deportation order.

The new student housing, still incomplete, of which Eddie Moore has been so proud, appears to have been built on a wetland, with resulting delays that have postponed its opening for yet another year, until August, 2004. The arrest of a VSU business-school student on September 2, 2003, for alleged rape and attempted murder unsettled the local community, although the devastation wrought by *Hurricane Isabel* drew attention away from such issues. Enrollment decreased substantially for the 2003-04 academic year.

On the other hand, a VSU physics professor, Dr. Anthony S. Arrott (formerly of Simon Fraser University), has designed a new form of magnetic memory that may revolutionize the computer industry, and a new Ed.D. degree program in Education Management has been initiated. The legislature approved funding for construction of a new engineering building. Thus VSU moved into another academic year amidst uncertainty, hope and despair, and with a potentially explosive atmosphere on campus. The 2003-04 academic year turned out to be mostly forgettable, except for the ongoing administrative war on Jean Cobbs and one hopeful surprise: by secret ballot in April, the VSU faculty elected biology professor Dr. Shaukat Siddiqi, a member of the Virginia Association of Scholars and sometime litigant against the Moore administration, to chair the Faculty Senate. Dr. Siddiqi won by two votes over the candidate supported by the VSU administration.

Chapter Eleven

Beyond Reason: Racial Politics at the University of Toronto

Martin Loney

Orthodoxy, of whatever color, seems to demand a lifeless imitative style... When one watches some tired hack on the platform mechanically repeating the familiar phrases.... One often has a curious feeling that one is not watching a live human being but some kind of a dummy.... A speaker who uses that kind of phraseology has gone some distance into turning himself into a machine. The appropriate noises are coming out of his larynx but his brain is not involved.... If the speech he is making is one that he is accustomed to make over and over again, he may be almost unconscious of what he is saying as one is when one utters the responses in church. And this reduced state of consciousness, if not indispensable, is at any rate favorable to political conformity.
— George Orwell, *Politics and the English Language*, 1946

I have made equity and diversity cornerstones of my presidency. Furthermore throughout my adult life I have put a great deal of personal energy into issues of diversity... We must be resolved that the new faculty we recruit will reflect the students and the society.... The watchword for such

recruitment must be excellence.... Exceptional people will be drawn to our enterprise precisely because they will feel at home in an academic community that celebrates diversity.... Department heads will come to understand, as most do now, that one of the critical criteria used to assess them will be their success in attracting diverse faculty to their departments. During departmental reviews, reviewers, often from outside the university, are asked to evaluate and comment on a number of issues, one of which is: "the extent and effectiveness of measures to recruit and retain students and faculty from demographic groups underrepresented in the units and programs.".... We will need to be vigilant and unrelenting in holding the course. I look forward to engaging your support as we work to transform the University of Toronto in the coming years.
— University President Robert Birgeneau, speech, 2001

The Tyranny of Diversity

Westhues's study of the University of Toronto's actions against Herbert Richardson and his commentary on similar cases of academic mobbing raise serious questions about the real nature of academic freedom in the contemporary university. This contribution is intended to examine other trends which supplant merit as the determining factor in academic appointment and circumscribe the range of acceptable views on some of the hot-button issues of the day. I have selected the University of Toronto as my case study. The fact that this is the venue of Richardson's trials and tribulations is fortuitous, the principal reason is that while the apostles of biopolitics are to be found on every campus, at the University of Toronto they are now in charge.

In the last twenty years Canadian universities have become preoccupied with issues of race, gender and diversity even as women have become a rapidly growing majority of the student body and visible minorities have been disproportionately successful in gaining access. Faculty positions are increasingly filled by those who present the requisite biological attributes, irrespective of merit. The claim that white males have secured an unfair advantage in recruitment may rest on poor science but it has provided a veneer of legitimacy to social engineers seeking to privilege some groups over others. The consequence is that while equity programs and the flotilla of diverscrats, anti-harassment officers and affirmative action specialists have become more and more pervasive, equity, in the sense of treating candidates according to universal norms, has been under sustained attack. Diversity of thought is scarcely mentioned; on the questions of equity and diversity it is actively discouraged.

The consequences extend beyond the decline in the quality of faculty, to the university curricula and the integrity of the institution itself. Preferential policies and the accompanying emphasis on multiculturalism and diversity necessitate a continuing monologue which reiterates and endorses at the highest level the fraudulent claims of preferential hirers. In the ruling ontology diversity is not a question of vigorous intellectual debate between competing perspectives but lies within the biological destinies and sexual preferences of faculty members and students. The emphasis on the enduring claims of race and gender constitutes a fundamental reversal of the liberal paradigm of the 1960s, which heralded a society in which individuals were to be judged on the basis of individual characteristics not group membership.

It might be thought that the call to arms by the University of Toronto's president, promising to "transform" the university in the name of diversity, reflected widespread discrimination in recruitment of students and faculty, a campus on which women and visible minorities were marked largely by their absence. In fact, beyond President Birgeneau's fevered rhetoric is a campus on which visible minorities and females are substantially overrepresented, a point to which we will return. The discrimination that exists is directed at those who can make no biologically-based claim to special treatment and to those with the temerity to reject the new orthodoxy.

The contemporary Canadian campus is actively hostile to those who challenge the claims of grievance groups. The rapid spread of women's studies and the growing feminist presence in other disciplines create (to borrow a favorite feminist phrase) a chilly climate for those who challenge the prevailing pieties. The propagation of feminist truths is no longer confined to a few courses, it is now possible to pursue a university degree largely immune from the troubling presence of critical thinkers.[1] Feminists played a key

---

[1] A contemporary advert for a position at the University of Victoria captures the emphasis on ideology over scholarship which characterizes such appointments: "The Women's Studies Department of the University of Victoria invites applications for a tenure track position at the assistant professor level, commencing July 1, 2004. We are particularly interested in

role in articulating the politics of racial grievance in Canada (Loney 1998), now new areas are being defined. The University of Toronto offers a program in Equity Studies, which brings together a range of like-minded ideologues. Program graduates are being groomed to take their place among the legion of myopic zealots who police Canadian society. They will find jobs in human rights commissions, grievance groups funded by various levels of government, municipal, provincial and federal human resource departments as "experts" on equity and diversity and of course in the burgeoning bureaucracies which universities dedicate to such issues (there are no less than 12 equity officials at U of T). U of T's was the first program of its kind, other universities quickly followed. In 2003, even the small Nipissing University, in North Bay, announced a new faculty position in the area. As in women's studies, traditional academic criteria are less important than a shared vision and the biological attributes that are the prerequisite for authenticity and credibility. The assumption that the proper role of the university is to teach students the skills required to understand complex and competing interpretations, to weigh evidence and retain a healthy scepticism in the face of those who offer universal panaceas, is in question. It is challenged by a feminist epistemology that believes the professorial mission is to reveal truth.

Faculty who might be inclined to challenge the claims of biopolitics face not simply collegial criticism or student rebuff but institutional sanction. A professor who questions the high level of criminal activity by Canadians and immigrants of Jamaican or Somali origin risks report to a battery of university officers able to bring the offender to account. Far better to follow the approach of Frances

---

individuals who can contribute to furthering an integrative *feminist analysis*. The successful candidate will have a Ph.D. or equivalent, a record of *feminist scholarship*, a demonstrable commitment to teaching in an interdisciplinary, undergraduate Women's Studies program, ability to draw on experiential knowledge in research and teaching, and willingness to help in the development of a M.A. program .... The department is strongly committed to both excellence and equity and to increasing the diversity of approaches and perspectives in teaching and research. Thus, *diversity and equity issues will be a factor in the selection process.* Preference will be given to a specialization in lesbian/queer studies and sexualities. However those with specializations in women's health and embodiment, feminist political economy, globalization or some combination thereof as applied to any field of inquiry are also invited to apply." (AUCC website, August 2003, emphasis added)

Henry, the doyenne of Canada's race-relations academics, and transform the issue of ethnic crime into one of racist policing and press coverage (Loney 1999, Henry and Tator 2002). A vigorous debate about such hot-button issues as immigration, gender differences or Islamic extremism places faculty at risk.

In the Summer of 2003, Andrew Andersen, an untenured political science professor at the University of Victoria, was accused by two students of being 'racist'. According to an e-mail he sent students he was accused of "spreading hatred towards minorities in general and Muslims in particular." Andersen claimed his contract was not renewed, the university reported that the review of the complaints by the Dean of Social Sciences would be completed in the Fall. Some students quickly moved to support Andersen while others, according to the student newspaper, urged the need to respect "the complaints of students who feel excluded or uncomfortable in the classroom." David Ball, who, according to the newspaper, had helped establish the wonderfully Orwellian, Political Science Open Dialogue Committee "as a safe space for students with concerns," was in no doubt of the importance of the complaints: "what we're saying is that this is an extremely serious issue – this is not something to be thrown around with uninformed petitions and campaigns on behalf of the professor" (*Martlet*, July 17, 03). This touching concern for any hurt feelings, real or otherwise, begs the question of how higher education can proceed in such a sensitive environment. Are professors to be lyrical about the virtues of capitalism lest they offend the progeny of the bourgeoisie? How then will they address the sensitivities of those whose parents are horny-handed union militants? In the meantime the University of Victoria's pusillanimous response sends a clear message to other professors reckless enough to court controversy. (For other case examples see Fekete 1994, Loney 1998).

Increasingly race and gender extremists have sought to silence their critics through the range of sanctions available to university administrators and their battery of officials with equity, anti-harassment, diversity and status of women functions. The hounding of Ken Westhues by radical feminists and administrators at Waterloo University was paradigmatic of the new policing of Canadian universities. The alleged offences may be vague but attach to them any hint of racial or gender insensitivity or an absence of sufficient commitment to the lifestyles of sexual minorities and conviction is all but guaranteed – if not finally in some official forum certainly in the powerful forum of popular opinion.

Racial and gender activists in Canada can also turn to sympathetic human rights commissions whose members and staff share a common messianic vision when it comes to eradicating incorrect thought or behavior. In this environment, not surprisingly, some find charges of racism and sexism a potent weapon with which to seek more personal ends.

In 1994, UBC psychology professor Don Dutton invited Fariba Mahmoodi, a mature student to his apartment to discuss research. She subsequently wrote to Dutton threatening to destroy his career if he did not get her into the graduate program. Dutton took the letter to the university's Equity Office, which did nothing. Subsequently Mahmoodi filed a complaint with the same office that Dutton had tried to seduce her at the apartment. The Office commenced an investigation which culminated six years later when the B.C. Human Rights Tribunal found Dutton guilty of "creating a sexualized environment" at his apartment, though it found no evidence that he had physically seduced her.

On top of six figure legal fees and six years of investigation the tribunal fined Dutton $13,000. Evidence from another professor, James Steiger, that Mahmoodi had, in the presence of witnesses, threatened to charge him with racial discrimination if he failed to pass her was ruled "inadmissible" since its probative value would not outweigh its potential damage to the complainant. Reviewing the case, Steiger concludes that such tribunals constitute a powerful force for constraint: "Say the wrong thing, be charged with a Human Rights violation, and you may end up spending several years defending yourself under indeterminate conditions.... The power of such a system to repress freedom of speech is disturbing, and similarities to certain totalitarian societies are frightening" (Steiger 2000: p. 7).

Faculty need not only to avoid giving offence, those with wider ambitions must enthusiastically endorse the claims of racial and gender grievance. Male faculty seeking advancement cannot fail to be aware of how much their careers depend on echoing the prevailing Zeitgeist.

Riding the Wave: Making a Career in the Modern University

While Dean of Science at MIT, Robert Birgeneau responded to allegations that MIT discriminated against women scientists by setting up a committee to investigate the issue. Nancy Hopkins, who had first raised the issue of gender discrimination in 1994, after failing to secure the additional laboratory space she had requested, chaired the committee. Six of the nine members were senior women scientists who would gain from any recommendations for improved pay, research grants, and laboratory and office space. The resulting report lacked hard data but was replete with feminist imagery including "a common finding for most senior women faculty was that the women were 'invisible'." Tenured women faculty reported feeling "marginalized and excluded from a significant role in their department" (Lopez 2000). Birgeneau quickly moved to address the report's concerns endorsing its findings: "It's data-driven and that's a very MIT thing" (*Massachusetts News*, April 2000). Hopkins received an invitation from the Clintons to visit the White House, an endowed chair, substantial increases in pay and research funding, and more laboratory space.

Others failed to share Birgeneau's enthusiasm. A subsequent report for the Independent Women's Forum by Patricia Hausman and James Steiger found: "compelling differences in productivity, influence and grant funding between the more senior males and females" in their study, which they argued could account for any salary differences, though the MIT report had offered no data on such differences (*Massachusetts News* Feb. 6, 2001). Another reviewer, Judith Kleinfeld, professor of psychology at the University of Alaska, dismissed MIT's report as "junk science." MIT refused to release any data claiming, says Kleinfeld, "that such data as sex differences in laboratory space is confidential" (Kleinfeld 2000). Kleinfeld concluded that the report contained no hard evidence but was "a political manifesto masquerading as science, an ideological tract draped in the robes of MIT's international prestige."

The report may have lacked substance, but Birgeneau's role in the farrago garnered much praise. Announcing his appointment as its next president, the University of Toronto noted that Birgeneau had not only established the committee to analyze the status of women in the in science: "Well before the completion of the final report Birgeneau facilitated collaboration between faculty and administration to begin redressing inequities." Birgeneau, U of T proclaimed, was now "a focus for advice and counsel throughout North America" (Bloch-Nevitte 2000). Professor Hopkins, not surprisingly, was very enthusiastic, telling the *University of Toronto Magazine*: "he's creative, a bit bold, definitely not dull. He's also brilliant" (Lawler 2000).

Critic Daphne Patai captured the trajectory succinctly: "Birgeneau's rapid move from MIT to Toronto says it all: careers are to be made – or unmade – over the political orthodoxies of the moment" (Lopez 2000).

So eager was the university to appoint Birgeneau that it offered him a salary 50% higher than his predecessor Robert Pritchard. Birgeneau also secured a salaried position for his wife, who would be assisting him with entertaining and other social functions. Birgeneau was in no doubt that his mission at Toronto was to continue to endorse the causes that had already served him so well. Birgeneau also proved a quick study, recognising that the issues of supposed gender inequity which had long preoccupied Canadian universities were increasingly taking second place to the demands of those who apprehended a pandemic of racism in hiring, student enrolment and the curricula.

Affirmative action programs in the United States, whatever their shortcomings, have been driven by the undeniable legacy of slavery and the continuing disproportionate impoverishment of black Americans. Slavery was marginal to Canada's development and largely ended by the beginning of the 19th century. Canada certainly had no lack of bigots in the early years of the 20th century, whether directing themselves to the exclusion of Chinese immigrants or later to the shameful internment of Japanese Canadians during the Second World War. Nonetheless by the 1980s, Canadian-born visible minorities were at least as successful as other Canadians. Earnings comparisons, taking into account such factors as age, education and area of residence demonstrate no race-based earnings penalty (Boyd 1992, Hum and Simpson 1999). In contrast to the United States the beneficiaries of preferential policies (including black Canadians) are overwhelmingly free migrants and their descendants, not those who can trace their lineage back to slavery. Visible minority Canadians are disproportionately successful in accessing educational resources. None of this deterred Birgeneau from making race and preferential hiring programs the central focus of his presidency.

According to the *Toronto Star,* Birgeneau advised university administrators in January, six months before he would take office, that "if they did not share his views on diversity they may as well step down" (*Toronto Star,* Jan. 9, 2000). A month later, commenting on a report by the Ontario Human Rights Commission (OHRC) into complaints of racial discrimination in the physics department (see below) Birgeneau returned to the theme. Universities, he claimed, had not been "sufficiently aggressive" in diversifying their faculties; too many were drawn from the ranks of white males. He told the *Toronto Star* that in meetings with administrators he had made his position clear: "diversity is one of the high priorities that I expected everybody in the leadership position at the university to be committed to. If they weren't they should find something else to do" (*Toronto Star* Feb. 8, 2000). Birgeneau refused any specific comment on the merits of the case brought against the physics department but his comments certainly offered an endorsement to racial activists who had denounced the university's hiring policies. In fact, as we will see, the data provide no support for Birgeneau's meretricious philosophising but as the MIT experience suggests, hard data are not an essential prerequisite for action.

Subsequently, as controversy over his remarks gathered, Birgeneau, not for the last time, claimed he had been misquoted: "I do not want in my administration people who discriminate, that is people who consistently favor one sociological sub-group over others" (*National Post* Feb. 26, 2000). This was a curious clarification since what President Birgeneau intended, in common with other preferential hirers, is precisely the pursuit of such discrimination in favor of women and visible minorities and other favored groups. Birgeneau's frequent references to diversity and his endorsement of the claim that university faculty were insufficiently diverse, coupled with his warning to department heads that their careers depended on compliance, leave no room for doubt.

Mythologizing the Diversity Case at U of T

Birgeneau's much publicised commitment to diversity needs to be set in the context of the actual demographic make-up of the U of T. Birgeneau's comments suggest a university which has failed to respond to Canada's rapidly changing ethnic composition – a campus where students and faculty from minority groups face unfair treatment, where white males rule supreme. If this were true, the comments would have justification. If not, it is reasonable to ask why Birgeneau is engaging in inflammatory demagoguery.

The university's data indicates that some one in four of recent faculty hires is a visible minority and women applicants are more likely to succeed than men. If lack of representation is prima facie evidence of discrimination then the group with the obvious case for redress is white males. In contrast, Birgeneau believes "achieving

greater diversity in faculty hiring will be one of our major challenges"
(Birgeneau 2002). U of T's president is more satisfied with the
'diversity' of the student body, where "about 50% identify themselves
in categories generally described as visible minorities." Such self-
identification exercises consistently understate the real number, a
point acknowledged by the University of Toronto in a review of the
adequacy of its own data on faculty self-identification (University of
Toronto 2000: Executive Summary).

Fifty eight per cent of students in U of T's undergraduate program
are women, 56% of the students in graduate programs. In short, at U
of T women are 43% more likely to be admitted to undergraduate
programs and 36% more likely to be admitted to graduate programs
than men. The visible minority population of Metropolitan Toronto
(37%, 2001 census) is far larger than the national figure (13%).
Canada's largest university historically has recruited extensively from
the wider province. 2001 census data indicate that 19% of the
population of Ontario are members of a visible minority. The
university also recruits in smaller numbers in other provinces. There
is no escaping the conclusion that just as males are dramatically
underrepresented, so are white students. Curiously absent from the
university's many well-funded outreach programs is any attempt to
redress these issues. Instead Birgeneau blithely assures his audience
that the university "is, in microcosm, a mirror of the world itself"
(Birgeneau 2002).

U of T's visible minority enrolment is high and, it could be
argued, unrepresentative of the wider Canadian picture. Are visible
minorities marginalised in education? Certainly for those who believe
Canada remains a profoundly racist society with an education system
that is too white and a curriculum that is too Eurocentric that must be
the assumed outcome. The obvious comparison is between visible
minorities born-in Canada and other born-in-Canada groups, where
language competence and educational access will be broadly similar.
1996 census data indicate that 47.5 per cent of Canadian-born visible
minorities, in the 25-34 age group, had university education compared
to only 26.6 per cent of other Canadian-born. Canadian-born visible
minorities also had the lowest level of high school non-completion,
about half that of other born-in-Canada groups (Canadian Race
Relations Foundation 2001: p. 16).

In a statement on diversity published in the student newspaper,
Birgeneau gave voice to the circumlocutions characteristic of the
debate. Eschewing any commitment to affirmative action plans that

involved quotas, Birgeneau (2002) wrote instead of "supports for our departments to become more innovative and broad-based in their faculty searches" and "proactively recruiting potential faculty members from visible minority cohorts." Quotas or not, the university has recruited more visible minority faculty than might have been predicted from their availability. A Performance Indicators for Governance report from the Office of the Vice-President and Provost estimates on the basis of a generous interpretation of availability data that visible minorities should constitute "at least 20%" of new hires. Data from department chairs indicates that for the 1999/2000 and the 2000/2001 years the proportion of visible minority hires was 28% (University of Toronto 2002a: p. 62).

Subsequently Birgeneau, in a speech marking the International Day for the Elimination of Racism, suggested another benchmark: "our university's success will in good part be measured ultimately by how representative our faculty is of our student body and of our country.... We must be resolved that the new faculty will reflect the students and the society that they serve" (Birgeneau 2001). The suggestion that the university faculty should reflect the student body could only mean that at least 50% of the faculty should be visible minorities. How this could reflect the wider society is unclear. University self-report data underestimate representation but 1996 census data indicate that 12% of Canadian university faculty were members of a visible minority (University of Toronto 2002a: p. 62), slightly exceeding their wider demographic representation (11% in 1996). Birgeneau's benchmark is not (perish the thought) a quota, but who could doubt that efforts must be directed to reaching the "target." Indeed, perhaps recognising the difficulty of meeting such an ambitious target from a purely domestic source, Birgeneau urged the use of "opportunity appointments. This will allow us to bring to the University of Toronto significant numbers of world class researchers and educators from groups that are currently underrepresented" (Birgeneau 2001). Young, white, Canadian males graduating with a Ph.D. are to take second place to those with no ties to Canada whose biological attributes fit Birgeneau's racial vision.

Birgeneau's pronouncements on diversity in hiring are the more notable for his failure to inform himself of the relevant demographic data. Those who are obsessed with representing diversity should be expected to familiarise themselves with the population they seek to represent. Reporting the university's 'successes' in racial hiring Birgeneau boasted: "Recent data reveal that of our new hires in the past three years, close to 50% were visible minorities in Applied Sciences and Engineering, 21% in Arts and Science and 19% in Medicine.... This compares to a visible minority population of *approximately 20 percent nation-wide*" (Birgeneau 2001, emphasis added). Birgeneau's figure is out by more than 50%. 2001 census data indicate that 13% of Canadians are members of a visible minority.

Women, as noted, have also fared unusually well at U of T. An analysis of new hires from October 2000 to September 2001 breaks recruitment down into five groups, according to the proportion of women recently graduating with PhDs. If biological diversity is indeed an important institutional goal it might be expected to affect not only instances where women or visible minorities are perceived to be underrepresented but also areas which are, for example, increasingly female-dominated. In the first group where women are a majority (which includes education, nursing, psychology and social work) there were 117 male applicants and 197 female applicants. 36 females and 11 males were interviewed, 14 females and two males were appointed, for a female success rate of 7% and a male 'success' rate of 2%. In the most 'male-dominated' category (which includes computer science, physics and engineering) there were 969 male applicants and 106 female applicants. 23 women and 138 men were interviewed, three females and 23 males were hired, for a female success rate of 3% and a male success rate of 2% (University of Toronto 2002b, table 13). In the male-dominated group women enjoyed an advantage; in the female-dominated group the male disadvantage is striking.

The list of those who might expect to find favor in Birgeneau's diverse utopia is not limited to women, visible minorities, aboriginals and the disabled. In his speech advocating a faculty representative of the student body Birgeneau urged those making hiring decisions to also think about "members of the LGBTQ community." At Canada's largest university the sexual preferences of academic candidates are now to be considered in making appointments.[2]

---

[2]In spite of his best efforts Birgeneau still seems some way behind the ball. Neil Worboys, president of the B.C. Teachers Federation, defending the suspension of a teacher who had, outside the classroom, had the temerity to criticise gay life styles, responded: "His views are antithetical to our position about the inclusion of gays, lesbians, transgendered and two spirited peoples in our society" (Wente 2003) It seems the claims of "two-spirited people" (native gays etc.) still await recognition at U of T.

Birgeneau may have told the *National Post* that he didn't want people in his administration consistently favoring one group over others, but white male applicants, with more conventional sexual identities, might reasonably conclude that a wide variety of groups took preference over them.

The Disadvantage Myth

Nationally there is a wide range of evidence to attest to the advantage of women in new hires at Canadian Universities. A survey in British Columbia of Simon Fraser University and the University of British Columbia reported that women were 29% of applicants and 41% of hires. Looking at her findings and a range of other evidence, Doreen Kimura, emeritus professor of psychology at Simon Fraser University, concluded: "It is clear that women are not being discriminated against in hiring in any Canadian university.... This holds true for Science disciplines in both biological and physical sciences, women were over-hired" (Kimura 2002). Seligman, reviewing eight years of data at the University of Western Ontario, found the "results in each of the years remarkably consistent. Women had almost twice the chance of being hired as did men" (Seligman 2001).[3]

The argument that women and visible minorities faced discrimination in university recruitment and are thus victims of historic disadvantage and entitled to preferential treatment rests on a flawed understanding of labor market dynamics. Nonetheless it is essential to the legitimacy of the preferential hiring case. The Canadian Charter of Rights and Freedoms is viewed as one of the great legacies (if not the principal legacy) of Pierre Trudeau's Liberal governments. Section 15, "Equality Rights", explicitly permits programs which seek "amelioration of conditions of disadvantaged individuals." The accompanying explanation explicitly endorses affirmative action for women and visible minorities and others who "may have suffered as a result of past discrimination" (Canada 1982). In practice it is not necessary to offer any empirical proof of such past disadvantage; it is simply assumed, even where those benefiting from preferential policies are in fact recent immigrants. Their putative claim to redress for historic disadvantage is entirely race-based.

---

[3]For a fuller discussion on women in Canadian universities see Loney 1998, pp. 288-325.

In Canada, in the post-war period, faculty recruitment largely mirrored the composition of the pool of Ph.D. graduates. This contained relatively few women or visible minorities. Changing social mores and the growing economic pressures on single-income families resulted in a significant increase in female labor-force participation and a rapid increase in the number of women pursuing post secondary education. Changes in Canada's immigration policies encouraged immigration from Asia, Africa and the Caribbean, resulting in a rapid and continuing increase in the numbers of those officially defined as "visible minorities." These changes did not immediately translate into proportionate increases in employment in university faculties for either group. The reasons are obvious, though they escaped the attention of preferential hiring advocates, for whom the "underrepresentation" of women and the alleged underrepresentation of visible minorities was prima facie evidence of "systemic discrimination." Hiring on merit will, all things being equal, result in proportionate representation of the qualified pool in *new* hires but it will not affect the make-up of the workforce already in place. Rapid increases of visible minority and female representation in the pool will only slowly translate into similar representation in the larger workforce unless there is rapid staff turnover.

Systemic discrimination is widely alleged but it remains ill defined.[4] The proof of systemic discrimination lies not in the identification of any single act of discrimination. It is rather a conclusion drawn from any outcome which fails to reflect the preferential hirers' belief that, absent discrimination, women, men and diverse ethnic groups will all be proportionately represented in each occupation at each level. It is, in short, tautological. Evidence that women or visible minorities are not present in any occupation, in the same numbers as in the wider population, is sufficient. From this perspective the very small number of women working in underground mining operations stems not from career preferences, which largely exclude a job which is physically demanding, dangerous, dependent on shift work, and frequently undertaken at remote locations, but systemic discrimination.

---

[4]Canada's Society for Academic Freedom and Scholarship was sufficiently mystified by the notion of systemic discrimination that it asked its members for help posing the question: "What is the meaning of 'systemic discrimination' and how does it apply, or not apply to universities in Canada?" (*SAFS Newsletter*, no. 25, April 2000, p. 3)

The real reason for the predominance of white males in Canadian university faculties is historical: at the time when many current incumbents and most senior academics were recruited, white males were the overwhelming proportion of applicants. In 1972-74, for example women comprised only 11% of the qualified pool from which universities could recruit (Irvine 1996: p. 260). In contrast to feminist claims, women were nonetheless disproportionately successful, comprising 19.6% of the appointments in that period (*ibid.*). Women have also been much more successful than men in securing appointment without a Ph.D. Twenty eight per cent of full-time female faculty lack a Ph.D., 16% of males. Among part-time faculty 50% of males have a Ph.D. but only 29% of females (Statistics Canada 2001).

As late as 1980, when the major wave of postsecondary expansion and faculty recruitment had already passed, only four per cent of Canadians were classified as visible minorities, a figure that tripled in the next 20 years. There is no evidence that visible minorities faced barriers to appointment; to the contrary, they have fared better than a careful analysis of availability might have suggested. Employment data are generally accurate in capturing the gender of employees but consistently understate the numbers of other so-called designated groups. Nonetheless, data from a number of universities in 1990-1991 show a range from 6% to 12% in appointments. In a case in which the author was involved at Ottawa's Carleton University, the university appointed visible minority women without Ph.D.s or scholarly publication in preference to white males with both. University data suggested that visible minorities, far from experiencing discrimination, had been disproportionately successful in securing appointment to the university faculty. The Ontario Human Rights Commission made no attempt to assess such data but upheld the discriminatory recruitment as a measure to achieve "equality of opportunity" (Loney 1998: pp. 269-274).

Dances with Diversity

Birgeneau's attempts to clarify his views on affirmative action and diversity failed to end the controversy. Some found his comparison in his *National Post* interview of the situation of women to that of Jews at the end of the Second World War far-fetched. Jewish academics and students had certainly faced discrimination. Montreal's McGill University, for example, required higher entry marks for Jewish students, but all that was demanded was treatment based on merit. If Birgeneau simply intended to hire on merit why all the fuss?

Was Birgeneau really suggesting that those who disagreed with his views on affirmative action favor discrimination? One professor emeritus certainly thought so: "That is you're a racist or a sexist or whatever. To say that openly would be too patently absurd even libelous so it's turned into an insinuation or a smear. The universities – and they're not alone – are full of people so petrified by that smear that, sheep-like, they fall silently into line behind affirmative action policies" (Zakuta 2000).

The Society for Academic Freedom and Scholarship (SAFS), a persistent critic of non-merit based hiring, suggested that while there are many legitimate views on diversity and equity, Birgeneau's insistence on the superiority of his own was a violation of academic freedom (SAFS 2000).

U of T psychologist John Furedy, a former SAFS president, subsequently rebutted Birgeneau's frequent attempts to portray diversity as synonymous with excellence, arguing that the diversity at issue was simply a manifestation of "identity politics" and not any commitment to intellectual diversity. Furedy pointed out that the all-male economics department at the University of Chicago "with its seven Nobel laureates" might seem an example of excellence (Furedy 2002).

One student wondered whether Birgeneau himself might need to be sacrificed on the altar of diversity. Responding to Birgeneau's comment to a *Varsity* reporter that "if U of T had more visible minorities on its faculty, it would produce greater research" she asked: "Does this mean that U of T would be better off if it fired Dr. Birgeneau, a white man as far as I can tell, and replaced him with someone a bit darker?" (Margolis 2000)

Racial Politics and U of T's Physics Department

The controversy over Birgeneau's views was re-ignited soon after his arrival with the announcement of a settlement between the university and disgruntled physicist Kin-Yip Chun. Dr. Chun, aided by student and faculty sympathisers, had for years been alleging racist treatment at the hands of his colleagues, specifically his failure to secure a faculty (rather than research) position. Chun's claims had been examined by three different investigations. The first in 1994, conducted for the University of Toronto in 1994 by Dr. Cecil Yip, the then Dean of Medicine, found evidence of irregularities in Chun's appointment as a research associate and the recruitment process for new faculty, but no evidence that race was an issue. The second, by the Canadian Association of University Teachers (CAUT), lacked access to many of the relevant documents and the co-operation of some of the key figures. Dr. Chun, whose lawyer Raj Anand was a former head of the Ontario Human Rights Commission, had already filed a complaint with the OHRC, and the Physics Department staff refused to meet with CAUT investigators. The CAUT found no evidence of direct discrimination but *prima facie* evidence of so-called systemic discrimination. The third report from the OHRC also identified systemic discrimination.

The strongest piece of evidence adduced in both reports is what the OHRC calls the computer-virus incident. This occurred in 1991, when a member of the department found that his computer had been accessed without authorisation and infected with a virus which he believed might have been introduced by a visiting academic from China. There is some dispute as to whether the virus really emanated from China but the posted warning included no ethnic opprobrium, it simply referred to the presumed geographic origin. The claim might in other circumstances have been that the virus came from Russia, Italy or the UK. Nonetheless if there is a smoking gun buried in these reports this is presumably it, though the OHRC report that the geophysicist, whose warning notice triggered the incident, strongly protested the accusation that he harbored any racial prejudice.

The finding of systemic racism appeared to rest (inevitably) on the observation that the Physics Department is largely white and male, *prima facie* evidence of the existence of an old boys' network. This, the OHRC claims, "effectively screens out racial minority persons, as well as other minority persons who are unable to tap into this network" (Loney 2000). This certainly captures the mantra of the race industry but is not supported by the evidence offered in the report. In one of the competitions on which the Commission provides detailed information, racial minorities were well represented on the selection committee, and women and visible minorities were represented on the short-list in the same proportion as in the wider applicant field. The successful candidate was reported to be of Albanian ancestry, a group that might be presumed to be included in "other minority persons."

The OHRC took six years to investigate Dr. Chun's allegations, during which time the Physics Department and the University remained under a cloud. The announcement of a settlement with Dr.

Chun was presented as a victory by U of T's new president. Chun received a faculty appointment, $100,000 in compensation, $150,000 in legal fees and $250,000 in research funding. The physicists who had born the brunt of Chun's allegations were less impressed. Dr. Azuma, chair of the department at the time of Chun's first application and chair of the search committee at the time of his third application, is of Japanese descent; his father was sent to a work camp in British Columbia during the Second World War. He told *Globe and Mail* columnist Margaret Wente, "I know what racism is. It's been my life." He also told her, "There has never been in 40 years in my tenure at the University of Toronto a shred of evidence of racism among my colleagues" (Wente 2000). Other physicists expressed concern that Chun had not withdrawn his allegations and was free to play the race card again if things were not to his liking. Wente concluded, not unreasonably, that the university had paid a high price to settle: "It includes the devastation to the morale of dedicated faculty. It includes an implicit invitation to anyone who feels abused to play the racial blackmail card" (*ibid.*).

Chun's supporters felt vindicated by the settlement and used the reports into the affair to support demands for racial quotas in hiring, with 30 per cent of new appointment at U of T reserved for "scholars of color."

Not all Plain Sailing

Birgeneau could have arrived at U of T, taken some time to familiarise himself with the institution's record and confronted its critics with hard evidence. No doubt this would have been unpopular in some quarters though it seems reasonable to assume that many of the university's students and faculty would welcome being portrayed in terms that suggested they were not knuckle-dragging rednecks. Birgeneau chose to do exactly the opposite, seeking to place himself at the forefront of ill-informed demands for institutional change. Not surprisingly this gave added urgency to the demands of those who were endlessly alert to race and gender injury. If U of T's new president had declared diversity his priority it must be because those who criticised the university for its lack of inclusiveness were right.

In November of 2002 the university's governing council agreed to a presentation from Murphy Browne, a representative of Toronto's Organization of Parents of Black Children. Why the council agreed to hear Ms. Browne is unclear; her purpose was to call on the University to join in the attack on the Conservative provincial government's educational policies. It is worth asking if a representative of a less fashionable group would have received a welcome. Consistent with the mau-mauing that frequently accompanies racial politics (Wolfe 1971) Ms. Browne started by noting that she didn't see many people present who looked like her. U of T's president was quick to reassure her, "My black friends tell me that I look like you on the inside, just not on the outside." Having thus assured Ms. Browne that "some of my best friends are ...," he moved to defend the university's record on diversity, noting that "White students too often go to other universities because we are so diverse" (*Globe and Mail*, Nov. 9, 2002). In the ensuing furore Birgeneau sought to retreat, calling his remark a "colossal misstatement."

Birgeneau had, in fact, done no more than give voice to the often unspoken assumptions of preferential hirers and diversity peddlers. The elite groups who are at the forefront of these campaigns distrust the instincts of less sophisticated citizens. If there is no plethora of bigots, or at least the unreflective prejudices of white males, why the need for such an array of special measures and sanctions? Birgeneau called his meeting with the protesting female scientists at MIT "akin to a religious experience" (Kleinfeld 2000); others have not had a similar epiphany and must no doubt remain suspect.

Birgeneau's apologia failed to end the matter. Two weeks later Murphy Browne was a guest at Occupying Space, an event organised by the Association of Part-time Undergraduate Students (APUS). A number of artist/activists had been invited: "the performers expressed their concerns about racism, poverty, discrimination against part-time students, President Birgeneau's recent offensive comments, and other equally pressing and challenging problems" (Mysko 2002). The performers reportedly "expressed justifiable outrage at the unjust treatment of part-time students and minorities on U of T's campus" and planned similar future events (*ibid.*). Clearly the university's fulsome pursuit of diversity and its enthusiastic recruitment of visible minority students had been insufficient.

Conclusion

The legacy of biopolitics at U of T, as elsewhere, is not the elimination of discrimination or any genuine embrace of diversity; it is the entrenchment of the politics of grievance. In an institutional environment which is antithetical to genuine intellectual inquiry, particularly in areas where the results are at variance with the new diversity orthodoxy, ambitious individuals will be quick to play the race and gender card. Hypocrisy is the central value. To openly discriminate against individuals because of their group membership is monstrous; to do so under the banner of progress and equity is redolent of the claims of the totalitarian regimes so admirably satirised by Orwell.

Bibliography

Birgeneau, R., 2001. "Equity and Diversity at the University of Toronto," 21 March.

Birgeneau, R. 2002. "Strength inDiversity," U of T *Varsity*, 12 Nov.

Bloch-Nevitte, S., 2000. "Robert Birgeneau begins term as U of T's 14th president," news@uoft, July 4.

Boyd, M., 1992. "Gender, Visible Minority and Immigrant Earnings Inequality: Reassessing an Employment Equity Premise." In Satzewich, V. ed., *Deconstructing a Nation: Immigration, Multiculturalism and Racism in 1990s Canada*. Halifax: Fernwood.

Canada, 1982. *Charter of Rights and Freedoms: a Guide for Canadians*. Ottawa: Supply and Services.

Canadian Race Relations Foundation, 2001. *Unequal Access*. Toronto.

Fekete, J. 1994. *Moral Panic: Biopolitics Rising*. Toronto: Robert Davies.

Furedy, J., 2002. Letter, *University of Toronto Bulletin*, May 6.

Henry. F., and C. Tator, 2002. *Discourses of Domination: Racial Bias in the Canadian English-Language Press*. Toronto: University of Toronto Press.

Hum, D., and W. Simpson, 1999. "Wage Opportunities for Visible Minorities in Canada," *Canadian Public Policy* 25.

Irvine, A., 1996. "Jack and Jill and Employment Equity," *Dialogue* 35.

Kimura, D., 2002. "Preferential Hiring of Women," *Newsletter*, Society for Academic Freedom and Scholarship, April.

Kleinfeld. J., 2000. "MIT Tarnishes its Reputation with Gender 'Junk Science,'" *Massachussets News*, April.

Lawler, A., 2000. "A Class Reunion," *University of Toronto Magazine*, autumn.

Loney, M., 1998. *The Pursuit of Division: Race, Gender and Preferential Hiring in Canada*. Kingston: McGill-Queen's.

Loney, M., 1999. "Reporting on the colour of crime," *National Post*, 29 Sept.

Loney, M., 2000. "Desperately seeking racists," *National Post*, 9 Feb.

Lopez, K. J., 2000. "Glass Ceilings and Foggy Science," *Heterodoxy*, February - March.

Margolis, S. F., 2000. "Is Diversity All That Great?" Letter, U of T *Varsity*, 2 Oct.

Mysko, B., 2002. "Occupying Space: Finding our voices through the Arts," *The Medium Online*, Vol 29, Issue 14.

Orwell, G., 1975. *Collected Essays.* London: Secker and Warburg.

SAFS, 2000. "Press Release Re President Designate University of Toronto," *Newsletter*, Society for Academic Freedom and Scholarship, April.

Seligman, C., 2001. *Summary of Recruitment Activity for All Full-time Faculty at the University of Western Ontario by Sex and Year.* London: University of Western Ontario, April 2001.

Steiger, J., 2000. "Out of balance: BC Human Rights Tribunal," *Newsletter*, Society for Academic Freedom and Scholarship, April.

Statistics Canada, 2001. Part-time University faculty, data provided by T. Omiecinski and M. Wendt, personal communication.

University of Toronto, 2000. *Employment Equity Report 1998-1999.*

University of Toronto, 2002a. *Performance Indicators for Governance.* Office of the Vice-President and Provost.

University of Toronto, 2002b. *Employment Equity Report 2000-2001.*

Wente, M., 2000. "Black day for white faculty," *Globe and Mail*, Sept. 14.

Wente, M., 2003. "Is this man fit to teach?" *Globe and Mail*, Aug. 7.

Wolfe, T., 1971. *Radical Chic and Mau-mauing the Flak Catchers.* New York: Bantam Books.

Zakuta, L., 2000. "Imposed diversity: Antithesis of a University," *Newsletter*, Society for Academic Freedom and Scholarship, April.

Chapter Twelve

Forget about Academic Fraud, Were You Sexually Harassed?

Irving Hexham

Introduction

Although a large and growing body of literature documents and discusses the implications of academic fraud by students,[1] fraud by established faculty members has received little or no attention.[2] The first part of this paper explores the question why academic administrators often seem more than willing to press charges of sexual harassment against distinguished faculty members while doing everything in their power to avoid taking action in cases of serious academic fraud. The second, concluding part makes some practical suggestions for improving the situation in Canadian universities.

---

[1]Cf. Don McCabe, "Cheating in Academic Institutions: a Decade of Research," *Ethics & Behavior* (2001) 11, No. 3, 219-232 (with L.K. Trevino & K.D. Butterfield).

[2]My own impression of the situation was confirmed in personal correspondence with Don McCabe, Director of the Center for Academic Integrity at Duke University (5/7/2002).

Beware of Administrators Offering Help[3]

Over a decade ago a friend of mine, I will call her Professor Kingston, from an Eastern Canadian University, decided to organize an international academic conference on a topic of public concern. To finance the conference she needed to obtain a Canadian Government Social Sciences and Humanities Research Council Conference Grant (SSHRC). The author of several important books, she wrote the grant application incorporating into it some of the findings of her recent research. Then, according to her university's regulations she needed to find an academic unit willing to host the conference.

At first she thought of hosting the conference through her own department but before the final preparations were made the head of a larger unit approached her suggesting that his unit was more suitable as the host for the type of interdisciplinary conference she had in mind. Excited that a well-respected scholar and head of a major academic unit, whom I will call Professor Snatch, wanted to support her work, she agreed. As a result he became the university official responsible for countersigning her grant application.

When she took the application to Professor Snatch, he surprised her by saying that he would take a few days to read it and would then forward it to the university's research services duly signed. This arrangement, he suggested, would save her time because one of his secretaries would duplicate the signed grant without her having to do any more work. When she said that she preferred to do this work herself he insisted that this was normal procedure and that she need worry herself no longer.

Building a Reputation on the Backs of Others

A few days later Professor Snatch's secretary, Ms. Faithful, called Professor Kingston to say that she had discovered a discrepancy in the budget. Therefore, she suggested that Professor Kingston go into the office to sort out the problem. Minutes later another telephone call informed Professor Kingston that there had been a bomb threat and that the office block in which the unit was situated was to be evacuated. Therefore, Ms. Faithful. said she would meet Professor Kingston at a local coffee bar.

---

[3]The following account, which is based on the experience of a friend of mine, is true. The details have been changed to protect privacy.

When the two met, Ms. Faithful presented Professor Kingston with a print copy of the grant folded over to the budget page. Professor Kingston quickly resolved the problem; then, wanting to take a last look at her handiwork, she turned to the front page. To her horror she discovered that she was no longer the author of the grant. Instead someone had replaced the first page with another that made Professor Snatch both the author of the grant and the university official that gave approval to the project.

Thinking that this must be some sort of secretarial mistake, Professor Kingston immediately pointed out the problem to Ms. Faithful, who explained that Professor Snatch had instructed her to make the changes. Ms. Faithful added that this was Professor Snatch's "normal practice" when submitting other people's grant applications for conferences to be hosted by his unit. When Professor Kingston asked, "Why would anyone give him permission to claim the authorship of their own work?" Ms. Faithful replied, "Didn't Professor Snatch ask your permission? I always thought this is what we were supposed to do and that everyone agreed to such an arrangement." When Professor Kingston said, "Nobody ever suggested this to me and I would never agree to such an arrangement," a confused Ms. Faithful ruefully commented, "Come to think of it, I've never discussed this with anyone other than Professor Snatch. I just assumed everyone knew what was going on."

Still thinking that perhaps she had misunderstood something, Professor Kingston's next step was to call Professor Snatch, who was working at his home office. He immediately told her that he had made the changes "to help" her obtain the grant. He insisted it had a much better chance of success if submitted in his name than in hers. This, he said, was because he had an excellent success record for conference grants with SSHRC. When Professor Kingston protested that she, too, had an excellent success record with research grants, and preferred to take her chance with SSHRC by submitting the application under her name, Professor Snatch suggested that they meet for lunch to discuss the issue.

A couple of days later the agreed meeting took place. Instead of making any concessions, Professor Snatch simply reiterated his claim that he had an excellent success record and that the grant was far more likely to succeed under his name than under hers. When Professor Kingston refused to be convinced and insisted that Professor Snatch restore the original first page, he became positively abusive and suggested that if she wanted to receive any further

SSHRC awards she ought to agree to his terms. Professor Kingston could hardly believe what she was hearing and left the meeting in a state of shock.

"Were you Sexually Harassed?"

Her next move as to arrange a meeting with the vice-president academic to complain about what she believed was serious academic fraud on the part of Professor Snatch. At that meeting the VP academic's one concern was whether she had been sexually harassed. When she said, "No, he is harassing me academically not sexually," the VP immediately lost interest in the case and told her to reach her own agreement with Professor Snatch.

Faced with an impasse, Professor Kingston informed the VP academic that she had decided to inform SSHRC about the whole affair. This suggestion brought an immediate response: the VP academic suddenly found a way to allow Professor Kingston to go ahead with her conference through another academic unit. At the same time she was told not to contact SSHRC because this would do "great harm" to the reputation of the university. Professor Snatch, she was told, would now be disciplined.

Believing that the VP academic had realized the true situation, Professor Kingston agreed to the new arrangement only to find that although a new unit took over the conference, Professor Snatch was allowed to continue to pressure her to work with him. At the same time Professor Kingston and her husband began receiving anonymous phone calls, where someone laughed into the phone but said nothing, at all hours of the day and night. When this was reported to the police, she was told that they came from public telephone booths in the neighborhood of the university but that the police were unable to locate the caller. To this day Professor Kingston believes that Professor Snatch made the calls. They abruptly ended when it became clear that she would not yield to his pressure. On this matter, however, she has to admit she cannot be certain and that the timing of the calls could have been a strange coincidence.

The Discovery of Plagiarism

Professor Kingston's husband, Professor Wordsmith, worked by coincidence in the same field as Professor Snatch, whom, until the dispute with his wife, he greatly respected and admired. When it became clear that Professor Snatch saw nothing wrong with his behavior, Professor Wordsmith remembered that he had been struck by a strange turn of phrase in one of Professor Snatch's books. Explaining an academic dispute, Professor Snatch had written that one of the protagonists "turned pink inside." The only other person Professor Wordsmith had ever heard use this peculiar expression was his own Ph.D. supervisor, the late Professor Distinguished in England.

Prompted by the treatment of his wife's grant application, Professor Wordsmith looked up the expression once again in Professor Snatch's book. Sure enough there was a footnote at the end of the paragraph to Professor Distinguished. When Professor Wordsmith checked the paragraph in question against the original, he found that almost all of it was a direct quote from Professor Distinguished's book but without the necessary quotation marks. After making this discovery he checked various other passages only to find that almost every paragraph in all of Professor Snatch's various books consisted of slightly changed quotations without the required quotation marks. Clearly, Professor Snatch was a plagiarist. To be absolutely sure, he ordered a copy of Professor Snatch's Ph.D. thesis by interlibrary loan. Upon examination, he found that it, too, was extensively plagiarized.

What is plagiarism?

What Professor Wordsmith saw in Professor Snatch's work was relatively easy to recognize and demonstrate. This was plagiarism that involved the direct appropriation of groups of words, phrases and entire sentences from other people's publications without due acknowledgement and the appropriate use of quotation marks.

Plagiarism, as Professor Wordsmith says, is the deliberate attempt to deceive the reader into thinking that they are reading the original work of an author when in fact that author is simply reproducing the work of another It is the appropriation and representation as one's own the work and words of others. Academic plagiarism occurs when a writer repeatedly uses more than four words from a printed source without the use of quotation marks and a precise reference to the original source in a work presented as the writer's own research and scholarship. Continuous paraphrasing without serious interaction with another person's views by way of argument or the addition of new material and insights is also a form of plagiarism in academic work.

Blatant plagiarism is plagiarism that hits you in the face. It is the type of fraud that can be seen immediately by anyone who cares to check the references used by a scholar against the text they claim to be citing. That is, it is plagiarism that is so obvious that anyone with a minimal degree of intelligence and a passion for learning is bound to spot it. This is what Professor Wordsmith discovered in Professor Snatch's work.

Taking plagiarism seriously

Allegations of plagiarism at Texas A&M University (*The Chronicle of Higher Education*, November 5, 1999, pp. A18-20) highlight the failure of academics and university administrators to address the issue of plagiarism with the seriousness it demands. For example, after reviewing the evidence, Professor Michael Schwartz, a sociologist at the State University of New York, is reported to have said: "You have to be uncomfortable when exact words are used and not put into quotes. But this is not some kind of high crime" (op cit. p. A19). Defending this type of argument, scholars like Professor Schwartz claim that they are "more concerned with the theft of ideas than of actual words" (op. cit).

This is a cop out. Surely Schwartz knows that individual words and ideas often overlap. It is far harder to prove plagiarism in terms of the use of similar words and the theft of ideas than it is to show that someone is using exact phrases from another person's work without quotation marks or appropriate references. It is almost impossible to prove the theft of ideas because they circulate within social communities and even when a communal influence is absent, similar circumstances often lead to the generation of similar ideas. Therefore, to insist on ideas while ignoring actual words simply makes it easy for academic plagiarists to ply their trade. The use of other people's words without quotation marks is far more easily recognized; so, too, is the continuous paraphrasing of someone's work.

To avoid the obvious conclusion that a colleague is a fraud, many academics argue that provided some reference to the original author is made then a writer cannot be accused of plagiarism even if they failed to tell their readers that they were actually quoting, without quotation marks, and not simply citing, another person's work. Legally, this argument does not wash. The inclusion of a footnote or some other form of reference without appropriate quotation marks when the words of another author are being used is no defense against the charge of plagiarism. This was clearly stated by the judge in the case of *Napolitano v. Princeton University Trustees* (Cf. Ralph D. Mawdsley, *Legal Aspects of Plagiarism*, Kansas, National Organization on Legal Problems of Education, 1985).

Academics who defend plagiarism in this way are like the Bank Manager who says that the fact that an employee returned $100,000 to the bank after successfully speculating on the Stock Exchange with the Bank's money is not an embezzler. Neither the police nor courts will accept this type of equivocation. Why should it be different with academic plagiarists?

The Decision to Report Professor Snatch's Fraudulent Work

Faced with continued hostility from Professor Snatch and the threat that his wife would never receive another SSHRC grant, Professor Wordsmith made a formal complaint of academic fraud against Professor Snatch. In doing so he prepared a long dossier of over 50 pages containing numerous examples of plagiarism.

When he submitted his complaint to his dean, the dean was at pains to point out that if the complaint proved unfounded he, Professor Wordsmith, could face civil legal charges as well as disciplinary measures from the university. Therefore, the dean suggested that he consider withdrawing the charge. From Professor Wordsmith's perspective, things seemed too far gone for that to happen and he was sure of his ground. So he went ahead with the charge, thinking that it was the only way to protect himself and his wife from the threats of Professor Snatch.

Administrative Justice

The formal university hearing took almost four months to complete. During this time Professor Wordsmith took the precaution of watching the library copies of key texts to see if anyone on the committee of inquiry actually compared his dossier with the original texts. He also sent copies of his dossier to a small group of academics he trusted, including myself, asking for their candid opinions. In all cases they reported that there seemed to be a clear case against Professor Snatch and that the charges were fully justified.

A week before the inquiry, his dean phoned Professor Wordsmith to say that he had "just learnt" that the head of the committee of inquiry had served on an important SSHRC committee with Professor

Snatch, but that he did not believe this would color the man's judgment. When the inquiry took place, Professor Wordsmith was not asked to appear before it. Nor, so far as he could tell, did anyone on the committee take any of the key texts out of the library to check the claim of plagiarism against the original texts. Further, he learned from a colleague that the day before the inquiry, Professor Snatch spent an entire afternoon discussing some undisclosed issue with the university lawyer.

About six weeks after the close of the inquiry, the dean informed Professor Wordsmith that he had received the committee's report but was undecided what to do about it. When Professor Wordsmith asked what conclusions had been drawn, the dean told him that he was not free to disclose any further information. In fact it was another six months, during which time Professor Wordsmith was very worried in case the committee had ruled against him, before he heard anything further. Then, after his third or fourth request for information, the dean told him that the committee had concluded that he did have a case and that the charges were not malicious. As a result he need not fear legal or disciplinary action based on his complaint.

Nevertheless, the dean said that the committee had decided the examples of plagiarism submitted to it were actually due to carelessness brought on by the overwork of a distinguished scholar. This despite the fact that many of the examples came directly from Professor Snatch's own Ph.D. thesis and included typographical errors copied from the works he plagiarized. Further, the committee diverted attention from the main charge by concentrating on a number of minor technical issues in the complaint that avoided serious discussion of the central issue of academic fraud.

After receiving this information, it was unclear to Professor Wordsmith why his dean had taken so long to inform him about the results of the investigation. Sometime later Professor Wordsmith heard on the university grapevine that the vice-president academic was very angry about Professor Snatch's fraud but unwilling to take public action for fear of alienating granting agencies like SSHRC, which are known to have strict standards about academic honesty. As a result, according to the grapevine, pressure was put on Professor Snatch to move to another university. This he did some months later when he obtained an excellent position in Western Canada that in reality was a form of promotion.

The Consequences: SSHRC Grants

Professors Kingston and Wordsmith, on the other hand, did not receive another SSHRC research grant for almost nine years. Of course, they cannot prove that this was due to Professor Snatch's intervention. What they can show is that they made repeated applications and on several occasions received excellent external reviews, but were always downgraded at the committee level. Further, it was clear to them that although Professor Snatch did not sit on any of these committees, some of his friends did. This is not to suggest that he told anyone not to support them. What they think most likely is that he, or friends of his, simply spread rumors about them and generally downgraded their work.

Beyond the problem with SSHRC, which it must be stressed was not the fault of SSHRC officers who were kept in the dark about this issue, Professor Kingston did not seem to suffer any real problems. Professor Wordsmith's situation was very different. Sometime after the Inquiry was complete and Professor Snatch had left the university, his department head came to see him on university business. A chance remark provoked an outburst of venom in which the head accused him of trying to harm Professor Snatch.

Believing that he was unable to openly discuss the matter due to university rules, Professor Wordsmith arranged a meeting between himself, his dean, and the department head. The outcome was disappointing because the dean refused to say anything of significance and left the situation more or less as it was before the meeting. To be fair to the dean, it needs to be pointed out that he indicated that the reason he was unable to say anything was that he was following instructions from someone else, presumably the vice-president academic or even the university president.

The Consequences: Administrative Harassment

Over the next ten years Professor Wordsmith suffered continual mild but very real harassment. This took the form of unsubstantiated reports of student complaints and various other minor but irritating issues being raised about his marking and other issues. He also learnt from his graduate students that a later department head, who was also a friend of Professor Snatch, invited them into his office where they were quizzed about their relationship with Professor Wordsmith and asked if they had any complaints. Fortunately they did not and were actually annoyed by what they saw as an attempt to recruit them to spy on Professor Wordsmith.

After the failure of this head to solicit complaints from graduate students, Professor Wordsmith found that other of his graduate students were subjected to harassment by some faculty members. He also found that very few students who applied to work with him were ever accepted into the department's program. Although he complained about this situation, neither the dean nor anyone else was prepared to take his complaints seriously.

Faced with clear administrative hostility, Professor Wordsmith began to wonder whether he had overreacted in the case of Professor Snatch. Although the plagiarism was clear, perhaps there was something he didn't know. Perhaps this type of work was far more common and acceptable in Canada and the United States than in Europe. After all, some people defended the plagiarisms of Martin Luther King on the grounds that he was a preacher and preachers tend to borrow from others. Therefore, he began to doubt his own judgments. To check himself and his understanding of scholarship, Professor Wordsmith then began to examine the works of a number of other prominent scholars of the same rank and standing in his field as Professor Snatch. To his relief he discovered that all of them maintained the same standards of scholarship that he considered normal.

After making this discovery, Professor Wordsmith received a manuscript for review from a well-known commercial publisher. When he read it, he immediately saw that it was plagiarized. Therefore, he called the editor who had sent him the manuscript to discuss the situation. The editor's comments surprised him. He said that the press regularly received manuscripts that contained plagiarism and that he estimated that between 10% and 20% of academics were fraudulent. Therefore the press had a strict policy of rejecting such works. Then the editor added that to his dismay he often found that such works were picked up by academic presses and published without any changes to the manuscript.

On the basis of this conversation, Professor Wordsmith carried out some further tests on the works of less prominent people including the head of department who was harassing him. This time he found that, as the editor suggested, between 10% and 15% of the texts he examined showed signs of blatant plagiarism. Later he read Wilfried Decoo's *Crisis on Campus* (2002), further confirming his findings. Because he does not see himself as a whistleblower, Professor

Wordsmith did not report these cases; rather he began to think of practical ways to prevent such abuses in the future.

Therefore at a meeting of his faculty he suggested that they ought to adopt a new policy governing future applicants for academic posts. Among other things, he argued that applicants ought, as is the practice in Europe, provide the university with a certified copy of their degree certificates and submit copies of all their major publications for examination by the appointments committee. This idea was scornfully dismissed by the dean, who responded with the comment that Professor Wordsmith appeared to lack trust in his colleagues.

The dean also said that Professor Wordsmith showed a lamentable lack of collegiality. If someone applied for a job from another Canadian university, it had to be assumed that their referees and graduate committee had thoroughly checked their work. Therefore there was no need for an appointments committee to carry out its own investigation. The fact that such checks are routine in most universities throughout the world because experience shows people cheat was dismissed on the grounds that to appear to question someone's credentials is unacceptable.

When Professor Wordsmith related this event to a colleague in another faculty, the man responded by saying that he had sat on a Ph.D. thesis committee as an external examiner when a case of plagiarism arose. He decided to fail the student but the dean of that particular faculty, supported by the dean of graduate studies, intervened. The professor was removed from the committee, and the thesis was passed.

Is Racism a Factor in Administrative Harassment?

Professor Wordsmith is an immigrant to Canada from Australia, where he obtained all of his degrees. He worked for several years in Australia and the United States before emigrating to Canada. Thinking about his own case and that of his wife made him aware that in every instance where charges of misconduct were pressed by administrators at his own university, they were made against professors who were outsiders. That is, they either obtained their graduate degrees and/or were born outside of Canada. When he asked colleagues at other universities if the same pattern held true in their experience, all of them said that it did. From this observation he believes that his university is in the grip of what nineteenth-century people called racism; as far as he can see, from the admittedly limited amount of evidence available to him, so are most Canadian universities.

In its original nineteenth-century meaning, "racism" was not restricted, as it is today, to questions of skin color. Rather it included all forms of discrimination based on ethnic and national characteristics. Thus conflicts between white South Africans of English and Dutch origins were seen as a "race problem," as were similar tensions between English and French Canadians. Seen in this light, it seems plausible that a racist elite very largely controls academic life in Canadian universities. This elite appears to dislike and discriminate against professors who were born and/or obtained their graduate degrees outside of Canada. Harsh as this judgment may sound, it is the only way he can explain the fact that every accusation of sexual harassment that led to severe punishment involved someone who was either educated and/or born outside of Canada.

What Constitutes "Sexual Harassment"?

To a very large extent, Professor Wordsmith observes, academic administrators decide which cases of sexual harassment they will treat seriously and which they will dismiss as unimportant. This is clearly the case because he know of several instances where Canadian-born professors have flaunted their affairs with female students without any action being taken against them. The difference between these cases and other cases where a professor is disciplined, usually for making some sort of remark that is deemed unacceptable, appears to depend entirely on the attitude of the administrator concerned and not on the seriousness of the complaint.

In at least three cases, he knows female students who complained to the appropriate department heads and deans only to find that they became subjects of derision. Warned by the administrator to whom they confided that taking their case outside the university would involve high legal costs, and ruin any hope that they had of an academic career, in every case the students involved abandoned their complaints and quest for justice.

Professor Wordsmith also observes that when cases of supposed sexual harassment were pursued, there was considerable evidence that other faculty members, department heads, and even deans, actively encouraged student complaints. Further, students who made such complaints received considerable material benefits in terms of research grants and paid teaching assignments. But other students who refused to play ball by not responding to hints that they ought to complain about a particular professor found that they were treated as second-class citizens who received only the very minimum financial support from their departments.

Professor Wordsmith says that in all the cases he has witnessed, complaints were pressed against scholars with outstanding research and publishing records by department heads who were academically weak both in terms of their graduate education and subsequent publications. On the other hand, the victims of the complaints were very active scholars educated at first-class institutions. This leads him to conclude that an element of jealousy is involved in the decision whether to press or dismiss complaints involving charges of sexual harassment against a professor.

University Administrators and Academic Fraud

If university administrators use sexual harassment as a way of enhancing their power, as Professor Wordsmith believes they do, the question immediately arises as to why they avoid making similar use of charges of plagiarism? Indeed, why do they avoid confronting the issue if between 10% and 20% of academics gained their positions on the basis of fraudulently obtained credentials? The answer to these questions seems to be that the discovery of blatant plagiarism in the work of an established faculty member raises serious questions about the entire academic enterprise.

To admit that a long-time faculty member's work contains blatant plagiarism is also to admit that numerous people failed to do their jobs properly in the first place. The fact is that from the time a student enters university until his or her ultimate promotion to the rank of full professor, his or her work is theoretically put under the microscope numerous times. Therefore, admitting that blatant plagiarism exists in such a person's work is to admit that many other scholars have failed in their duty as M.A. and Ph.D. supervisors, members of examining committees for graduate degrees, members of hiring and promotion committees, and department heads and deans.

In most cases it is a relatively simple task to check for blatant plagiarism. All it involves is testing a random sample of a writer's references against the texts they cite. Yet, apparently checking a student's work for plagiarism is far too hard for many supervisors who allow theses that contain blatant plagiarism, obvious to anyone who does a basic check, to be accepted as passable theses. This means these people ought to be held responsible for not doing their jobs. But, of course, no one bothers to reprimand an academic who approves a fraudulent thesis.

Equally important is the fact that before anyone becomes a full professor they must go through what is theoretically a rigorous selection process. The graduating Ph.D. student has to convince a selection committee that they are worth employing. Surely, it is reasonable to assume that before hiring someone a university department assigns at least some of its members to read the work of all interviewees to ensure that it is of a high quality. But, as can be seen from the evidence presented by Professor Wordsmith, this does not happen. Once again, asking professors to guard against academic fraud by tightening up the hiring process is too much for most of them, who are too busy to do their jobs properly. Such people, it seems, select candidates on their apparent collegiality rather than actual achievements.

After the hiring process is over, assistant professors must apply for tenure after three or so years of teaching. At that time all of their work is supposed to be reviewed and critically analyzed. Clearly, this does not happen in many cases because far too many plagiarists are granted tenure. Another series of supposedly rigorous hurdles has to be overcome for promotion to associate and then full professor. At each stage the candidate's work is submitted to the department head, an examining committee and the dean. Nevertheless, for all the rigors of the process few people are ever caught out as frauds. This can only mean that most heads, committee members, and deans are far too trusting and actually fail to thoroughly check a candidate's work.

It also needs to be noted that many academics asked to review manuscripts for publishers or grants for granting agencies clearly read these documents and comment on the arguments presented without checking for plagiarism or other forms of fraud. Therefore the "peer-review" process is actually not working. To be fair, some publishers do catch plagiarisms and reject manuscripts only to find that another publisher or journal picks it up.[4]

All of this leads us to recognize that the prevalence of academic fraud calls into question the entire peer-review system for academic journals and books. When frauds act as reviewers, the system is

---

[4]A senior editor at a major American publishing company told me that his company frequently rejects manuscripts because of plagiarism only to find that they are published without any alteration by other presses.

clearly flawed. Further, the fact that so many blatant frauds get published shows that few reviewers ever check the sources used by colleagues.

If Professor Wordsmith's observations are correct then academic fraud and the misuse of sexual harassment charges is evidence that Canadian universities are in crisis. Therefore it is time to make some practical suggestions that, if implemented, will help reduce the possibility of academic fraud and the misuse of power by administrators.

The central problem seems to be that many university administrators are actually failed teachers and researchers who went into administration because it was the only way they were able to gain promotion to the rank of full professor. Among this group he also believes a significant number are probably academic frauds because by entering administration they are able to protect themselves from possible discovery. As managers, many of these people are as incompetent as they were as university teachers and researchers. Yet because academic administrators are exempt from any external review process they are able to consolidate power and avoid the scrutiny they deserve.

University Administration and the Present Crisis

To appreciate how the present crisis developed, it is clearly necessary to understand the way the administration of Canadian universities has developed since the 1960s. Traditionally, and even today in continental Europe, university administration was divided between the practical day-to-day running of what is essentially a large business enterprise, and academic affairs. The day-to-day management of universities was left to professional managers and administrative staff hired for their skills as managers. Academic affairs, such as decisions about hiring new faculty, promotion through the ranks, course design and curriculum, were left to academics.

Under this arrangement academics normally held full-time teaching and research appointments while administering academic departments and even faculties. At the faculty level a dean was often, but not always, given some course release and was only appointed for a short period of time between one and three years. Presidents and academic vice-presidents were given more course release but even then were expected to maintain some teaching responsibilities and continue as active researchers. Here, too, the period of appointment was relatively short with the expectation that after completing their term of office they would return to a normal teaching department.

In this situation issues of salaries, space allocation, budgeting, etc. were not the responsibility of academics, such as department heads and deans, but rather of the central administration that was staffed by nonacademic professional managers and support staff. Thus there was a clear distinction between academic and day-to-day decision-making.

The late 1940s and 1950s saw rapid population growth leading to demands for the expansion of higher education that began in the mid-1960s and continued well into the 1970s. To meet the demand for new university and college places, graduate schools expanded rapidly with the result that many ill-qualified people were hired by universities in a desperate attempt to meet the demands of an ever increasing student population. After obtaining their doctorates and entering the ranks of the full-time faculty, it came as a shock to many people that they were expected to be both good teachers and with a publication record that proved their research abilities.

The only escape from the pressures of research was to enter academic administration and claim that administrative and teaching duties prevented ongoing research and publishing activities. Once this was conceded by university administrations, the next step was to argue that to expect administrators, such as department heads and deans, to continue working with a full teaching load was too much. Therefore, they were gradually given an increasing amount of release time until today it is normal for a department head to teach only one course per term or, very often, per year, and for deans to do no teaching at all. The success of these maneuvers, which took place over a long period of time, led other faculty to follow suit and create even more administrative positions that released them from the normal expectations of teaching and research. Thus posts like undergraduate advisor, graduate advisor, associate dean, etc. rapidly developed.

Because good teachers and researchers are primarily interested in teaching and research few objected to deadwood faculty moving into administrative positions. At least in such posts they fulfilled some type of role and took some pressure off other faculty. But as the deadwood occupied academic administration, it quickly became clear that the only way they could justify course release and freedom from publishing expectations was by assuming new roles and authority.

Increasingly, from the 1970s on, tasks that were once performed by secretaries and officers of the central administration were transferred to academic administrators. In the process the cost of such tasks escalated because highly paid professors were doing the work of support staff who received a third of their income. At the same time, as academics moved into new areas of administration the salaries of academic administrators began to increase.

Traditionally, department heads were given a small honorarium for their administrative responsibilities. Officially this is still the situation. In fact, department heads are now given large annual increments to compensate for the fact that because of their administrative duties they were unable to compete with other faculty for annual increments based on their teaching and publication record. Since such administrative increments are a permanent addition to a person's salary, the reward for administration is high indeed. As a result many people who ought to be earning salaries under $80,000 in terms of their actual achievements are drawing salaries of around $120,000 as a result of their administrative activities.

Anyone who doubts these claims has only to check the cv's and lists of publications of department heads, deans, vice-presidents and even university presidents. Contrary to the public perception, many people in university administrative positions are actually very poor academics with abysmal research records. Yet increasingly it is these very people who sit on government boards and committees that decide the future of higher education in Canada.

Regenerating Canadian Universities

To regenerate Canada's universities, Professor Wordsmith believes that the government needs to address the issue of university administration by failed academics and replace the present system with good management. To this end he proposes the following reforms:

- The day-to-day running of universities ought to be administered by professional managers and support staff without academic pretensions. Given the fact that full-professors-turned-administrators earn far more than normal managers, this step alone will save provinces a large amount of money, possibly halving the current costs of academic administration. The separation of academic administration from other forms of administration involving the day-to-day running of the university will result in better management, an increase in the number of faculty available for teaching duties, and huge financial savings.

- Academic administration ought to be restricted to academic issues such as decisions about curriculum, research agendas, and so on. To use highly paid academics to decide issues like the allocation of space and even the way rooms are to be decorated is a waste of time and money when the job can be done at much less cost by nonacademic staff.

- No academic under the rank of dean ought to be given release time from teaching except where they have brought in special funding to finance a research and writing project. All other administrative tasks, such as advising students, ought to be regarded as part of a faculty member's normal duties. The implementation of this requirement would immediately see a considerable increase of the number of courses offered by departments as everyone would carry a full teaching load. As a result, in most departments it would be like hiring at least one or more new faculty members.

- Deans ought to be expected to teach at least one course per term and continue to maintain a research and publishing program. Further, at least one of the courses taught by a dean ought to be a relatively large undergraduate class to avoid them escaping from teaching duties by "supervising" a few graduate students, while in reality doing no teaching.

- Academics who become vice-presidents ought to be required to teach one normal undergraduate class in their field each year and maintain a reduced research and publishing program to ensure that they do not lose touch with the realities of university life.

- University presidents ought to be seen as figureheads who represent the university in the community. Therefore, there is no need for an able academic to become the president and the job is most likely best done by a well-respected community figure with experience outside of academia.

- Since academics in state universities are public servants, all salaries ought to be published and publicly available. The cv's and lists of publications of all faculty ought to be published in a standard format on the Internet and all of the basic publications of faculty members, including copies of their M.A. and Ph.D. theses, ought to be available on the open shelves of the university library where they are employed. Such a procedure will quickly show who is really working and allow questions to be raised about the appropriateness of academic appointments, thus hindering the ability of deadwood to move into key academic posts.

- All promotions through academic ranks ought to be based on academic criteria alone. No one ought to be promoted from assistant to associate or from associate to full on the basis of administrative work. The basic administrative tasks required to run an academic department ought to be seen as a normal part of any academic job that everyone does. Similarly, good teaching, which is sometimes promoted as a substitute for research, ought to be excluded from promotion criteria because all professors should be good teachers. Every faculty member ought to be a good teacher and share in normal administrative duties. Doing something that is part of the job ought not to be grounds for promotion. Failure by a faculty member to fulfill normal administrative tasks and/or poor teaching ought to prevent promotion. Thus someone who fails to advise students or is a poor teacher ought not to be promoted. Similarly, someone who spends a lot of time with students and is a good teacher does not deserve to be promoted unless they produce solid research that shows up in academic publications.

- Since innovation and creative thinking is essential for research it is vital that departments do not become ingrown. Therefore, all faculty hiring involving tenure-track appointments must be done on an open basis involving national and international advertising. Departments ought to seek a diverse faculty. No more than 15% of a department's faculty members ought to be former students of that department. Most important of all faculty must be hired on the basis of academic achievement and merit.

- Academics accused of academic fraud usually claim that they are unable to fight the charges in court because university administrators have access to seemingly unlimited funds that allow them to drag out legal cases thus making it impossible for an ordinary person to challenge them in court. There is also evidence that when administrators, like Professor Snatch, are accused of misconduct such as plagiarism they are provided with advice from university lawyers. Yet no one seems to keep a check on university legal fees. Indeed few published university budgets give any indication of how much is spent on legal fees and why the expenditure was necessary. To prevent what appears to be the blatant abuse of public funds in defending the indefensible a close watch ought to be kept on university spending in this area and the use of university lawyers to provide support to administrators.

- Finally, Provincial Governments ought to establish a university ombudsman who can keep a sharp watch over the activities of administrators who at present appear to be totally unaccountable to anyone other than themselves.

Chapter Thirteen

The Postmodern Classroom: Risk and Shame in Higher Education

Nathan Young

For better or worse, postmodern criticism is now thoroughly woven into the substance and style of teaching in the humanities and social sciences in North American universities. While many faculty and sessional teachers disavow theories of postmodernism and (many fewer still) areas of knowledge are somewhat resistant to the postmodern critique, undergraduate and graduate students are invariably exposed to and engrossed in the concepts, the methods and methodologies, and (dare I say it) the logics of this collection of perspectives. My purpose here is not to advocate or condemn the place of postmodern criticism in the classroom or in pedagogical style. In a very real sense, there is no turning back the clock on the integration of postmodern critiques of morality, knowledge, and social organization into teaching materials and classroom dialogue. Instead, I hope to make a contribution to thinking about some new dilemmas of teaching and learning, particularly in the humanities and social sciences, that are raised by these new ways of thinking about the social world.

In this essay, I will argue that while postmodern criticism makes valuable contributions to academic thought and research, the *logic* of certain aspects of this criticism has consequences for relationships in the classroom. More specifically, I will argue that the postmodern emphasis on knowledge and language, united in the concept of discourse, enables a social critique capable of penetrating all institutions and relationships. More extreme versions of discourse theory, particularly those that link the speech and actions of individual people to broad societal power relations or historical legacies of dominance, challenge the social achievements of teaching and learning by suggesting that all relationships, including those in the classroom, are potential objects of criticism.

Postmodern thought challenges education in several ways. The first challenge, as prominent theorist of education Gert Biesta has argued (1995: p.164), is based in the "strong ... bond between the project of education and the project of modernity." Education "as a project" – as a pursuit engaged by people and by institutions – is at root about a faith and commitment to some form of progress at personal and societal levels. At a personal level, education fits into and drives narratives of self (biographies), and promotes those most modern of values: self-awareness and self-criticism (cf. Giddens 1991). At a societal level, education is inseparable from ideas about change and progress – the twin notions that subsequent generations will inherit a legacy of knowledge and values that they will in time build upon and supersede.

Among scholars of education, much has been written about the effects (real or imagined) of postmodern thought on the modernist "projects" of education (Aronowitz and Giroux 1991; Biesta 1995, 1998; Bloland, 1995; Gur-Ze'ev 1998, 2002; Tinning 2002). However, looking at higher education today, even in the humanities and those social sciences that have been remarkably open (and vulnerable) to postmodern criticism, I see little evidence of revolutionary challenge to the personal and societal "projects" of education. Even the most postmodern of topics taught by the most ardent opponents of modernist rationality in my mind still reflect the core beliefs of education: that what is taught in some way helps students towards a personal future that is full of both uncertainty and promise, and in some way helps to build a better world in which to live.

One advantage of writing on postmodernism in late 2003 is that the near-obsessive debates on relativism that dominated the early intellectual life of this school of thought (see Roseneau 1992), have *for the most part* receded. Teachers and students who are engaged with postmodern criticism are passionate about real issues, and are enthusiastic pursuers of personal and societal change. Furthermore, the format of university teaching has remained remarkably stable. Educators who identify with postmodern thinking may experiment with different class guidelines and evaluation schemes, but the "project" of formal education through formal means continues. I will therefore focus on a second challenge to education posed by postmodernist thought. This is not a challenge to the ends, aims, or means of education, but to practices of teaching and learning themselves. In this essay, I will argue that teaching and learning in the liberal arts is challenged by the incorporation of postmodern criticism into the classroom itself. Specifically, postmodern criticism's emphasis on the hidden mechanics of language, knowledge, and action threaten the capacity of some students to engage in the interpersonal accomplishments that are teaching and learning in the university classroom.

Discourse

Discourse is one of the primary concepts of postmodernist thinking, and discursive analysis is one of its primary methods of research. On the one hand, this concept and method are great sources of intellectual force and strength for the postmodern critique of social organization. For instance, discursive analysis directly questions the power basis of fundamental assumptions about roles and everyday behaviors. In doing so, it sheds important light on the interweaving of power, knowledge, and social practice. On the other hand, I will argue that the notion of discourse and the logic of discursive analysis are so broad and "portable" that they are easily applied to all kinds of speech and action. First, however, I will clarify this discussion by making very rough distinctions between three forms of discourse theory.

I will term the first form of discourse theory "institutional," because the primary phenomenon under scrutiny is indeed the institutional construction and dissemination of knowledges (in the plural). According to Ericson and Haggerty (1997: p.83),

> Discourse is the institutional construction of knowledge, which takes place within a social organization of territories, material objects, people, rules, formats, and technologies. What are constructed are representational frameworks:

classifications and categories that stand for objects, events, processes, and states of affairs in the world. These frameworks provide the basis for shared understanding, including an understanding of what knowledge is required to enhance, modify, or deny representation.

The institutional origins of discourses have been a main emphasis of postmodern critiques of knowledge for many years. For instance, Foucault's *Madness and Civilization* (1965), *Discipline and Punish* (1977), and *The History of Sexuality, Volume One* (1978) are each primarily preoccupied with the "institutional construction of knowledge" about the human body and human conduct. Importantly, moreover, institutional discourse theory also examines how this knowledge merges with everyday social practices and "lay" thinking and language. Such merging has two main effects. First, it serves to justify the existence and "expert status" of the institution in question. Second, it creates new means and categories for the exercise of control, surveillance, and discipline over a given population. The incorporation of expert knowledges about, for instance, human biology and "nature" into lay speech, relationships, and practices becomes a part of how people govern themselves and others. To sum, the emphasis of this form of discourse theory is primarily on the creation and diffuse exercising of institutional power on and through given populations by means of plural knowledges. Discourse analysis in this case means both examining the effects of such knowledges on human behavior, and unpacking the content of those knowledges in order to expose their underlying assumptions and logics.

I will term the second form of discourse analysis "relational," because it investigates how relationships *among* people are mediated by discursive frameworks. This approach builds on the idea that institutional knowledges work their way into categories and practices for everyday thinking and conduct. However, the relational form extends the analysis by directly addressing how such knowledges affect social exchanges within and between groups and among individuals. In other words, the relational approach investigates *privilege*. Arguments about privilege, familiar to scholars of inequality, posit that the "institutional construction of knowledge," which is a power-laden practice, ultimately reflects the interests of dominant groups. Thus, as these knowledges move into the mainstream and embed themselves in "common sense" and everyday social practices, they reinforce the existing power relations of the broader social world. As these institutional knowledges come to "make sense" to *most* people, this "making sense" is of great benefit to *some* people, in terms of status, material standing, and even personal autonomy; while to others, the same knowledges are directly harmful to life chances and freedoms of self-expression.

Importantly, privilege is not simply a result of institutional knowledges, but is an ongoing process that affects all relationships and actions. The notion of privilege therefore contends that people speak and act from different places in discursive "webs" or networks of power. In other words, when a person calls upon a "framework of shared understanding," necessary for all kinds of social action, that person also evokes (most often unintentionally) their own location in a discursive web. Postmodern thinking suggests that such discursive locations tend to be determined by identifiers "of the body" or of conduct, most obviously those of gender, ethnicity, and sexual orientation. Therefore, these identifiers give relative weight to whatever that person is actually saying or doing. Dominant groups have privilege because they have more "behind" what they say and do, while the actions of subordinate groups are downplayed or marginalized through the same process. The objects of analysis under this form of discourse theory are a person's speech and actions themselves: as they originate in certain discursive locations, resonate with certain discursive codes or frameworks, and are received by others embedded in their own locations.

The third form of discourse theory, which I will term "representational," builds on the assertions about power and everyday social action made by the "institutional" and "relational" approaches. It recognizes that the claims of powerful institutional actors create discourses that merge with "lay" knowledge and social practices, and it agrees that people act from different discursive locations in unequal webs and networks of power based in large part in biological/social indicators. Yet the representational approach carries these assertions further in its tendency to argue that relationships among people are *conduits* for discursive frameworks of power. In other words, this approach posits that people's speech, action, and identities do not simply originate in, but are inseparable from, societal relations of power and historical legacies of domination. Thus, while arguments about privilege contend that people's actions and identities *start* from different positions of advantage and disadvantage, arguments about representation suggest that people's actions and identities *embody* unequal power relations and historical legacies. Simply by speaking or acting (both of which rely on the "shared understandings" given in

Ericson and Haggerty's definition of discourse), a person is directly involved in the regulation of others through the reproduction of certain knowledges, and thus the reproduction of certain relationships of power.

The representation perspective encourages analysis of the discursive context of speech and action over their substantive content. Importantly, this means that what individuals say or do can be "explained" by reference to their location relative to dominant knowledges and power relations. While this may seem extreme, investigations of how location dominates a person's knowledge, subjectivity, and capacity to "understand" the plights of others is now a legitimate line of inquiry in the humanities and social sciences. It has been investigated in every discipline, including history (Wishart 1997), literary theory (Curti 1998), fine arts (Sawin 2002), psychology and psychoanalysis (Zakin 2000); and it is a cornerstone of queer theory (cf. Turner 2000), standpoint theory (Smith 1974; Haraway 1988; Harding 1991), and some feminist analyses of race and ethnicity (hooks 2000).

This discussion of theories of discourse is by no means exhaustive. It is, however, an important step in understanding the challenges of postmodern criticism to teaching and learning in today's university classroom. To be clear, I see significant intellectual validity and promise in the "institutional" and "relational" approaches to discourse analysis. These contribute to critical analyses of social institutions and knowledges, and provide frameworks to help understand social organization. At the same time, I will argue in the remainder of this essay that the "relational" and "representational" perspectives pose a serious challenge to the "project" of education because of their logic and their portability. Specifically, the tendency to ubiquity inherent in the concepts of privilege and embodiment makes it difficult to keep the rigors of the postmodern critique separate from the often-intense relationships that are central to teaching and learning in the university.

The Classroom

The university classroom is not a place, nor is it simply a setting for practises that could alternately be called "teaching" and "learning." Rather, the classroom is best thought of as a set of interpersonal relationships. Biesta (1998) in fact argues that education as a practise is ultimately "impossible,"

Yet the impossibility of education, the fact that it cannot be conceived as a technique, that its outcome cannot be predicted, can also be seen as an essential characteristic of all human interaction.

Biesta's point is that even the most structured classroom, with the most rigid lecture and rote learning format, is ultimately unpredictable in its results and character because all teaching and learning is an achievement of human interaction, and therefore of multiple persons. Classrooms are rife with formal roles, rules, and methods of ranking and evaluation. Nevertheless, classrooms should be thought of as structured settings for ultimately unpredictable social exchange. As any teacher intuitively knows, the "character" of a classroom can be slow in showing, can change through the course of a term or even a single session, and feeds off the personalities and comfort of students and instructor. Put simply, the interpersonal relationships that make education an "impossible" practise also determine the quality of learning as a social accomplishment among persons.

Thinking about education as an intersubjective accomplishment broadens the walls of the classroom. First of all, it makes us think beyond the obvious relationship between teacher and student. The teacher, by virtue of role and power, is of course the primary actor in any classroom. Yet learning (as well as teaching) happens in the presence of all people in the classroom. The "human interactions" mentioned by Biesta encompass the actions, body language, and conversation among students and between students and teacher. Equally important, moreover, are relationships prior to or outside of the classroom. Students who know each other from other classes or other social settings carry these relationships into the "human interactions" that anchor learning. While it is an old axiom to argue that learning is never restricted to the classroom, it is less common to think about teaching and learning as an accomplishment of the conjunction of "selves" with outside experiences, biographies, and prior relationships. It is precisely the intersubjective nature of teaching and learning that renders education "impossible," spontaneous, and of great consequence for all participants.

The notions of privilege and embodiment challenge the interpersonal achievements of teaching and learning. As mentioned earlier, the logic and methods associated with these concepts are very portable, and their emphasis on relationships, knowledge, and language makes it difficult to strictly define the object of critique.

Thus, the primary challenge posed by postmodern thinking lies in its encroachment on relationships in the classroom. Indeed, the classroom is particularly vulnerable to the incursion of notions of privilege and embodiment because teaching and learning are based in the intense exchange of language, knowledge, experiences and interpretations.

Without doubt, the criticism of knowledge is a cornerstone of the human interactions and intersubjective accomplishments of teaching and learning. And while ideas about *people's* ideas have always been a part of the curriculum in the humanities and social sciences (for instance, Marxist class consciousness, economistic rationality, and historical embeddedness), the logics of privilege and embodiment introduce the spectre of rigorous scrutiny of *a person's* ideas through their speech and action *in* the classroom. Therefore, the danger of the postmodern critique lies in its extension to the point that, as stated by Foucault (quoted in Dreyfus and Rabinow 1983: p.231-2), "if everything is dangerous, then we always have something to do." An insistence on *everything as dangerous* brings the critique directly to bear on speech and thought as found in the smallest of settings: the person. And the call that *we always have something to do* invites the application of this critique to the person with as much vigor as to the grandest institution. The classroom, as a setting for human interaction, is severely affected by this ethos.

Risk

In Westhues's (2004: p.158) discussion of covenantal relationships among teachers and students, he uses the term "risk." Writing about the teaching experience of theologian Herbert Richardson at St. Michael's College and the University of Toronto, Westhues states,

> [Richardson] sought to engage students more deeply, to challenge their assumptions about religion and life, to awaken them to new possibilities for themselves and the world, to give them gifts they would never forget. He wanted every course to be a meeting of minds in some new place. He risked exposure of his own person toward this end, and expected students to take the same risk.

The risks in question here are the risks of intersubjectivity. In this discussion, Richardson confronts the impossibility of education by pursuing the spontaneity and unpredictability of human interaction in the classroom. Importantly, moreover, Westhues writes that this risk involves most of all the "exposure of his own person." In other words, the pursuit of intersubjectivity means risking one's self – one's moral and intellectual narrative – to possible challenge and change.

In the postmodern classroom, where the critique of knowledge, language, and power applies both to institutions and to the discursive locations of persons, the dynamics of risk-taking in intersubjective engagement change. On the one hand, the risks to students and teachers remain the same. As I argued earlier, the postmodern ethic still invests a deep faith in education as a personal and societal "project." Indeed, much of the appeal of postmodernist thought lies in the transformative energy of its critique: that the spread of these tools for thinking and interpreting the social world contributes to better living and a better society that is more sensitive to difference. Thus, as with any pedagogical style or scheme, students and teachers in the postmodern classroom risk their personal moral and intellectual narratives when they engage in the "human interaction" of a classroom engaged with postmodernist ideas. Yet, on the other hand, notions of privilege and embodiment introduce a powerful emotional block to the intersubjective accomplishment of teaching and learning – a block that can utterly preempt any risk-taking among certain participants in the classroom. This block is shame, or the feeling of an abstracted culpability or implication in the dominance of others.

Shame

Shame, like most human emotions, is treated rather mechanically by the social sciences. In sociology, the study of human organization and relationships, it is almost completely absent. In psychology, it tends to be closely associated with fear and other "abnormalities" of perception and personality (cf. Lutwak et al. 2003). A recent essay by sociologist Thomas Scheff (2003) tries to resuscitate the notion of shame and advocates its rethinking as "the premier social emotion" (p. 239). Scheff argues that shame is the primary consequence of human social nature, of the fact that we are constantly "living in the minds of others" (p. 244). This leads him to conclude that shame is a form of conscience, and therefore a stabilizer of the social bonds that link people to one another and to social ideals.

Although I do not agree with Scheff's interpretation of the positive social role of shame as the "master emotion of everyday life," his contention that shame is a social regulator of behavior is very plausible, although his emphasis is somewhat misplaced. In my mind, shame is indeed a "social" or interpersonal emotion that is rooted in seeing oneself through the imagined eyes of critical others. Yet it is a mistake to think about the primary effect of shame in terms of the stability of social bonds. Shame can certainly promote social stability, but it does so by silencing and muting. Its conservatism is therefore not at all based on "the social bond," but on the effect it has to depress the participation of certain people, or simply to depress certain kinds of participation, in creative activities or other social exchange. In this light, shame seems antithetical to the spontaneity – the risk – of teaching and learning as intersubjective accomplishments.

The notions of privilege and embodiment introduced by the postmodern critique are inseparable from shame in the classroom. Embodiment in particular implicates certain people's actions, regardless of intent, in the exercising and reproduction of dominant relations of power. This means that the participation of some students and teachers in classroom debate and interaction can be severely qualified by "criteria" beyond their control. I say "can be" because it is by no means always or even often the intention of teachers or students to claim that a person's thoughts and speech are either grounded in or equivalent to actions and legacies of dominance. Despite some high-profile cases of extreme views about how people embody or represent broad social relations, few teachers or students in the postmodern classroom would purposely denigrate a person for *being* an embodiment or representation. Instances such as Boston College professor Mary Daly's twenty-five year practice of barring male students from her Women's Studies classes remain rare, and are criticized by professors of all traditions and political leanings.[1]

Importantly, however, direct or purposeful accusation is not a requisite for experiences of shame. Shame is a form of empathy and projection on behalf of the shamed, where one sees oneself critically through the imagined eyes of others. Thus, because the rubrics of privilege and embodiment insist that representation is for the most part unintentional, and, most importantly, unavoidable, people whose biological selves are linked with legacies of oppression or unjust

---

[1]Daly's practice was challenged in 1999 by a male student. In response, Boston College removed Daly's courses from the college's calendar for the subsequent term, claiming that she had retired. Daly insisted that she had not retired but requested a paid leave of absence following repeated attempts by the university to dismiss her. A confidential settlement was reached in 2001, ending Daly's affiliation with Boston College.

institutional practices are opened up to experiences of shame – of imagining what their speech and actions represent to critical others.

The effects of shame on the intersubjective classroom are not trivial. Shame is not simple bashfulness, nor is it discomfort, nor is it an abstracted embarrassment for self or for others. Shame is not something that is felt "in the moment" – it is not contingent on the situation or topic of classroom debate. Instead, I agree with Giddens (1991: p. 9), who links shame to the ongoing and lifelong "reflexive project of the self." By this, Giddens means that shame bears directly on feelings of the "adequacy of narratives of biography" (p. 65). Shame deeply affects how we understand ourselves, our actions, and our personal relationships with others. Thus, the challenge of the postmodern classroom is *not* one of explicit or implicit discrimination, reverse discrimination, or any other overt form of action to silence or pre-empt the participation and engagement of certain people in the intersubjective accomplishments of teaching and learning. Instead, the shame that is fostered among certain people by the postmodern critique acts, in Giddens' terms, on "the integrity of the self."

> Shame bears directly on self-identity because it is essentially anxiety about the adequacy of the narrative by means of which the individual sustains a coherent biography. (65)

Far from reinforcing social bonds in the manner envisioned by Scheff, shame makes people question their relationships with others because it assaults their sense of control over the personal narratives that guide actions and intentions. The logics of privilege and embodiment reinforce this, because they suggest that a person's discursive location is of more consequence to others than is the content and intended meanings of their speech and actions. A person can understand their actions to be reasoned, fair, and inclusive – these principles can stand at the core of one's own narrative of self – yet the logics of privilege and embodiment insist that all actions are *first* embedded in relationships of power that the person can never fully understand, let alone control.

Shame closes the university classroom to certain people and to certain types of participation. Historically, this was the case when older assumptions about the essences of gender and race made women's and minority members' engagement with teaching and learning very difficult. To its credit, the postmodern critique has definitively demonstrated the power of techniques for institutional administration (including universities) to shame those without social power. Furthermore, for these students shame was often accompanied by active discrimination. Today, few reasonable scholars would claim that comparable discrimination is being levelled at those who "represent" or embody dominant social relations, nor are these students shamed through a lack of social power.

Yet the problem of representation fosters shame through the same kind of moral displacement experienced in the classroom by the disadvantaged in earlier times. For instance, older styles of academic and pedagogical thinking suggested that certain people were limited by *the essence* of their biology. Assumptions about the limits of personal capabilities were imposed on students *as* women, *as* minorities, *as* disabled persons. Shame was therefore somewhat double-sided: there was shame at the condition of inferiority, but there was also a deeper shame – a shame of being denied the capacity to take on full moral responsibility for the content of one's thinking and actions. In other words, these students faced a shame of who they were, as well as a deeper shame of being denied autonomy over one's own "narrative." In the postmodern classroom, there is a similar duality stemming from a similar moral displacement. For the people who, following the logics of privilege and embodiment, "*know*" what they represent in the imagined eyes of critical others, there is a shame directed at self. Yet, as in times past, there is also the shame of an *imposed* inability to take full moral control over one's own thinking and speaking. Because privilege and embodiment are unconscious and/or unintentional – because they stem from location in discursive webs of power – a person's thoughts and actions are not just their own. They belong in significant measure to the institutional frameworks and historical legacies in which they are "based." There is thus shame of a legacy or embodiment, but also the inability, projected through the imagined eyes of critical others, to step outside of "location" and take moral ownership of one's own relationships and actions.

Silence and Anger

Shame closes the university classroom – it chokes off the participation of certain people in the risk-taking involved in the controlled "exposure" of narratives of self, and it diminishes the spontaneity of intersubjective interactions. Shame deeply affects those who feel it, but it also has significant consequences for everyone in the classroom. Specifically, shame can lead to silence and to anger, neither of which contribute to positive environments for teaching and learning.

First, shame silences because it prefixes speech and action. Again, shame manifests in the speaking or acting person's views of themselves in the imagined eyes of others. Shame thus silences by changing the meaning of a person's contributions to the intersubjective classroom. As I argued above, shame stems in large part from the denial of a person's moral autonomy over *both* themselves and their relationships with others. Under conditions where meaning becomes so detached from intention, and where imagined criticism prefaces any potential risk-taking in the classroom, silence, partial or total, becomes more amenable to the health of "narratives of self" than is engagement with others. The silence of any portion of a classroom lessens teaching and learning because it severely limits the human interaction that stands at the heart of education.

Second, and in some respects more serious, is the consequence of anger. Psychology tells us that one very human response to feelings of shame is to blame identifiable others (Lutwak et al. 2003). Scheff writes that much of the power of shame as a social emotion stems from its taboo, or the fact that people feel an intense "shame about shame" (2003: pp. 240, 249). However, as I argued earlier, shame in the postmodern classroom does not resonate primarily from direct accusations or from extreme views about embodiment held by a minority of students and teachers. In the postmodern classroom, shame resides in how certain persons imagine themselves to appear (as representations) in the eyes of others. This imagination is rooted in the *logic* of a critique that moves from a critique of institutional knowledge, to a more personal critique of privilege, to assertions about embodiment. In other words, the issue of embodiment or representation does not need to be raised in a given classroom for its spectre to be present. Notions of privilege and embodiment are a part of current postmodern thinking, and they cannot be barred from *any* classroom in the liberal arts. Importantly, however, anger at representation, or the "shame of shame" that some students and teachers feel in the classroom, is too often directed at specific people. When shame of shame produces anger, that anger often *makes* a target – and such targets are usually undeserving of blame. Shame and anger, together or apart, have no place in the classroom and are antithetical to the intersubjective accomplishments of teaching and learning.

Difference and Differentness

Throughout this essay, I have argued that the postmodern critique is both a valid form of social inquiry and criticism, and, through the logic of some of its chief concepts and methods, a danger to open teaching and learning based in the controlled personal risks involved in human interaction. Postmodern thought has entrenched itself in the university curriculum in the humanities and social sciences, but I will end here by arguing against that part of the postmodern critique that insists on the "locatedness" of all knowledge and that considers persons *first* as acting from discursive "intersections" of broad social and historical relations. Ironically, in some respects it has been easier to integrate arguments about privilege and embodiment into the classroom than to integrate postmodernism's promising *institutional* critiques. This is demonstrated in the following quotation from Richard Bernstein (1991: pp. 51-2), writing about the ethical challenges posed by postmodern thinking to open communication and interaction.

> Dialogic communication presupposes moral virtues – a certain "good will" at least in the willingness to really listen, to seek to understand what is genuinely other, different, alien, and the courage to risk one's more cherished prejudgements. But too frequently this commonality is not really shared, it is violently opposed. [Instead], a false "we" is projected.... Sometimes what is required to communicate – to establish a reciprocal "we" – is rupture and break – a refusal to accept the common ground laid down by the "other."

I agree with the spirit of this appeal for all participants in human dialogue and debate, in our case in the university classroom, to demonstrate "good will," a "willingness to really listen," and to "risk one's more cherished prejudgements" when engaged in human interaction. However, I strongly oppose the language interwoven with Bernstein's call for civility, empathy, and respect of pluralism. Specifically, I object to the language of "genuine otherness," "differentness," and "alienness." First of all, the terms hint at essentialism. But more importantly, these terms are part of the problem under discussion here – the problem of how intellectually valid postmodern criticism comes to impose upon the "human interactions" that guide teaching and learning.

Indeed, much of the validity of postmodern criticism stems from its concern with pluralism. By shedding light on the margins, by exploring the roots and consequences of modernist logic for disadvantaged groups, and by challenging accepted categories and concepts of thinking, the collection of theories and methodologies generally thought of as "postmodernism" have made real contributions to academic knowledge and to the quality of life of many disadvantaged people. Yet this pluralism, this concern with *difference*, is too frequently carried over (as in the quote from Bernstein) to thinking about *differentness*. This distinction is anything but semantic. A concern with difference involves an appreciation of, but not necessarily an uncritical stance towards, the validity of different interpretations, perspectives, rationalities and logics. In this respect, difference is entirely compatible with the "project" of education (with the pursuit of personal and societal aims through the pursuit and advocacy of knowledge), and enriches the classroom by introducing new elements to the intersubjective accomplishments of teaching and learning. An insistence on differentness, by contrast, suggests that fundamental and unbreachable boundaries exist between people based on their position relative to others. The problems of privilege and embodiment, where people are considered as inseparable from their location in discursive webs of power, are imported into the classroom through the idea of differentness. Obsession with differentness leads to the wider application of these concepts to all aspects of social life, including the classroom.

The challenges facing both students and teachers in the postmodern classroom are complex. First, the recognition of difference as an ethical principle in the classroom is a worthwhile pursuit that ought to be encouraged, but at the same time the fetish of differentness must somehow be excluded. Unfortunately, teachers and students who actively encourage free-ranging or intense debate and dialogue on issues such as pluralism risk damaging complaints or informal reprisals from other participants in the classroom. This sensitivity to the identity and comfort of "listeners" in the classroom is a reality of teaching and learning in today's university. Secondly, moreover, I have argued that the logic of postmodern criticism, including the logics of privilege and embodiment, are present to a certain degree in *all* classrooms of the humanities and social sciences. Postmodern narratives are very powerful, and their failure or unwillingness to distinguish between critiques of macro phenomena and micro relationships makes them both portable and easily appealed to in debates on almost any topic. Third, the consequences of the logics of privilege and embodiment, which include shame, silence, and anger, are felt first at the level of the individual. It is a painful irony that those who feel shame at the invocation of their "selves" with legacies and relationships of dominance are those who are most empathetic or inclined to consider themselves in the imagined eyes of critical others. The fact that shame often never shows (silence), or is masked by other emotions (anger), only furthers the challenges to the postmodern classroom.

So what is to be done? As always, primary responsibility for the classroom resides with the instructor. First, instructors have a duty and obligation to set rules of discussion and debate in the classroom so that ideas may be presented and critiqued without reference to persons, motives, or embodiment. This is no easy task, particularly as each student today brings some awareness of postmodern criticism into the classroom. Second, I strongly advocate that instructors, to the furthest extent possible, abandon considerations of the "comfort" of students in the classroom. Let me immediately clarify: everyone needs to feel comfortable in the classroom i.e., secure in their narratives of self. To risk one's narrative is a matter of individual decision and discretion, but that potential must always be available to everyone in the classroom. "Being comfortable" thus means not being excluded from this risk-taking, it means being in an environment of mutual respect for personal and intellectual integrity.

The notion of comfort, however, has taken on new meanings in the postmodern classroom, to the point that the minutiae of course content and classroom dialogue can be analyzed for shadows of offence to postmodern sensibilities. It is again a sad irony that this pursuit of offence, which goes well beyond a speaker's intent and into the motivations of their discursive locations, fosters "postmodern" shame. In the past, the fight against shame in the classroom was in large part a struggle against an essentialism that denied personhood. Today, it is against rubrics that similarly offer explanations for a person in advance of their speech and action. Any remedy must involve the utter abandonment of any suggestion that people cannot think, feel, and act on their volition and contribute positively to the intersubjective accomplishments of teaching and learning.

Acknowledgement

I would like to thank Christina Wilson and Derek Phillips for the many conversations that have contributed to the ideas in this essay. I would in particular like to thank Ken Westhues, whose humanism inspired me into sociology. This essay draws on my memory of his pamphlet, *The Risks of Personal Injury in Liberal Arts Education: a Warning to Students* (now published at http://mueller.educ.ucalgary.ca/westhues/), which I read in his Inroduction to Sociology class at the University of Waterloo in 1996.

References

Aronowitz, Stanley and Henry Giroux, 1991. *Postmodern Education: politics, culture, and social criticism.* Minneapolis: University of Minnesota Press.

Bernstein, Richard, 1991. *The New Constellation: the ethical-political horizons of modernity/postmodernity.* Cambridge, UK: Polity Press.

Biesta, Gert, 1998. "Say You Want a Revolution... Suggestions for the Impossible Future of Critical Pedagogy," *Educational Theory* 48: 4, 499-511.

Biesta, Gert, 1995. "Postmodernism and the Repoliticization of Education," *Interchange* 26: 2, 161-183.

Bloland, Harland, 1995. "Postmodernism and Higher Education," *Journal of Higher Education* 66: 5, 521-559.

Curti, Lidia. 1998. *Female Stories, Female Bodies: narrative, identity and representation.* London: Macmillan.

Dreyfus, Hubert and Paul Rabinow, 1983. *Michel Foucault: beyond structuralism and hermeneutics.* Chicago: University of Chicago Press.

Ericson, Richard, and Kevin Haggerty, 1997. *Policing the Risk Society.* Toronto: University of Toronto Press.

Foucault, Michel, 1978. *The History of Sexuality, Volume One, An Introduction.* New York: Pantheon Books.

Foucault, Michel, 1977. *Discipline and Punish: the birth of the prison.* New York: Vintage Books.

Foucault, Michel, 1965. *Madness and Civilization: a history of insanity in the Age of Reason.* New York: Vintage Books.

Giddens, Anthony, 1991. *Modernity and Self-Identity: self and society in the late modern age.* Stanford: Stanford University Press.

Gur-Ze'ev, Ilan, 2002. "Bildung and Critical Theory facing Post-modern Education," *Journal of Philosophy of Education* 36: 3, 391-408.

Gur-Ze'ev, Ilan, 1998. "Toward a nonrepressive critical pedagogy" *Educational Theory.* 48: 4, 463-486.

Haraway, Donna, 1988. "Situated Knowledges: the science question in feminism and the privilege of partial perspective," *Feminist Studies* 14 (Fall), 575-599.

Harding, Sandra, 1991. *Whose Science? Whose Knowledge? Thinking from women's lives*. Ithaca: Cornell University Press.

hooks, bell, 2000. *Feminist Theory: from margin to center* (2nd edition). Cambridge, MA: South End Press.

Lutwak, Nita, J. Panish and J. Ferrari, 2003. "Shame and Guilt: characterological versus behavioral self-blame and their relationship to fear of intimacy," *Personality and Individual Differences* 35, 909-916.

Roseneau, Pauline, 1992. *Post-modernism and the Social Sciences*. Princeton: Princeton University Press.

Sawin, Patricia, 2002. "Performance at the Nexus of Gender, Power, and Desire," *Journal of American Folklore* 115: 455, 28-61.

Scheff, Thomas, 2003. "Shame and Self in Society," *Symbolic Interaction* 26: 2, 239-262.

Smith, Dorothy, 1974. "Women's Perspective as a Radical Critique of Sociology," *Sociological Inquiry* 44: 1, 7-13.

Tinning, Richard, 2002. "Towards a 'Modest Pedagogy': Reflections on the Problematics of Critical Pedagogy," *Quest* 54, 224-240.

Turner, William, 2000. *A Genealogy of Queer Theory*. Philadelphia: Temple University Press.

Westhues, Kenneth, 2003. *Administrative Mobbing at the University of Toronto*. Lewiston, NY: Edwin Mellen.

Wishart, David, 1997. "The Selectivity of Historical Representation," *Journal of Historical Geography*. 23: 2, 111-118.

Zakin, Emily, 2000. "Bridging the Social and Symbolic: Toward a Feminist Politics of Sexual Difference," *Hypatia*. 15: 3, 19-44.

Part Five

Eliminative Techniques

Editor's Introduction

Among teenagers, also among wild and domestic fowl, mobbing is normally carried out by overt, transparent, violent means. Mobbers encircle the target, scream invective, and take turns assaulting the target physically to the point of total humiliation, debilitating injury, elimination, even death.

Among professors, mobbing almost never takes this form. It would not work. Norms against violence in colleges and universities are so strict the mobbers would discredit themselves. Their target would be seen as a victim, and they as deserving of punishment.

An academic mobbing usually unfolds more like the 1973 film, *The Sting*, wherein Robert Redford, Paul Newman, and some other crooks gang up on a crooked target named Shaw. The object is to get Shaw's money, but not by violent attack. Such a film would not have won Oscars. Instead, Shaw is fleeced in a scheme so convoluted and clever that he never knows what hit him, even at the end.

The cleverness of real-life academic mobbers does not quite measure up to Newman's in the film. Many are not even aware of what they are doing. Some behave as captives of an ideology. Others think they are just following policies. Only a few are devious and purposeful. Nonetheless, events somehow conspire, through twists, turns, and convolutions over months or years, to maneuver the target into a steadily more defenseless position, to the point of the same outcome as from the violent mobbings of teenagers: total humiliation, debilitating injury, elimination, even death.

It takes a quick and sharp wit to understand what is going on, the kind possessed by Joan Friedenberg. It is plain from her chapter below that she is not the sort of professor who kowtows to managerial oligarchies. Openly and without apology, she opposed the oligarchies at her university – insisting on meritocratic principles, filing grievances over policy violations, even joining in a lawsuit to have the Board of Trustees declared illegally constituted. In 2000, her opponents on campus coalesced and undertook to get rid of her. In her essay, Friedenberg details their techniques, using the framework I sketched in my book (reprinted as Chapter 2 of the present book). Few targets of academic mobbing would be able to assume so cooly analytic a posture toward their own hard experience. Her analysis of the use of a psychologist-consultant to discredit her is not just compelling but eery and sickening.

In Chapter 15, John Mueller describes a different technique for discrediting targeted professors, the Research Ethics Board now built into the structure of most colleges and universities. Mueller begins by recalling an academic mobbing case of the kind most of us were told about in graduate school, a story from the bad old days – which we have now, it was implied, moved far beyond. Mueller shows that this is not the case, that psychology professors get mobbed also in the present day, only on different hot-button issues and through different mechanisms, in particular charges of ethical misconduct in research. The cases he reviews – Justine Sergent at McGill, Louis Pagliaro at Alberta, Elizabeth Loftus at Washington, and others – suggest that one of the most serious risks in contemporary social scientific research is to the researchers themselves: the risk of being ganged up on by colleagues and administrators, obstructed, harassed, and humiliated if the work is good.

Techniques of violent mobbing are standard, banal, easy to list: shoves, punches, kicks, stabs, gunshots, and so on. Techniques of nonviolent mobbing are limited only by the imaginations of people working in complex organizations. The success of an academic mobbing depends on disguise. By exposing this, as Friedenberg and Mueller have done, one begins to turn the mobbing back.

Chapter Fourteen

Political Psychology at Southern Illinois University: the Use of an Outside Consultant for Mobbing a Professor

Joan E. Friedenberg

In recent years, scholars in the U.S. and Canada have begun to address the phenomenon of workplace mobbing and as a result there is a growing literature now available to victims, human resources professionals, and scholars. German industrial psychologist Heinz Leymann, who pioneered the research on workplace mobbing, estimated that 15% of Swedish suicides were directly attributable to workplace mobbing (Davenport, Schwartz, & Elliott 1999). Davenport *et al.* estimate that 4 million Americans are victims of workplace mobbing while Hornstein (1996) estimates that as many as 20 million Americans are victims of it. Davenport *et al.* (1999, p. 40) characterize mobbing as a "malicious attempt to force a person out of the workplace through unjustified accusations, humiliation, general harassment, emotional abuse, and/or terror....a ganging up by the leader(s) – organization, superior, co-worker, or subordinate – who rallies others into systematic and frequent mob-like behavior."

Westhues (2004) characterizes workplace mobbing as a conspiracy of employees who "humiliate, degrade, and get rid of a fellow employee, when rules prevent the achievement of these ends through violence" (p. 42). This conspiracy of employees is usually supported, if not led, by administrators. One way in which employers contribute to the mobbing of an employee is by engaging an outside consultant to strengthen a case against the targeted person. Consultants can lend legitimacy to the mobbing process by giving the appearance that they are outside experts who through a supposedly objective process somehow almost always end up agreeing with an employer's decision to eliminate or otherwise target an undesirable employee. And many consultants are only too happy to comply, often discarding any pretense that professional ethics will be followed. Consultants who assist employers in mobbing employees can be either experts in a particular field (who will conclude that the targeted employee is incompetent), private investigators (who can help determine that the targeted employee is somehow engaged in illegal or unethical behavior such as misusing workplace equipment and supplies and leaves), or mental health professionals (who can determine that a targeted employee is mentally unfit).

As an example of hiring experts from a specific professional discipline, universities often engage experts from specific academic fields to conduct program reviews. In such cases, the consultant rarely has expertise in conducting reviews and instead has expertise in the academic discipline. These consultants review a particular department and render observations regarding the department's weaknesses and strengths and offer recommendations for improvement. In such a program review, the consultant can easily conclude that a certain individual is incompetent or that a program or department should be eliminated. As an example, at Southern Illinois University Carbondale, a consultant was once hired by an administrator to review the School of Law. The consultant concluded that a particular staff member in the law school should be removed from his position. Written evidence from the grievance hearing that followed suggested that the consultant had been a longtime friend and colleague of the administrator and that he had engaged her services precisely because he wanted to terminate this particular staff person. Her report read something like, "I agree with you that so-in-so should be removed." (Later, the consultant thanked the administrator in writing for the flowers he had sent her.)

Private investigators are sometimes engaged when an employer is attempting to uncover evidence that a targeted employee is cheating or lying about something, hiding something, or is in some way behaving unethically enough to warrant dismissal. For example, Westhues (2004) relates an incident in which a private investigator was retained by a university to follow a professor who was on sick leave to see if the professor was actually sick. In my own case, my department chair, Glenn Gilbert, recommended in a memo that a private investigator be engaged to see if I was using the printer in my office inappropriately and if I really observed the Jewish religion, since I had complained about repeated late Friday afternoon faculty meetings. In addition, he suggested engaging an additional investigator to find out why I had left my previous employment. (Needless to say, in both cases, I would have cheerfully provided my employers with any of the information they sought.)

A third kind of consultant used to target employees is the mental health professional. I believe that using mental health professionals to target employees for mobbing should be an even more serious concern and it would probably not be an exaggeration to say that that this kind of consultant use is actually dangerous – for the targeted individual, for the mental health profession and for society as a whole.

When one imagines officials using mental health professionals to target undesirable individuals, one almost always thinks of totalitarian governments such as the former USSR, China, and Cuba. There is a long and ugly precedent of using mental health professionals in those societies to target politically undesirable people and have them placed in mental institutions involuntarily. Human rights groups refer to this practice as "political psychiatry" (Human Rights Watch, 2002). Victims of political psychiatry usually fit any of the following five categories: 1) people who have filed grievances or complaints against employers or officials, 2) labor organizers, 3) people who have publicly criticized officials, 4) members of minority religions, and 5) whistle-blowers (Bezlova, 2002; Pan, 2002).

For example, Gosden (1997) reports that in the early 1970s, psychiatrists in the West had become concerned about the fact that the incidence of schizophrenia in the USSR was nearly double that in the West. It was later revealed that the Soviets had "discovered" a unique form of mental illness that fit the profile of a political dissident. Soviet psychiatrists became so involved with controlling dissidents that an entire system of special psychiatric hospitals was established and run cooperatively with the KGB. Human rights groups alleged that over 3,000 political dissidents were inappropriately committed to mental institutions in the former Soviet Union, resulting in its condemnation by and subsequent resignation from the World Psychiatric Association from 1983 until Gorbechev came into power and initiated reforms.

As in the former USSR, according to the New York-based Human Rights Watch and the Geneva Initiative on Psychiatry (GIP), a Netherlands-based international foundation (2002), China is currently holding and torturing thousands of political and religious dissidents in mental institutions, dissidents who, for the most part, committed such offenses as using anti-government slogans, trying to establish trade unions, or participating in the Falun Gong religious movement.

Similarly, Brown and Lago (1992) explored the use of psychiatrists and psychiatric hospitals in Cuba to punish dissidents. They found that dissidents with no prior history of mental illnesses were interned in psychiatric hospitals with criminally insane patients and given high doses of electroshock treatments without the usual muscle relaxants, in addition to psychotropic drugs. After examining patient surveys at the Havana Psychiatric Hospital, they concluded that 4 percent of patients there were actually political dissidents.

This problem of political psychiatry became so critical that in 1996, the World Psychiatric Association passed the Madrid Declaration that "all forms of psychiatric diagnosis and treatment on the basis of the political needs of governments are forbidden" (Bezlova, 2002).

Surprisingly, mental health professionals are also used in North America to accomplish similar ends. Indeed, Westhues (2004, p. 153) reports that a whistle-blower member of a Canadian police force became the target of administrative mobbing and elimination with the help of a psychologist who, without ever even having met the officer, signed a report indicating that he was mentally ill.

Political Psychology at SIUC

In this essay, I report on and analyze a case where a consulting psychologist abetted the mobbing of a professor at Southern Illinois University Carbondale. In this instance, the psychologist performed a function similar to psychiatrists in the countries just discussed, and I was the object of the mobbing. As I will show, my circumstances approximated those of victims of political psychiatry.

An ironic feature of mobbing is that the complaints one's persecutors make are maddening in their vagueness and lack of specificity. This makes it difficult to decide what needs to be included in a digestible history of a mobbing. In what follows, I give the minimum context I believe necessary to comprehend my case and understand how political psychology became involved in it. I will first discuss my perceptions of some general features of the university and its administration, to indicate why administrators became involved, and then turn to the particulars of my department to indicate why antagonism to me was available for administrators to tap.

Southern Illinois University

My university has long been beset with conflict between its faculty and administration, with the latter being censured by the AAUP in the mid-1970s. Since that time, continued hostilities caused the faculty to unionize as a way of reducing capricious and arbitrary administrative behavior. In the governance structure of the University, department chairs are agents of the Board of Trustees, as are all administrators above them, and all are paid at levels intended to secure their allegiance to the Board and distinguish them from faculty. The premium for a chair, for instance, is approximately 54% above a similarly ranked faculty member. Indeed, joining the administration is one of the few means faculty possess to increase salaries that are low in comparison to peer institutions.

In this context, an "old boy" network of administrators and faculty encouraged a go-along-to-get-along culture within the university. This network closed ranks against faculty who protested, through grievances, capricious treatment by their chairs. Faculty grievances are routinely denied as they pass up administrative levels, eventually to become the subjects of expensive arbitration. Faculty had hoped that a new Chancellor hired in 1998, Jo Ann Argersinger, would be able to dismantle this network and improve relations with the faculty, but she was dismissed by the system President, Ted Sanders, after only 11 months in office, in part for being insufficiently antagonistic toward the faculty and its union. Her dismissal caused a storm of protest in which I was an active participant. As part of this, I was recruited to participate with two other faculty in a lawsuit that asked to have the then-sitting Board of Trustees declared illegally constituted under a provision of Illinois law that prohibits domination of the Board by members of one political party. I appeared in published photographs standing directly behind President Sanders at a news conference holding a sign requesting his removal. I became quite involved with union membership recruitment drives and made public speeches revealing what I knew about how the university administration, in my opinion, mismanaged the university's resources. I wrote several letters to the editor and guest columns for the three local papers criticizing the administration and applauding the benefits of unionization; I filed several Freedom of Information Act (FOIA) requests for budget information to expose administrative salary increases, university vehicle use by administrators, and their entertainment expenditures. I served on the union's grievance committee and participated in collective action activities, including all informational pickets, and helped develop chants and posters for picketing. I also handed out union leaflets at university events.

Argersinger was replaced by an interim Chancellor, John Jackson, who was, in my opinion, the arch representative of the old boy network in the University, and had been Dean of my college when I was hired. Jackson served briefly as Provost under Argersinger, until his apparent recalcitrance to change caused his removal. His appointment as Interim Chancellor upon Argersinger's removal spelled the return of the old boy network to a dominant position, as did the selection of a new interim Provost, Margaret Winters, who had previously served as the Administration's chief negotiator in bargaining against the faculty union. As will become clear shortly, the installation of these particular individuals meant that the University was being run by people who had quite direct ties to my department and its history of difficulties, to which I now turn. I will subject these difficulties to structural and historical analysis.

The Linguistics Department

I was hired from outside the University in 1994 to direct its Center for English as a Second Language (CESL). CESL is a division of the Linguistics Department, in which I became a full professor, and to whose chair, Associate Professor Paul Angelis, I reported as CESL director. CESL as a division was mainly staffed by teachers with MAs in TESOL, most of whom had degrees from our own department. These teachers were on temporary contracts that, after a considerable trial period, became de facto permanent but without tenure. Despite the fact that the CESL faculty had little direct contact with the Linguistics department chair, voting rights accorded CESL members, who sometimes outnumbered linguistics professors, gave them de facto control over who would be chair, in effect causing any who would aspire to that position to cultivate CESL support. That is, former graduate students in the department had significant control over the selection and retention of their former professors' chair, as well as considerable influence through their inclusion on linguistics department committees, on their former professors' merit increases and who would become their professors' TAs. Additionally, this structure introduced the likelihood that CESL teachers would find themselves beholden to the department chair given their non-tenure-track status.

At the time I arrived, the larger Department (Linguistics and CESL) was controlled by a small influential group of some faculty from both Linguistics and CESL. This group had strong ties to the Dean of the College (who later became Provost and then Interim Chancellor), John Jackson. I gradually discovered that the aim of this group was to reward friends and punish enemies, and it was protected in doing so by the favor of the Dean. Whenever I attempted to institute meritocratic policies that by coincidence favored its enemies, the group complained about me to the Dean.

When Jackson moved up to the Provost's office, he was replaced by his Associate Dean, Robert Jenson, who had equally strong ties to this influential group. To complete this structural portrait, when Jackson stepped in as Interim Chancellor, his selection for Interim Provost, Margaret Winters, was tied to Linguistics, having both a cross appointment in the department and a husband who was a member of it and interested in becoming its chair. In addition, another Associate Vice Chancellor, Kyle Perkins, had tenure in the Linguistics department. This guaranteed that not only my challenges to the higher administration, but my activities in the department, would be closely monitored by key players in the administration.

In turning from the department's structure and linkages to its history, I will focus on four events that I believe motivated my mobbing by colleagues in the department. It was in the course of these that I appealed for intervention by a psychologist, an appeal that allowed administrators to turn what should have been conflict resolution into political psychology.

The department had a long history of intramural acrimony, as I eventually learned from retired members and colleagues from my field who had served as external program reviewers. When I tired of fighting the influential group in my department, a group that was, in my opinion, mean-spirited towards colleagues and students and outdated and inflexible in its approach to intensive English instruction, I requested a change of assignment from CESL Director to a fulltime teaching and research position in Linguistics. Paul Angelis, a career associate professor, had been chair for about 18 years, and had become used to routinely ignoring provisions of the departmental operating paper that were, no doubt, irksome to him (e.g., he did not allow committees to elect their own chairs, voted inappropriately as only an ad hoc member of search committees, and did not follow tenure and promotion and merit guidelines). He also violated the operating paper by creating a new 12-month associate chair position (for a department of about 6) and appointing Geoffrey Nathan (husband of Margaret Winters, the associate vice chancellor who later became interim provost) to that position. When operating paper violations were brought to Angelis's attention quietly in the privacy of his office, he disregarded them. When they were brought to his attention during meetings, he raised his voice and threatened to have faculty removed. I filed a grievance against Angelis for, mainly, repeatedly refusing to follow the operating paper. It was dismissed up the chain of command until it was heard by the University's Judicial Review Board, which decided in my favor unanimously, adding that there seemed to be an atmosphere of intimidation in the department. Shortly afterward, and independent of this, Angelis failed in reelection and was removed as chair. He may have held his removal in part against me. This was the first of the four events

The second involves another grievance. Geoff Nathan, husband to Associate Vice Chancellor (later to become Interim Provost) Margaret Winters, served a semester as interim chair. He had served as a witness for Angelis during my previous grievance and, in my opinion, continued the custom of flouting our operating paper. I filed a grievance against Nathan for violating the merit guidelines of our operating paper by using capricious and arbitrary criteria to assign my merit. Although I was miffed about what I perceived to be a politically motivated, unfairly low merit review, in this case, I was more interested in filing the grievance to help interpret and, hopefully, strengthen vaguely worded sections of the collective bargaining agreement, than I was about the pittance I might gain in additional salary. This grievance was dismissed by interim dean Robert Jensen (a close friend of Nathan and Winters), but, remarkably, resolved by interim provost Thomas Guernsey who found in my favor before it advanced to arbitration. Losing this grievance clearly angered Nathan, who complained about it to a new dean nearly a year later (*Friedenberg vs. Winters et al.*, deposition of Shirley Clay Scott, 2003).

The third incident involved a slight I was forced to deliver to CESL faculty by the new collective bargaining contract. Since CESL faculty were not among the tenure-track and tenured faculty and, therefore, not in the bargaining unit, they could no longer have more than an advisory vote on amendments to the Departmental Operating Paper. It is my impression that the CESL faculty felt disenfranchised because they were not part of the bargaining unit and deeply resented my enthusiasm for the union. Indeed, at the end of one tense meeting in which this issue was discussed, CESL term faculty member Floyd Olive preceded me out the door and pushed the door back hard on me. Tensions in the department worsened and included slammed doors, shouting at faculty meetings, threatening phone calls, the stalking of a colleague of mine, a faculty member aiming her moving truck at me while I was walking to class, and my missing mail. Glenn Gilbert, who had lost the bid to be interim chair to Geoffrey Nathan and who aspired to become the next permanent chair, began disseminating email attempting rather overtly to rally the CESL faculty against me by accusing me unfairly of attempting to disempower the CESL faculty through operating paper amendments.

Departmental relations had become so bad at this point that I went with a colleague to then Chancellor Argersinger to appeal for intervention. Argersinger committed to engaging an outside expert to conduct mediation or conflict resolution for our department and asked provost Thomas Guernsey to coordinate the effort with the department chair, now Glenn Gilbert. A few weeks later, Chancellor Argersinger was removed as chancellor, and although Provost Guernsey did his best to bring about counseling and conflict resolution for the department, he too left his position and was replaced by Margaret Winters before any real progress was made. During this time, things in the department were almost intolerable, as Gilbert moved my office from the linguistics department area to the history department, "next to Jo Ann Argersinger," and scheduled the move during the Jewish High Holy Days, a move that was unnecessary and, in my opinion, designed to humiliate and harass me. After my office was moved from the department area, I began missing mail. Gilbert was delaying approval of my sabbatical application and I later learned that he had been trying to find an excuse to turn it down (allegedly because he believed I would use my sabbatical time to file grievances instead of carry out research), including resorting to having his wife, Sharon, contact a leading member of the Jewish community to inquire about my competence to conduct research on Jewish themes. (Amusingly, when asked in a sworn deposition how Gilbert's wife Sharon could have gotten a hold of my sabbatical application, Dean Shirley Clay Scott stated, "I don't think it's a reasonable assumption to say that he [Glenn Gilbert] shared the application with her [Sharon Gilbert].") (*Friedenberg vs. Winters et al.*, deposition of Shirley Clay Scott, July 30, 2003, p. 137:14-15). In addition to these indignities, I was subjected to harsh shouting by CESL term lecturer, Floyd Olive, simply for raising my hand while he was speaking during a meeting (while the chair and others said nothing), to continued dissemination of embarrassing email about me by the chair; was the subject of shouting and eye-rolling at meetings and having doors slammed closed when I walked by, was the subject of accusations concerning missing department materials (that were later found in Chairman Gilbert's home), and was reprimanded for not attending meetings scheduled on Jewish holidays.

After considerable pressure from my department (initiated by me) to engage a counselor, Interim-Provost Winters produced a set of potential counselors for us to consider. The department unanimously selected Dr. Debra A.G. Robinson, director of the counseling center at the University of Missouri, Rolla, a licensed psychologist and officer in the Consulting Psychology Division of the American Psychological Association. Dr. Robinson looked to be ideal, given her involvement with organizations and her direct experience with universities. Gilbert continued to delay bringing her to campus, however, despite my continued protests. He and interim provost Winters finally informed us that Dr. Robinson would begin her work with the department during the Fall 2000 semester, after I would begin a 12-month sabbatical leave. This timing was a great disappointment to me, since I had hoped to leave behind departmental problems and the consequential effects they had on my health, before taking my sabbatical leave.

The fourth event, which took place after Debra Robinson had been selected and scheduled but before she arrived, involved yet another grievance. After doing everything in his power to damage my relations with faculty through gossip and innuendo, Gilbert wrote in my merit review that my service was soured by my "adversarial positions" and assigned to me merit ratings that, once again, appeared to be politically motivated (i.e., capricious and arbitrary). This grievance was resolved to my satisfaction through arbitration. Later, I filed a harassment complaint against Gilbert for the office move, missing mail, emails, etc., which the university's Affirmative Action director, Seymour Bryson, refused to investigate.

The "Counseling" and "Conflict Resolution" Process

Psychologist Debra A.G. Robinson was on campus from August 28 to 29, 2000, to hold private interviews with both the Linguistics and CESL faculty. I noticed when I was signing up for a meeting time that interim provost Winters (union opponent and wife of Nathan) had scheduled meetings between Dr. Robinson and select administrators, including former interim dean Robert Jensen (close friend of Nathan and Winters, who dismissed my ultimately successful grievance against Nathan), John Jackson (close ally of Winters and Nathan and of Ted Sanders, who fired chancellor JoAnn Argersinger), Margaret Winters herself, and current Dean Shirley Scott. Missing were former provost Thomas Guernsey and former chancellor Argersinger, who were the administrators chiefly involved in looking into the problems in the Linguistics department and who had originally approved outside counseling and conflict resolution for it. It is worth mentioning again that Guernsey had previously found in my favor when I filed a grievance against Nathan (husband of the new interim provost Winters). Because of the selective administrative involvement, the "counseling" began to take on the appearance of a "put-up job" although I had full confidence that a competent and ethical psychologist who worked at a university herself would sniff out political manipulations.

I arrived at my office a few minutes before my appointment. Psychologist Robinson arrived shortly after and began asking me some questions that appeared to be based on a written list. I wanted to make specific complaints against specific people in my department, but Dr. Robinson instructed me not to name names and to simply answer her questions. I found her questions to be limiting, but did my best to cooperate.

At one point in the session, Dr. Robinson asked me about my sabbatical research. She indicated to me that she could discern a visible change in my face when discussing my sabbatical research, an observation that was probably true because I actually felt different (i.e., happier) when I thought about and discussed my research.

I told Dr. Robinson that there had been many conflicts and that things had gotten so tense in the department that I was sometimes fearful for my safety. I told her I was in the process of writing a harassment complaint against the department chair. She advised me to "stop filing grievances" and to concentrate only on my research. This advice surprised me because I had not told her about any other grievances and because I felt that she knew too little about the substance and basis for my grievance to make such a hasty and decisive recommendation.

Dr. Robinson also asked me for suggestions for the department and I provided her with several regarding the structural make-up of the department, as well as recommendations on how to cut down on gossip and to increase civility in the department. Near the end of the interview, I asked Dr. Robinson what the next step would be. She asked me what I thought it should be. I told her that I thought it was important for the department to establish ground rules for communication and civil behavior. Dr. Robinson indicated that there would be a group meeting and that she thought she would have the faculty brainstorm ways in which they thought they could behave better towards one another. I indicated to her that for a long time I had advocated (audio) tape recording our meetings as a way to either prevent uncivil behavior or to document it and perhaps learn from it. She then suggested that video recording would be even more effective since we could watch our non-verbal behaviors towards one another. I enthusiastically endorsed this idea and told her that I was frequently subjected to eye-rolling at department meetings. I had the impression that she would recommend our video-taping our future meetings. I had the impression from Dr. Robinson that changing departmental behavior would be a process and that she would be returning periodically to work with us.

At the end of the session, I remarked to Dr. Robinson that I was extremely distressed around my colleagues, I dreaded the thought of dealing with departmental conflicts during my sabbatical leave, and that I had an inclination not to attend the group meeting, although I would likely comply with any rules of behavior the department came up with to make life more civil. Dr. Robinson indicated to me in a very enthusiastic way that I should not attend the group meeting and that I should just concentrate on my research and enjoy my sabbatical.

At no time did Dr. Robinson indicate that there would be any limits on confidentiality, that she would be disseminating our responses, or that she would be making a report to the university administration. I left the private session with Dr. Robinson believing only that she would be working with the faculty directly in a process of helping us through counseling and conflict resolution to get along better.

After the session ended, I engaged in some small talk with Robinson as we walked to the car. I did not remember which university she was affiliated with and whether she was also affiliated with the psychology department of her university. I asked her what her position was at the university and she responded, "I'm an administrator, Joan." I sensed this response was the result of her being told that I disliked administrators, otherwise she would have said something like, "I'm head of the counseling center."

Approximately one month later, Dr. Robinson met with several members of the Linguistics and CESL faculties as a group. Although I did not attend this meeting, it was my understanding from my private session with Dr. Robinson that the primary purpose of this meeting was to have the faculty brainstorm some ground rules for getting along together better. I assumed that Dr. Robinson would put forth the suggestion that departmental meetings be video recorded for the time being. However, one of my colleagues contacted me by telephone after this meeting and indicated to me that Robinson had listed and disseminated all our responses to her in the private sessions and that, close to the end of the group meeting, Dr. Robinson indicated that she would be sending a report to the university administration. My colleague was not happy that our responses were revealed, even anonymously, since we are a small department and listing what we said could only serve to fuel more gossip and assumptions about who said what. My colleague indicated to me that Paul Angelis, Geoffrey Nathan, Colleen Brice, Kim Wilhelm, and Floyd Olive complained about me during the meeting, with Paul Angelis insisting repeatedly that Dr. Robinson mention my name as the source of the department's problems in her report to the administration. My colleague told me that Kim Wilhelm asked why I had not attended the meeting and that Robinson never said a word about counseling me to stay away, which surprised me.

Two days later, on September 29, 2000, on the eve of Rosh Hashana, Glenn Gilbert forwarded by email a report by Robinson to members of the linguistics and CESL faculty, as well as to secretaries, administrators, and faculty from other departments who had adjunct status in linguistics (but who had no knowledge of or involvement with the counseling and conflict resolution). The following excerpt of Robinson's report is written in the original and syntax and other errors have not been edited.

> Throughout the session faculty brought up issues and concerns. Although there was disagreement among the various viewpoints, people listened and allowed others to speak. Several faculty expressed the opinion that Joan

Friedenberg was the sources of their problems. Her name was mentioned at a higher frequency than any other name during the individual interviews as well. This points to the need for meeting of the faculty with a university official, possible Dean Scott, to allow faculty to openly discuss their fear of and anger towards this faculty member. It would be important for this official to have a direct conversation with Joan to discuss the impact she is having on departmental faculty as a whole and address the personal ramifications of her behavior. Assistance to change the destructive behaviors should be offered if she so desires. The group was told that you cannot change someone who does not wish to change and that tenure confers some privileges related to job security. (*Friedenberg v. Winters et al.*; Plaintiff's Deposition Exhibit #16)

I found these words shocking and, immediately upon reading them, experienced dizziness, palpitations, and dry mouth. I felt a sense of even greater outrage when I noticed the extent of the distribution list, among them people I had never even met. I felt as if I had been gang raped. But probably worse than the embarrassment was the realization that things would never improve at work and would likely grow even worse.

I immediately shot off an angry and sarcastic response to Robinson (*Friedenberg v. Winters et al.*; Plaintiff's Deposition Exhibit #18) accusing her of conducting a witch hunt on behalf of the administration. I indicated that I should be told the specifics of my so-called destructive behavior and suggested it was no more than filing a couple of (successful) grievances. I complained that she had invited the faculty to vent their anger towards me, when, in fact, some of them had been doing that quite vigorously already. I suggested to her that if the administration was so interested in getting rid of me it should transfer my husband and me to our other campus in Edwardsville or offer an early retirement package. I then complained to her that she misspelled my family name, using a German spelling instead of a Jewish one.

A few minutes later, I sent Robinson a second email informing her that Gilbert was disseminating her draft report throughout the campus. Robinson responded to my first email by inviting me to tell her more about what I would like so that she could help by including it in her special (i.e., secret) report to the administration (*Friedenberg vs. Winters et al.*, Plaintiff's exhibit #31). Sensing that she was trying to compromise me in some way, I stopped communicating with her. She never responded to my email complaining about the wide distribution of her report. I later learned, to my astonishment, that this psychologist had been forwarding my email to the department chair, dean and interim provost.

Later in the day, CESL term lecturer Floyd Olive took Robinson's open invitation to mob me further by writing and distributing a letter about me, likening my hand-raising four months prior in a faculty meeting, to a school child who was worried about having a personal hygiene accident. Although I knew nothing about mobbing at the time, in retrospect, I had become a classic victim of it, in September 2000.

Mobbing

Heinz Leymann (in Davenport *et al.* 1999, pp. 36-37) developed a comprehensive "Mobbing Typology" consisting of 45 mobbing behaviors that are grouped by five degrees. Davenport *et al.* (1999, p. 41) provide a list of ten key factors of the mobbing syndrome and Westhues (2004, p. 30) provides a helpful checklist of ten clues that mobbing has occurred. For purposes of this paper, I will apply Westhues's ten clues to my own situation.

1. High-achieving target. Westhues suggests, as do Davenport *et al.*, (1999) that mobbing targets are successful people who are popular in other circles. In my case, modesty aside, I have consistently received among the highest evaluations for teaching, research, and service in the department. I have more publications and grants than anyone in my department and the wall in my office, literally covered with plaques and certificates of appreciation, suggests that my efforts have been valued, at least by some.

2. Lack of due process. Westhues contends that in most mobbing cases established procedures are not followed, although there is often an effort to make it appear that they are. Unsubstantiated accusations about me were made with no opportunity for me to respond, yet, according to notes taken in relation to a December 2000 meeting and an affidavit by university chief counsel Peter Ruger, Ruger met with interim Provost Margaret Winters, Department Chairman Glenn Gilbert, and College of Liberal Arts Dean Shirley Clay Scott to lay out a plan for my termination. Again, to this day, I have never actually been accused of anything, making it impossible for me to respond in any way. And no established procedures have ever been used to address my supposed shortcomings. It is my belief that despite the fact that my "crimes" were all legally protected activities (e.g., union organizing, filing grievances, expressing opinions critical of officials, filing FOIAs, and suing the Trustees), at least one member of the University administration has been attempting to trump up charges such as unprofessional conduct, misuse of university resources, insubordination, and incompetence to terminate me.

3. Odd timing. Westhues contends that mobbers attack when the victim is least likely to be able to defend herself. Indeed, in my case, the mobbing occurred while I was on leave and not present. I had even been told by the psychologist not to attend the group meeting. Similarly, Westhues's own mobbing occurred while he, too, was on sabbatical leave (Westhues 1998).

4. Resistance to external review. Westhues indicates that impassioned mobbers try to avoid outside scrutiny of their actions. Here, the university insisted that an internal grievance I subsequently filed against interim provost Winters be "closed" to observers and when approached by reporters about this case, the university has refused to comment.

5. Secrecy. Eliminators, according to Westhues, like to keep their proceedings secret. Robinson ended up developing a second "confidential" report that was kept by the university administration. The university attempted to get a protective order for Robinson's report when I requested it as part of the discovery for legal action I had taken. This report was the only communication that even vaguely alluded to why the university was so unhappy with me. The problem, though, was that the majority of the part about me was based on complete fabrications, which was the likely motivation for the university's extraordinary efforts to keep it a secret from me and others.

6. Unanimity. Psychologist Robinson said in her deposition that my name was mentioned as a source of problems "**90 percent of the time**" (*Friedenberg vs. Winters et al.,* Deposition of Debra A.G. Robinson, p. 123). Similarly, CESL teachers Catherine Caldwell and Kim Wilhelm, agreed with Robinson's assessment with their respective statements that claim "there was **overwhelming group consensus** that Joan's name needed to be documented as the primary source of our dysfunction as a department." (Catherine Caldwell to Kent Robinson, 9/18/01; *Friedenberg vs. Winters;* Respondent's exhibit #4) and "**nearly everyone** at the meeting was in **strong**

agreement that …some mention should be made of this particular problem (person)" (Kim Hughes Wilhelm to Kent Robinson, 9/17/01; *Friedenberg vs. Winters;* Respondent's exhibit #3). And although unanimity supports a case for mobbing better than diversity of opinion does according to Westhues, in my case colleagues reported that only about a third of the faculty actually complained about me, although those who did complain claimed to be representing the views of everyone. In addition, deposition testimony indicates that other people were complained about during the "counseling" although they were not named.

7. **Fuzzy charges**. Charges cited in elimination cases are usually vague and numerous and sometimes imagined, according to Westhues. Despite requesting from Robinson some specifics about my "destructive behavior," to this day, I have never been informed about what I did to merit the exclusion and attacks. Robinson's secret final report alludes only to my filing grievances and to not supporting my colleagues' tenure and promotion bids. While I had filed three (successful) grievances in the six years prior to Robinson's visit to our campus, most of my tenure and promotion votes were positive and the couple that were negative were not supported by others either, including the administration. During his deposition, former department chair Glenn Gilbert indicated that the only real problem with me was that I had made requests (that were not belligerent in any way) not to have departmental meetings late on Fridays due to my observance of the Sabbath, that I had once raised my hand during a department meeting while someone else was speaking, and I had filed grievances (*Friedenberg vs. Winters et al.*, Deposition of Glenn Gilbert 2002, pp.80-99).

8. **Prior Marginalization**. Westhues distinguishes between conventional social control and mobbing in that with the former the crime comes first and is then followed by the apprehension of the criminal, while with the latter the "criminal" is identified first and then the "crimes" come to light. Although I had alienated members of the departmental group shortly after arriving on campus, real marginalization did not begin in my case until I filed a grievance and unionization began and until I exercised my right to request information under the Freedom of Information Act, participated in union activities, published opinion pieces in the newspaper critical of the administration, and joined in the suit against the Trustees. By the time Robinson had arrived on campus, I had been marginalized already for nearly three years, including, as mentioned, having my

office moved out of the department area; having doors slammed closed when walking down the department's hallway; having a door thrown closed on me when leaving a meeting; being shouted and spat at, and subjected to eye-rolling and then receiving letters of reprimand when I did not have the stomach to attend; being called names, such as "little twerp," having important meetings scheduled on Jewish holidays and then receiving letters of reprimand for not attending; missing both incoming and outgoing mail; being the target of untrue rumors about tenure and promotion votes and misleading gossip about proposals for operating paper wording; being blamed for missing department materials, and having a colleague scare me with her pickup truck on a campus street. Ironically, it was because of all of the prior marginalization that I was the one who requested the services of a counselor/conflict resolver for the department, a counselor who would only end up aiding in the mobbing process.

9. Impassioned rhetoric. Westhues (2004) indicates that the more excited the language used against the target, the less likely is there a basis for mobbing and the more likely there is nothing but a collective will to destroy. In addition, he points out that most mobbing rhetoric focuses on the person and not on any particular acts the person committed (p. 28) and it frequently creates the appearance that people have reason to be frightened of and therefore need protection from the targeted employee (p. 227). These generalizations are clearly supported by the statements about me below

- "...allow faculty to openly discuss their **fear** of and **anger** towards this faculty member (Debra A.G. Robinson, 9/28/00; (*Friedenberg vs. Winters et al.*, Plaintiff's Deposition Exhibit #16).
- "Assistance to change the **destructive** behaviors should be offered if she so desires." (Debra A.G. Robinson, 9/28/00; (*Friedenberg vs. Winters et al.*, Plaintiff's Deposition Exhibit #16).
- " Members of this department are **terrified** of Joan who is a **powerful** tenured full professor" (Geoffrey Nathan to Debra Robinson,9/29/00; *Friedenberg vs. Winters et al.*, Plaintiff's Deposition Exhibit # 66). .
- "...how we are to cope with the **turmoil** she has introduced and continues to **stir up.**" (Geoffrey Nathan to Debra Robinson, 9/29/00; *Friedenberg vs. Winters et al.*, Plaintiff's Deposition Exhibit # 66).

- "Joan Friedenberg's **attacks** are **dangerous** for the morale and integrity of the department." (Glenn Gilbert to Debra Robinson, 9/29/00; *Friedenberg vs. Winters et al.*, Plaintiff's Deposition Exhibit #19).
- "the cost of **picking up the pieces left from our disintegration** would be far more than the cost of doing whatever it takes to ...**get her out** of the university..." (Glenn Gilbert to Debra Robinson, 9/29/00; *Friedenberg vs. Winters et al.*, Plaintiff's Deposition Exhibit #19).
- "I question Friedenberg's **professional competence... she should be removed** from this committee..." (Glenn Gilbert to Dean Shirley Clay Scott, 9/13/01; *Friedenberg vs. Winters et al.*, Plaintiff's Deposition Exhibit #20).
- "What I viewed as especially serious ... was F's **attacks on a student** if that would serve her ends." "She is **unscrupulous** when it comes to the university's primary mission—giving students a good education. This suggests F is **professionally irresponsible** and beyond that, **incompetent,** and this might be another factor in the case to **have her terminated.**" ... ..." (Glenn Gilbert to Kent Robinson, 9/17/01; *Friedenberg vs. Winters et al.*, Plaintiff's Deposition Exhibit # 23).
- "We might be able to **charge her** with **misuse of university property** and resources." (Glenn Gilbert to Kent Robinson, 9/17/01; *Friedenberg vs. Winters et al.*, Plaintiff's Deposition Exhibit #23).
- "Once again **her Jekyl and Hyde personality** promptly emerged but there was no easy way to get rid of her." "She hides behind academic freedom, first amendment rights, the Jewish faith, and the Faculty Association." "**In hurting, stalking, and devastating others** as she has done..." (Glenn Gilbert to Kent Robinson, 9/17/01; *Friedenberg vs. Winters et al.*, Plaintiff's Deposition Exhibit # 23).
- "For the sake of our faculty and students, I would again urge you **in the strongest terms** to **reassign Friedenberg out of our department.**" (Glenn Gilbert to Shirley Clay Scott, 5/10/01; *Friedenberg vs. Winters et al.*, Plaintiff's Deposition Exhibit #21).

- "Her behavior ... is almost **beyond belief.**" (CESL teacher Catherine Caldwell to Kent Robinson, 9/18/01; *Friedenberg vs. Winters;* Respondent's exhibit #4)
- "...**overwhelming group consensus** was that Joan's name needed to be documented as the primary source of our **dysfunction** as a department." (Catherine Caldwell to Kent Robinson, 9/18/01; *Friedenberg vs. Winters;* Respondent's exhibit #4)
- "...nearly **everyone** at the meeting was in **strong agreement** that in order to be true to the data gathered, some mention should be made of **this particular problem (person).**" (CESL staff member Kim Hughes Wilhelm to Kent Robinson, 9/17/01; *Friedenberg vs. Winters;* Respondent's exhibit #3)

10. Backbiting. Westhues contends that rumors and "whispering campaigns" are common attributes of the elimination process (p. 32). I remember walking down the linguistics hallway one afternoon after my office had been moved to the area that houses the history department, and seeing a group of faculty huddled in the middle of the hallway. Upon seeing me approach, the group immediately dispersed and hid away in their respective offices. Additionally, I discovered in Robinson's secret report to the administration that she had been told that I had been fired from my position as CESL director, presumably for poor performance, and that I had not supported most of my colleagues' tenure and promotion bids. These assertions were simply untrue and obviously designed to encourage and justify my mobbing. Department Chair Gilbert routinely wrote and disseminated email making a variety of untrue accusations about me.

The Effects of Mobbing

Needless to say, I became quite distressed by the psychologist's legitimizing and assisting my colleagues' and the administration's mobbing of me. I felt betrayed by the psychologist and by the entire field of psychology. I still find it difficult to believe, a sign of naiveté on my part, that a licensed psychologist could behave in this way. In the weeks and months that followed the incidents of September 29, 2000, I suffered from depression, insomnia, significant weight loss, rashes, bouts of diarrhea and constipation, and nightmares that people were coming after me. I did not want to go out in public and did so only out of town, when someone locally needed my help, or when it involved my synagogue. Otherwise, almost all socializing took place in my home with close friends or in their homes. I sometimes replayed the incident of reading Robinson's draft report over and over in my mind and felt sickened once again. I lost interest in intimacy with my husband and even wet the bed on a couple of occasions. I began to suffer panic attacks and still do today, necessitating occasional calls to 911. I have become paranoid about being followed, fired, or harmed and have difficulty concentrating. Three years later, I have gained only half my weight back. I suffered so much anxiety that I began picking at my cuticles and biting the side of my tongue, habits that are still difficult to control. I also suffer from the return of an arrhythmia that I have not had in many years and am on medication to control it. Medication now also helps my insomnia.

Life at work has improved by my being awarded a large federal grant that has "bought" me a good deal of freedom from administrative control. However, I still feel physically sick each time I go to campus and I have never been invited to participate on a single college or university committee again. The dean has informed my department that she plans to eliminate it. I plan to retire as soon as I turn 55, and to leave the area, if I am not successfully eliminated first.

For evidentiary purposes, I engaged a forensic psychologist to assess my damages and after administering to me numerous unpleasant tests over many months, he concluded that I suffered from Post-Traumatic Stress Disorder, chronic with noteworthy interpersonal hypervigilance, adjustment disorder with depressed mood along with depression and anxiety, and that the incident of September 29, 2000 substantially contributed to these impairments.

Indeed, the findings of the forensic psychologist are consistent with the literature regarding common effects of workplace mobbing, including post-traumatic stress disorder (Davenport *et al.* 1999; Westhues 2004; Name & Namie 2003). Leymann, as reported in Westhues (2004), found in his research on workplace stress that the worst threat to worker health and safety is "The threat of collective, frequent, enduring hostile communication, of being isolated, silenced, ridiculed, gossiped about, threatened, harassed..." (p. 42).

Responding to the Mobbing

There is a growing literature on ways to respond to mobbing, including how to cope with it and ways to fight back (Davenport *et al.*

1999; Westhues 2004; Westhues 1998; Namie & Namie 2003). These measures include, among others, resigning; taking legal action; enlisting the help of friends, family, and a good therapist; and informing the media. I have taken a comprehensive approach by seeking support from close friends and family members, engaging the help of my family doctor and a good therapist, exercising more, and by attempting to expose my university's and the psychologist's behavior through internal grievance boards, a state agency, professional credentialing organizations, the mass media, the legal system, by word of mouth, and by educating. For the purposes of this paper, I will discuss my experiences with professional credentialing organizations, the legal system, the mass media, word of mouth, and what I call education.

Professional Credentialing Organizations

According to the American Psychological Association, the primary purpose of the APA Ethics Code is to "protect the public by deterring unethical conduct by psychologists."

I filed complaints against psychologist Robinson with the Missouri State Committee of Psychologists, as well as the American Psychological Association (APA). Although the APA opened a case against Robinson, it later dismissed it on the grounds of insufficient evidence. The Missouri State Committee of Psychologists also dismissed my complaint, but without explanation.

I have come to believe that professional accrediting agencies exist mostly to protect their member professionals and not the public. When I filed complaints with these organizations, Robinson would have access to all documents I submitted, but I would not have access to any filed by her, even if I subpoenaed them. In addition, psychologist Robinson was given the opportunity to respond to my complaints, but I was not given the opportunity to respond to her responses. For example, if Robinson had indicated that she never visited our campus or met me and that all my allegations were phony, I would have no knowledge of these statements and therefore not have an opportunity to prove otherwise. Westhues (2003, personal communication) also indicates that complaints against the mental health professionals who, without having met a whistle-blower police officer, signed a report indicating that he was mentally ill, were also dismissed by the Complaints Committee of the Ontario College of

Physicians and Surgeons and the Complaints Committee of the Ontario College of Psychologists.

It is important to point out that perhaps the single most critical principle to follow when fighting workplace mobbing, whether it be with credentialing agencies, the legal system, internal judicial boards, government judicial boards, or the media, is perseverance. After *both* credentialing organizations dismissed my charges, Robinson was forced to submit to a sworn deposition through my legal action against her and to justify her conduct. It was then that I became aware of her defense: that despite maintaining a current license as a psychologist, serving as an officer in the APA, and serving as the director of her university's counseling center at the time, Debra Robinson maintained that she does not consider herself to be a psychologist. Prominent psychology ethics expert Gerald Koocher disagreed and it is important to mention how emotionally therapeutic reading Koocher's report, excerpted below, was for me:

> The essence of my opinion is that Dr. Robinson, by her own admission under oath in deposition testimony, acknowledged acts of omission and commission that clearly constitute a breach of the professional duty she owed to Dr. Friedenberg. In so doing, Dr. Robinson's conduct fell substantially below the usual professional standards expected of psychologists in consulting practice. In attempting to defend her conduct, Dr. Robinson made assertions regarding psychologists' ethics that are significantly inaccurate and seem calculated to deny responsibility for her actions.

Koocher went on to say that Robinson should have known the appropriate conduct expected of a psychologist, that her assertions that she was not functioning as a psychologist at SIUC are invalid, that she should have known that her methods of data collection would have adverse consequences for me, that she created a forum for the hostile scapegoating of me, that she had an obligation to clarify to me and to others any limits on confidentiality that might apply to our communications with her, that she failed to retain significant records and data germane to the SIUC consultation; that she disseminated information that I reasonably assumed would be treated as confidential, that her responses about what consulting psychology entails seem "disingenuous, at best" and a "feeble attempt to avoid being held accountable for her professional errors," that she exhibited

"inappropriate casualness" in adhering to the APA code of conduct
and "inadequate professional responsibility." Koocher concludes:

> In summary, it is my professional opinion that Dr.
> Robinson's consultation to SIU was indeed professional
> work of a nature that triggered all ethical obligations
> delineated by the APA *Ethical Principles of Psychologists
> and Code of Conduct*. It is also my opinion that Dr.
> Robinson has at minimum acknowledged failure to follow
> proper notification, confidentiality protection, and record
> retention requirements. In addition, by failing to clarify
> relationships and limits of confidentiality, and by
> subsequently releasing information in the manner described,
> Dr. Robinson caused foreseeable harm to Dr. Friedenberg.
> The harm resulted from behavior on the part of Dr.
> Robinson that was clearly in violation of well-accepted
> professional standards (*Friedenberg vs. Winters et al.*,
> Expert Witness Report by Gerald Koocher, April 5, 2003).

On April 30, 2003, I submitted both the deposition transcript and
Koocher's report to the APA requesting that the case against
Robinson be re-opened, given the evidence from her deposition and
Koocher's written analysis of it. As of this writing, I have received
only an acknowledgment from the APA that my request was received.

The Legal System

Depending on the legal system can be even more frustrating than
depending on professional credentialing agencies because it is costlier
and potentially no more fair. Davenport *et al.* (1999) outline realistic
disadvantages and benefits of seeking legal recourse, including the
fact that legal recourse is expensive, stressful, long, and uncertain.
Davenport *et al.* point out that potential advantages include not
allowing oneself to be victimized, helping to prevent future
administrative abuses, and the possibility of recouping lost wages and
benefits. Another benefit of seeking legal redress is that having an
ongoing lawsuit allows for more opportunity to expose the abuses in
the mass media. Put simply, the media seem uninterested in covering
stories that are not in court. The potential beauty of using courts in
this way is that if one does not find justice in court or compensation
for one's damages, it is still possible to find justice in the "court" of
popular opinion, through the media. The literature on mobbing
suggests that most courts are biased in favor of employers (Westhues

1998; Namie & Namie 2003). Nevertheless, keeping my case in the system helps me to promote it to various mass media outlets and expose my university's and the psychologist's conduct. Other mobbing victims may be, understandably, less inclined to have themselves exposed in the mass media for fear that it may damage their ability to secure future employment.

Davenport *et al.* (1999) point out that unlike in many European countries, mobbing is not covered under any laws in the U.S. However, they offer other possible legal options, depending on the nature and likely causes for the mobbing, including federal civil rights laws that prohibit discrimination and laws against hostile work environment, defamation, and wrongful discharge.

I filed a malpractice lawsuit in state court against Robinson and a federal lawsuit (conspiracy to chill my speech) under the *First Amendment of the U.S. Constitution,* the *Due Process Clause of the Fourteenth Amendment of the U.S. Constitution,* and *Title 42 of the United States Code, Section 1983,* against former interim provost Margaret E. Winters, former department chair Glenn Gilbert, and psychologist Debra A.G. Robinson. Southern Illinois University has provided the three defendants in the federal case with free legal representation, despite the fact that two of the three are not affiliated with SIU in any way (defendant Winters had already left SIUC and moved to Wayne State University in Detroit to become the Associate Provost for Academic Personnel; defendant Robinson continues to work at the University of Missouri-Rolla and has since been promoted from counseling center director to vice-chancellor for student affairs in addition to serving as the editor for APA's Division 13 newsletter, *The Consulting Psychologist*; and defendant Gilbert remains at SIUC, although he was removed as department chair as a consequence of a no-confidence vote by the department). These cases are still in the courts after three years and have not yet come to trial. The defendants in the federal case filed a motion to dismiss that was denied and the state malpractice case has been stayed until the federal case is resolved.

The Mass Media

Davenport *et al.* (1999) point out that the media may be instrumental in creating public awareness of the mobbing syndrome. But Westhues (2004) aptly demonstrates that the media can be hurtful to the mobbing victim as well. He observes that in the noted case of theology professor Herbert Richardson, media reports were clearly hurtful. Although it is not clear whether Richardson or his university initially contacted the media, there were apparently over 50 reports unfavorable to Richardson in the local newspapers that subsequently spread throughout a good deal of North America (Westhues 2004).

Notifying the local media (in my town and in the psychologist's town) turned out to be surprisingly helpful, and lengthy articles about the psychologist and the appearance of collusion by SIUC administrators appeared in the local campus newspaper with headlines such as "Professor sues counselor, files grievances against administrators for misconduct" (*The Daily Egyptian*, August 30, 2001); in the weekly Carbondale newspaper with the headline, "Consultant in Ethics Charge" (*The Carbondale Times*, August 29, 2001); in the campus newspaper at the University of Missouri-Rolla and in the daily newspaper in Rolla, Missouri with the headline, "UMR director sued by college professor" (*Rolla Daily News*, September 13, 2001). I did not inform the local daily newspaper in Carbondale (*the Southern Illinoisan*) because of my perception that its reporting is heavily biased in favor of the university administration and because of its repeated anti-union stands. In addition to these, the *Chronicle of Higher Education* has assigned a reporter to follow this story. Many of my colleagues are of the opinion that Winters lost her bid to change her status from interim provost to permanent provost because of all the negative publicity surrounding my case, resulting in her having to leave the university in order to stay in administration.

It is possible that my media experiences were more positive than Richardson's (Westhues 2004) because I took the initiative to contact the media and I was well prepared to provide the media with a good deal of documentation to support my case. It is my hope that future media reports of my case will expose the university's and the psychologist's conduct in the national arena and that this and other exposure will encourage my university and other workplaces, as well as mental health professionals, to behave more appropriately in the future, as well as encourage legal and credentialing organizations to take the problem of workplace mobbing and political psychology and psychiatry more seriously.

Finally, as evidence that the media can sometimes be troublesome, I should note that the student newspaper at the University of Missouri-Rolla reported in January, 2004, that Robinson had been promoted once again and that the lawsuit against her was found in her favor – this despite the fact that the lawsuit has not yet been tried.

Word of Mouth

I also sought to expose the mobbing and political use of psychology through word of mouth. Concerned that Robinson held such a casual view of confidentiality and that she might actually harm students at her university, I informed members of the University of Missouri-Rolla counseling center (called the Center for Personal and Professional Development), as well as Robinson's superiors, of my complaints against her with the APA and in State Court. I will, no doubt, be accused of doing this solely to embarrass Dr. Robinson. Indeed, Westhues (2004, pp. 34-35) observes, "Those who have sought a person's removal from respectable company often interpret anything that person does afterwards, even survival, as an attempt at revenge."

I also began sharing my story with others at my university who had similar problems, and with former university employees still in the area who had been terminated by my university. This sharing became quite beneficial as we also shared resources and contacts. I began reading books and other resources about workplace mobbing, psychologist ethics, and political psychiatry, and contacted some of the authors who then put me in touch with other victims of mobbing or political psychology. This sharing of resources with others was not only emotionally therapeutic, it provided me with more outlets to respond to the university's and the psychologist's behavior.

Education

Education about workplace mobbing and political psychology's role in it comes most often from writing and publishing accounts of it and making presentations. In 2002, I contacted members of the Consulting Psychology Division of the APA and offered to make a presentation at their annual meeting in order to alert consulting psychologists of the dangers of being drawn into, perhaps unknowingly, workplace mobbing situations. I even offered to make the presentation together with Robinson, with the idea that she might wish to take a healthy approach by admitting her mistakes and helping other consulting psychologists avoid being dragged into such situations. Not surprisingly, the organization was unable to schedule such a presentation, although one of the individuals I had been in contact with thought the endeavor worthwhile.

Political Psychology

As mentioned in the introduction to this chapter, common targets of political psychiatry are whistleblowers, union activists, members of minority religions, persons who file grievances and complaints against employers and officials, and individuals who publicly criticize officials. Interestingly, common targets of workplace mobbing are whistleblowers, people who are "different" (e.g. in religion, skin color, language, sex, or physical appearance), creative individuals who promote new ideas, and highly principled and inner-directed individuals who ask "too many" questions and who champion the underdog (Davenport 1999). According to these criteria, I would be an ideal target of both political psychiatry and workplace mobbing. I functioned as a whistleblower when I filed Freedom of Information Act Requests that exposed the use by administrators of University vehicles and I functioned as a whistleblower when I filed a grievance against Angelis for flouting the rules of our department's Operating Paper. I have been a union activist. I am a member of a minority religion, which I have made obvious on occasion, including when I interviewed for the position during Passover and brought along with me to meals, matzoh. I have written numerous letters to the editor and guest columns criticizing the university administration and Board of Trustees; I have filed grievances against chairs for repeatedly violating operating paper procedures and for using capricious and arbitrary criteria in merit evaluations, the latter usually as a way to strengthen vaguely worded portions of the collective bargaining contract; and I joined with other faculty to sue the Board of Trustees for being illegally constituted.

Although from an average administrator's point of view my mobbing might be justified, the fact is that all of my activities were motivated by a sincere desire to make the university a more humane, fair, civil, and equitable place and all of my activities were legally protected and for an important reason. The United States prides itself on freedom, especially freedom of speech. Free speech, in fact, may be our country's single most valued ideal. It is an ideal that both liberals and conservatives alike fight vigorously to defend. Freedom of speech is the ideal that has resulted in the most powerful and sweeping changes in our country, including the rights of African Americans to vote, swim freely at public beaches and pools, eat in restaurants of their choice, attend colleges of their choice and sit wherever they wish on busses.

Using a psychologist for political purposes to degrade, publicly humiliate, and label me as destructive and in need of help, to invite further mobbing of me, and recommend my removal is, in my opinion, nearly as dangerous and egregious as the behavior of political psychiatrists in totalitarian governments. One critical difference, though, is that the World Psychiatric Association has recognized the problem, labeled it, and taken action to condemn and stop it, at least when it occurs at the hands of governments. What remains to be seen is whether the World Psychiatric Association and its member countries will see fit to also condemn the political use of psychiatrists by employers and whether the psychological community will also begin to address this serious problem.

The American Psychological Association (APA) is composed of several divisions, including ones for "consulting psychologists" (Division 13) and for "industrial and organizational psychologists" (Division 14). Both of these divisions have members who potentially address workplace matters. Lowman (1998) provides numerous examples of ethical compromises in workplace settings. In one example, Lowman relates a case of a psychologist who was hired to promote better team-building in an organization. Deciding that one of the participants was difficult, the psychologist had the employee moved away from the others during an exercise and proceeded to lead a discussion about that individual's behavior. The employee later returned to the group angry and hurt. In his interpretation of this case, Lowman indicates the psychologist had violated at least two ethical standards: "Boundaries of Competence" and "Avoiding Harm" (p. 95). He goes on to say that "the facilitator as a professional psychologist, had the responsibility to protect the dignity and well-being of the participants;" "must assume responsibility for maintaining an environment that is supportive rather than destructive;" and had an obligation to "help the other team members understand the role they may be playing in precipitating the behavior" (p. 96). In his final analysis of the case, Lowman states that "Failure to attend to the needs of specific team members who are persistently being scapegoated or isolated from the team demonstrates limited understanding by the facilitator of the potential power groups can have even on psychologically healthy individuals" (pp. 96-97). Lowman concludes by saying that "psychologists learning such techniques as ... conflict resolution should be fully trained ... to minimize the likelihood of their engendering psychological problems on the part of team participants" (p. 97).

As the above example illustrates (as does the previously discussed report by ethics expert Gerald Koocher), the American Psychological Association has an Ethics Code that contains numerous standards immediately applicable to workplace mobbing situations. However, both the APA and state licensing organizations in both the US and Canada turn a blind eye when it comes to enforcing these ethical standards, at least in workplace mobbing situations. It is, indeed, a sad commentary that a field that is supposed to help individuals who may be the victims of workplace mobbing is actually partly to blame for creating the problem in the first place! There is an urgent need for both the psychiatric and psychological communities to identify the problem of "political psychiatry" and "political psychology," re-examine their practices as they relate to workplace mobbing, and take appropriate punitive measures against practitioners who violate clearly established ethical standards to satisfy the political needs of employers. Additionally, mental health professionals need to be made aware of the phenomenon of workplace mobbing so that they can better help its victims.

Acknowledgements

The author gratefully acknowledges the very helpful reviews of Professor Mark A. Schneider, Department of Sociology, Southern Illinois University; Carbondale, IL, USA; Professor Kenneth Westhues, Department of Sociology, University of Waterloo, Ontario, Canada; Professor Albert Melone, Department of Political Science, Southern Illinois University Carbondale, IL, USA; Attorney Darrell Dunham, Professor Emeritus, School of Law, Southern Illinois University, Carbondale, IL; USA; Attorney Robert McCormick, Murphysboro, IL, USA; and Dr. David Clarke, Editor, *Knowledge, Technology, & Policy,* USA and France.

References

American Psychological Association Ethical Principles of Psychologists and Code of Conduct, 1992. Washington, DC: author.

Bezlova, Antoaneta, 2002. "China faces music for psychiatric abuse," *Inter Press Service.*

Brown, Charles, and Armando Lago, 1992. *Politics of Psychiatry in Revolutionary Cuba.* Sommerset, NJ: Transaction Publishers.

Davenport, Noa, Ruth Schwartz, and Gail Elliott, 1999. *Mobbing: Emotional Abuse in the American Workplace.* Ames, IA: Civil Society Publishing.

Friedenberg vs. Winters, Judicial Review Board Hearing, Southern Illinois University, Carbondale, IL, April 25, 2002; respondent's exhibits.

Friedenberg vs. Winters, Robinson and Gilbert, United States District Court for the Southern District of Illinois, Civil Action No. 02-4199-JLF; Deposition of Debra A. G. Robinson; February 28, 2003.

Friedenberg vs. Winters, Robinson and Gilbert, United States District Court for the Southern District of Illinois, Civil Action No. 02-4199-JLF; Deposition of Margaret E. Winters, February 17, 2003.

Friedenberg vs. Winters, Robinson and Gilbert, United States District Court for the Southern District of Illinois, Civil Action No. 02-4199-JLF; Deposition of Shirley Clay Scott; July 30, 2003.

Friedenberg vs. Winters, Robinson and Gilbert, United States District Court for the Southern District of Illinois, Civil Action No. 02-4199-JLF; Deposition of Glenn Gilbert; February 10, 2003.

Friedenberg vs. Winters, Robinson and Gilbert, United States District Court for the Southern District of Illinois, Civil Action No. 02-4199-JLF; Report by expert witness Gerald Koocher, April 5, 2003.

Gosden, Richard, 1997. "Shrinking the Freedom of Thought: How Involuntary Psychiatric Treatment Violates Basic Human Rights," *Monitors: Journal of Human Rights and Technology,* Vol. 1, February.

Hornstein, Harvey, 1996. *Brutal Bosses and their Prey: How to Identify and Overcome Abuse in the Workplace.* NY: Riverhead Books.

Human Rights Watch & the Geneva Initiative on Psychiatry (GIP), 2002. *Dangerous Minds: Political Psychiatry in China Today and its Origins in the Mao Era.*

Lowman, Rodney, 1998. *The Ethical Practice of Psychology in Organizations.* Washington, DC: American Psychological Association.

Namie, Gary, and Ruth Namie, 2003. *The Bully at Work.* Naperville, IL: Sourcebooks, Inc.

Pan, Philip, 2002. "The Silent Treatment from Beijing: Mental Hospitals Allegedly Used to Quiet Dissidents, Falun Gong," *Washington Post,* 8/26.

Westhues, Kenneth, 2004. *Administrative Mobbing at the University of Toronto: The Trial, Degradation, and Dismissal of a Professor During the Presidency of J. Robert S. Pritchard.* Lewiston, NY: The Edwin Mellen Press.

Westhues, Kenneth, 1998. *Eliminating Professors: A Guide to the Dismissal Process.* Lewiston, NY: Kempner Collegium Publications, The Edwin Mellen Press.

Chapter Fifteen

Research Ethics: a Tool for Harassment in the Academic Workplace

John H. Mueller

In his book on administrative mobbing, Westhues (2004) analyzes in detail the events leading up to the dismissal of Herbert Richardson from the University of Toronto in 1994. In addition, many other cases are noted, and a pattern emerges. The way that a distinguished academic's career can end in dismissal seems to follow a strategy that Westhues describes as "mobbing." The targets for such elimination usually have a history as popular achievers in their discipline and department, then at some point they find themselves subjected to intense attack. The attack focuses on some minor proclaimed offense, but the criticism is personal and directed toward the individual rather than the alleged incident. The demonizing criticism is highly emotional in tone, typically about a minor issue, and the critics are intolerant of dissenters or public scrutiny. The target must be removed from polite company, and thus the mob begins its vigilante action. The outcome may be elimination from the faculty, but even in the case of vindication such an experience leaves a large scar on the individual and the workplace.

It is sad that there have been enough cases of academic bullying to fill a book, but one suspects there are even many more that have not reached the public eye, if anything the trend seems toward more such incidents rather than fewer over the years. Understanding mobbing requires, in part, acknowledging that universities have changed over the years, and so the environment in which one starts an academic career will inevitably change. Among these changes, Westhues (p. 154 ff.) notes the distinction between a "covenant" and a "contract." A covenant is a loose and even open-ended commitment to duties and goals, "a broadly defined relationship of trust, governed mostly by unwritten rules ... (with) reciprocal loyalties" (p. 161), as in marriage vows. This is an "old-fashioned" approach, which implies, among other things, a mutual obligation to resolve conflicts in a collegial manner between equals. In contrast, the modern legalistic contract is a technical, detailed arrangement which is unbalanced in power favoring one party, and which requires an adversarial approach to conflict resolution. Rather than resolving the conflict, the contractual approach focuses on either finding a loophole to absolve a party from the agreement, or finding a technicality to coerce a party into an action – the letter of the law rather than the spirit of the law.

Although the growth of the legal industry no doubt plays some part, this rigid and detailed road-map approach has become the campus arrangement of choice coincident with the rise of a professional-manager type of campus administrator, the administrator self-styled as an executive, hired not by the campus but by an external consulting firm. Campus administrators today come less often from within and more often from outside the institution, and when they leave office they return to the outside, a national churning of 90-day wonders. As a result, these transients have no shared investment in the institution's history, nor any commitment to an ongoing shared future. This is hardly the foundation of a good marriage or any other covenant.

Although one might at first think a vague agreement offers the greater opportunity for treachery, in fact the lopsided contractual environment provides a laundry list of possible missteps for an academic, that is, a variety of "traps" that an administrator or mob can spring to induce a "difficult professor" to depart. Thus the incident used for elimination is usually some minor contractual oversight, in the context of longstanding overall satisfactory-plus achievement, that is, a matter of no fundamental importance from the perspective of a covenant.

It is possible to see this transition over the years in terms of the expectations about research on campus, and I will describe some of the ramifications of this. There are some recent incidents that are very disturbing in regard to how contractual aspects of research activities may become the incident that provokes a dismissal effort. Westhues (2004) briefly noted one of these, Justine Sergent at McGill, and I will describe some others. However, first, there is an historical incident that precedes formal ethics reviews that indicates the longstanding vulnerability of researchers in the social and behavioral sciences, in particular, to "right-thinking" censorship.

Max Meyer: "A matter of no fundamental importance"

As a new academic in the late 1960s, I was assigned to teach the History of Psychology course at the University of Missouri. I learned of the sorry experience of Max Meyer, a former faculty member in that same department forty 40 years earlier. His case seemed mostly quaint at the time, but I used it in class because it provided some local-color interest for students, and because it seemed to illustrate progress in academe and society over the years. I now believe that the progress is an illusion, caused by focusing on sexual mores as the issue, whereas that was more a symptom. Aside from the sexual content of the controversy, the general mechanics that were involved then are not only alive and well but flourishing in the modern research ethics industry on campus. Recast in this light, Meyer's case reinforces the notion of harassment and mobbing as described by Westhues (1998, 2004), and documents that social science research has long been subject to criticism and censorship by self-appointed morals police.

Max Meyer (1873-1967) was born in Germany and studied with several German psychologists in the 1890s. In 1898, he disagreed with his mentor, Carl Stumpf, over a substantive intellectual issue, and was dismissed from the University of Berlin by Stumpf. Meyer moved temporarily to London, and then to the United States. He was eventually hired at the University of Missouri in 1900, where he stayed until the incident in question led to his departure in 1929. Much of this time he was the only person in the department, and pursued his interests in areas such as the psychology of music and hearing. The circumstances of his career have been chronicled by Esper (1966, 1967), and I will only highlight the key points from Esper's treatment.

Although acknowledged as an excellent scientist and teacher, Meyer in some respects would be recognizable as what has been termed the "difficult professor" (Westhues 2001). That is, he was very principled himself, and he expected the same of those around him. His high standards earned him respect, but his demanding approach also contributed to making him an intellectual isolate. It is said that he had few close friends on campus, and his professional contacts also were few and often strained. There are a number of anecdotes about his outspoken behavior at academic meetings, where his direct, objective, and generally accurate critiques were not well received.

Over the years, his frustration grew because his own work did not receive the respect that he felt it deserved. History seems to support him on this; that is, his ideas deserved better coverage. There seem to be several reasons for this lack of influence. In part the problem was that his interests (hearing and music) were outside the mainstream, plus his approach was quite mathematical and thus very difficult. Furthermore, he made a series of poor choices of publishing outlets, and then his limited social "networking" skills were not able to bridge such limited dissemination. Nonetheless he performed quite well for the university for three decades, until "the incident."

Moral panic: Save the Children

As described by Esper (1967, p. 115), "Meyer's productive and dedicated career at the University of Missouri came in 1929 to the sudden and crashing end which is a nightmarish possibility for every professor deficient in protective coloring who teaches in a university governed by politicians and businessmen and at the mercy therefore of those mass hysterias which newspapers can so easily whip up ...." Fekete (1994) succinctly describes the contemporary manifestation of this as a "moral panic."

In 1929, Meyer became a benefactor for a sociology student, O. Hobart Mowrer, who wanted to develop a research questionnaire. In taking a sociology course entitled "The Family," Mowrer's group was to pursue a research project on "The economic aspect of woman." This materialized as an anonymous 11-item questionnaire sent out to university students, 500 fraternity men and 500 sorority women, using campus mail with the approval of someone within the University.

Most of the questionnaire items were about things such as divorce, alimony, economic independence for women, splitting expenses on dates, whether women should be able to ask men for a date, and such. However, the questionnaire also involved three items dealing with attitudes about extramarital sex: (1) one's position on the establishment of a legal system of trial marriage, (2) one's attitudes about finding that a prospective spouse had indulged in illicit sexual relations previously, and (3) whether one's sexual relations were restrained most by religious beliefs, fear of pregnancy, pride, fear of disease, or fear of social disapproval. The preamble for the questionnaire started with the statement, "It has become increasingly apparent that there is something seriously wrong with the traditional system of marriage ...."

Meyer's involvement was minor, helping with the wording of a few questions, and then graciously providing some envelopes for the questionnaires, obsolete letterhead with Meyer's name on it. Such admirable "recycling" around scarce materials would have been common practice in that era. As copies of the questionnaire surfaced in the community, the local newspaper editor traced them back to Meyer. In an editorial (*Columbia Daily Tribune*, March 13, 1929), the questionnaire was denounced by proclaiming, "Even asking an opinion, and this of 500 girls, as to trial and companionate marriage is a desecration and an outrage." Further, the basic premise of the study was rejected: "We wonder who told this graduate student, hardly dry behind the ears, that there is anything wrong with the 'traditional system of marriage'?"

At this point in time, what Westhues (2004) has described as a "covenant" was more the nature of campus interactions between faculty and administrators than an itemized contract. Although most of us could have readily explained our limited role and smoothed the waters, such was not Meyer's style nor did subsequent developments encourage him to capitulate. Likewise, any competent administrator could have handled the incident. However, the University President of the day was in conflict with the Board of Curators and with many politicians in the state legislature, and so chose to inflame this minor and atypical incident to try to deflect attention from his own troubles.

Meyer was suspended without pay for one year, and the Sociology professor (H. O. DeGraff) who taught Mowrer's class was summarily dismissed. The American Association of University Professors (AAUP) was a rather new institution at the time (formed in 1915), and the concept of "academic freedom" was in its infancy. Nonetheless, the AAUP had successfully pursued similar cases, including another "difficult" psychologist, James McKeen Cattell at Columbia, who had been dismissed for expressing pacifist views during World War I (Gruber 1972). Two other high-profile scandals involving sexual behavior by psychologists were recent developments. One was John Watson at Johns Hopkins University, whose affair with his research assistant led to divorce and dismissal in 1920. Ironically, Watson followed James Mark Baldwin at Johns Hopkins University, who was caught in a bordello raid and dismissed in 1909. However, Meyer's case was different from these in that it involved his intellectual behavior rather than his sexual peccadilloes.

Examining Meyer's case at Missouri, the AAUP investigation (Carlson et al. 1930) concluded that the punishments were excessive, that the only defensible charge against Meyer in particular was "a lack of attention or judgment on *a matter of no fundamental importance*" in the context of a fine collective career. The AAUP concluded that Meyer could, perhaps, have anticipated that the content would be socially sensitive, but given his 30 years of highly competent performance he was entitled to far better treatment by the President and the Board. This is the essence of many mobbing incidents described by Westhues (2004), where a minor incident in the context of a distinguished career is escalated to harass the professor to depart.

Meyer spent part of his year of suspension at Ohio State University, but the campaign of derision followed him there. He then spent part of the year at the University of Chile, but rumors plagued him in South America as well. The controversy may have been fading somewhat on his return from Chile, and some faculty and alumni were even planning to welcome Meyer back to campus. However, Meyer, speaking at a national meeting of psychologists in the spring of 1930, told the details of his story publicly, and in the process he characterized some members of the Board of Curators as "senile." Local newspapers by this time sided with Meyer against the Board, but the Board now tried him for "insubordination" and dismissed him. Then, in a curious gesture to his competence, it was arranged that he become a "research professor [without salary] on permanent leave of absence," in a research institute working with deaf children in St. Louis. After two years there, Meyer became a visiting professor at the University of Miami for several years, and gave professional presentations even to age 90.

Post-Mortem

In response to a hypothetical inquiry years later, Meyer was asked if he would consider a return to the University to speak, and he is said to have replied that he "would not return unless he received an

engraved invitation from the Board, because after all they had let him
go for a mild version of what made Kinsey famous."

The university at first refused to give Mowrer his diploma, but
eventually relented. Mowrer became famous and served as president
of the American Psychological Association (1954). As some would
say, the best revenge is living well.

Finally, perhaps in the category of evidence for a just world, the
President lost his job because he had let the incident mushroom
publicly.

The Moral of the Story

When I first learned of this incident in the late 1960s, humans had
just landed on the moon, America was in the throes of social
movements such as women's liberation, bra burnings, the sexual
revolution, birth-control pills, open marriages, and the Berkeley Free
Speech movement. The controversy about Meyer seemed comical,
just dumbfounding – Meyer's attribution to senility seemed apt, even
generous. The students and I could feel smug about the social
progress that had been made in the forty years since the incident.
Whether spoken aloud or not, the consensus was that "It couldn't
happen today." Yes, I was a naive young academic. Now, adding
another 30 years of experience, I can smile again, but for different
reasons. Today, the same questionnaire – with the very same
preamble about the sorry state of marriage – could be administered in
a sociology class. The media criers would again be mixed in their
judgment, the university administration would again try to dodge bad
publicity, and politicians would again threaten to cut off funding
unless the corruption of our youth ceases immediately.

Social science research seems destined to raise questions that often
provoke the response that "*such research just shouldn't be done.*" For
example, those who have tried to gather data on sensitive topics such
as racial differences (e.g., Arthur Jensen, Phillipe Rushton, Richard
Herrnstein and Charles Murray) know all too well that not only must
the children be saved but so too must many sacred cows (cf. Hunt
1999; Tavris 2001). The turmoil surrounding Scott Lilienfeld's (2002)
effort to publish an article about child sex abuse illustrates that this is
a continuing problem (Tavris 2000). Likewise, a recent issue of *Child
Development* (August 2003) included an article on day care, but given
the nature of the results, apparently, it was published with nine
commentaries and an editorial. Not only should some research just

not be done, but some outcomes are undesirable. Mark Twain observed, "Sacred cows make the best hamburger," but there seem to be many vegetarians at work today.

However, today there is one difference from Meyer's day, in that we now have a new class of "gatekeepers" who would almost surely challenge a research effort such as his, namely the Research Ethics Bureaucracy. These new gatekeepers are now on campus instead of in the community, and the "ethics" reviewers operate quietly, out of the public eye, star-chamber style. Although a newspaper editor has a bully pulpit to plead for censorship, that plea is at least in the public domain, and thus is subject to assorted checks and balances. Sex may have been the sizzle in Meyer's case, but the substance was really how the institution and some of its members used an atypical and insignificant incident to trash the career of a competent colleague. In Meyer's case, the newspaper publicity was of some value even if it did not ultimately lead to justice, but today such opportunities for harassment are provided to a secretive and self-policing group of "colleagues" with no accountability. What better place to squelch "undesirable" research than *before* such research is even done?

Research Ethics Industry

My purpose is to examine academic harassment involving a specific tool, namely the restrictions on scholarship that have emerged over the past three to four decades in the "research ethics industry." In Canada, the research ethics boards (REB) have the mandate of ensuring safety for the participants in research activities (TCPS, 1998). In the United States, the Institutional Review Boards (IRB) serve a similar function. Initially these reviews were mainly concerned with medical research and high-risk procedures, and justifiably so. However, solely as a matter of bureaucratic convenience, the softer sciences became subject to such screening as well. The idea that medical research is not an acceptable model for all research continues to be ignored by research ethics bureaucrats.

As a result, we have a solution apparently lacking an associated problem. The most fascinating aspect of this thirty-year "experiment" is that no one bothered to collect data to demonstrate that there ever was a bona fide *need* for such reviews to begin with (Mueller and Furedy 2001a, 2001b), nor has anyone collected data to document that the regulations have actually *improved* the subject's research experience (certainly not in the social and behavioral sciences)! Over thirty years of work to improve research, with no research to show that it has done so – Meyer's attribution of "senility" doesn't quite fit that, maybe "dementia" comes closer? In defense of its own existence, the research ethics industry typically cites some deplorable historical incidents, such as the Nazi war research in World War II, as a rationale for today's REB reviews. In truth, this is an intellectually dishonest subterfuge, simply an effort to deflect criticism, because nothing that is done by REBs today would have prevented the historical incidents. That is, the only people who submit to the REB are those who are trying to do things properly; the violators and "mad scientists" are not slowed at all, so the behavior of the latter is beside the point. It is merely another instance of using a moral panic strategy (Fekete 1994) to achieve constraints on individual behavior.

In practice, the lack of accountability awards remarkable one-sided power to an REB. We, the researchers, are supposed to "trust their good intentions" (covenant), whereas we are expected to comply with a mine-field of highly specific regulations (contract) or face Draconian censure. The research ethics regulations now resemble the tax law in Byzantine complexity and in their proclaimed scope.The implementation of the regulations is left to the discretion of the local REB, and so local regulations may, officially or unofficially, add traps that the federal regulations do not really have. Further, as some of us may know too well, even if you get advice from the tax authorities they are not necessarily bound by it, and this "flexibility" seems to exist in the research ethics industry as well. Making up rules and "reinterpreting" them as you go along are among the advantages of a lop-sided contractual arrangement.

Further, the local boards are usually composed of *volunteers*, and if there is one thing we should know after all these years of social science research it is that volunteers are not "normal." That is, they come to this position of unaccountable power with some motivation, some agenda, and with an unmonitored license to pursue it. The adage that "absolute power corrupts absolutely" seems to apply, at least potentially, because federal agencies disclaim responsibility for abuses or misapplications by local REBs, whereas local REBs piously justify themselves by arguing that "the Feds make us do it."

Shifting Criteria: Safety vs. "Doing Good"

There may be some merit in medical research for reviews with respect to safety, but in practice REBs had to shift their focus in the social and behavioral sciences away from "public safety" to such nebulous goals as "worthwhile topics" and "socially desirable outcomes." Their concerns today seem adequately described as "censorship" rather than efforts to protect public safety. In so doing, the REBs have become another tool of the political correctness movement, one specifically concerned with screening research proposals. Research done without formal REB approval thus becomes a potential "incident" in Westhues's terms, quite aside from whether any public safety issue was involved, and even with an ethics review, missing a specific technicality has the same repercussion. Not only does the behavior of an REB circumvent the notion of academic freedom and freedom of speech, it more generally restricts an academic's freedom of association. The atmosphere also seems quite lacking in civility and due process: today's scholars face a situation where they are considered guilty (unethical) until they prove themselves otherwise. On the other hand, there are no penalties for the REBs, nor the institution that houses them; apparently they are infallible. This is about as far from a mutual covenant as one can imagine.

Compared to a generation ago, where the expectation of an academic's research activity might have been described as more like a "covenant," the present contractual arrangement has diminished the autonomy and flexibility that academic researchers enjoyed and which served universities and society so well historically. The present state of affairs was originated by federal grant agencies, that is, conditions were imposed in exchange for money. Fair enough perhaps, but the new breed of university administrators, bureaucratic managers with little or no scholarly commitment, then spinelessly extended the coverage to even nonfunded research and then classroom activity. The ethics industry has become thoroughly entrenched on campus. The issues are nebulous, the number of regulations continues to grow, and the lack of accountability all provide many potential contractual violations "of no fundamental importance" that may be used to harass a scholar. Research has become a contractual requirement, a job requirement or degree requirement, but one with quite lopsided expectations and penalties.

To illustrate the minor technicalities that REBs may claim authority over, consider some of these. A study approved for 200 subjects unexpectedly found that 300 subjects were available, hooray, except that the ethics committee claimed the need to re-review. Projects must be re-reviewed each year. A colleague was told that students would need to go through the review process in order to interview their grandmothers to write an essay. A colleague was recalled from his father's death bed, to sign forms in blue ink so as to distinguish the original. To such important concerns we can add the proof reading and etiquette changes that commonly arise in requests for revisions. Further, there is the endless pursuit of the *paper trail*: things that once could be resolved with a simple telephone call now require a new paper submission and re-review. That's how bureaucrats try to avoid being blamed for a problem, as opposed to solving a problem. Whether the paper trail protects the institution is questionable (*Nature* 2001), and clearly it does nothing for public safety. Small wonder that we frequently find that the ethics review process takes longer than the actual data collection in social science research. As part of this paper trail, the lengthy legalistic consent forms now intimidate normal people, they are incomprehensible, but what else would one expect when you blend modern academic "communicators" with legalese?

Further in the category of pointless technical details, a doctoral student examining factors related to intelligence test scores asked permission of the REB to get students' scores on Test X (a specific name brand, e.g., the WISC). However, some schools did not administer Test X, but gladly provided their equivalent scores obtained using Test Y (a different brand name). The external examiner of the thesis sanctimoniously opined that this would not have been allowed by her ethics board (with no corroboration). The student was obliged to re-analyze and re-write omitting the offending Test Y data. One wonders, had the student not mentioned any brand names, just "intelligence test scores," would that have been "ethical"? Another student had a project approved by the provincial department of education (which was responsible for funding and ultimately governing her university), only to find her local university ethics board insisted her project had to be re-reviewed – once is never enough when you are trolling for victims.

All of these and more illustrate the rich mine-field of minor technical problems that can be used against the researcher. Interestingly, the tactic of being obliged to deal with minor and apparently meaningless demands is a key part of the process whereby prison guards establish authority over prisoners, such as in Zimbardo's (1999) infamous prison experiment. As Zimbardo noted when the study was terminated, "All the prisoners were happy the experiment was over, but most of the guards were upset that the study was terminated prematurely." Contracts do not establish a "we're all in this together" atmosphere; there is no longer anything "collegial" about the campus research climate, there are lawyers and auditors everywhere, plus the morals police. The campus research climate has changed, the researcher has become a second-class citizen, a problem to be purified by the ethics board, and valued most by the university as an extension of the fund-raising office.

Whatever the case for medical research, there never was concrete evidence of a need for public-safety screening in the social and behavioral sciences (Mueller and Furedy 2001a, 2001b), nor is there any concrete evidence that the subject's research experience has been improved by over thirty years of accumulated regulations. In the absence of evidence for public safety benefits, one can justifiably wonder whether right-thinking censorship is not the actual mission. Certainly that temptation looms. A book need not be burned for there to have been censorship, nor does a research project have to be totally rejected. Furedy (1997) refers to this as "*Velvet Totalitarianism,*" and the condition is also captured nicely in the title of Jonathon Rauch's book, *Kindly Inquisitors.* You need not be beaten in jail to be coerced; for example, when a junior scholar's research proposal on odor and memory is described as "silly," the message is quite clear.

Rauch (1993) refers to "*Fundamentalist Totalitarianism,*" an unwillingness to take seriously the notion that you might be wrong. Although this may have a religious basis, it can have other forms – all that is required is that the right answers are already established by some overarching set of infallible assumptions. As Bertrand Russell observed, "Assumptions have all the advantages of theft over honest toil." Rauch also notes "*Humanitarian Totalitarianism,*" which involves the notion that "all opinions have a right to be respected." On the surface this sounds reasonable, even admirable, but in practice it also has come to mean that *any* criticism is hateful and hurtful. From this self-righteous platform, critics can be shunned or treated as harshly as necessary to assure "respect," defined as "silence." It is telling that such observations came from a journalist (Rauch) rather than an academic.

What has happened is that these ideologies have effectively *criminalized mere criticism.* These closed systems claim to know what is right and wrong for everybody else and thus provide the tools for those who feel that "such research just should not be done." This is upsetting for those of us who think that everyone has the right to criticize, and be criticized, and that no one has the right to force opinions on others. The result is that actual banning may not be necessary, because such influences on campus have cultivated a chilled atmosphere of self-censorship and deference among scholars. Speech codes (e.g., Kors and Silverglate 1998; Ravich 2003) contribute to this atmosphere on campus, and then the research ethics industry can censor further by its list of "ethical" restrictions on inquiry.

Is This Paranoid, a Conspiracy Theory?

As I looked at this endeavor (REB) over the past few years, on a few occasions I wondered, "Am I really seeing what I think I'm seeing?" Regrettably, I have had to conclude that there is at least the potential for serious abuse in the present process, and in fact there are some cases that validate that concern. Some of the problems stem from the general corrosive atmosphere created by the research ethics industry, not just specific REB actions, where an opportunist can capitalize on the fear of the research ethics technicalities. There are good reasons to believe that there are many of these abusive incidents, as I will discuss later. I will describe just three here, in chronological order, and illustrate how they seem to fit into the mobbing mold described by Westhues, except that "the incident" derives specifically from the research ethics industry (if not directly from an REB).

Sergent. Westhues (2004, p. 25) briefly describes the case of Justine Sergent, a young neuropsychologist at McGill University's Montreal Neurological Institute. As background, she was described as a young high-achiever, and her research was held in high esteem internationally. She advanced rapidly through the academic ranks at McGill, and was on the threshold of promotion to full professor when the incident occurred. What we know about this is publicly recorded in various articles that appeared in the Montreal *Gazette* from 1994 to 1997, and we have to take that public record at face value because there is no other.

Sergent's research involved hemispheric differences in brain function, and she used brain scanning (PET) to study cognitive processing. Sergent did get approval from the ethics committee for such research, using faces as the stimuli to induce cognitive activity in the brain. She then decided to extend the research to different stimuli (music), merely a replication with the same design, and apparently she did not seek approval for this extension. There was no issue of public safety in switching to music, which is the larger concern; a "covenant" of approval would cover such variation.

Looked at in one way, the issue was a judgment call about territory, that is, the range of coverage the REB has, a matter of no consequence, surely correctable with minimal negotiation. Such an assumption as Sergent made would not have been at all unusual ten years ago, but this heightened legalism is typical of changes in the research ethics industry since that time. From another perspective, the complaint is a perfect example of how a minor technicality can be trumpeted into a major shortcoming, thus becoming the "incident" for mobbing. Given her extensive good service to the university, a reasonable person would think the administration could have coached a valued scholar without the fuss of a formal reprimand, but that is not what happened. Bureaucratic managers do not define success as solving problems; rather their goal is to avoid being blamed for a problem, and thus many of these ethics regulations are in place to protect the regulators and managers, not because they affect the participant's experience (*Nature* 2001). Ironically, Sergent noted later that the REB did not have the mandatory content expert on board, that is, someone knowledgeable about PET scans. This seems not to have bothered the authorities, details being binding only for the researcher.

This tragedy began with a complaint in July of 1992, by a party unknown, about her assumption that re-review wasn't necessary, and this led to an official reprimand in January of 1993. Sergent appealed the reprimand that summer and the matter went to campus arbitration. Along the way, an anonymous letter was sent to the university, the press, and several grant agencies and major journals, alleging various fraudulent activities in Sergent's research. A news story on April 9, 1994, indicated that Sergent was continuing her work, and that no discipline had been administered other than the reprimand, and that was still the subject of arbitration. Four days later, on April 13, 1994, the news reported that she and her husband had committed suicide, some 20 months after the reprimand. She was 42 years old.

Nothing was ever reported to corroborate any wrong-doing, even though the university honored Sergent's request for a scientific audit to try to clear her name. Her position was difficult; she had formerly been a student at McGill, she was a woman in a male-dominated field, and she was a Ph.D. (Psychology) in a medical school setting, and she acknowledged that interpersonal interactions with some colleagues had been occasionally problematic. She believed that the action was a personal vendetta, rather than being about scientific conduct. Finally, Montreal had recently been treated to a scandal in which a medical researcher actually had falsified patient records, and Sergent felt she was being pressed into the same category. Indeed the anonymous writer was exploiting such an inference, and, in spite of subsequent tap dancing, the newspaper's initial coverage implicitly linked her to the other case – guilt by accusation. She was bitterly disappointed that she had had to hire a lawyer to interact with a university which she had served so well, but that is part of the pattern of mobbing. Friends suggested that she take a leave but she continued to try to work instead. When the matter became public in the news of April 9, 1994, that apparently was too much.

Words fail me every time I think about this case. Did anything of any value come of it? An inquiry into McGill's internal handling of the matter was suspended January 15, 1997. The university spokesman (Shapiro 1997) concluded thus: "It would be nice to have some sort of satisfactory sense of closure, but that's not how human beings live with each other sometimes. ... I felt that this was an unreasonable drain on the University's resources – we were spending a great deal of time and money on this matter without any prospect that it would clarify itself in any reasonable period of time. I didn't feel it was in the best interests of the University to continue." No covenant there, just the bottom-line manager, without a clue that it shouldn't have taken years to resolve in the first place. Another spokesman (Murphy, 1997) responded: "Some in the scientific world have asked questions about Dr. Sergent's time at McGill, but, no, those questions haven't caused MNI any difficulties in its efforts to continue to recruit world-class researchers." I was worried about that. Yes, it's a covenant, we're all in this together; whisk, wink, under the rug. Just weeks later, the audit into Sergent's records was suspended March 21, 1997, almost five years after the initial inquiry. There never had been, and there still was, no evidence of fraud in any official communication.

Is there more to this than meets the eye? There is no way to know, but on the public record, this is just reprehensible. Did anyone lose their job, or even get a reprimand as she did? What did federal regulators do to prevent this happening again? What did the federal regulators do to the university? However, we've preserved the careers of some bureaucrats, and that is the point of the one-sided contract. No, the REB did not hook up the exhaust pipe of the car, nor did the federal regulators, nor the university administrators. But that's why our criminal justice system acknowledges other levels of responsibility, such as "accomplice" and "aiding and abetting." As far as I am concerned, in this case the difference in responsibility here is "a matter of no fundamental importance."

Pagliaro. In March of 2000, Louis Pagliaro, an educational psychologist at the University of Alberta, described drug use in Edmonton schools (Gillis 2000). He based his statements on interviews with children, teachers, police, and drug counselors. He had made controversial claims in the past; like those, this assertion provoked renewed controversy. Following complaints by the police and school boards, the university ordered him to stop talking to the media about the alleged "drug epidemic." As seems to often occur in mobbing cases, the messenger is attacked rather than the message. The university told Pagliaro that he was under investigation for allegedly performing his interviews on unsuspecting participants, without approval by the university's mandatory ethics review process.

Pagliaro ignored the gag order and continued to make his case publicly. An independent investigator recommended the university drop the case against Pagliaro. However, the university requested that the investigator continue, trying to find a breach of some detail that would permit discipline or dismissal. That is, as in many mobbing cases, the investigation continued in spite of a lack of evidence, seeking some legalism whereby dismissal could proceed. In this case, it was not the REB directly harassing, but the many technicalities of the research ethics industry were being mined by others for that purpose.

Pagliaro (personal communication, Sept. 13, 2003) reports that "after a full year of active investigation, the provost decided that I had done nothing wrong and sent me a 2-line letter 'dismissing' the complaint .... I never received: an explanation ... (nor) ... an apology for the unnecessary stress that I suffered; nor any assistance from the (university) academic staff association ...." Given Pagliaro's many years of service, this seems sad for a matter that should have been squelched early on, but that lack of contrition seems typical of harassment exercises, the sentiment being more like, "We'll get you next time." Other aspects of this case can be found at the website (http://www.safs.ca/albertamain.html) of the Society for Academic Freedom and Scholarship (SAFS).

Loftus. Tavris (2002) reports a third instance where the research ethics climate was used to harass researchers, in this case Elizabeth Loftus, University of Washington, and Melvin Guyer, University of Michigan. This case is interesting, among other reasons, because it shows how academics are now far more restricted in terms of opportunity for inquiry than are investigative journalists. Loftus and Guyer decided to reexamine the evidence in a published study of an adult Jane Doe's alleged recovery of memory of childhood sexual abuse, an area in which Loftus had earned international recognition. Examining material in the public domain, Loftus and Guyer concluded that there likely had been no childhood abuse, and they published reports to that effect.

According to Tavris (2002), Guyer checked with the Michigan review committee, stating that he felt that he did not need their approval because he was not doing "research" but rather "intellectual criticism, commentary on a forensic issue, and an historical/journalistic endeavor," and the IRB committee chair agreed. However, a month later, Guyer received another letter, advising him that the research was not exempt, and that it was disapproved, and that a reprimand was to be recommended. Almost a year later, a new IRB chair advised Guyer that there was to be no reprimand and that the project was indeed exempt. Isn't it curious, it's exempt but you still have to apply for a decision, another technicality, and the decision is never binding? Then this exempt decision makes it possible for critics to disingenuously proclaim that, "Oh my, this project wasn't approved by an IRB." True enough, but because it didn't have to be! Further, collaboration across multiple institutions invariably creates another potential trap whereby approval elsewhere is not good enough; the prevailing local attitude is always "We are more ethical than they are" – truly ethical imperialism.

Across the continent, the University of Washington received an email from Jane Doe (allegedly) arguing that her privacy had been violated. The author of the original report, her therapist, had been showing a video of her in public presentations, whereas Loftus and Guyer had never referred to her by her actual name, so this seems a baseless concern. Nonetheless, this started a 21-month ordeal. With just minutes notice, the University Officer of Scholarly Integrity and her department head invaded Loftus' office and seized her files. How easy it was for the university to ignore any privacy concerns, not to mention any presumption of innocence. This intrusion speaks volumes to the one-sidedness of the contract. Just try to get access to IRB files! There was no reciprocity whatsoever, and the raid on her office shames any notions of transparency and accountability in the research ethics industry. But there is perhaps a take-home lesson to be learned here, namely that now there is another reason for a home office besides tax deductions: *keep your important professional data and computer at home,* where at least a legal process is required to get to it. A word to the wise is sufficient: do it, now.

As Loftus tried to determine the charges against her, it was five weeks later that she finally learned that the invasion was not about the alleged privacy complaint as such, but something more nebulous and far-reaching: "possible violations of human subjects research." Lawyers tried to subpoena her personnel file; because they were from out of state, the request had no legal authority and the university could have and should have rejected it, but Loftus had to hire her own lawyer to resist. As Tavris notes: "This was the modus operandi at both universities: keep the charges secret, keep changing the charges, keep the meetings secret, keep the accused in the dark." This is common in mobbing cases, not to mention chillingly reminiscent of the machinations of governmental regimes historically not in favor in North America. As in other cases, the University of Washington violated its own rules, which required a committee to be formed within 30 days and a conclusion reached within 90 days, not 21 months. Ignoring the inconvenience of the contract is acceptable for one party, whereas even following the rules may not be enough for the other party.

Over a year later, the University of Washington committee concluded that Loftus was not guilty of scholarly misconduct, but nonetheless recommended to the Dean that she be banned from publishing and required to take remedial education in ethics. You're innocent, but a little indoctrination can't hurt, and shut up! Several weeks later, July 3, 2001, the Dean wrote a letter exonerating her of all charges and waiving the remedial ethics requirement, noting that this work did not "constitute research involving human subjects." But he still advised her not to contact Jane Doe's mother again nor interview anyone else about the case without prior approval! Consider how asinine this is, expecting Loftus and Guyer to get Jane Doe's permission to contact Jane's mother, who is not only an adult but Jane's "adversary." Freedom of association indeed, how paternalistic can one be!

Loftus and Guyer knew there were adversaries in the outside world, those whose living depended on promoting the validity of the repressed memories notion, but "colleagues" as the enemy within, along with the vigor of their actions, is a surprise. Once again, years of productive careers are ignored, innocent people have to hire lawyers, and one's institution turns out to be more a part of the problem than a solution. Credible evidence is not required to start an inquiry, just an accusation, and the accused must prove innocence, justice à la the the burning of witches at Salem. It makes one wonder about the curriculum in the institution's Law School, is it accredited?

Loftus has since moved to the University of California, Irvine, but litigation continues against Loftus, Tavris, and others. The experience of a student working with Loftus at one time further illustrates the guilt-by-association mobbing strategy (Coan 1997). As Westhues notes, to merely risk association with a pariah is to become part of the mobbing. This is clearly a vendetta to silence, not a quest for truth. As such it is a problem in legal ethics and administrative ethics, and perhaps journalistic ethics, rather than research ethics.

Others. There are other such cases. For example, there was the 1994 effort by the Simon Fraser University administration to force a graduate student, Russel Ogden, to disclose confidential research information at the request of a third party, the Vancouver coroner (Lowman and Palys 1998; Palys and Lowman 2000). After the prolonged legal battle, Ogden received an apology and a Master's degree from Simon Fraser. However, Ogden later sued for and won damages from Exeter University in England as well, because the university failed to honor its commitment to support him as he explored a network of people conducting assisted suicides for his Ph.D. (Todd 2003). Both institutions failed to follow their own agreements and policies with regard to confidentiality and anonymity, until forced to do so by external legal adjudication. Kors and Silverglate (1998) have shown that speech codes do not survive external challenges, nor apparently do some of the games of the research ethics industry. But why is inquiry more free off-campus in the real world than within a university?

There is also the case of whistle-blower Nancy Oliveri (*cf.*, for example, Jimenez 2000), who did what most in the real world consider to be the ethical thing, and then became a target herself. She went public about the apparently harmful effects of a drug after her supervisors did nothing. The letter of the law here may actually have been somewhat against her (see Furedy 1999, 2000), in that she had signed some secret contracts re nondisclosure, but the complexity of such a situation made things ripe for abuse and controversy, as well as honest confusion. These secret contracts seem ill-advised at a university in general, and while she may in a legal sense have breached that contract, from the perspective of public safety I am still inclined to consider her to have done the ethical thing in a larger context, without much institutional support.

It is necessary to rely on public evidence in these cases because the actual proceedings are "confidential" – to protect the authorities, not the researchers. The whole story in these cases thus remains buried in secrecy, but the main public points in these cases converge. Minor, at most, issues of research ethics were escalated to try to eliminate a "difficult" professor, in spite of years of good service. Institutional safeguards were ignored and harassment continued in spite of the lack of evidence. Censorship, silencing a faculty member, was clearly the issue, *not* public safety. Good intentions seem a pathetic defense from the research ethics industry, as censors always claim to be doing it for the good of the rest of us. These problems are especially acute in the social sciences, but no doubt research ethics harassment occurs in medical research as well, again with the researcher left as the scapegoat by the institution when problems arise. However, I have restricted my discussion here in part because there are true safety issues in medical research, whereas in the social sciences and humanities the process is clearly about ideological control rather than safety.

The Meek Will Inherit the University

These cases should be enough to make the point that "ethics" regulations of unproven value make handy tools for harassment. You aren't paranoid if they really are out to get you. Given the lack of evidence on effectiveness of these ethics boards, researchers understandably have been inclined to opt out of the process – rather than volunteer for REBs, for example. However, the fact is that there are very few mechanisms for meaningful input from researchers even if or when they want to participate. Communications and ethics review mechanisms now operate on the presumption that researchers are unethical and must prove their innocence. Any number of discussion formats exist on how to manage the researchers, how to keep them from sneaking something by the reviewers, what new rules can be imposed, and how important it is to identify unforeseen risks (chew on that for awhile). But there is no forum to consider whether the rules accomplish really anything for public safety. Not only do researchers not feel interested; the sentiment that their involvement is not wanted, and even that the researcher is the problem, is quite clear.

As sad as that is, there is every reason to believe that the relationship will deteriorate even further, and that there will be more ugly incidents where research ethics issues are used to harass researchers, whether these reach the public eye or not. One must realize that the cases noted above were senior scholars who could go public, having at least some protection by tenure. It is certainly reasonable to believe that such incidents involving junior scholars and students are far more numerous but invisible because they are unable to complain publicly. Further, because of their inexperience, junior faculty and students lack a meaningful perspective on what constitutes a reasonable, collegial question as opposed to inappropriate censorship. And, of course, the predilection to "confidentiality" effectively hides instances of such abuse.

In these witch hunts there was considerable loss for the researchers – time, expense, and psychological health – but apparently there were no consequences to the universities for behaving this way. Given the lack of consequences to the institutions for such abusive treatment of researchers, there is no reason to expect such malicious witch hunts to disappear in the future. To the extent that (a) we continue to permit the fuzzy goal state (ethics and social engineering instead of safety), (b) fail to document effectiveness, (c) fail to discipline the REBs and/or institutions, and (d) employ university administrators with no stake in the future of the institution, much less the researchers (*viz.* Max Meyer), it seems likely that in the future there will be more such incidents of researcher harassment rather than fewer.

Adapting to such a campus climate will shape faculty behavior in predictable ways. Specifically, it seems reasonable to see a Darwinian faculty selection process occur as a result of this censorious climate. Some faculty may capitulate and carry on, but it would not be surprising that many, especially senior, faculty move their scholarly efforts to outside consulting activity, books, or other venues that avoid having to confront unwarranted constraints on intellectual inquiry by ethics review boards. Or, just as the tax codes produce an "underground economy," some may just ignore "bad laws." In the case of graduate students, do such experiences encourage students to consider continuing a career in academic research? Not likely, their own experiences with ethics reviews for their Honors projects cause them to rethink plans for an academic research career. Blend in observations of their faculty mentors being treated as Loftus and others were, plus the constraints of speech codes and related manifestations of political correctness in coursework, and it becomes fairly easy to see a Darwinian selection process at work in defining the nature of future academic researchers. I say this not because I think it desirable, but because I know that humans adapt their behavior to constraints in ways that are describable, and we know this from research that predates the research ethics industry, like it or not (e.g., Thorndike and Skinner)!

Subject matter expertise will become less important to campus success, and instead a very critical trait for academic survival will be *deference*. Research activities will be restricted to conventional "safe" and popular questions, using noncontroversial methods that fit within the ideologically proscribed limits of right-thinking "ethicists." Policy bureaucrats and the new class of professional campus administrators will have prevailed, and the meek will inherit the university. Perhaps some future historian will label this upcoming era "The call of the mild." The garrulous, "difficult" professors, the characters dedicated to rigorous inquiry, like Max Meyer, will disappear. Then the executives of the university will be able to put their feet up on the desk, relax, and "manage," but will students and parents still value such a totalitarian university experience?

Why does academic inquiry need to be so constrained to no apparent benefit, when the constraints in fact produce demonstrable harms in the form of faculty harassment? Until there is true evidence of benefits to public safety, not ideology, the only clear purpose of the research ethics enterprise is censorship. How long it will be before campus researchers will be required to submit their data back to the ethics committee, *before* publication, so undesirable *outcomes* can be kept from the public eye? Why have we let this go on for over 30 years? How much longer will we let it go on? The basic problem will not be solved by more paper, royal commissions, tweaking the process, or the like. The sorriest aspect of the research ethics climate is the unwillingness to accept that the possibility that the entire bureaucracy was never necessary nor has it been of any value, at least in the social sciences. Except perhaps from the perspective of those who wish another way to harass colleagues.

We have devoted 30 years to *complying* with regulations, and apparently not a day to the *effectiveness* of regulations. There are no data demonstrating need or effectiveness, whereas the negative "side effects" of the research ethics climate are demonstrable. There is a medical dictum that applies perhaps, "First, do no harm." The savage damage to careers such as that outlined above would seem to justify the equivalent of formatting the hard drive for the research ethics regulations, or is collateral damage to innocent researchers just the price we pay in the name of ideology? I hope not. The research ethics enterprise is an affront to intellectual integrity, and it deserves to be dismantled entirely until it can be shown to be needed, effective, mutually accountable, and at least in accord with basic principles of civility and legality. The present 30-year long experiment is a failure.

References

Carlson, A. J., *et al.*, 1930. "Academic freedom at the University of Missouri: Report on the dismissal of Professor DeGraff and the suspension of Professor Meyer," *Bulletin of the American Association of University Professors*, 16, pp. 143-176.

Child Development, 2003. Day care issue. 74(4).

Coan, J. A., 1997. "Lost in a shopping mall: An experience with controversial research," *Ethics and Behavior*, 7(3), pp, 271-284.

Columbia Daily Tribune, March 13, 1929: editorial entitled "A filthy questionnaire," and article entitled "Sex secrets asked of M.U. Students."

Esper, E.A., 1966. "Max Meyer: The making of a scientific isolate," *Journal of the History of the Behavioral Sciences*, 2, pp. 341-356.

Esper, E.A., 1967. "Max Meyer in America," *Journal of the History of the Behavioral Sciences*, 3, pp. 107-131.

Fekete, J., 1994. *Moral panic: Biopolitics rising.* Montreal: Robert Davies.

Furedy, J.J., 1997. "Velvet totalitarianism on Canadian campuses: Subverting effects on the teaching of, and research in, the discipline of psychology." *Canadian Psychology*, 38, pp. 204-211.

Furedy, J.J., 1999. "Dr. Olivieri and the public interest," *Varsity* (University of Toronto), November 29, 1999.

Furedy, J. J., 2000. "A price too high?" *University of Toronto Bulletin*, March 27, 11.

Gruber, C. S., 1972. "Academic freedom at Columbia University: The case of James McKeen Cattell," *Bulletin of the American Association of University Professors*, Autumn, pp. 297-305.

Hunt, M, 1999. *The new know-nothings: The political foes of the scientific study of human nature.* New Brunswick, NJ: Transaction.

Jimenez, M., 2000. "Oliveri case referred to regulatory body," *National Post*, April 28, 2000.

Kors, A. C., and H. A. Silverglate, 1998. *The shadow university.* New York: Free Press.

Lilienfeld, S. O., 2002. Special issue. *American Psychologist*, 57(3).

Lowman, J. and T. Palys, 1998. "When research ethics and the law conflict," *CAUT* [Canadian Association Of University Teachers] *Bulletin*, June.

Montreal Gazette, 1994-1997. Articles, editorial and op-eds on Justine Sergent, April 9 to November 24, 1994; articles January 16 and March 21, 1997.

Mueller, J. H., and J. Furedy, 2001a. "Reviewing for risk: What's the evidence it is working?" *Observer*, 14 (September), 1, pp. 26-28.

Mueller, J. H., and J. Furedy, 2001b. "The IRB review system: How do we know it works?" *Observer*, 14 (October), pp. 19-20.

Nature, 2001. Editorial, "Time to cut regulations that protect only regulators," *Nature*, 414, 379.

Palys, T. and J. Lowman, 2000. "Ethical and legal strategies for protecting confidential research information," *Canadian Journal of Law and Society*, 15(1), pp. 39-80. See also www.sfu.ca/~palys/Controversy.htm

Rauch, J., 1993. *Kindly Inquisitors*. Chicago: University of Chicago Press.

Ravitch, D., 2003. *The language police*. New York: A. A. Knopf.

Tavris, C., 2000. "The uproar over sexual abuse research and its findings," *Transaction*, 37(4).

Tavris, C., 2001. *Psychobabble and Biobunk: Using psychology to think critically about issues in the news*. New York: Prentice-Hall.

Tavris, C., 2002. "The high cost of skepticism," *Skeptical Inquirer*, 26, 14(4), pp. 41-44.

Tri-Council Policy Statement, 1998. *Ethical Conduct for Research Involving Humans*. Online at www.nserc.ca/programs/ethics/english/policy.htm

Todd, D., 2003. "Academic wins ruling on assisted suicide research," *Vancouver Sun*, Nov. 1, 2003, B3.

Westhues, K., 1998. *Eliminating professors: A guide to the dismissal process*. Lewiston, NY: Edwin Mellen.

Westhues, K., 2001. The difficult professor: A pernicious concept. CAUT Legal Conference, March 2-3, Ottawa, ON.

Westhues, K., 2004. *Administrative Mobbing at the University of Toronto*. Lewiston, NY: Edwin Mellen.

Zimbardo, P. G., 1999. Stanford Prison Experiment. Online at www.prisonexp.org/

Part Six

Techniques of
Resistance and Recovery

Editor's Introduction

In the last decades of the twentieth century, the poor, powerless, helpless victim of abuse became an icon, displayed to demonstrate the oppressiveness of existing structures and to justify laws and programs designed to heal survivors' wounded psyches. The movement against workplace mobbing and bullying has reflected this cultural trend. Heinz Leymann established a clinic in Sweden for psychological treatment of mobbing victims, and similar clinics have been established more recently in Germany.

The truest victims of workplace mobbing are those who die as a result of it: by suicide, for example, or from stress-induced stroke or heart attack. The word *victim* is also properly applied to those mobbing targets whom the process leaves so depressed, so numb to everyday realities, or so dependent on drugs or alcohol that they are incapable of getting back on their feet themselves. Post-traumatic Stress Disorder is a real and serious psychological injury, which counselling and other kinds of professional treatment can help alleviate. Clinics have their place.

It is no favor to most targets, however, certainly not to most of those in academe, to treat them as victims. The experience of being mobbed has robbed them of control of their working lives. What they need is to regain control, to take stock of the resources they have left and put them to good use, recovering active, productive roles in the society at hand. Losses and scars remain, but life itself is a gift. Skills in research, teaching and writing are special gifts.

The first technique Brian Martin suggests in Chapter 16, for turning a mobbing back, is to get the facts of the matter out in the open. This is personally therapeutic and politically essential. He claims that Herbert Richardson's insistence on a public dismissal trial, and my publication of a book on it, were ways of making the attack on Richardson boomerang. He is right. The present book serves the same purpose for other cases and for workplace mobbing in general. All the contributors, especially the indomitable authors of first-person accounts, have taken giant steps toward undoing harm, just by exposing dark facts to the light of day. Martin's review of five major ways attacks are steeled against the boomerang effect, a review informed by his decades of meticulous scholarship in this area, is a sound practical guide for how to right administrative wrongs.

Workplace mobbing has sometimes been likened to clerical sexual abuse, both being problems formerly hushed up but now recognized, thanks to targets speaking out. In St. John's, Newfoundland, one outcome of scandal in the 1980s over clerical sexual abuse was the commitment of $1 million a year to Memorial University by the Catholic archdiocese, to establish a Chair in Child Protection in MUN's School of Social Work. Kathleen Kufeldt (a high achiever in her field, like other targets represented in this book) was recruited from Calgary to fill the chair, only to be mobbed out of it by administrators and colleagues. In Chapter 17, she tells the story and draws lessons for surviving, recovering from, and rising above such a bump in one's career and life. Kufeldt's experience corroborates Martin's point that "it is wise to avoid official channels" in seeking redress of workplace mobbing. She adds to Martin's analysis an identification of attributes both personal (intelligence, healthy self-compassion) and social (supportive family and community) that enable targets to show the same resilience as many people who were abused as children. Maybe Memorial University should establish a Chair in Adult Protection. Kufeldt would be a good choice to fill it.

Chapter Sixteen

The Richardson Dismissal as an Academic Boomerang

Brian Martin

Attacks sometimes recoil against the attacker, a process that can be called the boomerang effect. St. Michael's College's dismissal of Herbert Richardson can be considered to be a type of attack and hence analysed in terms of a boomerang effect. Kenneth Westhues's book provides a rich resource for examining boomerang dynamics in an academic dismissal case.

Attacks can boomerang when they are perceived as unjust by participants and observers. This is most obvious in the case of violent attacks on peaceful protesters. In 1930, Gandhi led a lengthy march with the stated aim of making salt from the sea, an unlawful act in violation of the British rulers' monopoly on salt production. In India, the salt laws were widely seen as unjust in themselves, and the march generated huge support throughout the country. At the culmination of the march, Indian satyagrahis (nonviolent activists) presented themselves to the police, who beat them mercilessly, with many protesters taken to hospital. Due to independent reporting, the police beatings of nonresisting protesters caused an upsurge in support for the Indian independence movement in India, Britain and elsewhere. It also weakened the resolve of the British colonial administrators in India (Dalton 1993).

Other famous cases where attacks against peaceful protesters
backfired include:

- the shooting of hundreds of demonstrators in 1905 in Russia
  — so-called Bloody Sunday — which caused a massive
  increase in opposition to the Czar;
- the police shooting of protesters in Sharpeville, South Africa
  in 1960, which generated enormous outrage internationally;
  and
- the shooting of mourners in a cemetery in Dili, East Timor, by
  Indonesian troops in 1991, which stimulated a big increase in
  international support for the East Timorese liberation struggle.

The reaction against violent attacks on peaceful protesters is so
predictable that Gene Sharp, the world's leading nonviolence
researcher, included it as a stage in his dynamics of nonviolent action
(1973). Sharp called this reaction "political jiu-jitsu," in analogy to
the sport of jiu-jitsu in which contestants turn their opponents'
weight and strength against them.

Sharp restricted his attention to nonviolent action, but it is
possible to observe similar jiu-jitsu processes in other arenas. For
example, the beating of Rodney King by Los Angeles police in 1991
was captured on video by witness George Holliday. When broadcast
on TV, the beating triggered a massive public reaction against the
participating police and against the police department generally.
Similarly, the use of torture, if revealed, can recoil against the
torturers, their masters, and the companies and governments
supplying torture technology (Martin and Wright 2003). Censorship,
which can be interpreted as an attack on free expression, can backfire
(Jansen and Martin 2003). For this expanded application of the
concept of political jiu-jitsu, I use the term *backfire* or *boomerang*.

Any violation of a social norm has the potential to recoil against
the violator. In sociology as well as popular culture, most attention is
given to norm violation by relatively powerless or stigmatised groups,
such as criminals or the unemployed. In the examples given above,
though, it is powerful groups, such as police, militaries or
governments, that have violated norms.

The dismissal of an academic can be interpreted as an attack on
the academic or on academic freedom, and thus can potentially
boomerang. The dismissal of Richardson, if it had occurred quietly,
would have had few repercussions for St. Michael's College. But a
highly publicised dismissal, even if it gets rid of the academic, can
generate negative attitudes towards the employer.

Determining whether, or to what extent, a dismissal boomerangs, is a fascinating and challenging task. However, my focus here is on something slightly different: boomerang dynamics. Boomerang effects are not just events or consequences: they can be studied as a dynamic process. Attackers often realise, consciously or unconsciously, that their actions can be counterproductive, and thus seek to limit these consequences. At the same time, targets of attacks, and their supporters, may act to stimulate outrage from an attack.

By examining a range of cases (Jansen and Martin 2003; Martin and Wright 2003), it is possible to discover a variety of techniques by which attackers can inhibit a boomerang effect, namely through (1) cover-up, (2) devaluation of the target, (3) reinterpretation of events, (4) use of official channels, and (5) intimidation and bribery. Targets have various means to counter each of these techniques. In each of the following sections — one for each of these five techniques — I give several general examples and then apply the ideas to the Richardson dismissal process.

Cover-up

If an attack is not widely known, it cannot be widely perceived as unjust and cannot generate significant outrage. Therefore, the most effective way to prevent a boomerang is to keep the attack secret. In the case of the Dili massacre, the Indonesian military controlled all media and communication out of the occupied East Timor. However, a western filmmaker, Max Stahl, videoed the shooting and was able to smuggle the videotape out of the country, enabling it to be broadcast internationally.

Police beatings occur all the time. In the years prior to the Rodney King beating, the Los Angeles Police Department paid out millions of dollars in court settlements and judgements in cases involving alleged use of excessive force by police. The Rodney King beating backfired in a much bigger way because of the Holliday video.

A key reason that torture is almost always carried out in secret is because it is widely seen to be unjust. Covering up torture is the most effective way to prevent outrage. Amnesty International and other human rights organisations use publicity as a powerful means of opposing torture.

For getting rid of an academic without repercussions, the cover-up is a powerful tool. If few people know about the reasons, the processes and the outcome, then the potential for generating outrage is minimal. Many academics cooperate in a cover-up because they are ashamed by the criticisms of their performance and because they are not accustomed to seeking publicity. Indeed, most academics avoid public engagement, much less publicity, seeking recognition only among peers through scholarly publications and conferences. This means that if discreet efforts are made to get rid of them, many are inclined to go quietly. For them, going public is not dignified. Scholarly self-image can get in the way of the quest for justice or even for survival.

In some cases when academics sue for wrongful dismissal, they reach a settlement with the university that includes a payment to them only upon acceptance of a silencing clause, namely a settlement condition that restricts future public comment about the case. Silencing clauses are potent means for cover-up.

From this it is possible to generalise: the most effective attacks on academics and on academic freedom are *Things Which Are Done in Secret,* to quote the title of Marlene Dixon's 1976 book on academic eliminations at McGill.

Richardson did not cooperate with his antagonists by going quietly. By fighting their attempts, he raised the stakes and greatly increased the potential for a boomerang, as shown by three examples.

First, in 1987, when Richardson was privately encouraged to leave St. Michael's, he stayed in his job. If, instead, he had left, the elimination would have occurred with no publicity, indeed virtually no awareness that anyone had been opposed to Richardson.

Second, Richardson pushed for and obtained an open tribunal. This raised the stakes for the attackers, making it far more difficult to hide the process. Richardson was not gagged by a clause in a settlement and the tribunal's report is available for scrutiny.

Third, after being dismissed, Richardson did not avoid publicity. Instead, through Mellen Press he published Westhues's book, which over the long term is likely to increase the boomerang against St. Michael's.

These examples show that boomerang can be seen as a process that can begin long before an overt attack and last far longer than a formal outcome. Even today, the Turkish government refuses to acknowledge the genocide of the Armenians in 1915. Cover-ups can last a long time. Likewise, for those opposing unjust attacks, it is never too late to expose what happened.

Westhues mentions the case of Liam Donnelly, a Simon Fraser University swimming coach dismissed for sexual harassment and date rape. "Then Donnelly went public with graphic offers of sexual favors that Marsden had sent him *after* he was alleged to have raped her." (Westhues, p. 4). Media coverage, especially television, is extremely powerful in countering cover-ups and maximising backfire. A film of Richardson's life and dismissal holds the greatest potential for increasing the boomerang against St. Michael's.

Devaluation

An attack can be less shocking, or even be seen as legitimate, if the target is perceived as lacking value. Consider a poorly performing, foul-mouthed academic, someone much more difficult to admire than Richardson. Dismissal of such an academic is less likely to trigger outrage than of a model scholar, even though the dismissal process is equally improper in each case. Therefore, devaluation of the target is a powerful means of inhibiting boomerang.

Within South Africa in 1960, blacks were not treated as equals by most of the white population. Therefore, when police shot and killed perhaps a hundred black protesters, this did not cause as much of an uproar as if police had killed even a few white protesters.

Rodney King, who was seriously beaten by Los Angeles police, was often called a "black motorist" in news reports. Supporters of the police were more likely to call him a "felony evader," a devaluing description. Police supporters regularly referred to King's prior criminal record. Subsequent to the beating, King was investigated or arrested several times in ways that compromised his credibility (Owens 1994).

The extermination of the Jews under the Nazi regime was preceded and accompanied by a sustained process of devaluation. Hitler and other Nazi leaders attempted to paint the Jews as subhuman, for example by calling them "vermin." Devaluation is a predictable feature of genocide.

These examples illustrate that there are many roads to devaluation. It can be a facet of prevalent social attitudes or it can be a carefully engineered process. It can occur before an attack or be pursued afterwards, or both. It can be promoted by labelling and slander but also by actions that stigmatise the target.

Devaluation of academics can occur in a similar range of ways, including via general attitudes, through specifically promoted associations or labels, and at any stage in an attack. Needless to say, devaluation is relative to an audience and is constantly subject to both reinforcement and challenge. A person devalued in the eyes of some, due to characteristics or labelling, might achieve greater value in the eyes of others.

I use the term *devaluation* to refer to something quite serious. Although a sociologist might have lower status than a molecular biologist, both are highly valued in western societies. On the other hand, an illiterate or intellectually disabled person is likely to be seriously devalued, with consequent impacts on the person's life opportunities or even survival.

It would seem a tall order to devalue Herbert Richardson, a confident, reflective and high-performing academic. His scholarly output puts most colleagues to shame. But no matter how outstanding a person's capability and performance, it is possible to bring them down and hence to reduce the boomerang effect from an attack.

A potent tool for devaluation is "malicious gossip and whispering campaigns," listed under the heading "Back-biting" by Westhues as one of ten clues that a process of exclusion counts as elimination in his terms (pp. 30-32).

Richardson's role as a Protestant in a Catholic college would have had complex effects on his status, which might be lowered in the eyes of some Catholic colleagues and administrators but raised in the eyes of Protestants elsewhere. Given the level of concern about minorities, an attack on an isolated Protestant is likely to generate heightened concern, just as the beating of a black Rodney King by white police generated increased outrage due to people's inference of police racism. Richardson's role as an isolated Protestant might help to explain why he was subject to attack — Westhues certainly makes a powerful case in this regard — but it does not constitute strong evidence of inhibition of a boomerang effect through devaluation.

Richardson's association with the Unification Church and similar groups would have had a serious effect on his status. Westhues describes the "smearing of the Unification Church" (p. 124), a process of devaluation, and some of this rubbed off on Richardson. Westhues notes (p. 125) that Richardson's invitations to give lectures evaporated after he defended the Unification Church, a good indication that he had been tainted by association.

Richardson's reputation also suffered greatly due to the *Lingua Franca* article. Westhues describes how the article became more hostile to Richardson through different versions and details some of its misrepresentations, for example concerning the choice of Edwin Mellen for the name of Richardson's press. Whatever the means by which the article came to be published, it certainly had a damaging effect on Richardson, making him seem a less deserving victim.

Within the context of the tribunal, Richardson's contributions were minimised by the focus on his particular alleged deviations from procedure, rather than his overall performance assessed in context. This was not a process of devaluation of the person *per se* but rather one of setting aside valued dimensions of Richardson's role.

In summary, Richardson's reputation was damaged most of all by his association with the Unification Church and by the *Lingua Franca* article. This damage no doubt made it easier to dismiss him. But in the wider society, Richardson's contributions were sufficiently great to make devaluation a difficult method for reducing backfire from the dismissal.

Reinterpretation

When an attack can potentially be seen as unjust, attackers may interpret the situation in a very different way. If they can convince others of this alternative explanation, boomerang is inhibited.

The savage beatings of nonresisting satyagrahis in India in 1930 caused numerous injuries, with protesters sent to hospital; British authorities in India said that the protesters were faking their injuries. After the Sharpeville massacre, South African police attributed the incident to agitators. Police involved in the beating of Rodney King claimed that it was King who was "in control" during the incident, and that the beating, though harsh, was completely justified by King's threat to the police.

In some cases, the attacker's reinterpretation is a lie that can be readily exposed by any independent observer, as in the case of the beating of salt march satyagrahis in India. In other cases, though, the attacker's perspective seems genuine though lopsided from the point of view of outsiders. Though there were more than 20 law enforcement officials at the scene of the Rodney King beating, the officer in charge of the arrest thought that King was on PCP — giving him extraordinary strength — and that his behaviour, such as not going into the prone position, signalled a threat (Koon, 1992).

In yet other cases, it is difficult to assess the genuineness of the attacker's claims, even when they seem outlandish. The US military attack on Iraq in March 2003 was publicly justified on the grounds that the Iraqi government possessed weapons of mass destruction that posed an immediate threat to the US, hence warranting a pre-emptive attack. For months before the invasion of Iraq, US officials made strong pronouncements about the threat from Iraq. Afterwards, though, many questions were raised about the basis for these claims. Probing the psychology of US officials at the time remains a virtually insuperable challenge, barring release of documents or testimony showing that they were saying one thing privately and another publicly.

In the case of academics, it is standard for attackers to interpret the situation in a way that justifies their actions. Officials *never* say, "Professor Z was exercising her academic freedom, so we dismissed her." They *rarely* say, "Professor Z spoke out in an unacceptable way, so we dismissed her" and even then they might add, "This has nothing to do with academic freedom." What they more commonly say is, "Unfortunately, Professor Z's position was eliminated in a reorganisation" or "Professor Z's performance was substandard, so she had to be released" or "Funding shortfalls make it impossible to retain Professor Z's services." These latter sorts of justifications are far less likely to trigger outrage, as they do not indicate unfairness.

The degree of reinterpretation necessary depends on the potential for adverse reactions. If an academic has been severely devalued and has no allies, then an overt attack may not lead to repercussions. In some countries, radical academics are at risk of murder. But even ruthless regimes may seek to hide or reinterpret their actions due to pressures from human rights campaigners. "Disappearances" are less likely than open assassinations to recoil against the killers.

It is possible for attackers to misjudge the situation and be too blatant in their actions. This is a common source of boomerangs.

Richardson's occasional displays of temper were interpreted by some students not only as disturbing and unacceptable, but as indicating that he posed a threat. Personal behaviour is a rich source of interpretative diversity, with different observers often drawing entirely different conclusions from the same events.

In reporting his involvement with Edwin Mellen Press, Richardson separated scholarly and commercial dimensions, reporting only the scholarly side. The tribunal interpreted this quite differently, judging Richardson guilty of fraud for not following the reporting rules. The problem here is that rules do not interpret themselves, so it is often possible for attackers to offer a different but plausible explanation.

For an academic, setting up a scholarly press would normally be seen as a signal achievement. Richardson's attackers, though, creatively reinterpreted Mellen Press as some sort of shady operation and turned what would normally be an asset into a liability.

The tribunal also found Richardson guilty of a second charge, that he had committed fraud in his claims for taking sick leave. Westhues explains that Richardson needed to escape the stress of his situation at St. Michael's but that this did not preclude him from other sorts of vigorous activities. However, the tribunal adopted a different interpretation, namely that Richardson's actions during his sick leave indicated that he was not all that sick.

I have seen a number of cases in which academics have suffered acute stress at work and needed to get away from their offices. In some cases, they have been able to work productively in a different setting, yet suffer a relapse as soon as they return. This is quite compatible with what is known about trauma and recovery (Herman 1992). But for some colleagues, this behaviour may be interpreted quite differently: the stressed academic may be seen as a lazy impostor or as someone who just needs to "pull themselves together." There are some people who fake symptoms of stress or other illnesses, so there are no automatic answers in such situations. The key point here is that an academic under stress may receive not sympathy but rather further stress-inducing attacks.

Many academics, through their research and teaching, develop considerable experience in interpretation and reinterpretation of actions and motives. The tribunal presented a persuasive narrative about Richardson's failings. Westhues has presented a contrary narrative that places Richardson's actions in a much more favourable light. The tribunal's narrative inhibits boomerang from the dismissal; Westhues's narrative accentuates it.

Official Channels

An attack can generate immediate outrage from observers, if it is perceived as unjust. One way to inhibit boomerang is to justify the attack through some sort of official procedure, such as a commission of inquiry, a trial, a police investigation or an ombudsman's report. Official procedures give a stamp of approval to action taken. The most effective official channels are ones that are considered to have authority and to be fair-minded in dispensing justice.

In the aftermath of the Sharpeville massacre, the South African government set up a commission of inquiry to reduce the serious adverse effects of the massacre for its reputation as a democratic state. Following the beating of Rodney King, the Los Angeles government set up an inquiry. In addition, four police were charged with assault and tried. However, there are limits to the capacity of official channels to inhibit outrage. When a jury acquitted the four police officers, the discrepancy between the outcome and people's own judgement from watching the video of the beating triggered days of rioting in Los Angeles, causing massive damage and numerous deaths.

Attackers do not always obtain the endorsement they seek from official channels. The US government sought endorsement from the UN Security Council for its planned assault on Iraq. Because this was not obtained, popular antagonism to the attack was greater than it otherwise would have been, judging by opinion polls. In the end, the US government did not actually present a motion to the Security Council, obviously judging that a formal rejection would be more damaging than not bringing the matter to a vote.

Endorsement through official channels can inhibit boomerang even though the official channels are not neutral. The UN Security Council is a highly politicised body, subject to enormous pressure by the US government. But many people are not aware of this, believing that authorities are neutral and dispense justice. Similarly, courts are not neutral, serving those with wealth and power far more than the poor and dispossessed, but many people believe that the court system dispenses justice.

The belief in a just world is extremely deep and hard to budge (Lerner 1980). Many whistleblowers speak out fully expecting that their concerns will be fairly investigated and judged by bosses or regulatory bodies. These whistleblowers are shocked when they come under attack instead. Yet they continue to believe that there must be some higher authority that will provide justice, and so they continue to make appeals to ombudsmen, courts, politicians, auditors, anti-corruption bodies and others. Unfortunately, none of these appeal bodies gives more than a remote chance of success (De Maria 1999).

A tribunal was vital to minimising backlash from Richardson's dismissal. By following procedures, the dismissal decision was given an official stamp of approval. Most observers assume that a formal tribunal provides justice. Few bother to examine the actual process and to scrutinise the reasons given for dismissal. Westhues's account is invaluable precisely because it critically examines the reasons.

Imagine an alternative: summary dismissal without following any of the formal procedures laid out by the institution. This is very likely to backfire, as shown by the case of the dismissal of biologist Ted Steele from the University of Wollongong in 2001 (Martin 2002).

Next consider Richardson's counterattacks: his action for defamation against *Lingua Franca* and his appeal for judicial review of his dismissal. These were unfortunate for Richardson in several ways. First, he lost. Second, the court decisions gave additional official endorsement that his dismissal was fair, despite the fact that the courts did not look at the substantive issues involved. Third, as a consequence, the boomerang from his dismissal was dissipated rather than augmented.

The implication of this analysis is that in order to increase the boomerang effect, it is wise to avoid official channels and instead take one's case directly to potentially concerned audiences. Official channels usually serve those with more power, money and institutional centrality. Richardson would have gained more sympathy by not suing anyone, as Westhues is pained to emphasise.

The boomerang effect is not a goal in itself. There may indeed be good reasons to use official channels. But if one's primary goal is justice, then the experience of whistleblowers and others suggests that using official channels has a surprisingly poor chance of success.

Intimidation and Bribery

Attackers sometimes intimidate the victim, witnesses and others. If effective, this can inhibit boomerang. For example, police who use excessive force often charge their targets with assault or resisting arrest or threaten them with charges should they make a complaint. Sometimes witnesses are threatened too. After the Sharpeville massacre, South African police went through the township arresting anyone they could blame for the "disturbance." They also dragged anti-apartheid activists from the hospital. This intimidation helped reduce the willingness of witnesses to testify against the police at the commission of inquiry (Frankel, 2001).

In academia, these sorts of heavy-handed tactics are unusual in industrialised countries. But western academics can be cowed even without the threat of violence. Most academics are so concerned about their jobs, their grants, the respect of their peer groups, and their good standing with superiors that they are very unlikely to take an unpopular public stand, especially as a lone voice. Most academics are willing to acquiesce to dominant views without the need for explicit threats or attacks. The hurdles and peer pressures in an academic career serve as a way to create "ideological discipline" (Schmidt 2000). Unconscious self-censorship becomes a way of life.

Michiel Horn, author of *Academic Freedom in Canada* (1999), wrote to me that "Most academics are conformist Milquetoasts. If we weren't we wouldn't have entered academe." Obviously there are exceptions to this generalisation: a few individuals are willing to stick their necks out on behalf of colleagues, and in some places and cases a union or professional association offers principled defence.

An attack on an academic, whether a reprimand or dismissal, can serve as a form of intimidation. Many academics are deeply shamed by any official criticism and wish to go into hiding. Many leave rather than fight. It requires a robust character to survive psychologically in the face of widespread condemnation, especially to persist in the face of a degradation ceremony.

Intimidation did not work against Richardson. He ignored the strong suggestion in 1987 that he leave. He demanded an open tribunal. He counterattacked through legal actions. He continued his business. He published Westhues's book. All this indicates an exceptional character and unusual inner strengths.

For academics who would resist unjust attacks, or even just survive the everyday environment of a toxic workplace, developing this sort of inner strength should be a priority. Wyatt and Hare (1997) present one way of building this strength. Arguably, psychological skills for understanding and negotiating organisations should be in every curriculum, from primary school to university.

For inhibiting boomerang, bribery is the partner of intimidation. Those who cooperate with an attack may be rewarded by praise or promotions, or at least protection against similar treatment. In the most famous Australian academic dismissal case, the sacking of philosophy professor Sydney Orr from the University of Tasmania in 1956, some commentators allege that key figures who collaborated in the attack on Orr were rewarded by plum jobs (Eddy 1960). Bribery usually has to be inferred in the academic context, because there are no written promises or even conscious intentions. Westhues does not give any evidence of this sort of bribery at St. Michael's. This is not surprising given that he relies heavily on written documents of a sort that are unlikely to reveal unsavoury activities carried out behind the scenes. Another factor is defamation law, which inhibits reporting of such activities.

Intimidation and bribery can backfire if they are exposed. The first task is to survive intimidation. The next is to expose the intimidation so that it boomerangs against the attackers.

Conclusion

Looking at the process by which an attack can boomerang seems a fruitful way to examine the dynamics of Richardson's dismissal. Those who acted to get rid of Richardson used most of the standard methods that, as revealed in a wide variety of attacks, often inhibit boomerang. The attackers in the Richardson case attempted to cover up the attack, devalue the target and reinterpret the events. They used official channels. Though there is no public evidence that the attackers used intimidation and bribery, any attempt at dismissal is intimidating for most academics.

The model of attack and boomerang can be revealing even without making any judgement about the validity of the process and the methods. Boomerang dynamics operate on the basis of perceptions. A dismissal may be quite justified by the evidence and still boomerang if it is perceived as unjust. Likewise, a dismissal may be quite unjust and yet proceed without arousing concern, by effective inhibition of boomerang.

This analysis suggests what is likely to be effective in magnifying the boomerang effect. The first, most vital thing is to expose the attack. Richardson did this by refusing to go quietly and by demanding an open tribunal.

A second method is to counter the process of devaluation of the target. For example, Richardson and his supporters might have tried to use publicity to paint him as a courageous defender of religious freedom and as an inspiring if somewhat confrontational teacher. However, Westhues gives no mention of any pro-Richardson publicity campaign.

The third method is to advance one's own interpretations and undermine the attackers' interpretations. Richardson attempted to do this at the tribunal. To be more effective, his perspective needed to be taken to wider audiences.

The fourth method is to avoid relying on official channels to obtain justice. Perhaps Richardson could not have avoided the tribunal, but he could have used it as a platform for a publicity campaign. Organisational attackers hate adverse publicity more than anything.

Sympathy and outrage are more likely to be generated when people perceive a large, powerful organisation attacking an individual who does not strike back. Therefore, from the point of view of magnifying boomerang, Richardson's counterattacks — his legal actions — were ill-advised. They gave the appearance of justice and of a battle between equals.

The fifth method is to refuse to be intimidated. In this, Richardson succeeded remarkably well, by not leaving St. Michael's quietly, by pushing for an open tribunal and by publishing Westhues's book.

Looking at academic attacks in terms of the boomerang effect is just one perspective. Its great strength is in providing insight into the dynamics of a struggle and offering guidance for action. By itself, though, it does not provide background, context or an assessment of right and wrong. For these dimensions of the Richardson saga, Westhues's book is invaluable. The book can also be seen as a highly potent intervention in an ongoing process of academic boomerang.

References

Dalton, Dennis, 1993. *Mahatma Gandhi: Nonviolent Power in Action.* New York: Columbia University Press.

De Maria, William, 1999. *Deadly Disclosures: Whistleblowing and the Ethical Meltdown of Australia.* Adelaide: Wakefield Press.

Dixon, Marlene, 1976. *Things Which Are Done in Secret.* Montréal: Black Rose Books.

Eddy, W. H. C., 1961. *Orr.* Brisbane: Jacaranda Press.

Frankel, Philip, 2001. *An Ordinary Atrocity: Sharpeville and its Massacre.* New Haven, CT: Yale University Press.

Herman, Judith Lewis, 1992. *Trauma and Recovery.* New York: BasicBooks

Horn, Michiel, 1999. *Academic Freedom in Canada: A History.* Toronto: University of Toronto Press.

Jansen, Sue Curry, and Brian Martin, 2003. "Making censorship backfire," *Counterpoise* 7 (3), pp. 5-15.

Koon, Stacey C., with Robert Deitz, 1992. *Presumed Guilty: The Tragedy of the Rodney King Affair.* Washington, DC: Regnery.

Lerner, Melvin J., 1980. *The Belief in a Just World: A Fundamental Delusion.* New York: Plenum.

Martin, Brian, 2002. "Dilemmas of defending dissent: the dismissal of Ted Steele from the University of Wollongong," *Australian Universities' Review* 45(2), pp. 7-17 (http://www.uow.edu.au/arts/sts/bmartin/pubs/02aur.html).

Martin, Brian, and Steve Wright, 2003. "Countershock: mobilizing resistance to electroshock weapons," *Medicine, Conflict & Survival* 19, pp. 206-223.

Owens, Tom, with Rod Browning, 1994. *Lying Eyes: The Truth behind the Corruption and Brutality of the LAPD and the Beating of Rodney King.* New York: Thunder's Mouth Press.

Schmidt, Jeff, 2000. *Disciplined Minds: A Critical Look at Salaried Professionals and the Soul-Battering System that Shapes their Lives.* Lanham, MD: Rowman & Littlefield.

Sharp, Gene, 1973. *The Politics of Nonviolent Action.* Boston: Porter Sargent.

Westhues, Kenneth, 2003. *The Trial, Degradation, and Dismissal of a Professor: Administrative Mobbing in Academe* (pre-publication draft, essentially the same as first edition, 2004). Lewiston, NY: Edwin Mellen.

Wyatt, Judith, and Chauncey Hare, 1997. *Work Abuse: How to Recognize and Survive It.* Rochester, VT: Schenkman.

Chapter Seventeen

Eliminated but not Annihilated

Kathleen Kufeldt

This essay reflects a highly personal history. Much of its presentation is inspired by Herbert Richardson's experiences and parallels to it. Also, in its own way, it contributes to affirmation of Kenneth Westhues's theory building with respect to workplace mobbing and professorial elimination. Westhues's work is worthy of support in that it presents a positive contribution on two levels. First and most importantly it fulfils the *raison d'être* of academe, albeit one that becomes clouded in the sometimes internecine struggles that lie at the root of mobbing in universities. His powerful conceptualization, his theory building, and particularly the use of theory for human betterment are in the best traditions of scholarship. The second level is that of the individual. His work brings a voice of reason, sanity, and hope to those of us who are the targets. In my own and others' cases, it provides some counterbalance to the negative effect of contemplating painful and difficult events in our lives. We are no longer alone but part of a community who have been victimized, not because we did something wrong, but in most cases because we tried to do what was right. Guilt, isolation and confusion disappear in the bright light shed by his insightful analyses. Now it is my turn as I respond to the invitation to contribute this commentary.

In doing so I can follow, in a sense, in the footsteps of some who have experienced even darker persecution: Holocaust survivors. As Lowinger states in her introduction to *Tapestry of Hope,* "Through their stories, poems and personal accounts, the contributors record the darkest of times, not to dismay us but to show us that nothing can extinguish the spark that gives dignity to life" (2003, p. xi). In order to survive the elimination we have to keep that spark alive and resist annihilation. Sharing our stories, as some Holocaust survivors have done, may be an encouragement to others. Certainly, Westhues's earlier account (1998) served that purpose for me and for many others.

As I studied his theory building, I was captivated by Westhues's discussion of semantics, particularly his use of the term *elimination* as his central concept. Indeed, perhaps one could consider it as an important theoretical *construct* since his focus goes beyond the physical removal of professors. It includes the imposition of an almost intolerable burden. This burden is invoked not only by the attempted destruction of one's career, but by the interruption of productive research endeavours, shunning by one's colleagues, and gossip in the community of the particular discipline. Those who are eliminated are truly shoved out beyond the threshold. Hence I agree with him, his language does not constitute inappropriate hyperbole. Nor does my use of terms such as *internecine* and *annihilation.* The etymology of each is as enlightening as that of elimination, *ad liminem. Internecine* is derived from the Latin *internecare,* to slaughter or massacre. It has entered into modern parlance as activity or struggle within an organization that is mutually destructive to the participants. Indeed, whenever there is workplace mobbing or elimination, actual or intended, both sides suffer and the organization is the poorer for it. *Annihilation* is also derived from a Latin root, *nihil* meaning nothing and *annihilare,* to reduce to nothing. Mobbing has that intent. Some victims have indeed been reduced to nothingness, sometimes with loss of health leading to premature death, sometimes succumbing to such depths of demoralisation and despair that the "spark that gives dignity to life" (Lowinger 2003, p. xi) is extinguished though life itself goes on. In my own case, more than once I was close to complete physical breakdown but fortunately that spark survived and nurtured a determination to fight annihilation even though successfully eliminated. Westhues's earlier book (1998) was recommended to me by a good friend, also experiencing workplace mobbing, when the spark was flickering low. His insightful analysis and courageous endurance of his own ordeal helped fan the spark into life again. I became determined that the university would not succeed entirely in its efforts and so diverted my energies to maintaining productive scholarly activities, albeit unpaid.

The Incident – Fact and Fiction

In both his books Westhues described a process that moves through three phases, informal ostracization and harassment, an "incident." and finally a postlude, usually of protests, appeals etc.(Westhues 1998, 2003). In my own case the first two phases were reversed, though the postlude followed. There was first an "incident." This in its turn prompted harassment; included in this harassment was the successful triggering of mobbing, ostracization within the department, and eventual elimination. This flipping of events does not negate Westhues's description; rather it illustrates that the process itself can be invoked to eliminate someone who has become a PITA – Westhues's (1998) acronym for Pain in the Ass – to someone in a position of power. I was a relative newcomer to this University, so in a sense, perhaps I was seen by some as an outsider like Richardson, thus making the targeting easier for the perpetrator. Also, as I learnt subsequently, there was at least one other within the department who had coveted the position offered to me, and another who felt threatened by my profile within the community. Both became very active participants in the mobbing process. So what was this "incident" that could create such havoc?

It is necessary to backtrack a little. Because of demonstrated success in my field I had been successfully wooed to leave my former position with the promise that I would be given time and resources to focus the next few years on my major area of research and interest. For some time all went well. The Department Head, here referred to as Dr. Teflon,[1] seemed delighted: I was doing all that I had been recruited to do. So why an incident and what was it about it that could initiate the mobbing and precipitate such a dire outcome? In truth, there *was* a factual incident, known to me and to Dr. Teflon, but to few others. His reaction was to initiate a programme of harassment which included the construction of fictitious incidents which were

---

[1] I learnt during the mobbing process that his nickname was the Teflon Man, since nothing seemed to stick, adverse events slid off his back. That is why I have used the term here.

then broadcast amongst my colleagues and higher echelons of the University.

The initial incident was an innocent action on my part to investigate some anomalies in the trust account assigned to my work. The controller whom I approached checked the figures and discovered that relatively large sums of money had been transferred to an internal department account to which the Head had access. He was quietly advised to replace the money. This was done. The controller and I considered the incident closed. We did not bargain for the fact that I was perceived as a whistleblower – dangerous activity. The Greeks knew that. Modern society has been slower to wake up to the fact, or indeed to put in procedures to protect those who do so with good intentions.

Neither the controller nor I anticipated the anger that would be provoked and the ensuing revenge. The anger for the most part was never openly expressed. On the two occasions when it did emerge the degree of vitriol was shocking to witnesses, but alas it was never witnessed by those who were to become the mobbers. Whenever I approached Dr. Teflon to try to resolve whatever issue he had, as his nickname indicates, my approach would simply slide off him, conversation was diverted, and he, like Liza Dolittle's dance partner, would proceed to "ooze charm from every pore." In actual fact the psalmists describe better the behaviour of such as he: "No truth can be found in their mouths, their heart is all mischief, their throat a wide-open grave, all honey their speech."[2] For while the speech was indeed honeyed, the false rumours were circulated and the harassment continued. And "incidents" were fabricated. One fiction that was particularly successful in precipitating mobbing was an alleged failure to take on teaching assignments. I remember one occasion when I asked another member of the administration what the problem was, the reply that came back was, "Well you are not exactly pulling your weight around here!" This reply was particularly odd since this same person had on another occasion chided me for working too long hours and suggested that I tried to pace myself better!

The Mobbing

If Dr. Teflon's behaviour was hard to take, the workplace mobbing thus generated was even more demoralizing. My colleagues began to treat me like a pariah. One has since moved to another University and

---

[2]Psalm 5: 2-10, 12-13.

from the safety of that vantage point admitted to me that she bought into the mobbing mentality until she was herself victimized and could see through the stratagem. Somewhat shamefacedly she acknowledged that she didn't have the guts to speak out against the mob. At one time I approached another whom I thought was a friend to ask if he could help me make sense of the developing atmosphere. To my surprise I was subjected to an extreme burst of anger and refusal from then on to engage in any kind of conversation. When it became clear that elimination was to be successfully achieved some colleagues came by to preach and chastise – they had been part of secret committees struck to decide what should be done about me. It was clear that there were more fabrications than I had ever conceived of. The committees were established and used to precipitate mobbing, to justify the Department Head's actions, and, by giving its members a spurious sense of their own power, were able to intensify the negative atmosphere that had developed.

Who Are the Participants in a Mobbing?

Coloroso (2002) has produced an insightful portrayal and analysis of mobbing in schools, where it is more commonly known as bullying. She identifies the bully, the bullied and the bystander. Much of what she says can be applied to my situation, to Richardson's, and to that of others who have been first mobbed then eliminated. Here I will use her conceptualization to make analogies primarily to my own situation.

The Bully. Coloroso suggests that there are three markers or elements to the bullying, and sometimes a fourth. The three are an imbalance of power, the intent to harm, and the threat of further aggression, where both the bully and the bullied are aware that the aggressive behaviour is going to continue. These three were definitely present in my own case. The fourth element, as the aggression escalates, is that of induced terror. This did not happen, despite the fact, as Coloroso maintains, that the intent is to intimidate and maintain dominance. The lawyer I consulted in the fairly early stages warned me that nothing would change, that the intent was to get rid of me, and that if I acted immediately I would have grounds for a suit of constructive dismissal. With hindsight good advice. But like Richardson, I thought justice would prevail without recourse to a lawsuit. Besides, I was in the middle of some pretty important work, which I did not want to jeopardize by such an interruption. I suspect that in both my own and Dr. Richardson's case, the failure to induce terror provided yet another motive for the eventual elimination. There is probably not quite as much fun in bullying, or in workplace mobbing, if the desired effect of complete subjection and fear is not achieved.

The Bullied. Coloroso says that "Targets can be just about anybody," and lists twenty possible attributes of a potential victim (Coloroso, 2002, p. 43-45). I suggest that five in particular can create vulnerability in academe. These are a person:

- who is unwilling to fight – who prefers to resolve conflict without aggression;
- whose race or ethnicity is viewed by the bully as inferior, deserving of contempt;
- whose religion is viewed by the bully as inferior, deserving of contempt;
- who is bright, talented or gifted – targeted because she "stands out" – in other words, who is different;
- who is independent and unconcerned about social status, doesn't conform to the norm.

Certainly as I read about Herbert Richardson, and about Westhues's own struggles, it struck me that each of us would likely score four out of five – pretty high risk! I would maintain, however, that for bullying to flourish there has to be a certain organizational culture as well as a vulnerable target. I say this because I can recall some events in my own life history that failed to escalate in the particular contexts. The first occurred when I was about twelve. I was somewhat reserved, top of the class, but completely unconcerned about this and totally noncompetitive. One of my classmates said in friendly jest, "It's weird, you don't even look smart." But these attributes roused the ire of an older kid. I also met one other of Coloroso's qualifications for being bullied: "one who has superficial physical attributes that are different from the majority." I had braces on my teeth; these became the initial butt for attempted humiliation. Fortunately for me there was a school ethos that was protective toward the smaller and weaker, and that frowned on bullying. The would-be bully's cohorts distanced themselves, forcing withdrawal of the attacks.

The second event occurred much later in life at another University. At the time I was a relatively new academic, not yet on the tenure track, but applying whenever a vacancy was advertised. A series of minor harassments were inflicted by the Department Head: a friendly mentor advised me that as long as I kept on applying, I was preventing the Head from appointing his choice of candidate, presumed to be a former student of his. So the harassing behaviour was understandable and I must confess that I took considerable amusement from second guessing what the next move would be. Eventually there was an action serious enough that it needed to be taken to the Faculty Association. The tradition in that University was that senior administration and the Faculty Association saw themselves as working cooperatively to resolve problems for the general wellbeing of the institution. My problems were quickly resolved. The next application won me the position, and eventually the approbation of the Head. These examples augur well for Westhues's suggested solutions, both for prevention and education. They did not prepare me well for the events that led to my elimination. I hoped for too long, at great cost, for right to prevail.

The Bystander. Colorado describes bystanders as "the supporting cast who aid and abet the bully through acts of omission and commission" (2002, p. 62). Without them, as my early school experience illustrated, the bullying dies aborning. They are an essential part of the drama that is to be played out. These bystanders are the active or passive participants in workplace mobbing. Some have their own personal reasons for exacerbating the mobbing ("I wanted that position"; "his profile is diminishing mine"; "she's a ratebuster"). Some get caught up in the labelling and stereotyping that goes along with workplace mobbing ("this person deserves all he gets"; "she brought it on herself"). More insidious are situations such as those of Dr. Nancy Olivieri, where money flowing from corporate sponsorship is deemed to be more important than upholding ethical standards.

What about the passive bystanders? Some, though seemingly standing aloof, are actually enjoying the scene. Others are guilt ridden but fearful of taking on the mob, or of being mobbed themselves. Then there are the few who will defend the targetted person. But too often their fate in turn feeds into the fears of others who would like to help but lack the courage. I can think of two such people in my case. Each suffered sanctions. Dr. A. at that point had a relatively low profile in the field, and was able to move to a more congenial position elsewhere. Dr. B. on the other hand suffers/enjoys an extremely high profile, with a very respectable publication record and numerous public speaking and media engagements. In addition, Dr. B. scores five out of five for potential bullying in academe. Not surprisingly this professor has become the target for some unusually vicious mobbing that extends beyond the immediate institution to the entire field, such that attempts to obtain another position have to date been unsuccessful.

The dynamics that affect Dr. B's attempts to seek another position have also operated in my own situation. I have found that the mobbing behaviour extends into the larger community of the particular discipline and goes on, even after a successful elimination. For example, recently emboldened by a positive conversation with a program head concerning the value of my work and his desire to develop improvements in the field, I made a follow-up call to this person, assuming that we could work together. However, the response was that it would be impossible because of "ongoing issues." While I don't consider myself as suffering from post-traumatic stress, I was surprised at the depth of hurt and reactivation of old feelings of stress and despondency. I have to accept that I now work in a divided world. Fortunately for me the whispering, the innuendoes, and even past and recent attempts to wrest my programme of research from me are counterbalanced by a healthy reputation supported by those who know me well, admire the work, and are happy to continue to work with me.

The Postlude

Westhues's third phase in the mobbing and elimination process, the postlude, is currently being directed at Dr. B. There are encouraging signs that in his case some of the checks and balances in place will counteract any possible elimination. I myself, like Herbert Richardson, experienced a prolonged postlude before the final elimination was achieved. As I mentioned earlier, I ignored legal advice to sue for constructive dismissal and decided instead to grieve the harassment. After all, this recourse had worked before and worked in fact to my advantage. It transpired that in this University there was no remedy in the collective agreement for harassment; nevertheless the Faculty lawyer could identify several different grounds for grievance embedded in the harassment, each of which had to be dealt with separately.[3]

---

[3]This strategy had a subsequent negative rebound effect: the fact that so many grievances were launched helped create an image of a complainer, a true "Pain in the Ass."

There was also another significant difference. Unlike in my previous University, the negative actions directed at a complainant could continue until such time as the grievance was resolved – and the grievance procedures dragged on. My spouse and major supporter put it succinctly: "they can carry out a death sentence before the appeals have all been heard!" At one point it was recommended that I appeal a particular issue to a higher level of administration, since it was a relatively simple matter. I had been denied permission to leave campus to take overdue annual leave (before I had even asked for it!). I found to my dismay that my Department Head had recruited even this level to the mobbing team. I well remember being told, as my request was refused, "You have had your own way before, from now on you will toe the line!" So the rumours, accusations and innuendos had spread. Even changes in Department Heads achieved nothing. The pack was in full cry, although it did require some changes to the collective agreement to enable the mob to achieve elimination.

Resilience

Coloroso (2002) has informed us about vulnerability. In order to finish on an optimistic note, I would like to discuss the antidote, resilience. Where does the resilience come from to survive the pain of mobbing? What is it that promotes resilience in the face of such debilitating and devastating experiences? These are important questions: as Westhues states in his final chapter, mobbing is *unnecessary harm,* and its "incidence and intensity can and should be reduced for the sake of human betterment" (Westhues 2004, p. 292). I agree with him and believe that he has made a significant contribution to that end, and most likely to his own resilience. A study of both of his books and of Richardson's saga convinces me of these men's inherent goodness. In turn they reassure me that I possess goodness. Such certitude can help to build resilience. As I pondered these things I came across the following lines: "Prophets like Amos are closely tied to a people whom they cherish and for whose future they care deeply. And yet people like him are perceived as disturbers." (Prévost 2002, p. 410). Prévost therein provides a clue to both resilience and to the roots of mobbing in academe. The victims of mobbing have in various ways disturbed the status quo, the prevailing culture, or someone else's ambitions. They are disturbers. On the other hand, their commitment to that which they cherish enables them to transcend the actions of the mob. Other explorers of the concept of resilience would support this and have much to tell us about survival.

O'Connell Higgins (1994), Rubin (1996) and Silva-Wayne (1995) are three scholars who have studied resilience exhibited by victims of childhood abuse. O'Connell Higgins identifies elements of recovery:

- healthy self-compassion, with locus of responsibility on the abusers;
- sharing the extent of the abuse with trusted loved ones;
- being aware of what one can control in one's life;
- healing within the company of others.

Rubin provides nine examples of adults who have transcended an abused childhood within the family. Her use of the concept of marginality (perhaps another example of being *ad liminem*) is particularly interesting. She describes the abused child as marginalized within the family, but this very marginalization becomes, in her words, "a psychological bedrock" enabling the child to distance from and refuse to identify with the abusive family. Interestingly, in a recent conversation with Dr. B., I asked what was it that helped his survival in such a toxic milieu. His response echoed those of Rubin's respondents. He had turned the marginalization into a positive: distancing from the mob enabled him to concentrate or more productive pursuits. Both for him and for Rubin's people, alternatives become possible that are both comforting and distancing. Some alternatives identified by her and by other experts in the field are reading, writing, excellence in sports, or in the arts. Other attributes Rubin identified are personal attractiveness, intelligence and, similarly to O'Connell Higgins' findings, achieving an internal locus of control.

Silva-Wayne studied successful graduates of the foster care system and discerned the following contributors to their eventual success:

- use of positive role models, including fictional models;
- affiliation to supportive communities;
- having experiences which raised self-esteem;
- exposure to opportunities;
- use of protective thinking.

Her findings support Rutter's (1987) identification of resilience factors, including supportive relationships, task accomplishments and relationships that open up opportunities.

The findings of these various authors overlap and can be summarized into key attributes that have helped sustain survivors of mobbing in academe. To illustrate, I am presenting my own assumptions about how they apply to Richardson's, Westhues's, and my own cases.

- Personal attractiveness: success in engaging others;
- Intelligence: shown in their scholarly work;
- Supportive loved ones: marriage partners;
- Supportive community: enhanced by personal faith;
- Internal locus of control: experience put in perspective;
- Developing alternatives that raise self-esteem: Mellen Press; successful research; publications

Remedies

Remedies at the individual level are time-consuming, expensive, and hard to come by. In my own case, administrative grievance procedures at the eliminating University, as well as the Canadian Justice system processes, have been grievous disappointments. Nevertheless, I would advocate a continued fight for justice. Such fights, where successful, may provide useful precedents for subsequent victims. There are possibilities for remedies at the organizational and societal level. Westhues provides an excellent role model in this respect when he argues against the easier route of anti-oppression rhetoric (2004, p. 291). Instead he addresses the greater objective of human betterment, of the common good.

Westhues identifies three remedial approaches:

- Recovery of the target,
- Prevention,
- Education.

Recovery of the target is not straightforward. My own experience has shown that dependence on legal and natural justice creates its own stresses and frustrations. Much more productive is for friends and supporters to focus on the contributors to resilience. Prevention requires anti-mobbing laws, policies and procedures. Westhues expresses some scepticism about their efficacy, including a prognosis that they may generate "new techniques for punishing, stigmatizing and eliminating employees" (2004, p. 305). His recommended remedy is that of education. Education can identify mobbing for what it really is. It can also identify how destructive it is to the perpetrators and the institutions as well as to the target. And, "Education is a way of preventing mobbing in the still more basic sense of getting the facts of the matter out in the open" (Westhues 2004, p. 309).

Both Westhues and Coloroso have done a great deal to advance such education. Through their analyses and through the powerful metaphors evoked by their concepts they tell us not only what bullying and mobbing truly are, but also how destructive such activities are. The intended destruction is towards the targets, but the perpetrators, the mobsters, the bystanders and the very institutions themselves are thereby damaged.

Conclusions

Writing this paper has evoked pain; it has also been cathartic. It is a strange experience to stand back from one's experiences, to put oneself in the position of observer rather than prime participant. What it does is provide perspective. If Richardson and Westhues can survive, so can I. If their experiences can assist in the educative process, then it may be that mine also can do the same. At the very least it does support the central thesis of Westhues's work.

Working in academe is an exceptional privilege. Very few places provide that milieu where there is support to pursue and advance knowledge for the betterment of the human condition. Somehow too may Universities have lost sight of this fact. Fabrikant has been vilified but he correctly identified some of the corruption that has crept in. His resorting to violence is unacceptable, but his actions sparked the Canadian Tri-Council's efforts to advance and improve ethical standards. Somehow the academic culture has to be changed. Westhues has taken the first step. Despite his reservations, I believe that we also need to instigate anti-mobbing, anti-harassment policies and practices; if implemented hand in hand with the lessons he offers us, they may yet save the day.

References

Coloroso, Barbara, 2002. *The Bully, the Bullied and the Bystander*. Toronto: HarperCollins Publishers Ltd.

Lowinger, Kathy, 2003. "Introduction." In Lilian Boraks-Nemetz & Irene N. Watts, eds., *Tapestry of Hope: Holocaust Writing for Young People*. Toronto: Tundra Books, pp. xi-xii.

O'Connell Higgins, Gina, 1994. *Resilient Adults: Overcoming a Cruel Past*. San Francisco, CA: Jossey-Bass.

Prévost, Jean-Pierre, 2002. "Commentary for Fifteenth Sunday in Ordinary Time." In Louise Pambrun, editor-in-chief, *Living in Christ Sunday Missal.* Toronto: Novalis.

Rubin, Lillian, 1996. *The Transcendent Child.* New York: Basic Books.

Rutter, Michael, 1987. "Psychosocial resilience and protective mechanisms," *American Journal of Orthopsychiatry,* 57, 316-331.

Silva-Wayne, Susan, 1995. "Contributions to Resilience in Children and Youth: What Successful Child Welfare Graduates Say." In J. Hudson and B. Galaway, Eds., *Canadian Child Welfare: Research and Policy Implications.* Toronto: Thompson Educational Publishing, pp. 308-323.

Westhues, Kenneth, 1998. *Eliminating Professors: a Guide to the Dismissal Process.* Lewiston, NY: Robert Kempner Collegium, Edwin Mellen Press.

Westhues, Kenneth, 2004. *Administrative Mobbing at the University of Toronto.* Lewiston, NY: Edwin Mellen Press.

Part Seven

Strategies of Prevention

Editor's Introduction

The adage, "an ounce of prevention is worth a pound of cure," applies to workplace mobbing even more than to most ills. Leymann claimed that in all his research, he had not found a single case of a mobbed worker being accepted back into the workplace with an apology and compensation. My findings on academic mobbings are almost as bleak. Once an institution has eliminated a professor, kicked him or her outside the circle of respectability and paid employment, it finds taking the professor back almost impossible, no matter how wrong the eliminative decision is shown to have been. Financial compensation is sometimes obtained, or a post-termination expression of regret, but almost never a restoration of the pre-mobbing relation or a genuine reconciliation. This pathology has an air about it of chilling finality.

The harm it does to individuals and institutions therefore warrants serious and skilled effort to prevent mobbing from happening. The four chapters below reflect such effort. Each offers practical ideas for reducing the likelihood of the many ganging up on the one.

In Chapter 18, Dan Cohn-Sherbok argues persuasively that because British university policy forbids religious tests for theology professors, Richardson could not have been ousted there in the way he was from St. Michael's College, University of Toronto. Cohn-

Sherbok also highlights the importance of clear, fair disciplinary procedures, with the accused having the right of union representation.

In Chapter 19, Roman Dubinski makes an even stronger argument for faculty unions in the context of an insightful historical analysis of the University of Waterloo's evolution from "benign paternalism" in the 1960s to bureaucratic management in the 1990s. Dubinski accurately reports my views on how the incidence of mobbing can be reduced. He finds them impractical. Where we agree is on the necessity of multiple centers of power in campus political economy.

Dubinski was too modest to mention an important additional way mobbings are prevented and stopped: by strength of character, by the kind of decency, generosity, wisdom and courage he showed as chair of our faculty association's Academic Freedom & Tenure Committee from 1993 to 1996, and as my colleague-advisor during proceedings against me before Waterloo's now defunct Ethics Committee.

In counterpoint to Cohn-Sherbok's and Dubinski's confidence in rules of fair procedure and adjudication, Charmian Bondi and Jan Gregersen analyze in Chapter 20 what actually happened in Oslo, Norway, when a mobbed worker sued her boss. She lost – like many other complainants in similar adjudications. Procedural complexities trumped the substance of her claim. In the end, her humiliation at work was chalked up to "personality conflict," and the ruling came down in favor of the side with more power. The help of journalist Philip Mathias with editing this essay is gratefully acknowledged.

This book's final chapter is by law professor David Yamada, author of the definitive review of American legislation relevant to workplace mobbing and bullying, author also of a model statute that would outlaw the destructive social process that the present book is about. Yamada is keenly aware of the imperfections of any legal and judicial system. Such awareness lends credence to his argument for status-blind hostile work environment protection.

Public law and university policy must undoubtedly be counted among the instruments by which the incidence of workplace mobbing can be reduced. Organizational reform aimed at promoting shared, pluralistic, democratic governance in academe is another instrument. The most basic means of preventing workplace mobbing is education, so that all professors will at least know what it is, how it happens, and what havoc it wreaks. Practical education of this kind is the underlying purpose to which all the chapters in this book contribute.

Chapter Eighteen

Lessons from the British System for Preventing Cases Like Richardson's

Dan Cohn-Sherbok

Introduction

Kenneth Westhues has provided a fascinating and horrifying account of the ejection of the founder of The Edwin Mellen Press, Professor Herbert Richardson, from his teaching post at St. Michael's College at the University of Toronto. Outlining the intricacies of the process of exclusion and eventual elimination of Professor Richardson from the world of academe, Westhues has issued a warning to all academics of the dangers of institutional life. Throughout this work, he has illustrated the terrifying ordeal of mob rule in what is superficially a civilized environment. Yet there are, I believe, legal means of restraint which can protect professors from such an onslaught. Drawing on the procedures which govern relationships between teachers and managers in my own university, this essay seeks to demonstrate that mobbing can be thwarted by appealing to established procedures for dealing with situations of personal conflict.

The Herbert Richardson Case

Throughout his study Westhues emphasizes that Richardson had been singled out for attack. Initially, he alleges, St. Michael's College responded to his sabbatical plans by urging him to consider resigning from the University so that he could devote his talents to publication. In his letter of 7 January 1987, the Dean wrote:

> We would not be destitute now if you decided in the future to put your energies elsewhere. You would be well advised to talk with the University Bursar, Fr. Hale, or our President, Fr. McConica, to see what financial settlements might be made that would be equitable and just.[1]

As Westhues points out, Richardson did not acquiesce to this suggestion. Instead he went off for his one-year sabbatical, and returned to St Michael's. Yet, the Dean's letter had a deep impact on Richardson: he no longer regarded his academic job in covenantal terms. Rather, Richardson viewed his relationship with the College as a contract, binding on both sides. It was on this basis that the College subsequently was determined to dismiss Richardson for what they regarded as a breach of contract.

The first stage of the formal break with St. Michael's occurred when the College issued a 31-page document outlining its new bylaws pertaining to theology. All staff were required to sign and return a memorandum of agreement which stated that the Faculty of Theology exercises special responsibilities to the Roman Catholic Church to teach accurately its history, doctrines and tradition of ministries. Richardson, however, was not prepared to sign such a document. The Dean then sent him a letter asking that he attend to this matter, and later a further reminder. Unwilling to comply, Richardson wrote to the Dean in the fall of 1989, explaining that he would be represented by legal counsel concerning this issue.

With the arrival of a new President of the College, Richardson hoped that this impasse could be avoided. On 14 September 1990, he met with the President; four days later Richardson sent him a letter requesting that he be dropped from the Faculty of Theology and continue teaching and research through the Graduate Centre of Religious Studies and the Toronto School of Theology. For Richardson, the new bylaws constituted a breach of personal freedom: he could not agree that the magisterium of the Catholic Church had the right to determine how academics interpret and teach Scripture. In his view, this was what the Protestant protest was about — he simply could not deny his faith.

---

[1]Westhues, prepublication printing of *Administrative Mobbing...*, p. 173.

On his return from Britain, Richardson found no reply from the President. In November the Dean wrote to the President, indicating his uncertainty about how the College was to proceed. In his letter he noted that there had been complaints about Richardson's teaching and his method of grading. He also suggested that Richardson should give an account of his outside employment. In January 1991, the President proposed that Richardson be dropped from the Faculty and that his responsibilities be transferred to the Department of Religious Studies. In that capacity Richardson could continue to offer courses and pursue his research.

The formal stage of Richardson's dismissal commenced the following year. In a five-page letter sent to Richardson on 23 June 1993 from the vice-dean of arts and sciences of the University of Toronto, he was informed that the University was seeking to dismiss him. The letter spelled out the case against Richardson. In his study, Westhues outlines the charges in reverse order because the subsequent Evans tribunal upheld only the first two charges: abuse of medical leave and failure to report outside related activities. The fourth charge concerned scholarly misconduct and consisted of criticisms of Richardson's publications with the Edwin Mellen Press; the third criticism was of gross misconduct in teaching. Neither of these charges was upheld by the Tribunal as grounds for dismissal. The second criticism concerned Richardson's management of Edwin Mellen Press; and the first charge concerned the abuse of a medical leave — both of these charges were upheld by the Tribunal.

What is striking about the course of this process of elimination and dismissal is the apparent lack of formal disciplinary procedures. As Westhues illustrates, St Michael's College and the University of Toronto had become increasingly dissatisfied with Herbert Richardson's teaching, extra-curricular activities and research. Yet, the college authorities failed to take steps to remedy these problems. At no stage was Richardson encouraged to meet with his employers to explain his actions and to find a resolution to the difficulties. Instead, the University determined to rid itself of an irritating employee.

Disciplinary Procedures

By contrast with the lack of formal procedures exhibited in the Richardson case, my university is compelled to follow rigid guidelines for dismissal as outlined in the Staff Handbook distributed to all members of the faculty. Under Disciplinary and Dismissal

Procedure for Academic staff contained in section 7 of this handbook, Annexe 1 lays down a number of principles which are to govern relationships between members of staff. Point 1 emphasizes that it is the spirit and intention of the procedure agreement between the University of Wales and the Association of University Teachers (the union for all academic staff in the UK) "to foster the best possible relations between the University and the Association of University Teachers and to this end provide a mutually understood method of discussion, consultation and negotiation."[2]

Annexe 4 outlines the steps which are to be taken when a disciplinary case involving a member of staff is undertaken:

1. Normally disciplinary action for a minor offence is a recorded oral warning issued by a supervising officer. The Union concerned must be notified that an oral warning has been given. After such a warning, the Union concerned has the right to make representation to the Pro Vice-Chancellor.

2. The normal disciplinary action for a more serious offence or for an inadequate response to an oral warning is a written warning issued b the supervising officer. Copies of this warning should be sent to the Pro Vice-Chancellor and to the Union concerned. After this warning, the Union shall, in the event of a dispute concerning the warning, have the right to make representation to the Pro Vice-Chancellor.

3. A further transgression, or an inadequate response to a written warning will evoke a final written warning. This is to be issued by the Pro Vice-Chancellor and copies should be sent to the Union concerned. Again, after such a warning the Union shall have the right to make representation to the Pro Vice-Chancellor.

4. If a final written warning fails to evoke the required improvement or if the staff member commits a further offence, the matter is referred to a Disciplinary Committee consisting of a Chairman, a member nominated by the Trade Union of the member of staff, and the Pro Vice-Chancellor.

---

[2]Appendix 1 of Section 7 of the *Academic Staff Handbook of the University of Wales*, Lampeter, 2000.

5.   The member of staff whose conduct is the subject of the Disciplinary Committee shall receive not later than seven days before the meeting of the Committee a statement of his/her alleged failings and copies of other documents that may be used as evidence, together with details of the time and place at which the Committee is to meet. The staff member is to be informed of the composition of the Committee, given an opportunity to be accompanied at the hearing by a Trade Union representative or a friend as well as a legally qualified adviser. The staff member may be present to listen to all the evidence that is brought against him/her and may cross-examine those who have given evidence. Further, the staff member may give evidence and call witnesses on his/her own behalf.

6.   The Disciplinary Committee shall then consider the case and determine that the case be dismissed, the member of staff be suspended, or the contract of the member of staff terminated. The decision made should then be communicated to the staff member as well as the secretary of the Trade Union.

7.   A member of staff has the right to appeal against the decision of the Disciplinary Committee.

As can be seen, disciplinary cases must follow rigid guidelines — any breach of this process would invalidate the disciplinary case brought by university authorities. At every stage, from the first oral warning to the final written warning, staff members are given an opportunity to defend themselves with the support of Trade Union and legal representation. Even at the final stage when a Disciplinary Committee is summoned to evaluate the offence, a staff member is given the opportunity to challenge the charge. Further, staff members are permitted to appeal against the findings of this committee.

The Richardson Case and the British University System

If Herbert Richardson had been teaching at my university, the authorities could not have taken the same action as the University of Toronto administrators. Most importantly, British universities are not allowed to impose religious tests on academics in theology and religious studies departments. As we have seen, St Michael's College (as part of the University of Toronto) insisted that its teachers subscribe to theology bylaws which state that it is a condition of employment to teach accurately the history, doctrines, and tradition of ministries of the Roman Catholic Church.[3] Later paragraphs spell out the implications of these responsibilities: Catholic professors need to have obtained a mandate from the Superior-General of the Basilian Fathers, acting as delegate of the diocesan bishop, and the mandate depends on the demonstration of integrity of doctrine and uprightness of life. Non-Catholic professors have to have satisfied the Superior-General that they are knowledgeable about Catholic teachings and willing to share, in accord with the nature of their specific discipline, the special responsibilities of the Faculty of Theology.

My university authorities cannot introduce such religious standards because the Statutes of the University of Wales explicitly state that no religious test can be imposed on its employees. If the Vice-Chancellor of the University sent a similar letter to a faculty member, the Staff Handbook lays down procedures whereby that individual would be able to make a case against the Vice-Chancellor for violating the University's Statutes. There is simply no way that an individual's tenure could be threatened if he did not comply with the kind of religious norms imposed by St Michael's College. However, if a University administrator sought to impose such criteria, he could be dismissed for failing to uphold the Constitution of the University.

With regard to the type of charges levelled against Herbert Richardson, in every case disciplinary procedures would need to be carefully followed. In my university, student evaluation forms are handed out at the end of each course; they are then passed on to the Chairman of the Department. Any student complaint should be dealt with by the Chairman and the member of staff concerned. Ideally, a solution should be found. However, if difficulties continued, the Chairman would then be required to give an oral warning to the staff member — as we have seen, there is a rigorous formal procedure for such discipline. The same applies to any problem concerning scholarly research: there are procedural rules which specify how such dilemmas should be handled. If questions are raised about the integrity of publications, it is the Chairman's responsibility to deal with these issues when they arise. The same applies to an inadequate workload. Here, too, the Chairman must act in accordance with the disciplinary rules set out in the Staff Handbook. Similarly, if problems arise about an individual's activities during a medical leave,

---

[3]See Westhues, *ibid.*, pp. 186ff.

they should be dealt with immediately. At every stage, faculty members are entitled to representation at all meetings with administrators as well as negotiation with the Association of University Teachers.

The tragedy of the whole affair is not only the fact that a distinguished academic lost his job, but also that the University of Toronto was made to look arbitrary, dictatorial and prejudiced. The whole problem could and should have been solved by the following of clear, established, equitable procedures. Fortunately, the British University system enforces legal constraints on employers who are thereby prevented from engaging in the administrative mobbing of an academic that Westhues rightly deplores in his study of the Herbert Richardson case.

Chapter Nineteen

How to Minimize Workplace Mobbing: a Critique of Westhues

Roman Dubinski

Although we had been colleagues in the Arts Faculty of the University of Waterloo since 1975, I first met Ken Westhues in December 1993, when he approached me as Chair of the Academic Freedom and Tenure Committee of the Faculty Association of the University of Waterloo (FAUW). He sought my assistance in his dispute with a colleague and his department chair over an oral exam by one of his graduate students. Little did I know at the time that for the next three years, as Westhues's advisor and colleague, I would witness first-hand the process that he calls workplace mobbing. Unlike Westhues's exhaustive and contextually based analysis of the Richardson case, no such account of Westhues's own case has been written. But a fairly full account exists in *The Final Report of the Academic Freedom and Tenure Committee (Canadian Association of University Teachers) in the Matter of a Complaint by Professor Ken Westhues.* (Gannon 1996). I had submitted a lengthy brief to this Committee and published a briefer account in the *FAUW Forum* (Dubinski 1995). The report by the AF&T Committee of the CAUT found serious flaws in the processes of the Grievance and Ethics Committees at the University of Waterloo and concluded that Westhues had not been fairly treated.

Not only was Westhues involved in this dispute with his department, but in 1996, he was also accused by an undergraduate student of making racist comments in one of his classes. Though he sought to address the student's allegations informally, the student insisted that the Ethics Committee hear the case. Because of his previous unhappy experience with the Ethics Committee, Westhues presented a written statement to the Committee at its first meeting, and after he left he asked me to represent him. I was expelled from succeeding meetings of the Committee, which concluded its hearings without either Westhues or a representative present. The Committee found that Westhues was at fault and recommended that he take sensitivity counseling. The Provost rejected this recommendation and found that Westhues's comments were well within the bounds of academic freedom. But because he refused to co-operate with the Committee, the Provost fined him one month's salary. When Westhues appealed this penalty, the President appointed an independent adjudicator to hear his appeal. The adjudicator completely vindicated Westhues, threw out the fine, and awarded him a six-month paid leave (Mercer 1998).

During the same period that I was involved in Westhues's cases, I also served as advisor to Professor Len Friesen, whose case also showed clear symptoms of workplace mobbing and that did lead to Friesen's elimination from his position at Conrad Grebel College (affiliated with the University of Waterloo). I wrote a lengthy account of this case (Dubinski 1994a), concluding that financial expediency was a pretext for eliminating Friesen, while the real reason was to remove a professor who raised uncomfortable questions about the way the College was administered.

Like Richardson, both Friesen and Westhues survived the ordeal of elimination. Friesen received a public apology from the Board at Conrad Grebel College (see Westhues 2004, p. 296), was appointed as a History professor at neighboring Wilfrid Laurier University, and has since pursued an active and flourishing career. I know first-hand the torment Westhues suffered during the three years of his ordeal (see Westhues 1998). But rather than being crippled by this experience, Westhues turned his attention as a scholar to the study of workplace mobbing as a social phenomenon deserving close attention. By redirecting his research interests, Westhues has become a leader in this new field of studies, having now published two books on the subject. (Westhues 1998, 2004)

Readers of Westhues's book on the Richardson case must be impressed by the thoroughness of his research. Since I have not immersed myself in the documentation of the Richardson case, I have decided not to comment on Westhues's analysis. Instead I want to respond to his challenge and address the question of what needs to be done to subvert the process of workplace mobbing and to neutralize the eliminative passion.

Westhues believes that the way to check or subvert the endemic tendency in humans to mob individuals or seek their elimination is through education in the broadest sense, to awaken people to understand the process and seek remedies to avoid it. By getting the facts of the matter out into the open and available for scholarly and public scrutiny, Westhues contends that the subversion of mobbing and social elimination can be achieved. (Westhues 2004, pp. 307ff.)

In addition to education, Westhues proposes the establishment of a culture of reciprocity in workplace relations. Reciprocity for Westhues is similar to politics, that is, an ongoing process of negotiation and trade-off among workmates. Employees are encouraged to connect with one another in constructive human ways. The marks of reciprocity, argues Westhues, are argument, debate, friction, that is, conflict. Reciprocity means accepting as inevitable and good that colleagues have diverse viewpoints, therefore allowing them all to be expressed and debated. Reciprocity depends upon colleagues being able to work out agreements among themselves. (Westhues 2004, pp. 310ff.)

Westhues's concept of reciprocity derives from his distinction between a covenant and a contract. "A contract is the simpler relation. It means *quid pro quo*, tit for tat: an agreement freely made between two parties, actually, or as if in writing, to exchange one thing for another. Nothing but self-interest is required" (Westhues 2004, p. 154). "A covenant", writes Westhues, "is a larger, less specific, longer-term, more open-ended agreement beyond what words on paper can capture. It is an exchange of promises: to speak and listen to one another, to look out for each other's interest, to let one's very self be shaped by the other." (Westhues 2004, p. 155) Westhues laments the fact that our society values covenants less than contracts. In an attempt to replace traditional, authoritarian, dominative-submissive, master-servant relations of the past with contractual relations, our society has abandoned the notion that coercive relations of the past might be better replaced with covenantal relations. Westhues would like the covenantal relations of lifelong marriage or that between parents and children to define the relations between people in other contexts, especially in the workplace. In the academic setting, Westhues concedes that relations between students and teachers are often contractual, but are not always so. In some instances, especially between a thesis supervisor and student, the relationship is more covenantal than contractual (Westhues 2004, p. 155). In his call for reciprocity and covenantal relations, Westhues hopes that the tendency towards mobbing and elimination can be contained or minimized.

Westhues's vision of the way human relationships can be carried on has many noble and admirable aspects. But even he concedes that many in our world would call this vision idealistic and utopian. This is not to say that the vision should be abandoned, but to ask whether in the postmodern world of ideological conflict and the pursuit of individual self-interest it can achieve the kind of result Westhues hopes for.

Westhues is explicit in his criticism of the forces of postmodernism that dominate our society, forces such as secularism, scepticism, ideological conflict, denial of objective reality. His response is to long for a return to something like a brotherhood of man, where unconditional love, mutual respect, tolerance and acceptance of difference and diversity are the defining characteristics of the human community. In the academic world, he longs for a community of scholars, teachers and administrators united in their quest for knowledge, mutually respectful and supportive, tolerating differences and willing to work out conflict in a friendly, kindly way.

When I read Westhues's ideal account of relations in academia, my immediate thought was that this might work in a small liberal arts college of the past, but I was sceptical that it would work in a huge multiversity composed of numerous faculties with diverse interests, with professionalized administrations that run universities like large corporations, with large corporations exerting greater and greater influence on universities to maximize their commercial interests, with social forces like biopolitics that Westhues and others have written about (Westhues 1999), and with cost-cutting governments imposing budgetary pressures on universities.

The way I can respond to Westhues's vision is to reflect on my own thirty-two year career as an English professor at the University of Waterloo, during which time I became intimately acquainted with the culture and *modus operandi* of my workplace.

When I joined the university in 1964, it was then only seven years old. In the first decade or so of its existence, the faculty, staff and administration of the university functioned as a highly motivated group of pioneers bent on a mission to create a new institution. The spirit of collegiality and sharing of responsibility between faculty and administration seemed to be the rule, and there was tacit acceptance of a kind of benign paternalism in the operation of the university. As an institution incorporated under the laws of the Province of Ontario, the university was governed by an appointed Board that was entrusted with the power and authority to develop and implement the entire infrastructure governing how the university was to fulfill its mandate and in particular to determine the terms and conditions of employment of all its employees. In this early stage of the university's history, faculty and staff groups were allowed to make briefs to the Board on salary and other issues, but the final decision was the Board's. The Board also appointed senior administrators with only minimal or no input from faculty and staff.

This benign paternalism, as I have called it, could not last as the university grew in size and complexity, and as faculty, staff and students in the late sixties, not only at Waterloo, but also in campuses across the country, agitated for greater participation in university governance. The Board and administrators at Waterloo also began to realize that they needed to put in place various policies governing terms and conditions of employment for its faculty. The informal and somewhat arbitrary procedures governing hiring, promotions, tenure, salaries and a host of other issues seemed inadequate for an institution that aspired to find its place among the older and more established universities in Canada.

Faculty were intimately involved in academic matters through their participation in faculty councils and the university senate, but in matters concerning the terms and conditions of employment all decisions were the prerogative of the administration and the Board. To fill this vacuum, the Faculty Association mobilized in the late sixties and sought to negotiate a more meaningful participation in the determination of terms and conditions of employment. These negotiations, when I was President of the Association, led to a formal agreement in 1971 between the university and the Faculty Association which acknowledged the Association as representative of the faculty and set out in general terms the process to be followed in the establishment of policies governing terms and conditions of employment. A separate agreement established the framework for the annual salary negotiations. What the administration and the Board would not agree to, however, was a satisfactory dispute-resolution mechanism. The Association's proposal for third-party arbitration was rejected. The final decision in any dispute was to be made by the Board on the advice of the administration.

This failure to negotiate a satisfactory dispute-resolution mechanism led the Faculty Association in 1972, to explore the possibility of seeking voluntary recognition as a union under the terms of the Ontario Labour Relations Act. Since the university recognized the Association as representing the faculty, the legal advisor of the Association believed that it could invoke the voluntary recognition clause in labor law. The Association discovered, however, that an application to the Ontario Labour Relations Board would have been rejected because of a lack of clear distinction in its membership between those defined by law as employees and those defined as managers. For instance, several deans and the president were members of the Association.

The result of this phase of the relations between the Association and the administration was unsatisfactory. Though the administration now recognized the Association as a partner in determining terms and conditions of employment, it refused to support an adequate dispute-resolution mechanism. It was not surprising that whenever a dispute arose in the next decade or so, the Board always chose the administration's side.

By the mid-eighties, most activists in the Association recognized that the special plan negotiated in 1971 was not an adequate framework to regularize relations with faculty, mainly because of the lack of an acceptable dispute-resolution mechanism. At this juncture, the activists divided into two groups, one seeking to enter into negotiations with the administration to improve the existing agreement, and the other forming a separate organization, of which I was president, seeking certification under the Ontario Labour Relations Act. Once the new organization began its membership drive, the administration made several concessions that Association negotiators believed significant and were willing to accept. When the new Memorandum of Agreement was concluded and presented to the membership, the new organization lost its momentum and disbanded.

The new 1986 Memorandum of Agreement was another "special plan" outside the Ontario Labour Relations Act. Though it provided external mediation in salary disputes, arbitration was to remain internal. The mechanism for policy review was outlined, with no mechanism for dispute-resolution, though the Association had a veto power. A few years before this new arrangement, Grievance and Ethics Committees were established to hear grievances (but with no external arbitration), and external arbitration was agreed to in dismissal cases, but only at the appeal stage, and not before the decision to dismiss was taken. These provisions became part of the new "special plan."

When I returned to active involvement in the Association in the early nineties as a Board member and chair of the Academic Freedom and Tenure Committee, I gained first-hand experience of the limitations and deficiencies of this "special plan" of 1986. Experiences such as the administration's unilateral abrogation of an agreement on salary negotiations, the unhappiness of many individuals who sought justice from the Grievance and Ethics Committees but did not find it, the general dissatisfaction with the lack of professionalism and *ad hoc* quality of the grievance and ethics processes, the inordinate time taken to reform policies, the deficiency in the dismissal process, where individuals were denied fairness and due process – these and other irritants convinced me and other activists that major reforms were needed in the relationship between the administration and the Association.

In 1995, the Association Board re-opened negotiations with the administration on a new special plan. The hope was that the administration would agree to negotiate reforms in many of the policies and procedures governing terms and conditions of employment, and would agree to accept binding external arbitration as a means of resolving conflicts and disputes. It soon became apparent that the administration was reluctant to agree to the needed reforms. Consequently, the Association, with the approval of a majority of its members, began the process of seeking certification under the Ontario Labour Relations Act. When it would become certified, the Association hoped that as an equal partner it could insist on good-faith negotiations leading to a collective agreement that would include all the needed reforms and that would guarantee third-party arbitration to resolve disputes over the terms of the agreement. This decision to seek certification could not be seen as a radical or precedent-setting departure in the relations between administrations and their faculties, for faculty associations in nearly all Canadian universities were already certified. The University of Waterloo was one of the very few that was not. Certification had not destroyed any of the most treasured values of universities, and in many instances had markedly improved the relations between faculty and administration.

The campaign for certification resulted in a sufficient number of faculty signing cards to warrant the holding of an official vote administered by the Department of Labour. The vote was held in the spring of 1996. The result was that 55% of those voting rejected certification.

Though this vote was a setback for the Association, the fact that 45% had voted for certification sent a message to the administration. Negotiations on a new special plan were restarted. The result was a more satisfactory arrangement, though still not as legally binding as a collective agreement under labor law. One positive result, however, was that the administration agreed to abolish the Ethics Committee and allowed grievors to choose between the local Grievance Committee and an external arbitrator to hear their grievances.

If I have tested the patience of readers with this bit of history at the University of Waterloo, I apologize. It is not intended to be an authorized or official history. Its purpose has been to show the evolution of relations between the administration and faculty, as I experienced them, and also to reveal the growth of my sympathy for a legally binding arrangement under the Ontario Labour Relations Act.

Though a small majority of the faculty at Waterloo voted against certification, I remain convinced that a collective agreement given force by labor law remains the best protection an individual can have against arbitrary and unfair decisions by an administrator, or against what Westhues has described as mobbing or a passion for elimination.

Westhues obviously wouldn't agree with me. As part of his disapproval of contractual relations as opposed to covenantal ones, Westhues frequently reiterates his scepticism about the use of judicial or quasi-judicial tribunals in universities to resolve conflicts or disputes. I assume he would include third-party arbitration proceedings under labor law in this category. His scepticism derives from the imperfections of judicial proceedings both in universities and society at large, but more particularly because these proceedings "tend to reduce conflict to a binary variable: guilty or not guilty, win or lose, goodness on one side versus wickedness on the other. The complexity of life is lost. What is worse, the adversarial process tends to draw out from all concerned the impulse to evil, the tendency in all of us to separate certain others from respectable company and pretend that they are not like us" (Westhues 2004, p. 10).

I know that Westhues's bitterness about judicial proceedings in universities is colored by his own unhappy experiences with the Grievance and Ethics Committees at the University of Waterloo and by his assembling of numerous cases (especially Richardson's) in other universities where the defects of such proceedings were acute. As Westhues's colleague and advisor in the cases he was involved in, I too became aware of the gross deficiencies of the two quasi-judicial tribunals at the University of Waterloo (Dubinski 1994b). A brief account of the grievance process at the University of Waterloo before 1996 will explain the limitations and defects of these quasi-judicial tribunals.

In the normal course of events, if individuals experienced conflicts or had problems with decisions made by chairs, for instance, university policy required them to seek to find a solution first with the chair, and failing that to appeal to the dean. One would hope that administrators at all levels would be skilled in conflict resolution and would be sensitive to the need for due process and natural justice when dealing with complaints or grievances. The reality was that often due process was ignored or slighted. When individuals appealed to the next level of the administrative hierarchy, the common practice seemed to be that the higher administrator had either already approved or underwritten the decision of the lower administrator and was therefore unlikely to review or reverse the decision. The provost at the University of Waterloo made it perfectly clear when he explained that "what a grievance involves is an objection to some measure applied by the university and when you grieve an action of that sort then you are really grieving an action of the university . . . philosophically, what a grievance is, is a dispute of the actions taken by the university as a collective body" (Mercer, Appendix II, p. 35). What this statement suggested is that in most cases the administration acted as a unified body and was aligned against the individual with a grievance.

Individuals at Waterloo were offered another avenue when they had a grievance. They could take their case either to the Faculty Grievance Committee or to the Ethics Committee, though the jurisdiction of these committees was not clear. Both of these committees, however, were tied into the administrative hierarchy of the university and could only make recommendations. The Grievance Committee made recommendations to the president, who made the final decision without further appeal. The Ethics Committee was appointed by and reported to the provost. The provost made the decision, but individuals could appeal to the president without further appeal. Thus, the ultimate review of grievances against lower administrators rested with the higher administrators. The administration, which acted as a collective body, was vested with the power to review itself, hardly a fair process.

Individuals appointed to serve on these committees were very much amateurs asked to make judgments on complex issues. They might also find themselves involved in a network of relationships and responsibilities within the university, which might preclude them from taking an arms-length or independent position on the issues before them.

The processes of these committees were also troubling. Though they acted in a quasi-judicial capacity, they operated in an amateurish and *ad hoc* sort of way. Hearings were held *in camera*, and though they were taped, no transcripts were made. Since access to records of past hearings was difficult, it was virtually impossible to monitor whether the processes followed were consistent, fair, and observed the principles of natural justice. In Westhues's case before the Grievance Committee, limits were put on whom Westhues could or could not consult, while no such restrictions were put on the administrator. In fact, both the committee and the administrator consulted lawyers provided and funded by the university.

These and other deficiencies of these committees were pointed out to the university by the Academic Freedom and Tenure Committee of the Canadian Association of University Teachers. Here is one of its concluding comments about these committees: "All of these deficiencies (and others) have been brought to the attention of the faculty and administration at Waterloo on previous occasions. Now again, . . . a case [Westhues's] has arisen that demonstrates how far these policies have failed to provide proper and fair procedures for the redress of a grievance – with significant damage to the careers and reputations of a number of parties involved, wittingly or unwittingly, in the dispute, and to the reputation of the University of Waterloo itself" (Gannon, p. 7).

When one scrutinizes this review of former grievance procedures at the University of Waterloo, one can easily nod in agreement with Westhues's claim that judicial or quasi-judicial proceedings have little place, perhaps no place, in a healthy working environment. To support his claim Westhues has provided a documentary history of the Ethics Committee at the University of Waterloo and his experience with it on a web site (Westhues 2004a). If judicial proceedings are to be avoided, then, what mechanism would Westhues set up to handle conflicts and disputes? He proposes that decision-making should rest with administrators chosen by and responsible to the faculty, without pretense of emancipation from political process. Their decisions should be subject to ongoing critique, revision and sometimes reversal by the overt political action of governing boards, senates, student bodies, and individuals from both inside and outside the university. In rare cases, misconduct should be handled in a public court far removed from campus politics and subject to the constraints of due process, as spelled out in the criminal law. (Westhues 2004, p. 313.)

As I thought about this proposal, I had difficulty conceiving how it would work in practice. First, the suggestion that administrators should be chosen and responsible to faculty seems in line with the thinking of many faculty that administrators are actually faculty members on temporary leave, chosen by their colleagues to do a thankless job. Usually administrative appointments are for a fixed term, with option for a second term. What happens, however, when an administrator loses the confidence of his colleagues? To oust such an administrator will likely be a messy and divisive procedure and may actually be opposed by the Board. The fact that administrators are chosen by their colleagues does not guarantee that their decisions will always be fair and just. When an administrator makes a bad decision that provokes a grievance, how will the aggrieved individual seek redress under Westhues's scenario? He can appeal up the administrative hierarchy, and perhaps may find satisfaction, but what if the administrative hierarchy is already aligned against the individual? The individual, then, claims Westhues, may bring his case before the senate, the Board of Governors, student bodies and certain unspecified individuals both within and without the university. I have difficulty in imagining what form this process would take. Would the individual distribute a brief of his grievance to these bodies and ask to present his case before them? As far as I know, university senates deal mainly with academic matters and aren't equipped with procedures for passing judgments on individual grievances. Boards, in my experience, take their cues from administrators and aren't likely to take sides against them. Besides, many board members lack experience with the inner workings of a university. What addressing student bodies would accomplish is unclear to me. I'm also unclear as to the identity of the individuals both within and without the university that the grievor would approach. Perhaps what Westhues is suggesting is that by making his grievance public and engaging various bodies within the university, the grievor may hope to sway public opinion in his favor. I'm assuming that since Westhues hasn't mentioned one there is no faculty association, certified or uncertified, no collective agreement, and that each faculty member is on his own in seeking redress of his grievance. Perhaps the best the grievor can hope for is that some of his colleagues may launch a petition supporting him, or that students may demonstrate or organize a sit-in. Some sympathetic journalist may take up his case and give it wider publicity. Some of his colleagues at other universities may write letters of support and try to put pressure on the administration. Maybe all this activity is what Westhues means when he claims that all administrative decisions should be subject to overt political action. Westhues himself helped to organize a petition in support of mathematics professor Jack Edmonds, who believed he was unjustly fired. Perhaps Westhues hopes that any aggrieved professor can count on a massive outpouring of support from colleagues, both within and without the university.

The process that Westhues describes is likely to be extremely divisive and would probably convulse the campus. I'm sure that Westhues would argue that most grievances would be settled quietly and privately, but that in extreme cases the political process he describes would have to be activated.

Because he is so disillusioned by the failure of judicial and quasi-judicial processes, Westhues rejects the possibility that these processes, imperfect though they may be, may offer the best chance for aggrieved individuals to receive a fair hearing and disposition of their grievances. I think this would apply to individuals who are being mobbed or are facing elimination.

What I have in mind is a university that has in place a strong and vigilant certified union that has negotiated a collective agreement with the administration, an agreement that establishes an environment in which the work of teaching and research may proceed in the most creative way, that establishes procedures for regulating the terms and conditions of employment, and that has in place a grievance process to address conflicts or disputes that puts a premium on collegial, internal processes, but when these break down has recourse to binding external arbitration. This may not be a perfect solution, but it is the one that nearly all the universities in Canada have adopted. Although this model assumes that the relation between a faculty member and the university is a contractual one, Westhues's desire that relations should be covenantal should not be ignored. Good faith, mutual respect, trust and willingness to compromise need not be absent from contractual relations. It is when these break down that individuals need the protection afforded by a legal contract and by judicial proceedings that are fair and open.

I am not so naïve as to think that a certified faculty union will solve all the problems of workplace relations in a university. Unions are made up of individuals who themselves may be tempted to participate in a mobbing process. As Westhues has noted, the essence of life in a university must include friction and conflict. How to keep conflict creative and how to manage it when it becomes destructive is the question. All options to address this issue have limitations and are imperfect. Like Westhues, I too would hope that relations among faculty would resemble the covenant model he describes. But, unfortunately, most individuals have come to recognize that contractual arrangements offer them better protections than dependence on the good will of their fellows in a university community.

References

Dubinski, Roman, *et al.,* 1994a. *AF&T Committee Report on the Circumstances Leading to Conrad Grebel's Termination of Professor Leonard Friesen's Probationary Contract on the Grounds of Financial Expediency.* Waterloo, ON: Faculty Association.

Dubinski, Roman, 1994b. "Why Grievance Procedures Aren't Working," *FAUW Forum* (November).

Dubinski, Roman, 1995. "CAUT to Report on Westhues Grievance," *FAUW Forum* (October).

Gannon, Roger, *et al.* 1996, *Report of the AF&T Committee into the Complaint of Professor Kenneth Westhues.* Insert in *CAUT Bulletin.*

Mercer, Peter, 1998. *In the Matter of an Appeal by Professor Kenneth Westhues under University of Waterloo Policy 33 from the Decision of the Vice-President Academic & Provost, Dr. James Kalbfleisch, dated March 11, 1997. Arising out of the Report of the Ethics Committee dated August 25, 1996.* Waterloo ON: University of Waterloo.

Westhues, Kenneth, 1998. *Eliminating Professors: A Guide to the Dismissal Process.* Lewiston, NY: Edwin Mellen Press.

Westhues Kenneth, 1999. "A Test of the Biopolitics Hypothesis," *Sexuality and Culture*, 3 (*The Politics of Sexuality*): pp. 69-99. New Brunswick, NJ: Transaction.

Westhues, Kenneth, 2004. *Administrative Mobbing at the University of Toronto.* Lewiston, NY: Edwin Mellen Press.

Westhues, Kenneth, 2003a. Documentary History of the University of Waterloo Ethics Committee.
www.arts.uwaterloo.ca/~kwesthue/ethicscommittee.htm

Chapter Twenty

Lessons from a Lawsuit over the Harassment of an Employees' Representative

Charmian Bondi and Jan Gregersen

Victims of bullying campaigns should beware that judgments in the civil court are not always clear-cut. A prime example of this took place in Oslo, Norway, when an Employee, who claimed she was a victim of systematic harassment, brought her case to Oslo City Court. This Employee, a fifty-year-old lawyer and employees' elected Health and Safety Officer, sued a Norwegian government ministry, claiming compensation for long-term bullying by her boss, head of the Norwegian government agency where she worked. The judge ruled against the victim and she lost her case. In raising actions such as this one, an employee's biggest obstacle to winning can be that judges frequently do not understand the bullying phenomenon. Despite the fact that The Worker Protection and Working Environment Act of 1977 in Norway makes considerable provisions for employees' wellbeing in the workplace, the judge chose to disregard this.

In a Kafka-esque situation, the Employee, supported by her union, had to bring her case not against her boss, who was the actual perpetrator of the bullying campaign, but against the Cabinet Minister, head of the Department in charge of the government agency. To add to the confusion the Cabinet Minister who was summoned to the court in his capacity of head of the Department, was not the same Cabinet Minister against whom the action was raised.

In raising her action against the Minister, the Employee claimed Kr 1.5 million (approximately $150,000) in compensation for loss of earnings and damage to her health. She claimed that her boss (the Director of the government agency where she worked) had carried out a systematic bullying campaign against her over a period of two years. The employee claimed that her boss targeted her in many different ways in his harassment of her. He talked about her negatively behind her back. His body language was unfriendly. He constantly sneered at her and rolled his eyes heavenwards whenever she tried to raise any serious matters with him in her capacity of employees' elected representative. He systematically ignored her and conducted a whispering campaign against her. He denigrated her as a liar. She claimed his hostility toward her led to mental distress and psychosomatic disorders, forcing her to take frequent sick leave.

The problems grew steadily worse and the Employee came to realize it was not possible for her to solve them internally, so she approached the Norwegian Inspectorate of Work, and then the Ministry. She told the Ministry that employees were being made ill by a work environment that was poisoned by fear and insecurity. At the time of the action, she was on long-term sick leave herself, and to the present day she has not returned to work. Whether she will be permanently unfit to work remains to be seen.

The Employee acted in two capacities in the agency. She was a civil servant working as a legal adviser and she was also the employees' elected health and safety representative (required by Norwegian law). The bullying she endured was partly triggered by her decision to help the others.

As elected Health and Safety Officer, she felt obliged to represent her co-workers in their own complaints against management. These were principally that internal co-operation was poor and there was a breakdown of communication, all leading to a poisoned environment. Her vigorous efforts to improve the psycho-social environment of the employees led to increased confrontations with the Director. In Norway, the internal proceedings in such questions are regulated by the Worker Protection and Working Environment Act, and followed up by the Health and Safety Committee representing the employees. Both physical and psycho-social issues in the workplace are encompassed by this Act.

In court, the Director claimed that the Employee was a bad lawyer. He denied there were any personnel difficulties at the agency, and claimed that any problems that did exist in the workplace were caused by the Employee while acting as Health and Safety Officer. However, the Director had already dismissed one of his heads of section (who has also mounted a lawsuit); another worker who was drawn into the conflict was on sick leave. The Director had also worked in two other government ministries and his controversial style of management had given rise to problems for his subordinates in those workplaces, too, but this was ruled inadmissible by the court.

The court proceedings revealed a government agency in chaos, cloaked in an atmosphere of obsessive secrecy. There were whispering campaigns, isolation of targeted employees and widespread fear of reprisals among staff. The agency was also sharply split into two factions. On one side were the Director's supporters. On the other side were those who opposed him. Working conditions were much more difficult for those who were not on the Director's side.

The Employee's Union also complained on her behalf. But the Ministry replied that it was well aware of what was going on at the agency. And it had full confidence in the Director. As a result of this, the Employee in the capacity of the elected Health and Safety Officer and on her own behalf, brought the matter to court with the union's backing.

In the courtroom, the Employee's counsel (appointed by her Union) had to ask the Director to stop sniggering while she presented her client's case. Counsel told the court the Director had opposed her client in all her activities both in her capacity of legal adviser at the agency and in her capacity as the employees' properly elected Health and Safety Officer. Counsel then entered into evidence a letter written by the Director that stated in a moralizing tone that the Health and Safety Officer had to behave in an honest and decent way, but that she was clearly not capable of doing so. Counsel went on to say that the Director systematically presented her client in a bad light and made out she was a liar.

The Director declared the conflict was something the Employee had created herself, in her capacity as Health and Safety Officer.

A specialist in work and organizational psychology was appointed by the Court as expert witness. He carried out a thorough investigation of the Employee's background: education, previous workplaces, social relationships, children, husband, past illnesses, changes in other circumstances and any pressures put on her before the time she was diagnosed as unfit for work as Health and Safety Officer. The results of this examination indicated she had a steady background without any unusual emotional upheavals. The expert said he would characterize the Employee as physically and mentally fit in the period before she was appointed Health and Safety Officer.

He summarized his preliminary conclusions in a written report to the court:

- The Employee at age 49 was in good health on January 1, 2000.
- During her service as Health and Safety Officer, she was subjected to treatment by management that can be characterized as harassment.
- The harassment was so extensive and systematic that there was a 75% probability rate that it would cause damage to the health any average person.
- Management should have been aware that this harassment would cause long-term damage to the Employee's health.
- The Employee's current mental state was consistent with DSM.IV.TR309.81 and ICD-10 F.43.1, which are both symptoms of post-traumatic stress disorder. The expert's diagnosis also indicated severe psychological after-effects caused by the trauma. He said the Employee was at no greater risk of developing these illnesses because of her work as Health and Safety Officer. She was not predisposed to any psychological vulnerability. And he had not found any deviations from the normal in any of her behavior. He believed it was unlikely her condition would be helped by short-term courses of treatment. Her state of health thus appeared to be consistent with the medical requirements for long-term sick leave. This diagnosis was consistent with information provided by the doctor and the psychologist treating the Employee. The expert's only caveat was that evidence emerging in court could conceivably impact on his diagnosis, and he cited Robert Hare's Psychopathic Check List (PCL).

The Judge insisted the agency's Personnel Officer be present during the proceedings, even though he was to be called later as a witness. A Personnel Officer is primarily responsible for the psychological well-being of employees and that was pivotal to the issue at law in this case. The Employee's counsel opposed the continuing presence of the Personnel Officer, saying there was a risk he would tailor his evidence to match the Director's. The Judge overruled the objection.

The Employee's counsel said the Director had attempted to remove the Employee from her elected appointment as Health and Safety Officer. He stated that she had a communications problem that created difficulties between employees and management. The Employee as Health and Safety Officer was then barred from any meetings between the employees' representatives and management. The Director's excuse was that he didn't believe the Employee was still the Health and Safety Officer.

According to the Employee, the problems started when she was elected Health and Safety Officer and her path began to cross the boss's more frequently. As the HSO she vigorously upheld the rights of the other employees and indeed acted as whistleblower on several occasions. This triggered the bullying campaign and subsequent humiliation of the Employee over a long period of time. Her boss kept her on a lower salary grade than her colleagues of equivalent rank, and he accused her of spending too much time on her duties as HSO. Management suggested that she might take long-term leave of absence, but when she began to show interest in this as a solution to the working environment problems, the management retracted the offer. She was subjected to a series of disparaging actions by the Director. Interesting tasks were taken away from her. She was refused payment for her overtime and she was not allowed to attend external conferences or internal meetings which would normally be her right. The boss did his best to undermine her position and to ostracize her. This was an attack on her self esteem, attempting to make her a nonperson. In sum, this chain of negative actions could be regarded as an attempt at constructive dismissal.

When the original government agency was split into two separate agencies and new positions were created for lawyers and engineering inspectors, the Health and Safety Officer tried to protect the rights of the employees. This was because the Director refused to allow those already employed in the former government body to apply for the positions advertised for the new. Outsiders who had been selected for the new jobs were given higher salaries and more challenging tasks than those who were already there. This created a negative working environment, which the Employee as Health and Safety Officer raised with the Director on several occasions. She insisted that her complaint was made not in regard to herself, but on behalf of a large number of her colleagues. The regulations laid down in the Working Environment Act (see below) were not properly followed, she claimed.

The Employee told the court the Director's habit of rolling his eyes, sighing and sneering when she talked about health and safety issues made up a good part of his bullying and harassment of her. The Director categorically denied this behavior, giving the excuse that he usually smiled, but admitted he had a rather forceful manner.

When called upon to give evidence, the Director prevaricated by giving long explanations of the challenges facing the agency. He talked about engineering projects, new technical solutions, and other activities. This went on for some time, until the Judge interrupted him and asked him to return to the matter at hand. The Director then said he had difficulty recalling any confrontations at all with the "former" Health and Safety Officer. He denied any recollection of saying to the Employee: "Here is someone who is on her way out!" He denied preventing lawyers employed in the old government body from applying for better-paid positions in the new agency.

Counsel for the Director also denied all accusations of bullying and harassment on the part of his client. He said it was obvious that the two parties, the Director and the Employee, had serious problems communicating with one another, but it was difficult to see this as harassment. All attempts by the Director to reconcile with the Employee were rebuffed by her, the lawyer said. He declared the Ministry was prepared at any stage of the court proceedings to discuss a compromise with the Employee.

The Director's counsel also claimed the Employee had not understood the limits placed on her position as Health and Safety Officer. He said she was a free-acting person who tried to correct everything she thought was wrong, regardless of whether it came under her job description. One could understand why the climate at work became soured, he said. It impinged on the employer's right of control. He submitted that it was the Employee's intention to get rid of the Director, not the other way around.

The Director's counsel also insisted that a Health and Safety Officer must tolerate some turbulence in the workplace, because no workplace was completely placid. He said the case at hand illustrated the Employee's lack of a sense of reality and her inability to deal with any personal opposition. It seemed to him that 1,500 pages of documentation and 60 witnesses were out of all proportion to the case at hand. He asked the Judge to decide whether all these witnesses were really necessary. In the end, only 34 witnesses were heard.

A former head of the government agency in its original form testified on the Employee's behalf. His evidence was in stark contrast to the Director's. This witness presented a very positive picture of the Employee. He said she felt a great responsibility for her colleagues and spoke out for them. "We never had any disagreements," he stated categorically. After retiring from the agency, this witness served as consultant to the agency and could confirm that there was a great deal more turbulence within the new agency than there was in the old one. He described the Director's leadership style as authoritarian and forceful. He believed some people thought there was too little democracy in the agency.

Because of the complicated legal system concerning civil servants in Norway, the Employee was forced to bring her action against the Minister personally even though most of the complaints were about the Director. Thus when the Director was summoned to the court he was technically representing the Ministry – the Cabinet Minister at the time of the court proceedings held the formal position of defendant. The Minister (now a lady) did not appear personally – this is not unusual in such cases. However, it compounded the Kafka-esque situation that a recent change of government had taken place and the *former* minister was actually called as a witness. *He* testified that the unions had informed the Ministry that there was a great deal of conflict at the agency, and that he had specifically asked his Ministry to take up the problem with the Director, who was the employer actually responsible for the agency's employees.

The Judge's efforts to get the two sides to reach a compromise were in vain. Counsel for the Employee and Counsel for the Director (formally, for the Minister) were not even able to reach agreement on a definition of harassment.

The Judge's Decision

Summing up, the Judge said that the two parties had widely diverging views of how the situation should be resolved. According to the Employee, the problems began shortly after the Director joined the agency. She complained about events that affected her and other employees, as well as the general work environment. The Judge held that the Director's actions toward the Employee were the principal issue. He would not rule on the Director's actions toward other employees or on the general work environment. He also refused to consider allegations that the Director had had problems at his previous workplaces, saying simply there was not enough evidence.

The Judge chose to ignore the Employee's allegations that there was systematic discrimination against the old employees. He also disregarded her claims that the new employees received higher salaries and more interesting tasks. Nevertheless, he suggested that this had contributed to the Employee's negative view of the Director when she began her duties as Health and Safety Officer.

The first episodes that concerned the Judge were comments made by the Personnel Manager at the beginning of 2000, when it appeared that he had accused the Employee of "being out of touch with real life" and had declared her "unwanted" in the workplace. The Personnel Manager had also called a meeting on November 2, 2000, at which health and safety issues were to be discussed, and he had not invited the Employee as Health and Safety Officer to attend. But one of the Union representatives invited her to the meeting. She arrived late and the Personnel Manager remarked she had come to the wrong meeting. At a later date, there was a decision made that health and safety issues would not be dealt with at these personnel meetings, but the Employee continued to attend. The Personnel Manager told the court the Employee lacked a sense of reality. The Judge said the way the Personnel Manager had expressed himself was unfortunate, but did not view this episode as a form of harassment or any basis for compensation.

At another meeting, at which a survey of health and safety issues was scheduled to be discussed, there was palpable tension between the Employee and the Director. According to the Employee, the Director stated he had other channels of information than the Health and Safety Officer and did not want to listen to any of her suggestions. He also said communications between them were nonexistent.

Witnesses from among the employees suggested to the court that at a later meeting the Director's conduct could be regarded as bullying. The Director did not admit that any form of bullying took place, and the Personnel Manager supported him. The witnesses did not actually insist there was bullying, but declared there was unpleasant tension between the Employee and the Director, and the Director reacted to the Employee's health and safety concerns by sneering, by keeping his eyes on the ceiling, on the table, or on documents, and by rolling his eyes. The Judge did not conclude that this behavior was harassment. Nor did he regard it as harassment when the Director claimed in the Employee's presence that he did not know who was the Health and Safety Officer.

The Employee and the Director also broke into vigorous disagreement at another meeting that was called to elect employees to sit on the Health and Safety committees The Employee claimed that the Director had stated he had no confidence in her. The Director explained that he had expressed his frustration with her and her way of working, and the Employee decided to leave the meeting. She returned some time later, and the Director then confirmed that he had no confidence in her.

The Director also stated at that meeting that the head of the legal department at the agency also claimed he had problems communicating with the Employee, whose primary appointment was as one of the legal officers at the agency. At that meeting, there was a disagreement about what should be recorded in the minutes, which were thus regarded as unreliable. The Judge said it was unfortunate that the Director had stated openly that he had no confidence in the Employee as Health and Safety Officer, particularly when there were others present. This was damaging to the reputation of the Health and Safety Officer, who had to represent all the employees' interests. However, she was still supported by the employees who elected her, the Judge noted. He also pointed out that it was the Employee herself who raised the question as to whether the Director had confidence in her.

After a work environment survey had been completed, the external consultant who conducted it took the Employee aside. He asked her about her relationship with the Director and her duties as Health and Safety Officer. The consultant told her bluntly that she had lost the fight with the Director, and that her career prospects were permanently damaged. He recommended she resign as Health and Safety Officer. The Employee believed that the consultant's clear intention was to attack her at the instigation of the Director. The

Judge's view was that the consultant was responsible for his own actions as an external contractor. There was no evidence the Director was behind his remarks.

The Judge said complaints were made that the Employee spent too much time on her Health and Safety duties (as opposed to her work as a lawyer.) Management refused to pay her overtime for this work. The Judge did not regard this as harassment or a reason for compensation.

The Employee's superior asked her to take a leave of absence several times, so that the conflict could be resolved. She regarded this as a form of harassment, but the Judge disagreed. It could indeed be a way of getting rid of her as Health and Safety Officer, the Judge said, but it could just as well be an attempt to resolve the conflict in her best interests. This was not harassment or a reason for compensation.

The Judge recognized that there was an extremely bad relationship between the Director and the Employee. He found it probable that the Director had behaved in the way described by the Employee, and that this had occurred at several meetings. Whether the Director failed to acknowledge her or ignored her at these meetings was less clear, the Judge said.

The Employee stated that, as part of the systematic harassment she endured, she was kept at a lower salary than a colleague who had previously received the same salary and who had now been given a raise, whereas the Employee had not. She also claimed she was no longer allowed to attend certain meetings where health and safety issues were discussed. She regarded this as a form of harassment, but the Judge did not agree and pointed out that another colleague was also disbarred from these meetings. The Judge also concluded that it was not proven that the Employee was not allowed to take part in certain courses because of her duties as Health and Safety Officer.

The Employee claimed she was harassed while on sick leave when the agency's Medical Officer retracted his statement that her illness was work-related. In a conversation with the Medical Officer, she said he urged her to give up her duties as Health and Safety Officer and come back to work. The Employee claimed the Medical Officer had changed his opinion after management had spoken to him. This was revealed in an email from the Personnel Manager to the Director in which he hinted that the agency's contract with the Medical Officer should be reviewed if the Medical Officer provided the Health and Safety Officer with information about any problems in the agency.

The Director denied he had put pressure on the Medical Officer. He pointed out that a long time had elapsed between the email and the Medical Officer's change of opinion. The Judge said he could not conclude that the Director was responsible, since the Medical Officer was independent and not an employee of the agency. The Medical Officer was therefore responsible for his own actions. The Judge did not regard the Medical Officer's change of opinion as harassment because his intention was to get the Employee back to work before the sick leave became drawn out.

The Employee claimed that a letter written by the Director to the Norwegian Work Inspectorate was another example of harassment. In this letter, the Director gave an account of the controversial events at the agency and added his comments. The letter claimed the Employee used her position as Health and Safety Officer to create conflicts, that she told lies, that she consistently presented incorrect information, and that she was motivated by a desire for a salary increase.

The Judge said this letter was unfortunate, since the Employee was in a state of great mental distress. The Director then offered his regret. But the Judge believed the letter was written after the Employee had sent a summons to the Ministry to attend the court proceedings. The Employee had therefore set in motion this confrontation with the Director herself. The Judge could not conclude this was harassment or a reason for compensation.

The Judge concluded there was strong disagreement between the parties over who should have done what and when, and any initiative by either was condemned by the other. For this reason, the Judge could not blame the agency for its actions during the period in question. These actions were neither harassment nor reason for compensation.

The Judge held that the Director behaved in a reprehensible way on several occasions, and that he could have dealt with the Employee in a more flexible and considerate manner. A sign of a good leader, the Judge said, is the ability to manage people who disagree with him in a way that is beneficial to both parties. This is particularly important in the case of a Health and Safety Officer who must look after other employees' interests. The gravity of the situation was underlined when the employees' representatives commented on the negative treatment the Health and Safety Officer had received from the Director, the Judge said.

However, the Judge concluded that there was no basis for compensation. Despite the fact that some of the Director's actions were reprehensible, there were none that could be characterized as serious. And the Judge could not discern any planned system of harassment. Most of the complaints the Employee brought before the court had already been dealt with and she had accomplished some of her own objectives, such as the health and safety survey. A key line in the judgment reads: "The Court rules that this is first and foremost a personality conflict between the Director and the Employee. They failed to reach agreement because they are two very different personalities. The disagreement need not have been so great."

The Judge was also of the opinion that the Employee was partly responsible for her conflict with the Director. Her demeanor and behavior contributed to the negative climate, he said, just as much as the Director's. She easily became irritated and angry, and had a confrontational and direct manner. She was quick to contact the Ministry, and did not inform the agency's management before doing so. She defined her duties as Health and Safety Officer very widely so that she spent a great deal of time on them.

Despite the fact that the expert witness, a psychologist, had been appointed by the court, the judge chose to disregard his opinion. "This psychologist approached the situation from an angle different from the court's. His opinion as a therapist prevailed over his opinion as an expert witness reporting to the court," the ruling said.

The Judge reached the conclusion that, although there was some room for doubt, there was no responsibility under the Law of Torts, which in his view was the only Law under which the case could be brought to court, for any of the actions carried out by the Director or the agency's management. The problems between management and the Employee must be resolved by the agency, the Judge said, since there was no discernible reason to remove the Director. "In accordance with legal practice and theory, organisational responsibility cannot be linked to anybody's actions other than the Minister's. There is no claim that the Minister insulted the plaintiff," the Judge concluded.

The Ministry was acquitted. The Director was thus cleared of the charge of bullying the Employee out of her job and destroying her job prospects. Although the Employee lost, the Judge in an unusual ruling stated that in his opinion she had adequate reasons for bringing the case to court and both parties would bear their share of the costs.

The court proceedings lasted 22 days.

Epilogue

The Employee's Union has decided to appeal because the Judge was unable to clarify whether it was a case of bullying or not. He failed to look closely into the individual incidents and did not recognize that the Employee was constantly repudiated and unable to function as Health and Safety Officer.

The Union also believes the judgement was based on a false premise. The Judge was mistaken in regarding the situation as a conflict between two persons. The real issue lay in regard to the Working Environment Act, and the Judge failed to define harassment as he had been requested to do.

The question before the court was: How far can a top manager go in harassing a Health and Safety Officer who is an elected representative of the employees? The Court failed to give a satisfactory answer to this. The Union is emboldened by the judge's statement that there was such a strong element of doubt that both of the parties would have to bear their own legal costs, which is highly unusual.

The Government has decided the agency will be transferred to a town far outside Oslo, under a parliamentary decentralization policy whereby several agencies are being moved out of the capital. The decision has led to considerable resistance among the employees, and many have declared they are not prepared to move.

Commentary

The Employee in this case was not formally fired, but claims to have been squeezed out. In some countries this would be a case of constructive dismissal. In Norway, the Employee was obliged to bring a claim for compensation to court. Unlike dismissal cases, the burden of proof that any compensation is justified falls on the plaintiff. There have been several similar cases in the past, and the employee's claim has usually been dismissed. Many lawyers advise their clients against bringing such cases at all, as the risk of losing and the legal costs are usually very high, and any compensation awarded in Norway is usually rather low. In the language of economics that means Negative Expected Returns.

However, in this case the Employee started out with strong support from her Union, from several colleagues and from health professionals etc. In addition, she was also entitled to special legal protection as the employees' representative. In court, the Employee was also supported by the court-appointed psychologist and indeed to some extent by the Judge.

The question is: Why did she lose? The answer lies, not in the facts or what happened in the courtroom, but in the Judge's reasoning, which we will compare to recent bullying research presented in Ken Westhues's book, *Administrative Mobbing at the University of Toronto* (2004).

In this case, a boss is accused of having harassed one of his subordinates. The first question is: What is harassment?

Harassment

The judge did indeed use the phrase "harassment." But unfortunately, legislation in many countries confines this concept to discrimination against members of minority or vulnerable groups within society. As a Canadian researcher once put it: "If you are a white heterosexual male, then you have no protection against harassment." Professor Westhues writes "The policies proposed generally follow the model of existing laws and policies forbidding harassment or discrimination on the basis of sex, race, religion, sexual orientation, and so on. The goal is to implement status-blind policies of this kind, to make it illegal (or in organisations, a policy violation) to harass or demean anyone, regardless of the reason or basis for doing it" (p. 304). In Norway, as in many other Western countries, legislation does exist to protect vulnerable groups against harassment as such. Breaking these laws might be viewed as a criminal offence. Although the Director and the Employee are of opposite sexes in this case, there is no indication that gender differences played any role in the alleged harassment. If the Employee's case had somehow been related to sexual harassment, the Director's actions would have been examined more closely and that might have influenced the outcome.

Serial Bully

The court's view was that first and foremost it was the actions of the Director towards the Employee that should be considered, particularly those in which it was claimed he was the instigator. The Judge did not take into consideration the Director's actions towards other employees, nor the work environment in general. In this way he established a very particular way of viewing causes. A key question here should have been whether the Employee's health problems were related to the pscyho-social environment at the workplace or not. If the cause of sickness lay elsewhere, let us say, for example, a gas leak, the damage to bystanders does not necessarily prove that the gas had a bad effect on any particular person who was present. However, such a consideration would normally be taken into account. In this case, the experience of other people in the same workplace, which was claimed to be a health risk, was viewed as irrelevant, for unknown reasons.

In this case, a particular person was alleged to be the cause. Westhues writes "Tim Field (1996) writes about the serial bully, who goes after one, then another and another, like a vampire whose sustenance requires sucking blood from successive victims" (p. 46). This is close to the statement made by the psychologist in this case. He confirmed that the Employee suffered from Post Traumatic Stress Disorder and ruled out any other explanation than "stress experienced at work." However, when preparing his report, the expert had had little opportunity to observe the perpetrator or to hear the other witnesses' statements against the Director. Thus there is an inference from his reference to the "Psychopathic Check List" signalling that the boss might have been the worst kind of bully. (See R. D. Hare *et al.*, "The revised psychopathy checklist," *Psychological Assessment* 2, 1990, pp. 338-341.)

Despite the fact that the psychologist was appointed by the court as expert witness, the Judge viewed him as the Employee's man, and dismissed his evidence. By doing that, he not only disregarded the lay witnesses, but also the expert witness. Perhaps the Judge had an *a priori* conviction that serial bullies do not exist. In addition, he did not appear to be interested in the personal characteristics of the antagonists, only the interaction between them.

The Judge would then have had good reason to question whether the perpetrator's behaviour was the only reason for the Employee's health problems. On the contrary, the Judge might have viewed the incredible amount of documents and witnesses the Employee brought to court as an indication that she was painfully over-particular and that she had blown the situation out of proportion. But this collection of evidence is the recommended way of dealing with such cases. In his report the Judge also tends to ignore the emotional implications of the situation. Thus there is not much room for expert opinion from the psychologist either. And as the legal system is practised, the Employee is the Plaintiff and the burden of proof rests on her.

"Bullying" vs. "mobbing"

Let us try to link this case to another concept, which appears to be implied in this case. That is to say *bullying.* Based on the Employee's version of events, we see the pattern described as follows.

As the employees' elected representative her path began to cross the boss's more frequently. At one stage, in supporting the rights of other employees, she acted as a whistleblower against the boss. This was the trigger for the systematic harassment and humiliation of this woman, which took place over the period of two years when she was acting as Health and Safety Officer. The boss deliberately ignored her, denigrated her, and as she later discovered, kept her on a lower salary than colleagues with equivalent qualifications. She was accused of spending too much time on her duties as the employees' representative. His supporters tried to push her out into a long-term leave of absence, but when she began to show interest in this as a solution, that is to say a way of resolving the conflict, the offer was swiftly withdrawn. Interesting tasks were taken away from her. Payment for overtime was denied, as was participation in both external conferences and internal meetings that she would normally attend. This was clearly an attempt to ostracise her. Her boss undermined her position and her self-esteem, making her feel insecure and a nonperson. In summary, these actions could be regarded as constructive dismissal.

The Director accused her of being touchy and losing her temper easily. This behaviour, if true, was in all probability caused by the long-term attrition of her equanimity at her boss's hands. Over time, like Chinese water torture, the small assaults built up; the accumulated impact was devastating, resulting in severe mental stress and breakdown of health, so that she was forced to take sick leave.

The boss also attacked her by sending letters to the Norwegian Inspectorate of Work stating that she was unreliable, a liar and a problem-maker. He tried to damage her present and future career prospects. After seeking help in vain from the Norwegian Work Inspectorate and other bodies, she brought her case for compensation for ill health and loss of earnings to court.

As so often happens, the Judge in the Norwegian court was not familiar with bullies and their tactics. In his judgement, he stated that he regarded the Employee's claims of harassment as a series of trivial incidents. In his eyes, no single action could be regarded as serious or abusive. He failed to look at the overall picture, the systematic bullying and degradation as well as the consequences of the boss's actions over time. The chilling truth was that indeed no single action was serious. In fact in many cases the boss's actions were trivial, such as his constant sneering at anything she said, the rolling of his eyes, his deliberate failure to recognise her.

He also accused her several times of telling untruths. The Judge attached importance to the fact that there were a few single actions that were "reprehensible," but no actions that could be characterised as "serious." This reasoning reveals that the judge evaluated each incident by itself and did not look into the pattern as a whole.

Here's what Westhues writes about bullying: "It was precisely because the term 'bullying' connotes 'physical aggression and threat' that Leymann preferred not to use it, but to use 'mobbing.' The 'disastrous communication' towards targets in his research 'quite often is done in a very sensitive manner' (2004, p. 45). Leymann's concern was with the humiliation of a worker, not of any particular techniques used for this purpose. In empirical fact, he found that the most common techniques were completely nonviolent. They were words spoken and written politely, with a smile."

In other words, the judge was right that there was no bullying in the sense of physical aggression or threats. If he had viewed "harassment" in terms of *mobbing* (as Leymann sees it) the result might have been different.

The judge chose to regard it as a conflict situation with two sides fighting each other. He did not regard it as a situation of bullying and victimisation. In this way, the Judge ruled out the conclusion that the boss targeted his victim and forced her into certain behaviour.

Westhues writes that conflict can indeed develop as a desperate way to communicate, but adds: "Mobbing signals a near-total breakdown of reciprocal relations in a workplace. All the power is massed on the mobbers' side and drained completely from the target's side. The latter is not listened to, unless with groans of contempt." That is to say, reciprocal conflict and mobbing are two quite different phenomena. Because of the Judge's reasoning, the case seems to have been lost before it even started, no matter what evidence the Employee might have been able to present.

Lack of individual responsibility

The Worker Protection and Working Environment Act of 1977 states clearly: "Employees shall not be subjected to harassment or other improper conduct. " At the time the Law was drawn up, it was viewed as a breakthrough, and a model for other countries. It clarified the responsibility of employers, and for that reason, triggered considerable objections, as it was feared that employing anybody at all would become very risky. The authority to enforce the law was left to the Norwegian Work Inspectorate. Unfortunately, this institution is supposed to take care of physical risks as well as the psycho-social environment at the workplace, and claims to have too many duties to perform with its limited resources. If the Work Inspectorate were given the option of stopping chemicals hazardous to health or getting deeply involved in a case like this, its choice would seem predictable. In addition, the law is not precise and there seems to be a lack of effective ways to apply sanctions if it is violated. Here the judge ignores the Working Environment Law altogether by viewing the case as a compensation claim, raised by one individual against another. On this basis he is concerned only about the more general Law of Torts and avoids clarifying whether or not this was a break of employer's duties as specified in the Working Environment Law. From the Union's point of view the WEL may become meaningless and thus they have taken the case to the Court of Appeal.

The Judge agreed that the Director did not function well as a leader. Perhaps he couldn't have done any better, even if he had tried. Some people function worse than others, some are even useless, but after all, that is not illegal. However, the Employee's claim was not directed against the boss, but at the Ministry, or more precisely, its political leader, the Minister herself. The principle, as it is practised in Norway, is that the one at the top is responsible for what goes on further down. For that reason, there was no other way for the Employee to bring her claim.

However, the Judge acquitted the Minister by writing: "In accordance with legal practice and theory, organizational responsibility cannot be linked to anybody's actions other than the Minister's. It is not claimed that the Minister insulted the plaintiff." The Working Environment Act places the responsibility on the employer to maintain healthy working relations, that is to say on the Director. If complaints from employees are met by retaliations by the employer against their elected representative, this can hardly be viewed as anything but a very serious undermining of this law. In the present case employer's responsibility seems to be raised to a higher level, and the judge's comment above could well confuse foreign readers further. The present case is mainly based on the Norwegian Court's judgement, and this very quotation was originally written in an ambiguous way. Nevertheless, it seems clear that the Judge weakened the superiors'·responsibility (and the Employee's case) by making this statement.

The former Cabinet Minister confirmed that he was aware of the troubles in their agency. And something was done. The judge considered this sufficient. The fact that it had little effect appears irrelevant in this line of reasoning. As long as you do something, that's enough. Altogether this contributes further to the picture of a Kafka-esque trial where the *employer's responsibility* is placed nowhere and is completely overlooked.

Bullying and mobbing are not only about what somebody has done. They are also about what they haven't done. (See Charlotte Rayner *et al.*, *Workplace Bullying,* Taylor and Francis, 2002.) Westhues writes: "Each needs only to do his or her small part [in a mobbing]. A comfortable "diffusion of responsibility" (Darley and Latané 1968) kicks in. In the analogy of the chicken coop, each bird has only to inflict its own little nick on the one at the bottom of the pecking order. It is the cumulative effect, for which no individual can be responsible, that eliminates the target." (2004, p. 54). From the Employee's view in this case, there was a variety of harassers: those contributing actively, those who contributed passively and those who supported her only half-heartedly. In fact although the Employee's breakdown in health was caused by her bullying boss, it was exacerbated by the feeling that no one could stop him and that she had no way out.

The present case also tells us something about court's ability to settle such cases. As pointed out, the Judge may have insufficient knowledge about the phenomenon, and the formal requirements of such proceedings may turn out disadvantageous to people in such a situation. In addition there is the time aspect. It took a long time before the Employee was able to present her case in court. She is still queuing for her appeal case – almost four years after having left her workplace on sick leave. She even risks that the story will end up in the Supreme Court. All this waiting and uncertainty are extra burdens no matter what the final outcome may be. This supports Westhues's conclusion that the legal system is not the best way of settling cases of workplace bullying if there are any other alternatives. The question arising from the present story is whether there are better ways to approach the problem.

Legal Reference

Part 4, Worker Protection and Working Environment Act, 1977, Norway. Online at www.arbeidstilsynet.no/regelverk/lover/pdf/7529.pdf
Section 12, Workplace arrangements
1. General requirements
Technology, organization of the work, execution of work, working hours and pay systems shall be arranged in such a way that employees are not exposed to adverse physical or mental strain and that their possibilities of exercising caution and observing safety considerations are not impaired. Necessary means to prevent adverse physical strain shall be placed at the disposal of the employees. *Employees shall not be subjected to harassment or other improper conduct.*
Conditions shall be arranged so the employees are afforded reasonable opportunity for professional and personal development through their work.
Section 14, Duties of employer
The employer shall ensure that the establishment is arranged and maintained, and that the work is planned, organized and performed in accordance with the provisions laid down in out pursuant to this Act, cf in particular sections 7-13.

Chapter Twenty-One

The Role of the Law in Combating Workplace Mobbing and Bullying

David Yamada

Ken Westhues has written a tremendously thoughtful and provocative book about workplace mobbing and the stories of university professors targeted for extinction by their own institutions. Forgive my resort to an academic cliché, but this is an important work. There is so much here that invites comment that I must struggle to stay within the bounds of my general expertise.

Like Westhues, my own interest in abusive work environments was originally inspired (if that is the correct word) by behavior I witnessed in the academy. As a professor who specializes in employment and labor law, I have been centering my work on the legal and policy implications of workplace bullying. Thus, my main point of engagement with Westhues concerns whether the legal system can play a helpful role in responding to these behaviors.

Between the story of Herbert Richardson and the sidebar accounts sprinkled throughout the book, Westhues provides us with disturbing accounts of the twisted, bizarre dynamics that can lead to professors being mobbed, bullied, and abused. We see how academe, an environment that supposedly embraces vigorous exchanges of opinion, a diversity of perspectives, and rational discourse, can become a world turned upside down. But herein lies my central point of departure with the author. Buttressed by examples of mobbing in academe, Westhues then generalizes by arguing that any newly-created legal sanctions against abusive work environments will likely backfire and be used to persecute rather than protect the targets of these behaviors. I, on the other hand, believe that the law can play a useful role in preventing and responding to severe, intentional emotional abuse in the workplace.

I fully agree that any attempt to create legal protections against abusive work environments must be done carefully, with utmost attention to detail and to the risk of unintended consequences. I also recognize that virtually *any* law, placed in the wrong hands, is subject to misuse. However, I strongly caution against basing objections to legal protections against bullying and mobbing largely on the culture and dynamics of one industry, namely, academe.

The Naming Game

Before I get into the heart of my response, I would like to address very briefly the ongoing debate over what to call the kind of behavior that many of us are studying and writing about. Westhues observes that *mobbing* and *bullying* are the terms that are most frequently invoked, and he casts his lot with the former. In view of the subject matter of his book, I can understand why. However, I have preferred the term *bullying* because it appears to be more representative of the various combinations of parties and behaviors that may constitute an abusive work environment. The term *mobbing* connotes either spontaneous or planned group action, and thus I see it as being a type of bullying, not a synonym for it.

Accordingly, my comments below will intersperse the terms *bullying* and *mobbing*. However, I hope we do not become too hung up on names and labels. Work abuse, workplace aggression, and workplace harassment are among the other helpful terms that have been used to describe the same general set of behaviors and effects. Although adoption of a uniform term would help us to develop a more widely recognized "brand name," the more important thing for now is that we endeavor to understand and respond to the core dynamics of abusive work settings.

Laws and Policies

Westhues opposes the enactment of laws and the development of policies designed to respond to mobbing and bullying situations.

He believes that their "practical effect is probably just the establishment of additional institutional mechanisms for the wielding of managerial power, new techniques for punishing, stigmatizing, and eliminating employees that bosses and/or workmates dislike." Instead, he favors "education in the classic, liberal sense: offering people the concept of *mobbing* or *social elimination,* acquainting them with research findings concerning it, then encouraging them to reflect on this material freely and critically, in light of their own experience, to discuss it and debate it, and to draw whatever conclusions fit the contexts of their lives." These educational efforts, he holds, should extend well beyond training programs and workshops.

I agree that education is a valuable preventive measure, but I also believe that sanctions are necessary when education alone proves to be inadequate. Philosophically speaking, if bullying and mobbing behaviors lead to the kind of personal and professional suffering that Westhues describes, then society should deem this conduct to be wrongful. And if law is one of the clearest expressions of our social norms, then severe, hurtful, and intentional emotional abuse in the workplace should be illegal and subject to appropriate remedies.

Westhues further suggests that anti-mobbing policies and proposed anti-mobbing laws "are likely to function mainly as instruments for humiliating the humiliators." I must confess that, at least for situations in which we can fairly delineate between the perpetrator and target, this is lower on my list of concerns. While I would not want to facilitate the workplace equivalent of the mob taunting a prisoner on the way to the guillotine, I support measures that enable us to remove the worst offenders from positions in which they can act abusively towards others. Moreover, in the most severe instances of abuse, targets should be able to recover damages from the responsible parties. And if the offender suffers some embarrassment or even humiliation, then perhaps that shaming process will help to discourage others from acting in such a manner.

Ultimately, a combination of education that encourages a more humane workplace culture *coupled with* laws and policies that intervene when the educative function falls short may be the most comprehensive and effective response to bullying and mobbing behaviors. From that baseline, let us acknowledge that the devil is truly in the details in terms of designing legal sanctions that are effective, fair, efficient, and subject to minimal misuse and abuse. Accordingly, the role of the law in responding to hostile work situations, and the challenges of designing legal sanctions against bullying and mobbing that are substantively sound and procedurally fair, will comprise the bulk of my comments. I hope to show that legal protections in this realm are important and can be designed to respond to some, though concededly not all, of Westhues's concerns.

Academic Culture

Westhues's observations on workplace mobbing are inextricably intertwined with the nature of academic culture. Thus, it would be appropriate to flesh out how the academic workplace gives rise to these behaviors, and to relate them to the author's overall prescriptions for reducing mobbing. As a backdrop, we should begin by recognizing that the nature of service-sector work in general, and pressures generated by the Knowledge Economy, are making conditions ripe for workplace bullying. For one, stress has become a standard occupational hazard in service-sector work. As business writer Jill Andresky Fraser observes in her 2001 book, *White-Collar Sweatshop*, "unpleasant working conditions, difficult job demands, and rising career insecurities have combined to make stress the constant companion of many of today's white-collar men and women." Although bullying is no stranger to the assembly line, the very nature of service-sector work creates conditions that enable this behavior. Frequent, ongoing personal interaction between workers often becomes a basic element of a job. The more people interact, the more likely it is that personalities will clash and that individuals who are prone to bullying will have opportunities to do so.

To this we add the unique aspects of academic culture. In its idyllic form, academic life promises relief from the kind of stress associated with certain corporate work environments. Academic work itself can be immensely satisfying, and for many of us it becomes a calling. However, the academic environment can fall well short of those images of collegial discussions and intellectual community. Julius Getman, a University of Texas law professor, offers one of the most thoughtful critiques of academic life in his 1992 book, *In the Company of Scholars*. A noted labor-law scholar who is a chaired professor at his university, Getman has been a tenured faculty member at Yale and Stanford law schools, and he has served as general counsel and president of the American Association of University Professors (AAUP). On paper, at least, he would seem an unlikely critic of the academy, as he appears to have enjoyed the trappings of academic success. Nevertheless, he writes:

I thought that universities provided an opportunity for caring relations, a sense of community, an atmosphere in which ideas were shared and refined, an egalitarian ethic, and a style of life that would permit time for family, friends, and self-expression. The reality, as I discovered, was quite different. The academic world is hierarchical and competitive; achievement is generally ephemeral and difficult to measure. Much that is done in the name of scholarship or teaching makes little contribution because it is removed from reality and the concerns of humanity. Rather than feeling an automatic sense of community, I have often felt alienated. In particular, the desire for success and status has often conflicted with other goals of meaning, community, study, and reflection.

Academicians are adept at intellectual analysis, manipulation, and argumentation. When applied to the right tasks – effective teaching, thoughtful scholarship, and meaningful service – these skills reinforce the most socially useful aspects of the academy. But many of us who have spent meaningful stretches of time in the academy know what can happen when these skills are applied in hurtful and even malicious ways. The more commonplace but still disturbing situations need not rise to the level of vicious social and professional elimination depicted by Westhues. For example, in how many faculty meetings have we heard calmly reasoned but wholly illogical explanations for the most irrational or even bizarre positions and decisions? How many times have we witnessed candidates for faculty positions torpedoed or boosted by wonderfully articulate but remarkably wrongheaded comparisons, criticisms, and praises? I am convinced that some academicians become so adept at this mental game-playing that they could persuade themselves of the rightness of virtually any conclusion or opinion.

Of course, intellectually rationalized actions and explanations occur in many organizations. But in dysfunctional academic units, they often rise to an art level. A steady diet of faculty and committee meetings, administrative memos, and institutional self-promotion in these settings can condition us to become used to, and quietly accepting of, intellectual dishonesty and rhetorical "mal-manipulation." Call it Dilbert in Tweed, or perhaps the hellish side of paradise.

Because this kind of mental and verbal facility is often at the heart of both perpetrating and defending bullying and mobbing, academe becomes a natural petri dish for such behaviors, especially the covert varieties. So many decisions in the academy, including employee evaluation, compensation, scheduling, teaching and committee assignments, and support for research, are based upon very subjective judgments. Such an environment becomes a particularly attractive setting for the passive-aggressive bully and the quiet-but-deadly mob. Those who do not enjoy the protections of tenure (including junior faculty and most administrators) are particularly vulnerable to being targeted, and Westhues shows us that even the tenured are not immune.

In view of all this, it makes sense to me that Westhues, having immersed himself in these Kafka-esque accounts of academic mobbing, can imagine a world where laws and policies would be misused and misapplied. But I see this as more a reflection on academic culture than on the nature of legal sanctions in general. Unfortunately, virtually every standard, procedure, or policy in academic life is subject to the same kind of perverse twisting out of shape that Westhues envisions for laws and policies meant to curb mobbing. I think it is fair to argue that in less dysfunctional institutions, academic or otherwise, such sanctions would be applied in a more rational, if not perfectly fair, manner.

Bully Types and Bullying Scenarios

In considering the need for legal sanctions, it also may help us to examine the factual landscape more generally. In *Brutal Bosses and Their Prey*, Professor Harvey Hornstein assesses how economic pressures of the 1990s intersected with abusive bosses and concludes that the work environment of that period "ignited explosions of brutality from both innate bullies who thrive on their mistreatment of others and from overburdened bosses who might never have behaved that way in less stressful times." In this trenchant observation, Hornstein captures a lot of compelling points.

First, Hornstein suggests that some people who engage in bullying behavior do so because they find themselves in an acute, stressful situation. Under this pressure, they falter. Most of us, save the most saintly and self-controlled, are capable of engaging in some pretty rotten behaviors, and therefore we should give pause before we, in essence, mob the bully. I think this is what Westhues is getting at when he warns us not to become what we abhor. Working through this can make for humbling self-reflection; certainly my study of bullying has caused me to consider times when I have treated others poorly.

But Hornstein also acknowledges the existence of the "innate bully," or what others have called the "serial bully." Westhues acknowledges this variation, but in adopting the mobbing paradigm, I suggest that he is too dismissive of it. In such individuals, the impulse to eliminate their targets runs deep. The recurring results of their behavior, ranging from careers sidetracked to lives in ruins, are terrible to behold. In some instances, the innate bullies become the natural ringleaders of mobs. Oftentimes, their employers are too clueless or too cowardly to get rid of them. In dealing with such offenders, I have no problem with placing them where they can no longer hurt others, including showing them the door.

Perhaps an example best explains my position. The situations that triggered my interest in this topic involved a singular bully. On occasion he was assisted by a sidekick. Also in the picture was a higher-level administrator who was apprised of the bully's behavior by multiple sources but who chose not to do anything about it. None of the main four targeted individuals were mobbed in the sense suggested by Westhues. However, three of them left the institution, in large part due to how they were treated, and all four suffered considerable stress and anxiety. Furthermore, the bully surely demonstrated the kind of impulse to eliminate these individuals that Westhues so insightfully describes.

It follows that in weighing what types of legal protections may constitute an appropriate response to abusive work behaviors, we should consider scenarios involving both the individual bully and the multi-person mob. We also should ask where to draw the line between objectionable behavior that should implicate sanctions and objectionable behavior that should not.

The Legality of Cruelty

Unfortunately, it is clear that existing law does not provide adequate sanctions against severe bullying and mobbing. Several years ago, I did a survey of American state court decisions in which employees had sued employers and co-employees under a legal theory known as intentional infliction of emotional distress (IIED), concentrating on cases decided from 1995 through 1998. I had concluded that of all the possible legal claims for workplace bullying, IIED provided the best match between relevant legal doctrine and applicable factual scenarios. As stated in many of these cases, in order to prevail in an IIED claim, an individual must prove the following by a preponderance of the evidence:

1. The wrongdoer's conduct must be intentional or reckless;
2. The conduct must be outrageous and intolerable in that it offends against the generally accepted standards of decency and morality;
3. There must be a causal connection between the wrongdoer's conduct and the emotional distress; and
4. The emotional distress must be severe.

After reviewing and categorizing several hundred judicial decisions, I concluded that typical workplace bullying, especially conduct unrelated to sexual harassment or other forms of discrimination, seldom resulted in liability for IIED.

The most frequent reason given by courts for rejecting workplace-related IIED claims was that the offending behavior was not sufficiently extreme and outrageous to meet the requirements of the tort. In some cases, these findings were understandable. After all, bruised feelings and "everyday" incivility, however undesirable, should not be the stuff of legal proceedings, lest the courts become the ongoing arbiters of workplace interactions. But in other instances, it was extremely disturbing that courts found against employees who had been the targets of severe, ongoing, hostile, and harassing behavior, suffering considerable psychological, physical, and financial injuries.

In many of these decisions, the courts relied on the *Restatement of Torts*, an authoritative and oft-cited treatise on the law of personal injury. The *Restatement* holds that liability for IIED is appropriate "only where the conduct has been so outrageous in character, and so extreme in degree, as to go beyond all possible bounds of decency, and to be regarded as atrocious, and utterly intolerable in a civilized society." This means, of course, that only the most egregious and personally destructive conduct raises the specter of IIED liability, for "beyond all possible bounds of decency" and "utterly intolerable in a civilized society" are pretty tough standards to meet. In most cases of bullying and mobbing, this is hard to establish, even where the target has suffered extreme personal and professional harm.

Mirzaie v. Smith Cogeneration, Inc., a 1998 Oklahoma appeals court decision, is illustrative of how difficult it is to prevail in an IIED claim. In *Mirzaie*, the former employee claimed that his supervisor yelled at him in front of other company executives, called him at 3:00 a.m. and "browbeat him for hours," required him to "needlessly cancel vacation plans," refused to allow the employee to spend a day at the hospital with his wife after the birth of their son, intentionally called the employee's wife by the employee's former wife's name, and delivered the notice of termination two hours before the employee's wedding. There was nothing "in this working milieu," reasoned the court, "that would elevate the recited facts to the 'outrageous' level."

Similarly, in *Denton v. Chittenden Bank*, a 1994 decision, the Vermont Supreme Court rejected an IIED claim where the employee alleged that the supervisor "embarked on an insulting, demeaning, and vindictive course of conduct" that included, among other things, repeated ridicule and invasions of privacy. The Court held that even if all the allegations were true, a mere "series of indignities" did not constitute sufficiently outrageous conduct to prevail.

My "poster case" example of the reluctance of courts to grant relief even to the most severely bullied employees came in *Hollomon v. Keadle*, a 1996 Arkansas Supreme Court decision. This dispute involved a female employee, Hollomon, who worked for a male physician, Keadle, for two years before she voluntarily left the job. According to Hollomon, throughout her period of employment "Keadle repeatedly cursed her and referred to her with offensive terms, such as 'white nigger,' 'slut,' 'whore,' and 'the ignorance of Glenwood, Arkansas.'" Keadle often used profanity in front of his employees and patients, and called women who worked outside of the home "whores and prostitutes." Keadle threatened Hollomon's life "if she quit or caused trouble." She suffered from "stomach problems, loss of sleep, loss of self-esteem, anxiety attacks, and embarrassment." Unfortunately for Hollomon, the Arkansas Supreme Court found that Keadle's behavior did not amount to outrageous conduct and dismissed her case.

My survey also found that workers can lose their IIED claims because they did not show the requisite level of severe emotional distress, as *Harris v. Jones*, a 1977 Maryland Court of Appeals decision, aptly demonstrates. Harris was an assembly-line worker who suffered from a lifelong stuttering problem that gave him "great difficulty with longer words or sentences, causing him at times to shake his head up and down when attempting to speak." During a five-month period, his supervisor and co-workers continually mimicked, verbally and physically, his speech impediment. As a result of this behavior, "Harris was 'shaken up' and felt 'like going into a hole and hid[ing].'" His wife said that his nervous condition worsened during this time. Although, at trial, the jury found for Harris, the Maryland appeals court held that he had not demonstrated a sufficient level of emotional distress in order to prevail in his claim.

Of course, there have been instances where employees have prevailed on their IIED claims. These cases often have been grounded in allegations of severe sexual or racial harassment, or claims of retaliation for whistleblowing. However, this only highlights the pertinent void in the law. Targets of sexual or racial harassment also can avail themselves of employment discrimination laws as a basis for legal relief. Targets of retaliation often can invoke whistleblower provisions of various statutory protections. The typical target of "garden variety" bullying and mobbing, however, has considerably fewer viable legal options.

My research into the pertinent legal standards of other nations indicates that this void in the law transcends national boundaries. Gradually we are witnessing the emergence of legislative initiatives and regulatory standards that attempt to address abusive work behaviors, but we remain in the very early stages in terms of these developments. The International Labor Organization also has recognized bullying and mobbing as threats to the well-being of workers, but to date it has not recommended a comprehensive legal or regulatory response. I shall have more to say about my own attempt to design model legislation below.

Linking Employer Liability to Education, Awareness, and Prevention

Because employers are unlikely to face liability for typical workplace bullying, the law provides little incentive for them to act preventively and to respond effectively to complaints about bullying behaviors. Although some enlightened employers have started to consider the economic and human-resources costs of bullying, all too often this behavior is simply written off as a personality conflict and dealt with in uneven and often ineffective ways. In many cases, an inadequate response by the employer adds to the trauma experienced by the target.

The evolution of American sexual harassment law shows how well-crafted anti-bullying laws could help to prevent the abuse of employees. In two companion cases decided in 1998, *Burlington Industries, Inc. v. Ellerth* and *Faragher v. Boca Raton*, the United States Supreme Court held that employers can be held strictly liable for sexual harassment committed by their supervisors. The framework adopted by the Court offers powerful incentives for employers to adopt effective training and prevention programs. This framework could easily be adapted for virtually any status-blind harassment law.

In short, the Supreme Court held that in certain circumstances, an employer may avoid liability for sexual harassment by showing (1) that it "exercised reasonable care to prevent and correct promptly any sexually harassing behavior," *and* (2) that the "employee unreasonably failed to take advantage of any preventive or corrective opportunities provided by the employer or to avoid harm otherwise." By offering employers this defense, the Court created a concrete incentive for them to provide effective training and prevention programs and to respond promptly and fairly to complaints of sexual harassment. And, indeed, this has been the result. On the heels of the *Faragher* and *Ellerth* cases, many companies moved quickly to develop stronger training and awareness programs and to adopt more effective procedures for handling employee complaints of sexual harassment. In essence, the Court demonstrated that liability standards can be designed in a way that encourages employers to act preventively and responsively towards sexual harassment.

There is no reason why similar approaches for imposing liability should not apply to bullying and mobbing. In fact, it could be argued that sexual harassment is simply one form of bullying and mobbing, in that abusive behaviors in this context are distinguished by their sexual content or sexist intent. Placing some burden upon employers to prevent and respond to bullying behaviors would mean that all workers, not only targets of sexual harassment, would be more protected against abusive treatment of all kinds.

Another benefit of imposing liability on employers is that it can serve as a check on mob behavior. The risk of liability at least makes an organization think twice before "piling on" with the abusive actions of an individual or group. By contrast, the current void in the law tacitly encourages employers to take the path of least resistance, which often means doing nothing, and sometimes means going along with the mob.

Unfair Accusations, Twisted Applications, and Due Process

Running throughout Westhues's book is an undercurrent of deep consternation over how wrongful, baseless, or trumped-up accusations of wrongdoing have been the grounds for eliminating professors. I wish I had an airtight response to that concern, but I do not. In the wrong hands, almost any law or policy can be turned into a weapon against an innocent party or to deny an individual accused of wrongdoing a fair hearing. And surely there are plenty of instances where legal rules have been applied in ways that run counter to the best intentions of their drafters. The creation of anti-bullying laws and policies would not be exempt from these risks.

Unfortunately, the story of the law is filled with examples of absurd and unfair applications. One of my favorite examples in American law is the Sherman Antitrust Act of 1890, enacted for the purpose of curbing monopolies and restraint of trade at a time when wealthy and powerful individuals and corporations were engaged in an alarming aggregation of economic power. However, its first application – upheld by the United States Supreme Court -- was against labor unions. In *Loewe v. Lawlor,* the Court reasoned that individual workers who banded together through a union to boycott goods were engaging in illegal restraint of trade under the new antitrust law.

Certainly the comparatively nascent history of sexual harassment laws and their application gives reason for pause. Several examples provided by Westhues illustrate how the elevation of sexual harassment to punishable offense, whether in an academic administrative setting or a court of law, has opened the door to wrongful accusations that have severely damaged or even ruined the lives and careers of the accused. Furthermore, although the U.S. Supreme Court has wisely stated that reasonableness should be our benchmark for what determining what constitutes a hostile work environment, American employers have sometimes overreacted to the risk of liability by imposing draconian limitations on normal social interaction. In addition, some individuals have brought, and on occasion tribunals and juries have agreed with, sexual harassment claims for behavior that few of us would deem worthy of legal relief.

Despite these imperfections, it is far preferable that we have laws that protect against sexual harassment. Too many people, mostly women, have suffered in silence in the face of these behaviors, leaving bruised and battered psyches in their wake. It is important that we as a society proclaim our opposition to treating anyone in this manner. In addition, it is equally important that we continue to strive for the fair and reasonable application of these legal standards. Failure to do so results in miscarriages of justice and justifiable public cynicism towards, and even derision of, these hard-won protections.

The same can be said for bullying and mobbing. It is axiomatic that rules help us to establish boundaries between appropriate and inappropriate behavior. Without pronouncements, through laws and policies, that this behavior is wrongful and objectionable, we increase the likelihood that such instances become reduced to a behavioral free-for-all that simply gets labeled a "personality conflict." We also are telling the targets of the most severe forms of workplace mistreatment that we deem their suffering unworthy of compensation.

The wild card in all of this, of course, is whether the culture of the institution involved values fairness, integrity, and – yes -- moral courage. In all too many of the instances summoned by Westhues, these three qualities were missing. No wonder people were mobbed! These tales of academic elimination reminded me of the lynchings of black people in America's Old South, in that all the laws and procedures on the books were worthless towards saving them. In my view this does not mean that we should give up on developing fair legal standards and adjudicatory mechanisms. However, it does mean that when the mob mentality has taken over and the pertinent institution is too weak to withstand it, heaven help those who are on the receiving end, for they may be doomed.

In such cases, internal dispute resolution tribunals are simply minor obstacles on the way to the execution, literally or figuratively. Westhues raises some disturbing examples of university adjudicatory tribunals in action, but at times I found myself asking, *would the ultimate result have been the same regardless of procedural protections?* After all, a mob bent on elimination uses whatever tools are at hand, and it finds ways to navigate, or run roughshod over, disagreeable legal niceties.

Of course, in some instances the presence of a fair tribunal may help to keep a mob at bay. In this sense, Westhues's accounts of how in-house university tribunals helped to enable the departure of targeted professors raise important broader questions about the desirability of alternative dispute resolution mechanisms in resolving employment cases. For example, in the United States, the courts have become increasingly receptive to the growing use of mandatory arbitration clauses by employers. These "agreements" (which often are imposed unilaterally) require employees, as a condition of employment, to give up their right to file work-related claims in a court of law or appropriate public agency. Instead, claims must be submitted to binding arbitration. This practice is bitterly opposed by many employee advocates on the ground that workers will not be afforded a fair hearing if their claims are not subject to more public scrutiny and employers enjoy undue power to control the terms of arbitration.

The stories of the Richardson case and others provide ample reason to be concerned about dispute resolution mechanisms that, to adapt a popular phrase, block the sunlight. And when we factor in the remarkable ability of academicians to manipulate words, meaning, and interpretation, we see the inherent dangers in allowing decisions on such important matters to be made in settings that discourage openness and accountability. Certainly these risks are present in other industries and work settings as well. In-house tribunals, especially, should send out warning signals to all of us. Whenever possible, we should prevent process being used as the handmaiden of bullying and mobbing.

Model Legislation

After analyzing the existing state of American law with regards to workplace bullying, I wrote a model statute designed to fill the aforementioned gaps in the law while addressing the very real concerns about introducing stronger sanctions for bullying behavior. Dr. Gary Namie, co-founder of the Workplace Bullying & Trauma Institute and one of the central figures in bringing an awareness of this topic to an American audience, dubbed the bill the "Healthy Workplace Act" and took it to his home state of California in search of legislative support. The first tangible result of this effort came in February 2003, when California Assembly Member Paul Koretz filed Assembly Bill 1582, which represented a virtually verbatim adoption of the model statute.

Assembly Bill 1582 makes it "an unlawful employment practice ... to subject an employee to an abusive work environment." That short phrase activates a long series of definitions and sub-definitions designed to limit relief to targets of severe, intentional, hurtful behavior. For example, "abusive work environment" is defined as "when the defendant, acting with malice, subjects the complainant to abusive conduct so severe that it causes tangible harm to the complainant." From there, terms such as "malice," "abusive conduct," and "tangible harm" are defined with specificity.

Assembly Bill 1582 also holds employers strictly liable for abusive work environments created by their employees. However, it borrows heavily from the U.S. Supreme Court's decisions in the *Faragher* and *Ellerth* cases (discussed above) by providing that, in certain situations, employers may escape liability where they can demonstrate that they took adequate measures to prevent bullying and responded fairly when presented with a complaint about bullying behaviors. This, in turn, encourages employers to engage in training and education programs designed to reduce such behaviors. Furthermore, the bill includes provisions intended to reduce frivolous litigation and to limit employer exposure to unfair damage awards, including limitations on compensatory and punitive damages.

I make no claim that Assembly Bill 1582 represents a magic solution to abusive behavior in the workplace. If enacted, some targets of bullying and mobbing will still find it difficult to prevail in court, and some employers will face unwarranted lawsuits. Nevertheless, I believe it is one of the more thoughtful attempts to provide legal relief to severely bullied individuals and to encourage employers to act preventively and responsibly within this realm.

Acknowledging Intellectual Rigor, Common Ground, and Grace

Let me close on a note of appreciation. I am bowled over by the amount of factual detail, insightful and provocative analysis, and thoughtful reflection contained in the Westhues book. Students of the workplace and of academic culture would do well to consider it closely, for this is a work that "sticks to the ribs" by raising important and sometimes uncomfortable questions. I am sure that this book will have its share of critics, but it will be difficult for them to claim that it did not make them think and *rethink*.

I also happen to believe that Westhues and I likely agree on more points than we disagree when it comes to our analyses of mobbing, bullying, and work abuse. In some ways our perspectives may be complementary rather than contradictory. In considering solutions, perhaps Westhues and I share a bias towards our respective disciplines and can learn from each other. As a sociologist, he places more faith in education and communication and exhibits a healthy suspicion towards legal sanctions and legal process. As a legal scholar, I am skeptical that education will be sufficient and believe that the law must intervene to shape our behavior and give relief to injured parties. Maybe there is room for a multifaceted and balanced approach that reflects both of our perspectives.

Finally, we should note that Ken Westhues has written a book that attempts to reflect the teachings of its contents. He has made every effort to give credit where credit is due, to limit his disagreements to the merits, and to refrain from the kind of gratuitous bashing of contrary viewpoints that all too often is mistaken for genuine intellectual exchange. There are plenty of lessons in this book for all of us, not the least of which is how its author chose to engage his subject.

Selected Bibliography

Books, Treatises, and Articles

American Law Institute, 1965. *Restatement (Second) of Torts.* St. Paul, Minn.: American Law Institute Publishers.

Fraser, Jill Andresky, 2001. *White-Collar Sweatshop.* New York: W.W. Norton & Co.

Getman, Julius, 1992. *In the Company of Scholars: The Struggle for the Soul of Higher Education.* Austin, Texas: University of Texas Press.

Hornstein,Harvey, 1996. *Brutal Bosses and Their Prey: How to Identify and Overcome Abuse in the Workplace.* New York: Riverhead Books.

Namie, Gary, and Ruth Namie, 2000. *The Bully at Work.* Naperville, Ill.: Sourcebooks.

Yamada, David C., 2000. "The Phenomenon of 'Workplace Bullying' and the Need for Status-Blind Hostile Work Environment Protection," *Georgetown Law Journal*, Vol. 88, pp. 475-536.

Yamada, David, 2003. "Workplace Bullying and the Law: Towards a Transnational Consensus?" pp. 399-411 in Einarsen, *et al.*, eds., *Bullying and Emotional Abuse in the Workplace: International Perspectives in Research and Practice.* London: Taylor & Francis.

Primary Legal and Legislative Sources

Burlington Industries, Inc. v. Ellerth, 524 U.S. 742 (1998).
Denton v. Chittendon Bank, 655 A.2d 703 (Vt. 1994).
Faragher v. Boca Raton, 524 U.S. 775 (1998).
Harris v. Jones, 380 A.2d 611 (Md. 1977).
Hollomon v. Keadle, 931 S.W.2d 413 (Ark. 1996).
Loewe v. Lawlor, 208 U.S. 274 (1908).
Mirzaie v. Smith Cogeneration, Inc., 962 P.2d 678 (Okla. Ct.App. 1998).

California Assembly Bill 1582, 2003-4 session of the California legislature (Assembly member Paul Koretz, chief sponsor).

Notes on Contributors

(alphabetically by surname)

Jo Blase (Ph.D. Colorado 1983) is Professor of Educational Leadership at the University of Georgia. Her research interests include administrator-teacher interaction *vis-a-vis* school reform and supervisory discourse in education and medicine, leadership preparation, and democratic school leadership. Recent publications (with Joseph Blase) include *Handbook of Instructional Leadership: How Successful Principals Promote Teaching and Learning* (Corwin, 2nd ed., 2004), and "The Micropolitics of Instructional Supervision: A Call for Research," *Educational Administration Quarterly* (2002). Postal address: College of Education, University of Georgia, Athens, Georgia 30602. Email: jblase@coe.uga.edu

Joseph Blase (Ph.D. Syracuse 1980) is Professor of Educational Leadership at the University of Georgia. His primary research interests include principal-teacher relationships, school-level micropolitics, democratic school leadership, and principal mistreatment. Recent publications (with Jo Blase) include *Breaking the Silence: Overcoming the Problem of Principal Mistreatment of Teachers* (Corwin, 2002), and "The Phenomenology of Principal Mistreatment", *Journal of Educational Administration* (2003). Postal address: College of Education, University of Georgia, Athens, Georgia 30602. Email: blase@coe.uga.edu

Charmian Bondi (M.A. Edinburgh, Scotland) is an international journalist, counsellor to victims of destructive leadership, and researcher in workplace bullying and organizational problems. She is involved in establishing self-help groups for victims of workplace harassment. In 1998 she contributed to a book, identifying some of the patterns of workplace bullying. Her chapter with Jan Gregersen in the present volume was initially presented at the Fourth International Conference on Bullying in the Workplace, Bergen, Norway, in June 2004. Postal address: Jarlsborgveien 5, N-0379 Oslo, Norway. Email: charmian@online.no

Enrico Cavina (M.D. 1961, Liceo Classico 1955) retired in 2003, as Professor and Head of the Department of Surgery, University of Pisa. He is author or co-author of more than 250 scientific papers, reports, and chapters, and of monographs on general surgery, emergency and trauma surgery, laparoscopic surgery, telemedicine, and most recently, preparedness of hospitals for terrorism attacks. He is past president of the European Association for Trauma Emergency Surgery, Fellow of the American College of Surgeons, and founding head of the Telemedicine Project on Tilos, Greece. Postal address: PO Box 01 85002, Tilos, Greece, and Mazzini St. 150, 86010 Pontasserchio, Pisa, Italy. Email: ecavina@lycos.com

Dan Cohn-Sherbok (Ph.D. Cantab., D.D. Hebrew Union College – Jewish Institute of Religion), an American Rabbi, is Professor of Jewish Theology at the University of Wales at Lampeter. He has been a Visiting Professor at the Universities of Essex, Middlesex, St. Andrews, Durham, and Vilnius, and a Visiting Fellow at Harris-Manchester College, Oxford. He is author or editor of over 60 books, including *The Jewish Heritage, The Blackwell Dictionary of Judaica, Modern Judaism, World Religions and Human Liberation,* and the text *Judaism: History, Belief and Practice* (2003). Postal address: Department of Theology, University of Wales, Lampeter SA48 7ED, Wales, UK. Email: cohn-sherbok@pocketmail.com

Roman Dubinski (Ph.D. Toronto 1969) is Professor Emeritus and Adjunct Professor at the University of Waterloo. He was a member of the English Department at the University where he specialized in Seventeenth-Century English Literature. His publications include *Alexander Brome: Poems* (Toronto, 1982) and *A Chronological Bibliography of English Poetry Printed 1477-1642* (Waterloo, 1996). He was active in the Faculty Association of the University of Waterloo, serving as President in 1972, and Chair of the Academic Freedom and Tenure Committee from 1992 to 1996. Postal address: 209 Westvale Dr., Waterloo, Ontario N2T 1M9. Email: rdub@golden.net

Joan Friedenberg (Ph.D. Illinois 1979) is Professor of Linguistics and Director of the Bilingual Education Training for All Teachers Program at Southern Illinois University Carbondale. She is the author of 75 publications related to the problems and rights of immigrants. She has served as a consultant for the United States Departments of Education, Labor,

Immigration, and State, over ten state departments of education, over a hundred school districts, programs and community-based organizations, and several embassies overseas. Postal address: Department of Linguistics, Mailcode 4524, Southern Illinois University, Carbondale, IL 62901. Email: jefriedenberg@earthlink.net

Jan Gregersen (M.B.A. Norwegian School of Management) is a lecturer, counsellor to victims of destructive leadership, and researcher in workplace bullying and management. In cooperation with organized groups for victims of workplace harassment, he contributed to a 1998 book about the bullying pattern. He has published an essay of special relevance on the trials of St. Paul; an English version was presented at the International Conference on Bullying at Work at Birkbeck College, University of London, in 2002. The essay in this volume was presented at the Fourth International Conference on Bullying in the Workplace, Bergen, Norway, in June 2004. Postal address: Bergsvingen 5, N-1358 Jar, Norway. Email: Jan.Gregersen@hiak.no

Irving Hexham (Ph.D. Bristol 1975) is Professor of Religious Studies at the University of Calgary. Before becoming an academic he served an apprenticeship and worked as a manager with the British North Western Gas Board. His degrees are in addition to City and Guilds (1961) and Institute of Gas Engineers (1964) qualifications. He has published 21 books including *The Irony of Apartheid* (1981), *A Concise Dictionary of Religion* (1993), *New Religions as Global Cultures* (1997), *The Scriptures of the amaNazaretha of Ekuphakameni,* and numerous academic articles and book reviews. Postal address: Dept. of Religious Studies, University of Calgary, Calgary, Alberta T2N 1N4, Canada. Email: hexham@ucalgary.ca

Kathleen Kufeldt (Ph.D. Calgary 1981) moved her research program to the University of New Brunswick after being terminated from the Chair of Child Protection, School of Social Work, Memorial University of Newfoundland. As Adjunct Professor in the Muriel McQueen Ferguson Centre on Family Violence at UNB, she has co-edited a book and has a second forthcoming, has published eight book chapters, five monographs and five refereed articles. She has generated $1.6 million in research funds, and disseminates her research findings at national and international conferences, often by invitation or as keynote speaker. Local and national media frequently seek her views on child welfare issues. Email: kathleen.kufeldt@nf.sympatico.ca

Martin Loney (Ph.D. London School of Economics 1981), is a freelance researcher and writer for academic and public forums, notably the *National Post*. In the 1960s, he was a leader of Canada's radical student movement. He was fired as a security risk from a government research position in 1971

(the RCMP claimed he was the leader of the Extra Parliamentary Opposition, a nonexistent group it said was infiltrating the public service and preparing to overthrow the state). He later worked for World University Service, traveling to Rhodesia and South Africa to assist students fighting racist regimes. He served as General Secretary of Britain's National Council for Civil Liberties, and taught for 12 years at the Open University, where he was acting head of interdisciplinary social sciences, before returning to Canada, where academic positions have eluded him. Email: Martinloney@aol.com

Brian Martin (Ph.D. Sydney 1976), a physicist by training, is an Associate Professor in Science, Technology and Society at the University of Wollongong, Australia. He is the author of ten books and hundreds of articles in a range of fields, including nonviolence, dissent, scientific controversies, information issues, and democracy. Noteworthy here are *Suppression Stories* (1997) and *The Whistleblower's Handbook: How to Be an Effective Resister* (1999). He is international director of Whistleblowers Australia. His website is at http://www.uow.edu.au/arts/sts/bmartin/dissent/ Postal address: STS, University of Wollongong, NSW 2522, Australia. Email: bmartin@uow.edu.au.

Hugo A. Meynell (Ph.D. Cantab. 1963) taught at the University of Leeds in the Departments of Philosophy and Theology, until moving to the University of Calgary as Professor of Religious Studies in 1981. He was elected to the Royal Society of Canada in 1993. He is the author of thirteen books – on ethics, aesthetics, theory of knowledge, the philosophy and theology of Bernard Lonergan, and Handel's operas. His most recent book is *Postmodernism and the New Enlightenment* (Catholic University of America Press, 2000). Now retired, he lives in Calgary. Postal address: 107-320 24th Ave. SW, Calgary, Alberta T2S 0K2.

John Mueller (Ph.D., experimental psychology, St. Louis 1968) has been Professor of Applied Psychology at the University of Calgary since 1990. He taught previously at the University of Missouri. His areas of research include human learning and educational technology, also history of psychology and philosophy of science. He has done editorial work for numerous professional journals, grant agencies, and publishing companies. He has published over 100 articles and book chapters in professional outlets. He is a Fellow in both the American Psychological Association and the American Psychological Society. Postal address: Applied Psychology division, University of Calgary, Calgary, Alberta T2N 1N4, Canada. Email: mueller@ucalgary.ca.

Dhiraj Pradhan (Ph.D. Iowa 1972) holds a Chair in Computer Science at the University of Bristol. He previously held the COE Endowed Chair at

Texas A&M, and has taught at Oregon State, Stanford, and Massachusetts. Among his many honors are Germany's Humboldt Prize in 1990, and a Fulbright FLAD Chair in 1997. A fellow of several scientific associations, he holds two patents and is the author or co-author of many books including *Fault-Tolerant Computer Systems Design* (1996) and *IC Manufacturability* (2000), and of about 200 journal articles, book chapters, and conference papers. Postal address: Department of Computer Science, Merchant Venturers Building, Woodland Rd., University of Bristol, Bristol BS8 1UB, U.K. Email: pradhan@cs.bris.ac.uk

Carey E. Stronach (Ph.D. William and Mary) is Professor of Physics at Virginia State University, where he has taught since 1965, and is now the most senior member of faculty. He has been a visiting professor at the University of Alberta. He is author or co-author of 110 papers in his field, and was chairman of the *Ninth International Symposium on Muon Spin Rotation* held in Williamsburg, Virginia, in 2002. He has written two plays. He received the Patrick Henry Award from Virginia Governor Jim Gilmore in 2001. Long active in the Virginia Association of Scholars, he was elected president in 2004. Postal address: Department of Physics, Virginia State University, Petersburg, Virginia 23806. Email: cestronach@adelphia.net

Kenneth Westhues (Ph.D. Vanderbilt 1970) is Professor of Sociology at the University of Waterloo, where he has taught since 1975. A former chair of his department and winner of Waterloo's Distinguished Teacher Award, he has been a visiting professor at Fordham University, Memorial University of Newfoundland, and the University of Graz, Austria. He is author or editor of a dozen books, including *First Sociology* (1982), *Basic Principles for Social Science in Our Time* (1987), *The Working Centre* (1995), *Eliminating Professors* (1998), and *Administrative Mobbing at the University of Toronto* (2004), as well as about fifty book chapters and scholarly articles. Postal address: Department of Sociology, Univ. of Waterloo, Waterloo, Ontario N2L 3G1. Email: kwesthue@uwaterloo.ca

Daryl White (Ph.D., anthropology, Connecticut 1985) is Associate Professor and Chair of Sociology and Anthropology at Spelman College, where he has taught since 1985. His specialty is the study of religion, ritual, and other symbolic systems. He is co-editor (with O. Kendall White, Jr.) of *Religion in the Contemporary South: Diversity, Community, and Identity* (1995), and (with George Armelagos) of *Globalization and the Evolution of Emerging Disease* (forthcoming). He is the author of numerous articles in the anthropology and sociology of religion. Postal address: Department of Sociology and Anthropology, Campus P. O. Box 375, Spelman College, Atlanta, Georgia 30314. Email: dwhite@spelman.edu

O. Kendall White, Jr. (Ph.D. Vanderbilt 1975) is the William P. Ames, Jr. Professor in Sociology and Anthropology at Washington and Lee University. A former chair of his department, he is the author of *Mormon Neo-Orthodoxy: A Crisis Theology* (1987) and co-editor (with Daryl White) of *Religion in the Contemporary South: Diversity, Community, and Identity* (1995). He has also published several dozen articles and book chapters in the sociology of religion, especially on issues of race, feminism, and sexual orientation in Mormonism. Postal address: Department of Sociology and Anthropology, Washington and Lee University, Lexington, Virginia 24450. Email: whitek@wlu.edu.

Melvin D. Williams (Ph.D. Pittsburgh 1973) is Professor of Anthropology at the University of Michigan, where he has also held many administrative posts. He received Michigan's Career Service Award in 2004. He is the author of seven books, including *On the Street Where I Lived* (1981), *Community in a Black Pentecostal Church* (1984), *The Human Dilemma* (1992, 2002), and *The Black Experience in Middle-Class America* (2001), and of many scholarly articles. He is founder, director, and curator of the Belmar Neighborhood Living Museum, the area of his fieldwork for 40 years. He has also published field studies of the Songhees and Saanich First Nations of Vancouver Island. Postal address: Department of Anthropology, Univ. of Michigan, Ann Arbor, MI 48109. Email: mddoublu@umich.edu

David Yamada (J.D. New York University School of Law) is Professor of Law and Director of the Project on Workplace Bullying and Discrimination at Suffolk University Law School. He is member of the bar in Massachusetts and New York. He is a leading authority on the legal and policy implications of workplace bullying, mobbing, and abusive work environments. The best known of his articles is his exhaustive analysis of American employment law relative to workplace bullying, published in the *Georgetown Law Journal* (2000). His model anti-bullying bill has been introduced in several American state legislatures. Postal address: Suffolk University Law School, 120 Tremont Street, Boston, Massachusetts 02108. Email: dyamada@suffolk.edu

Nathan Young (Ph.D. expected 2005) is a doctoral candidate at the University of British Columbia. He holds a Killam Predoctoral Fellowship and is currently a co-investigator on a Community-University Research Alliance initiative addressing economic transitions in coastal British Columbia, funded by the Social Sciences and Humanities Research Council of Canada. He has published in the areas of environment and the sociology of science. Postal address: Department of Anthropology and Sociology, 6303 NW Marine Dr., Vancouver, British Columbia V6T 1Z1, Canada. Email: njyoung@interchange.ubc.ca